DATSUN
4-WHEEL DRIVE PICKUPS
1980-1982
SHOP MANUAL

By
ALAN AHLSTRAND

SYDNIE A. WAUSON
Editor

JEFF ROBINSON
Publisher

CLYMER PUBLICATIONS

World's largest publisher of books
devoted exclusively to automobiles and motorcycles

12860 MUSCATINE STREET · P.O. BOX 20 · ARLETA, CALIFORNIA 91331

FIRST EDITION
First Printing August, 1981

SECOND EDITION
Revised by Alan Ahlstrand to include 1982 models
First Printing February, 1983

Printed in U.S.A.

ISBN: 0-89287-344-2

Production Coordinator, Blesilda Jacinto

*Photos and illustrations courtesy of Nissan Motor Corporation,
U.S.A.*

.

COVER:
*Photographed by Michael Brown Photographic Productions,
Los Angeles, California.
Assisted by Bill Masho.
Truck courtesy of Low Manufacturing, Monrovia, California.
Truck driven by Spencer Low.*

CONTENTS

QUICK REFERENCE DATA

LUBRICANT VISCOSITY

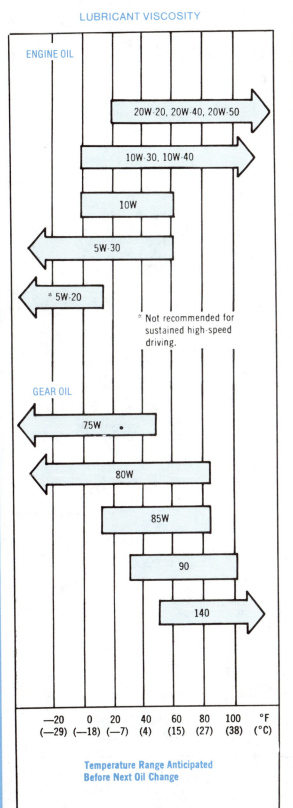

ENGINE OIL

20W-20, 20W-40, 20W-50

10W-30, 10W-40

10W

5W-30

* 5W-20

* Not recommended for
sustained high-speed
driving.

GEAR OIL

75W

80W

85W

90

140

| —20 | 0 | 20 | 40 | 60 | 80 | 100 | °F |
| (—29) | (—18) | (—7) | (4) | (15) | (27) | (38) | (°C) |

**Temperature Range Anticipated
Before Next Oil Change**

1980 VALVE ADJUSTMENT

Front

① ③ ⑤ ⑦

**Adjust these valves with No. 1
cam lobe pointing up.**

Front

② ④ ⑥ ⑧

**Adjust these valves with No. 1
cam lobe pointing down.**

1981-ON VALVE ADJUSTMENT

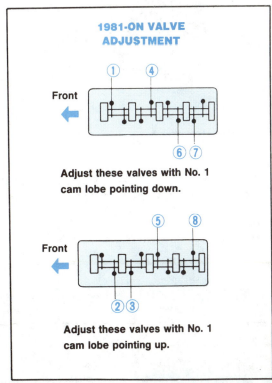

Front

① ④

⑥ ⑦

**Adjust these valves with No. 1
cam lobe pointing down.**

Front

⑤ ⑧

② ③

**Adjust these valves with No. 1
cam lobe pointing up.**

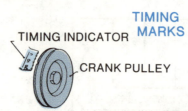

TIMING MARKS

TIMING INDICATOR

CRANK PULLEY

IDLE SPEED SCREW

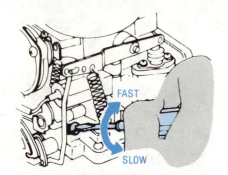

FAST

SLOW

NO. 1 TERMINAL (1981-ON)

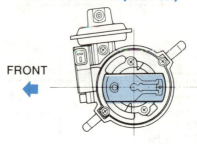

FRONT

DISTRIBUTOR LOCKBOLT

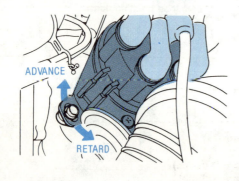

ADVANCE

RETARD

NO. 1 TERMINAL (1980)

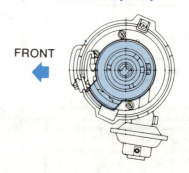

FRONT

ENGINE COMPRESSION SPECIFICATIONS

Standard compression	171 psi (12 kg/cm^2)
Minimum compression	128 psi (9 kg/cm^2)
Maximum variation between cylinders	Lowest reading within 80 per cent of highest

TIRE PRESSURES

Size	Load range	Pressure (psi)
G 78-15	B	28
G R 78-15	B	28

FUEL STOP CHECKS

Engine oil	Check level
Coolant	Check reserve tank level
Battery electrolyte	Check level
Windshield washer fluid	Check container level
Brake fluid	Check level
Clutch fluid	Check level
Tire pressures	Check

RECOMMENDED LUBRICANTS

Engine oil	API service SE
Transmission transfer case and steering gear	API GL-4
Differentials	API GL-5
Multipurpose grease	NLGI No. 2
Brake and clutch fluid	DOT 3
Antifreeze	Ethylene glycol base

APPROXIMATE REFILL CAPACITIES

Engine oil (including filter)	4.3 liters (4 1/2 qt.)
Transmission oil	
4-speed	1.7 liters (3 5/8 pt.)
5-speed	2.0 liters (4 1/4 pt.)
Transfer case oil	1.4 liters (3 pt.)
Differential	
Front	1.0 liter (2 1/8 pt.)
Rear	1.25 liters (2 5/8 pt.)
Steering gear	
Non-power	0.33 liter (3/4 pt.)
Power	1.0 liter (1 1/8 qt.)
Cooling system (including reservoir tank)	
1980	8.9 liters (9 3/8 qt.)
1981-on	10.2 liters (10 3/4 qt.)
Windshield washer tank	
1980	2 liters (2 1/8 qt.)
1981-on	1.85 liters (2 qt.)
Fuel tank	
1980	
Short bed	50 liters (13 1/4 gal.)
Long bed	64 liters (16 7/8 gal.)
1981-on	
Short bed	60 liters (15 7/8 gal.)
Long bed	75 liters (16 7/8 gal.)

TUNE-UP SPECIFICATIONS

Valve clearance
  1980
    Intake
      Hot   0.25 mm (0.010 in.)
      Cold   0.17 mm (0.007 in.)
    Exhaust
      Hot   0.30 mm (0.012 in.)
      Cold   0.24 mm (0.009 in.)
  1981-on
    Intake
      Hot   0.30 mm (0.012 in.)
      Cold   0.21 mm (0.008 in.)
    Exhaust
      Hot   0.30 mm (0.012 in.)
      Cold   0.23 mm (0.009 in.)

Spark plugs (NGK brand)
  1980
    U.S.
      Standard   BP6ES-11, BPR6ES-11
      Hot type   BP4ES-11, BPR4ES-11,
                                    BP5ES-11, BPR5ES-11
      Cold type   BP7ES-11, BPR7ES-11
    Canada
      Standard   BPR6ES
      Hot type   BPR4ES, BPR5ES
      Cold type   BPR7ES
  1981
    U.S.
      Standard   BP6ES
      Hot type   BP5ES
      Cold type   BP7ES
    Canada
      Standard   BPR6ES
      Hot type   BPR5ES
      Cold type   BPR7ES
  1982
    Intake side
      Standard   BPR6ES
      Hot type   BPR5ES
      Cold type   BPR7ES
    Exhaust side
      Standard and hot type   BPR5ES
      Cold type   BPR6ES, BPR7ES

Spark plug gap
  1980 U.S.   0.039-0.043 in. (1.0-1.1 mm)
  All others   0.031-0.035 in. (0.8-0.9 mm)

Ignition timing (at idle speed)
  1980 California   12 $\pm$2 degrees BTDC
  1980 non-California   10 $\pm$2 degrees BTDC
  1981   5 $\pm$2 degrees BTDC
  1982   3 $\pm$2 degrees BTDC

Idle speed
  1980 U.S.   600 $\pm$100 rpm
  1980 Canada   600 rpm
  1981-on   800 $\pm$100 rpm

DATSUN
4-WHEEL DRIVE PICKUPS
1980-1982
SHOP MANUAL

INTRODUCTION

This detailed, comprehensive manual covers all 1980-1982 Datsun 4-wheel drive pickups. The expert text gives complete information on maintenance, repair and overhaul. Hundreds of photos and drawings guide you through every step. The book includes all you need to know to keep your car running right.

Specific information for 1980-1981 models is contained in Chapters One through Thirteen. The Supplement at the back of the book contains information on 1982 models that differs from that in the main body of the book.

Where repairs are practical for the owner/mechanic, complete procedures are given. Equally important, difficult jobs are pointed out. Such operations are usually more economically performed by a dealer or independent garage.

A shop manual is a reference. You want to be able to find information fast. As in all Clymer books, this one is designed with this in mind. All chapters are thumb tabbed. Important items are indexed at the rear of the book. Finally, all the most frequently used specifications and capacities are summarized on the *Quick Reference* pages at the front of the book.

Keep the book handy. Carry it in your glove box. It will help you to better understand your truck, lower repair and maintenance costs, and generally improve your satisfaction with your vehicle.

CHAPTER ONE

GENERAL INFORMATION

The troubleshooting, tune-up, maintenance, and step-by-step repair procedures in this book are written for the owner and home mechanic. The text is accompanied by useful photos and diagrams to make the job as clear and correct as possible.

Troubleshooting, tune-up, maintenance, and repair are not difficult if you know what tools and equipment to use and what to do. Anyone not afraid to get their hands dirty, of average intelligence, and with some mechanical ability can perform most of the procedures in this book.

In some cases, a repair job may require tools or skills not reasonably expected of the home mechanic. These procedures are noted in each chapter and it is recommended that you take the job to your dealer, a competent mechanic, or machine shop.

MANUAL ORGANIZATION

This chapter provides general information and safety and service hints. Also included are lists of recommended shop and emergency tools as well as a brief description of troubleshooting and tune-up equipment.

Chapter Two provides methods and suggestions for quick and accurate diagnosis and repair of problems. Troubleshooting procedures discuss typical symptoms and logical methods to pinpoint the trouble.

Chapter Three explains all periodic lubrication and routine maintenance necessary to keep your vehicle running well. Chapter Three also includes recommended tune-up procedures, eliminating the need to constantly consult chapters on the various subassemblies.

Subsequent chapters cover specific systems such as the engine, transmission, and electrical systems. Each of these chapters provides disassembly, repair, and assembly procedures in a simple step-by-step format. If a repair requires special skills or tools, or is otherwise impractical for the home mechanic, it is so indicated. In these cases it is usually faster and less expensive to have the repairs made by a dealer or competent repair shop. Necessary specifications concerning a particular system are included at the end of the appropriate chapter.

When special tools are required to perform a procedure included in this manual, the tool is illustrated either in actual use or alone. It may be possible to rent or borrow these tools. The inventive mechanic may also be able to find a suitable substitute in his tool box, or to fabricate one.

The terms NOTE, CAUTION, and WARNING have specific meanings in this manual. A NOTE provides additional or explanatory information. A CAUTION is used to emphasize areas where equipment damage could result if proper precautions are not taken. A WARNING is used to stress those areas where personal injury or death could result from negligence, in addition to possible mechanical damage.

SERVICE HINTS

Observing the following practices will save time, effort, and frustration, as well as prevent possible injury.

Throughout this manual keep in mind two conventions. "Front" refers to the front of the vehicle. The front of any component, such as the transmission, is that end which faces toward the front of the vehicle. The "left" and "right" sides of the vehicle refer to the orientation of a person sitting in the vehicle facing forward. For example, the steering wheel is on the left side. These rules are simple, but even experienced mechanics occasionally become disoriented.

Most of the service procedures covered are straightforward and can be performed by anyone reasonably handy with tools. It is suggested, however, that you consider your own capabilities carefully before attempting any operation involving major disassembly of the engine.

Some operations, for example, require the use of a press. It would be wiser to have these performed by a shop equipped for such work, rather than to try to do the job yourself with makeshift equipment. Other procedures require precision measurements. Unless you have the skills and equipment required, it would be better to have a qualified repair shop make the measurements for you.

Repairs go much faster and easier if the parts that will be worked on are clean before you begin. There are special cleaners for washing the engine and related parts. Brush or spray on the cleaning solution, let it stand, then rinse it away with a garden hose. Clean all oily or greasy parts with cleaning solvent as you remove them.

WARNING
Never use gasoline as a cleaning agent. It presents an extreme fire hazard. Be sure to work in a well-ventilated area when using cleaning solvent. Keep a fire extinguisher, rated for gasoline fires, handy in any case.

Much of the labor charge for repairs made by dealers is for the removal and disassembly of other parts to reach the defective unit. It is frequently possible to perform the preliminary operations yourself and then take the defective unit in to the dealer for repair, at considerable savings.

Once you have decided to tackle the job yourself, make sure you locate the appropriate section in this manual, and read it entirely. Study the illustrations and text until you have a good idea of what is involved in completing the job satisfactorily. If special tools are required, make arrangements to get them before you start. Also, purchase any known defective parts prior to starting on the procedure. It is frustrating and time-consuming to get partially into a job and then be unable to complete it.

Simple wiring checks can be easily made at home, but knowledge of electronics is almost a necessity for performing tests with complicated electronic testing gear.

During disassembly of parts keep a few general cautions in mind. Force is rarely needed to get things apart. If parts are a tight fit, like a bearing in a case, there is usually a tool designed to separate them. Never use a screwdriver to pry apart parts with machined surfaces such as cylinder head and valve cover. You will mar the surfaces and end up with leaks.

Make diagrams wherever similar-appearing parts are found. You may think you can remember where everything came from — but mistakes are costly. There is also the possibility you may get sidetracked and not return to work for days or even weeks — in which interval, carefully laid out parts may have become disturbed.

Tag all similar internal parts for location, and mark all mating parts for position. Record number and thickness of any shims as they are removed. Small parts such as bolts can be identified by placing them in plastic sandwich bags that are sealed and labeled with masking tape.

Wiring should be tagged with masking tape and marked as each wire is removed. Again, do not rely on memory alone.

When working under the vehicle, do not trust a hydraulic or mechanical jack to hold the vehicle up by itself. Always use jackstands. See **Figure 1**.

Disconnect battery ground cable before working near electrical connections and before disconnecting wires. Never run the engine with the battery disconnected; the alternator could be seriously damaged.

Protect finished surfaces from physical damage or corrosion. Keep gasoline and brake fluid off painted surfaces.

Frozen or very tight bolts and screws can often be loosened by soaking with penetrating oil like Liquid Wrench or WD-40, then sharply striking the bolt head a few times with a hammer and punch (or screwdriver for screws). Avoid heat unless absolutely necessary, since it may melt, warp, or remove the temper from many parts.

Avoid flames or sparks when working near a charging battery or flammable liquids, such as brake fluid or gasoline.

No parts, except those assembled with a press fit, require unusual force during assembly. If a part is hard to remove or install, find out why before proceeding.

Cover all openings after removing parts to keep dirt, small tools, etc., from falling in.

When assembling two parts, start all fasteners, then tighten evenly.

The clutch plate, wiring connections, brake shoes, drums, pads, and discs should be kept clean and free of grease and oil.

When assembling parts, be sure all shims and washers are replaced exactly as they came out.

Whenever a rotating part butts against a stationary part, look for a shim or washer. Use new gaskets if there is any doubt about the condition of old ones. Generally, you should apply gasket cement to one mating surface only, so the parts may be easily disassembled in the future. A thin coat of oil on gaskets helps them seal effectively.

Heavy grease can be used to hold small parts in place if they tend to fall out during assembly. However, keep grease and oil away from electrical, clutch, and brake components.

High spots may be sanded off a piston with sandpaper, but emery cloth and oil do a much more professional job.

Carburetors are best cleaned by disassembling them and soaking the parts in a commercial carburetor cleaner. Never soak gaskets and rubber parts in these cleaners. Never use wire to clean out jets and air passages; they are easily damaged. Use compressed air to blow out the carburetor, but only if the float has been removed first.

Take your time and do the job right. Do not forget that a newly rebuilt engine must be broken in the same as a new one. Refer to your owner's manual for the proper break-in procedures.

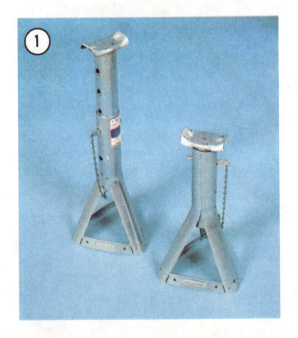

SAFETY FIRST

Professional mechanics can work for years and never sustain a serious injury. If you observe a few rules of common sense and safety, you can enjoy many safe hours servicing your vehicle. You could hurt yourself or damage the vehicle if you ignore these rules.

1. Never use gasoline as a cleaning solvent.

2. Never smoke or use a torch in the vicinity of flammable liquids such as cleaning solvent in open containers.

3. Never smoke or use a torch in an area where batteries are being charged. Highly explosive hydrogen gas is formed during the charging process.

4. Use the proper sized wrenches to avoid damage to nuts and injury to yourself.

5. When loosening a tight or stuck nut, be guided by what would happen if the wrench should slip. Protect yourself accordingly.

6. Keep your work area clean and uncluttered.

7. Wear safety goggles during all operations involving drilling, grinding, or use of a cold chisel.

8. Never use worn tools.

9. Keep a fire extinguisher handy and be sure it is rated for gasoline (Class B) and electrical (Class C) fires.

EXPENDABLE SUPPLIES

Certain expendable supplies are necessary. These include grease, oil, gasket cement, wiping rags, cleaning solvent, and distilled water.

Also, special locking compounds, silicone lubricants, and engine cleaners may be useful. Cleaning solvent is available at most service stations and distilled water for the battery is available at most supermarkets.

SHOP TOOLS

For proper servicing, you will need an assortment of ordinary hand tools (**Figure 2**).

As a minimum, these include:

a. Combination wrenches
b. Sockets
c. Plastic mallet
d. Small hammer
e. Snap ring pliers
f. Gas pliers
g. Phillips screwdrivers
h. Slot (common) screwdrivers
i. Feeler gauges
j. Spark plug gauge
k. Spark plug wrench

Special tools necessary are shown in the chapters covering the particular repair in which they are used.

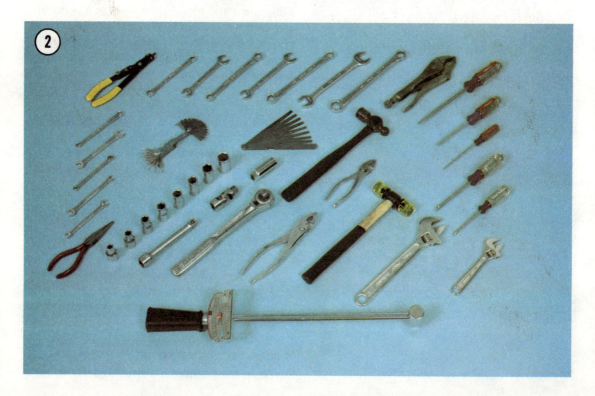

Engine tune-up and troubleshooting procedures require other special tools and equipment. These are described in detail in the following sections.

EMERGENCY TOOL KIT

A small emergency tool kit kept in the trunk is handy for road emergencies which otherwise could leave you stranded. The tools listed below and shown in **Figure 3** will let you handle most roadside repairs.

a. Combination wrenches
b. Crescent (adjustable) wrench
c. Screwdrivers — common and Phillips
d. Pliers — conventional (gas) and needle nose
e. Vise Grips
f. Hammer — plastic and metal
g. Small container of waterless hand cleaner
h. Rags for clean up
i. Silver waterproof sealing tape (duct tape)
j. Flashlight
k. Emergency road flares — at least four
l. Spare drive belts (water pump, alternator, etc.)

TROUBLESHOOTING AND TUNE-UP EQUIPMENT

Voltmeter, Ohmmeter, and Ammeter

For testing the ignition or electrical system, a good voltmeter is required. For automotive use, an instrument covering 0-20 volts is satisfac-

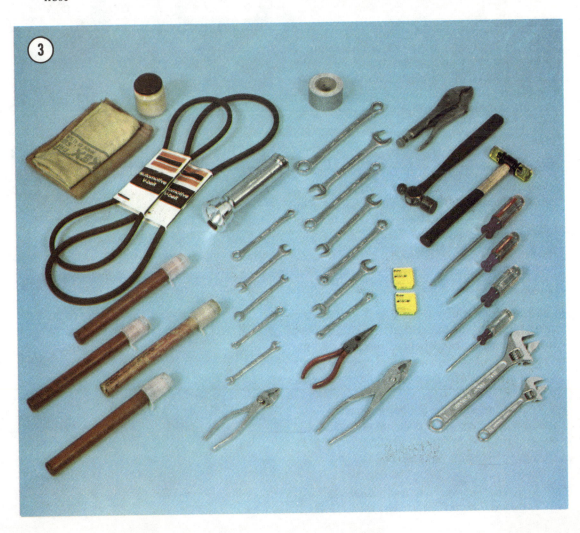

tory. One which also has a 0-2 volt scale is necessary for testing relays, points, or individual contacts where voltage drops are much smaller. Accuracy should be ± ½ volt.

An ohmmeter measures electrical resistance. This instrument is useful for checking continuity (open and short circuits), and testing fuses and lights.

The ammeter measures electrical current. Ammeters for automotive use should cover 0-50 amperes and 0-250 amperes. These are useful for checking battery charging and starting current.

Several inexpensive vom's (volt-ohm-milli-ammeter) combine all three instruments into one which fits easily in any tool box. See **Figure 4**. However, the ammeter ranges are usually too small for automotive work.

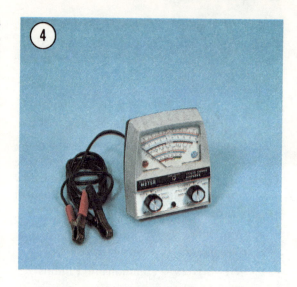

Hydrometer

The hydrometer gives a useful indication of battery condition and charge by measuring the specific gravity of the electrolyte in each cell. See **Figure 5**. Complete details on use and interpretation of readings are provided in the electrical chapter.

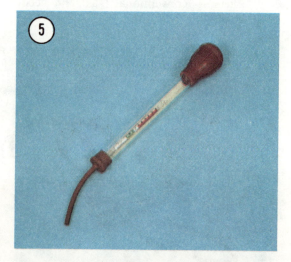

Compression Tester

The compression tester measures the compression pressure built up in each cylinder. The results, when properly interpreted, can indicate general cylinder and valve condition. See **Figure 6**.

Vacuum Gauge

The vacuum gauge (**Figure 7**) is one of the easiest instruments to use, but one of the most difficult for the inexperienced mechanic to interpret. The results, when interpreted with other findings, can provide valuable clues to possible trouble.

To use the vacuum gauge, connect it to a vacuum hose that goes to the intake manifold. Attach it either directly to the hose or to a T-fitting installed into the hose.

NOTE: *Subtract one inch from the reading for every 1,000 ft. elevation.*

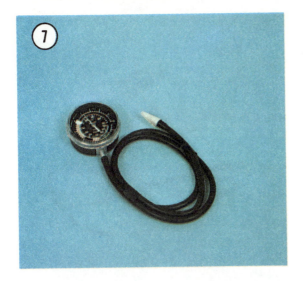

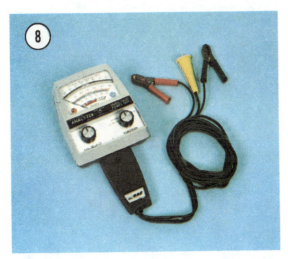

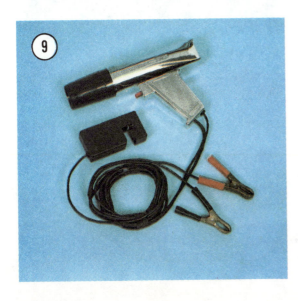

Fuel Pressure Gauge

This instrument is invaluable for evaluating fuel pump performance. Fuel system trouble-shooting procedures in this manual use a fuel pressure gauge. Usually a vacuum gauge and fuel pressure gauge are combined.

Dwell Meter (Contact Breaker Point Ignition Only)

A dwell meter measures the distance in degrees of cam rotation that the breaker points remain closed while the engine is running. Since this angle is determined by breaker point gap, dwell angle is an accurate indication of breaker point gap.

Many tachometers intended for tuning and testing incorporate a dwell meter as well. See **Figure 8**. Follow the manufacturer's instructions to measure dwell.

Tachometer

A tachometer is necessary for tuning. See **Figure 8**. Ignition timing and carburetor adjustments must be performed at the specified idle speed. The best instrument for this purpose is one with a low range of 0-1,000 or 0-2,000 rpm for setting idle, and a high range of 0-4,000 or more for setting ignition timing at 3,000 rpm. Extended range (0-6,000 or 0-8,000 rpm) instruments lack accuracy at lower speeds. The instrument should be capable of detecting changes of 25 rpm on the low range.

Strobe Timing Light

This instrument is necessary for tuning, as it permits very accurate ignition timing. The light flashes at precisely the same instant that No. 1 cylinder fires, at which time the timing marks on the engine should align. Refer to Chapter Three for exact location of the timing marks for your engine.

Suitable lights range from inexpensive neon bulb types ($2-3) to powerful xenon strobe lights ($20-40). See **Figure 9**. Neon timing lights are difficult to see and must be used in dimly lit areas. Xenon strobe timing lights can be used outside in bright sunlight. Both types work on this vehicle; use according to the manufacturer's instructions.

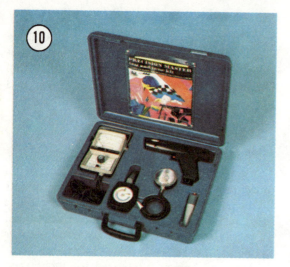

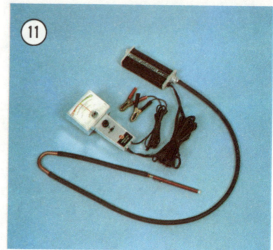

Tune-up Kits

Many manufacturers offer kits that combine several useful instruments. Some come in a convenient carry case and are usually less expensive than purchasing one instrument at a time. **Figure 10** shows one of the kits that is available. The prices vary with the number of instruments included in the kit.

Exhaust Gas Analyzer

Of all instruments described here, this is the least likely to be owned by a home mechanic. This instrument samples the exhaust gases from the tailpipe and measures the thermal conductivity of the exhaust gas. Since different gases conduct heat at varying rates, thermal conductivity of the exhaust is a good indication of gases present.

An exhaust gas analyzer is vital for accurately checking the effectiveness of exhaust emission control adjustments. They are relatively expensive to buy ($70 and up), but must be considered essential for the owner/mechanic to comply with today's emission laws. See **Figure 11**.

Fire Extinguisher

A fire extinguisher is a necessity when working on a vehicle. It should be rated for both *Class B* (flammable liquids — gasoline, oil, paint, etc.) and *Class C* (electrical — wiring, etc.) type fires. It should always be kept within reach. See **Figure 12**.

CHAPTER TWO

2

TROUBLESHOOTING

Troubleshooting can be a relatively simple matter if it is done logically. The first step in any troubleshooting procedure must be defining the symptoms as closely as possible. Subsequent steps involve testing and analyzing areas which could cause the symptoms. A haphazard approach may eventually find the trouble, but in terms of wasted time and unnecessary parts replacement, it can be very costly.

The troubleshooting procedures in this chapter analyze typical symptoms and show logical methods of isolation. These are not the only methods. There may be several approaches to a problem, but all methods must have one thing in common — a logical, systematic approach.

STARTING SYSTEM

The starting system consists of the starter motor and the starter solenoid. The ignition key controls the starter solenoid, which mechanically engages the starter with the engine flywheel, and supplies electrical current to turn the starter motor.

Starting system troubles are relatively easy to find. In most cases, the trouble is a loose or dirty electrical connection. **Figures 1 and 2** provide routines for finding the trouble.

CHARGING SYSTEM

The charging system consists of the alternator (or generator on older vehicles), voltage regulator, and battery. A drive belt driven by the engine crankshaft turns the alternator which produces electrical energy to charge the battery. As engine speed varies, the voltage from the alternator varies. A voltage regulator controls the charging current to the battery and maintains the voltage to the vehicle's electrical system at safe levels. A warning light or gauge on the instrument panel signals the driver when charging is not taking place. Refer to **Figure 3** for a typical charging system.

Complete troubleshooting of the charging system requires test equipment and skills which the average home mechanic does not possess. However, there are a few tests which can be done to pinpoint most troubles.

Charging system trouble may stem from a defective alternator (or generator), voltage regulator, battery, or drive belt. It may also be caused by something as simple as incorrect drive belt tension. The following are symptoms of typical problems you may encounter.

1. *Battery dies frequently, even though the warning lamp indicates no discharge* — This can be caused by a drive belt that is slightly too

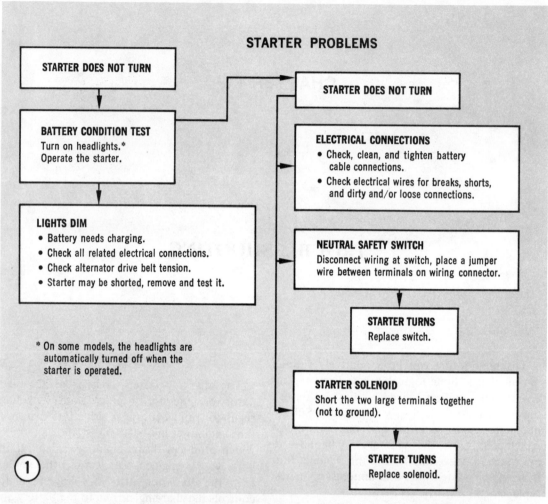

STARTER PROBLEMS

STARTER DOES NOT TURN

BATTERY CONDITION TEST
Turn on headlights.*
Operate the starter.

LIGHTS DIM
• Battery needs charging.
• Check all related electrical connections.
• Check alternator drive belt tension.
• Starter may be shorted, remove and test it.

* On some models, the headlights are
automatically turned off when the
starter is operated.

STARTER DOES NOT TURN

ELECTRICAL CONNECTIONS
• Check, clean, and tighten battery
cable connections.
• Check electrical wires for breaks, shorts,
and dirty and/or loose connections.

NEUTRAL SAFETY SWITCH
Disconnect wiring at switch, place a jumper
wire between terminals on wiring connector.

STARTER TURNS
Replace switch.

STARTER SOLENOID
Short the two large terminals together
(not to ground).

STARTER TURNS
Replace solenoid.

①

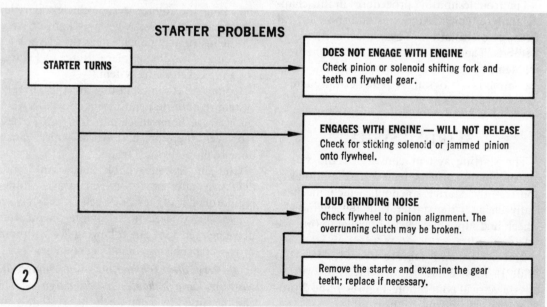

STARTER PROBLEMS

STARTER TURNS

DOES NOT ENGAGE WITH ENGINE
Check pinion or solenoid shifting fork and
teeth on flywheel gear.

ENGAGES WITH ENGINE — WILL NOT RELEASE
Check for sticking solenoid or jammed pinion
onto flywheel.

LOUD GRINDING NOISE
Check flywheel to pinion alignment. The
overrunning clutch may be broken.

Remove the starter and examine the gear
teeth; replace if necessary.

②

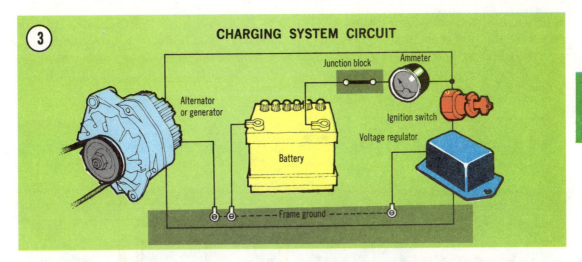

③ **CHARGING SYSTEM CIRCUIT**

Junction block

Ammeter

Alternator or generator

Ignition switch

Voltage regulator

Battery

Frame ground

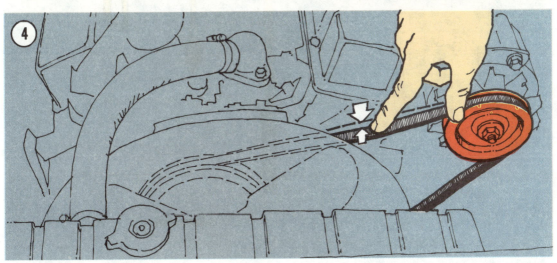

④

loose. Grasp the alternator (or generator) pulley and try to turn it. If the pulley can be turned without moving the belt, the drive belt is too loose. As a rule, keep the belt tight enough that it can be deflected about ½ in. under moderate thumb pressure between the pulleys (**Figure 4**). The battery may also be at fault; test the battery condition.

2. *Charging system warning lamp does not come on when ignition switch is turned on* — This may indicate a defective ignition switch, battery, voltage regulator, or lamp. First try to start the vehicle. If it doesn't start, check the ignition switch and battery. If the car starts, remove the warning lamp; test it for continuity with an ohmmeter or substitute a new lamp. If the lamp is good, locate the voltage regulator

and make sure it is properly grounded (try tightening the mounting screws). Also the alternator (or generator) brushes may not be making contact. Test the alternator (or generator) and voltage regulator.

3. *Alternator (or generator) warning lamp comes on and stays on* — This usually indicates that no charging is taking place. First check drive belt tension (**Figure 4**). Then check battery condition, and check all wiring connections in the charging system. If this does not locate the trouble, check the alternator (or generator) and voltage regulator.

4. *Charging system warning lamp flashes on and off intermittently* — This usually indicates the charging system is working intermittently.

Check the drive belt tension (**Figure 4**), and check all electrical connections in the charging system. Check the alternator (or generator). *On generators only*, check the condition of the commutator.

5. *Battery requires frequent additions of water, or lamps require frequent replacement* — The alternator (or generator) is probably overcharging the battery. The voltage regulator is probably at fault.

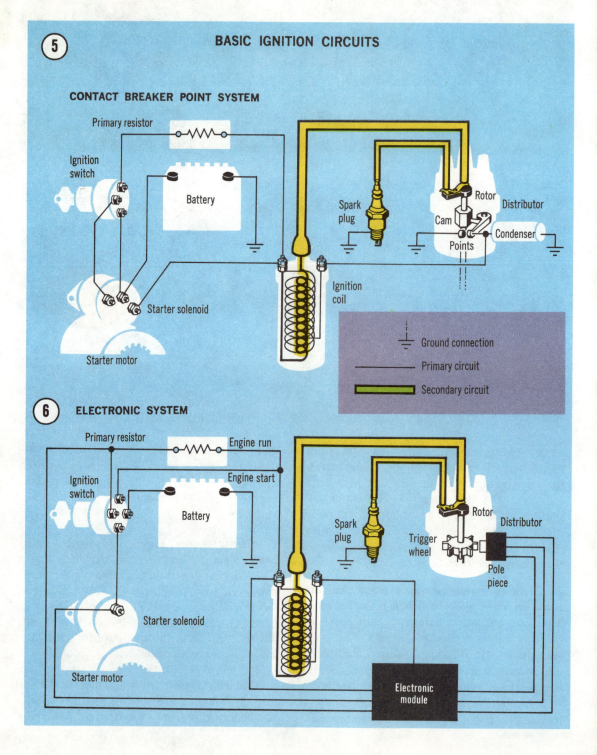

⑤ **BASIC IGNITION CIRCUITS**

CONTACT BREAKER POINT SYSTEM

Primary resistor

Ignition switch

Battery

Spark plug

Cam

Rotor

Distributor

Condenser

Points

Ignition coil

Starter solenoid

Starter motor

⎓ Ground connection

——— Primary circuit

▬▬▬ Secondary circuit

⑥ **ELECTRONIC SYSTEM**

Primary resistor

Engine run

Ignition switch

Engine start

Battery

Spark plug

Trigger wheel

Rotor

Distributor

Pole piece

Starter solenoid

Starter motor

Electronic module

6. *Excessive noise from the alternator (or generator)* — Check for loose mounting brackets and bolts. The problem may also be worn bearings or the need of lubrication in some cases. If an alternator whines, a shorted diode may be indicated.

IGNITION SYSTEM

The ignition system may be either a conventional contact breaker type or an electronic ignition. See electrical chapter to determine which type you have. **Figures 5 and 6** show simplified diagrams of each type.

Most problems involving failure to start, poor performance, or rough running stem from trouble in the ignition system, particularly in contact breaker systems. Many novice troubleshooters get into trouble when they assume that these symptoms point to the fuel system instead of the ignition system.

Ignition system troubles may be roughly divided between those affecting only one cylinder and those affecting all cylinders. If the trouble affects only one cylinder, it can only be in the spark plug, spark plug wire, or portion of the distributor associated with that cylinder. If the trouble affects all cylinders (weak spark or no spark), then the trouble is in the ignition coil, rotor, distributor, or associated wiring.

The troubleshooting procedures outlined in **Figure 7** (breaker point ignition) or **Figure 8**

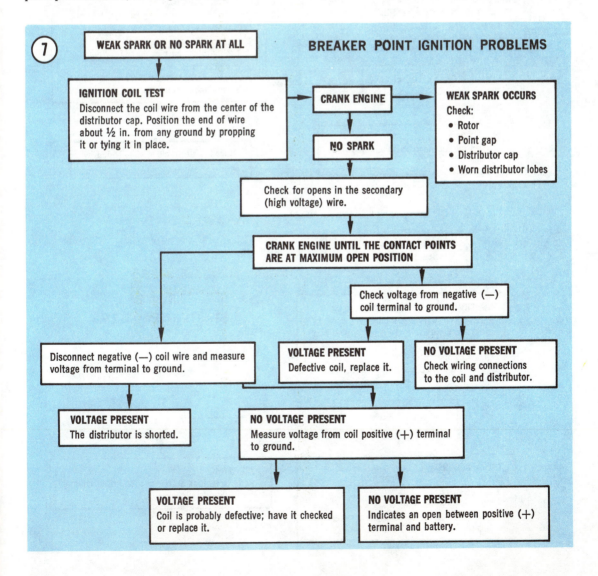

(electronic ignition) will help you isolate ignition problems fast. Of course, they assume that the battery is in good enough condition to crank the engine over at its normal rate.

ENGINE PERFORMANCE

A number of factors can make the engine difficult or impossible to start, or cause rough running, poor performance and so on. The majority of novice troubleshooters immediately suspect the carburetor or fuel injection system. In the majority of cases, though, the trouble exists in the ignition system.

The troubleshooting procedures outlined in **Figures 9 through 14** will help you solve the majority of engine starting troubles in a systematic manner.

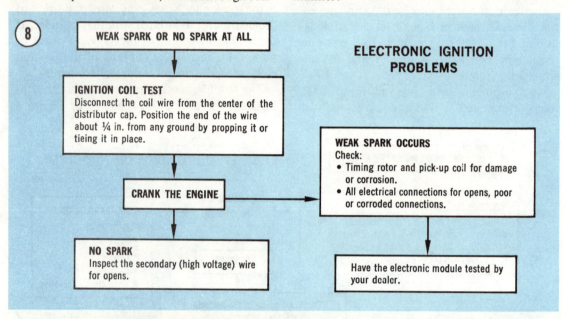

⑧ **ELECTRONIC IGNITION PROBLEMS**

WEAK SPARK OR NO SPARK AT ALL

IGNITION COIL TEST
Disconnect the coil wire from the center of the distributor cap. Position the end of the wire about ¼ in. from any ground by propping it or tieing it in place.

CRANK THE ENGINE

NO SPARK
Inspect the secondary (high voltage) wire for opens.

WEAK SPARK OCCURS
Check:
• Timing rotor and pick-up coil for damage or corrosion.
• All electrical connections for opens, poor or corroded connections.

Have the electronic module tested by your dealer.

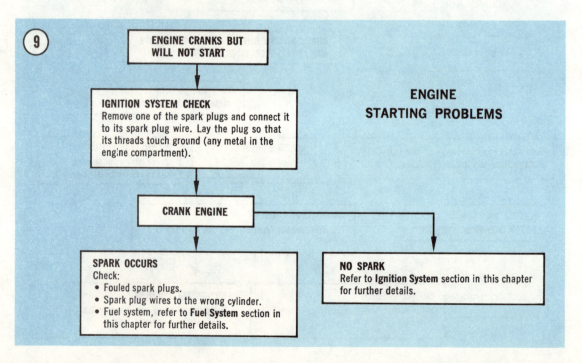

⑨ **ENGINE STARTING PROBLEMS**

ENGINE CRANKS BUT WILL NOT START

IGNITION SYSTEM CHECK
Remove one of the spark plugs and connect it to its spark plug wire. Lay the plug so that its threads touch ground (any metal in the engine compartment).

CRANK ENGINE

SPARK OCCURS
Check:
• Fouled spark plugs.
• Spark plug wires to the wrong cylinder.
• Fuel system, refer to **Fuel System** section in this chapter for further details.

NO SPARK
Refer to **Ignition System** section in this chapter for further details.

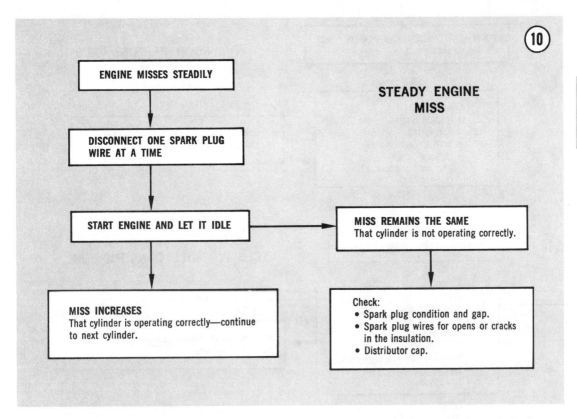

⑩

ENGINE MISSES STEADILY

STEADY ENGINE MISS

DISCONNECT ONE SPARK PLUG WIRE AT A TIME

START ENGINE AND LET IT IDLE → **MISS REMAINS THE SAME**
That cylinder is not operating correctly.

MISS INCREASES
That cylinder is operating correctly—continue to next cylinder.

Check:
• Spark plug condition and gap.
• Spark plug wires for opens or cracks in the insulation.
• Distributor cap.

2

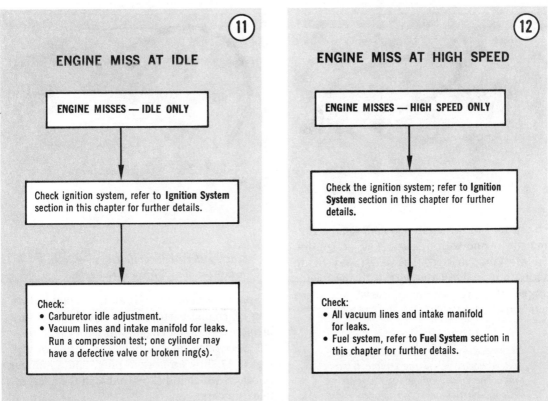

⑪

ENGINE MISS AT IDLE

ENGINE MISSES — IDLE ONLY

Check ignition system, refer to **Ignition System** section in this chapter for further details.

Check:
• Carburetor idle adjustment.
• Vacuum lines and intake manifold for leaks. Run a compression test; one cylinder may have a defective valve or broken ring(s).

⑫

ENGINE MISS AT HIGH SPEED

ENGINE MISSES — HIGH SPEED ONLY

Check the ignition system; refer to **Ignition System** section in this chapter for further details.

Check:
• All vacuum lines and intake manifold for leaks.
• Fuel system, refer to **Fuel System** section in this chapter for further details.

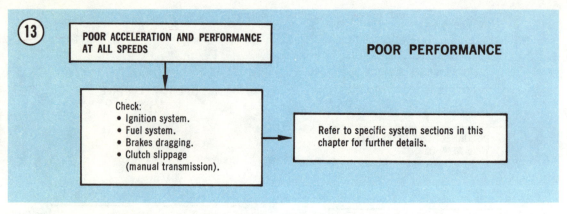

(13)

POOR ACCELERATION AND PERFORMANCE AT ALL SPEEDS

POOR PERFORMANCE

Check:
• Ignition system.
• Fuel system.
• Brakes dragging.
• Clutch slippage (manual transmission).

Refer to specific system sections in this chapter for further details.

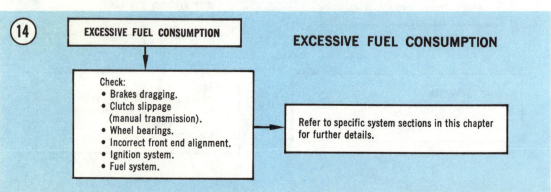

(14)

EXCESSIVE FUEL CONSUMPTION

EXCESSIVE FUEL CONSUMPTION

Check:
• Brakes dragging.
• Clutch slippage (manual transmission).
• Wheel bearings.
• Incorrect front end alignment.
• Ignition system.
• Fuel system.

Refer to specific system sections in this chapter for further details.

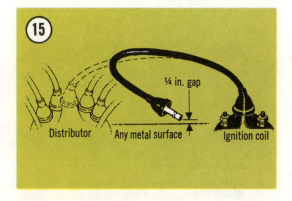

(15)

¼ in. gap

Distributor   Any metal surface   Ignition coil

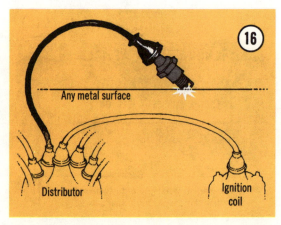

(16)

Any metal surface

Distributor   Ignition coil

Some tests of the ignition system require running the engine with a spark plug or ignition coil wire disconnected. The safest way to do this is to disconnect the wire with the engine stopped, then prop the end of the wire next to a metal surface as shown in **Figures 15 and 16**.

WARNING
Never disconnect a spark plug or ignition coil wire while the engine is running. The high voltage in an ignition system, particularly the newer high-energy electronic ignition systems could cause serious injury or even death.

Spark plug condition is an important indication of engine performance. Spark plugs in a properly operating engine will have slightly pitted electrodes, and a light tan insulator tip. **Figure 17** shows a normal plug, and a number of others which indicate trouble in their respective cylinders.

NORMAL
- Appearance—Firing tip has deposits of light gray to light tan.
- Can be cleaned, regapped and reused.

CARBON FOULED
- Appearance—Dull, dry black with fluffy carbon deposits on the insulator tip, electrode and exposed shell.
- Caused by—Fuel/air mixture too rich, plug heat range too cold, weak ignition system, dirty air cleaner, faulty automatic choke or excessive idling.
- Can be cleaned, regapped and reused.

OIL FOULED
- Appearance—Wet black deposits on insulator and exposed shell.
- Caused by—Excessive oil entering the combustion chamber through worn rings, pistons, valve guides or bearings.
- Replace with new plugs (use a hotter plug if engine is not repaired).

LEAD FOULED
- Appearance — Yellow insulator deposits (may sometimes be dark gray, black or tan in color) on the insulator tip.
- Caused by—Highly leaded gasoline.
- Replace with new plugs.

LEAD FOULED
- Appearance—Yellow glazed deposits indicating melted lead deposits due to hard acceleration.
- Caused by—Highly leaded gasoline.
- Replace with new plugs.

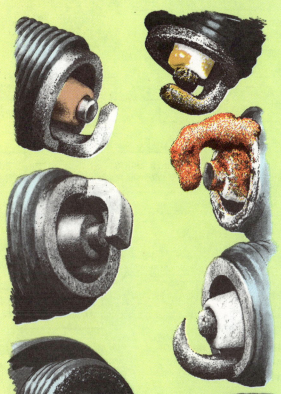

OIL AND LEAD FOULED
- Appearance—Glazed yellow deposits with a slight brownish tint on the insulator tip and ground electrode.
- Replace with new plugs.

FUEL ADDITIVE RESIDUE
- Appearance — Brown colored hardened ash deposits on the insulator tip and ground electrode.
- Caused by—Fuel and/or oil additives.
- Replace with new plugs.

WORN
- Appearance — Severely worn or eroded electrodes.
- Caused by—Normal wear or unusual oil and/or fuel additives.
- Replace with new plugs.

PREIGNITION
- Appearance — Melted ground electrode.
- Caused by—Overadvanced ignition timing, inoperative ignition advance mechanism, too low of a fuel octane rating, lean fuel/air mixture or carbon deposits in combustion chamber.

PREIGNITION
- Appearance—Melted center electrode.
- Caused by—Abnormal combustion due to overadvanced ignition timing or incorrect advance, too low of a fuel octane rating, lean fuel/air mixture, or carbon deposits in combustion chamber.
- Correct engine problem and replace with new plugs.

INCORRECT HEAT RANGE
- Appearance—Melted center electrode and white blistered insulator tip.
- Caused by—Incorrect plug heat range selection.
- Replace with new plugs.

2

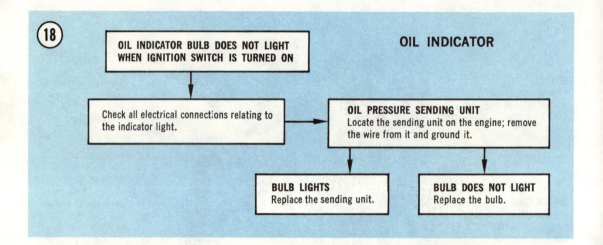

ENGINE OIL PRESSURE LIGHT

Proper oil pressure to the engine is vital. If oil pressure is insufficient, the engine can destroy itself in a comparatively short time.

The oil pressure warning circuit monitors oil pressure constantly. If pressure drops below a predetermined level, the light comes on.

Obviously, it is vital for the warning circuit to be working to signal low oil pressure. Each time you turn on the ignition, but before you start the car, the warning light should come on. If it doesn't, there is trouble in the warning circuit, not the oil pressure system. See **Figure 18** to troubleshoot the warning circuit.

Once the engine is running, the warning light should stay off. If the warning light comes on or acts erratically while the engine is running there is trouble with the engine oil pressure system. *Stop the engine immediately*. Refer to **Figure 19** for possible causes of the problem.

FUEL SYSTEM (CARBURETTED)

Fuel system problems must be isolated to the fuel pump (mechanical or electric), fuel lines, fuel filter, or carburetor. These procedures assume the ignition system is working properly and is correctly adjusted.

1. *Engine will not start* — First make sure that fuel is being delivered to the carburetor. Remove the air cleaner, look into the carburetor throat, and operate the accelerator

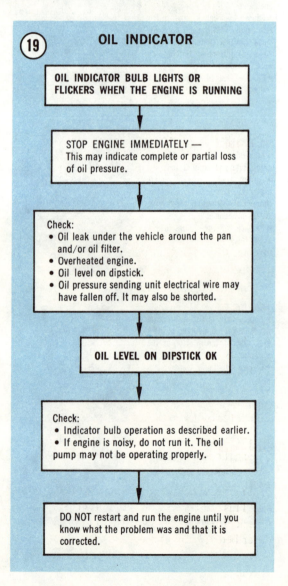

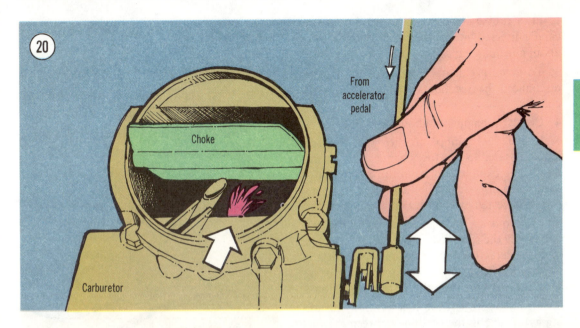

linkage several times. There should be a stream of fuel from the accelerator pump discharge tube each time the accelerator linkage is depressed (**Figure 20**). If not, check fuel pump delivery (described later), float valve, and float adjustment. If the engine will not start, check the automatic choke parts for sticking or damage. If necessary, rebuild or replace the carburetor.

2. *Engine runs at fast idle* — Check the choke setting. Check the idle speed, idle mixture, and decel valve (if equipped) adjustment.

3. *Rough idle or engine miss with frequent stalling* — Check idle mixture and idle speed adjustments.

4. *Engine "diesels" (continues to run) when ignition is switched off* — Check idle mixture (probably too rich), ignition timing, and idle speed (probably too fast). Check the throttle solenoid (if equipped) for proper operation. Check for overheated engine.

5. *Stumbling when accelerating from idle* — Check the idle speed and mixture adjustments. Check the accelerator pump.

6. *Engine misses at high speed or lacks power* — This indicates possible fuel starvation. Check fuel pump pressure and capacity as described in this chapter. Check float needle valves. Check for a clogged fuel filter or air cleaner.

7. *Black exhaust smoke* — This indicates a badly overrich mixture. Check idle mixture and idle speed adjustment. Check choke setting. Check for excessive fuel pump pressure, leaky floats, or worn needle valves.

8. *Excessive fuel consumption* — Check for overrich mixture. Make sure choke mechanism works properly. Check idle mixture and idle speed. Check for excessive fuel pump pressure, leaky floats, or worn float needle valves.

FUEL SYSTEM (FUEL INJECTED)

Troubleshooting a fuel injection system requires more thought, experience, and know-how than any other part of the vehicle. A logical approach and proper test equipment are essential in order to successfully find and fix these troubles.

It is best to leave fuel injection troubles to your dealer. In order to isolate a problem to the injection system make sure that the fuel pump is operating properly. Check its performance as described later in this section. Also make sure that fuel filter and air cleaner are not clogged.

FUEL PUMP TEST (MECHANICAL AND ELECTRIC)

1. Disconnect the fuel inlet line where it enters the carburetor or fuel injection system.

2. Fit a rubber hose over the fuel line so fuel can be directed into a graduated container with about one quart capacity. See **Figure 21**.

3. To avoid accidental starting of the engine, disconnect the secondary coil wire from the coil.

4. Crank the engine for about 30 seconds.

5. If the fuel pump supplies the specified amount (refer to the fuel chapter later in this book), the trouble may be in the carburetor or fuel injection system. The fuel injection system should be tested by your dealer.

6. If there is no fuel present or the pump cannot supply the specified amount, either the fuel pump is defective or there is an obstruction in the fuel line. Replace the fuel pump and/or inspect the fuel lines for air leaks or obstructions.

7. Also pressure test the fuel pump by installing a T-fitting in the fuel line between the fuel pump and the carburetor. Connect a fuel pressure gauge to the fitting with a short tube (**Figure 22**).

8. Reconnect the primary coil wire, start the engine, and record the pressure. Refer to the fuel chapter later in this book for the correct pressure. If the pressure varies from that specified, the pump should be replaced.

9. Stop the engine. The pressure should drop off very slowly. If it drops off rapidly, the outlet valve in the pump is leaking and the pump should be replaced.

EMISSION CONTROL SYSTEMS

Major emission control systems used on nearly all U.S. models include the following:

a. Positive crankcase ventilation (PCV)

b. Thermostatic air cleaner

c. Air injection reaction (AIR)

d. Fuel evaporation control

e. Exhaust gas recirculation (EGR)

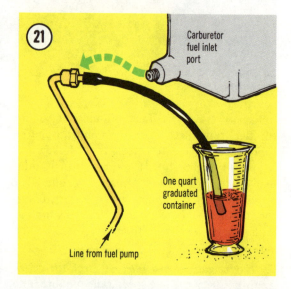

Carburetor fuel inlet port

One quart graduated container

Line from fuel pump

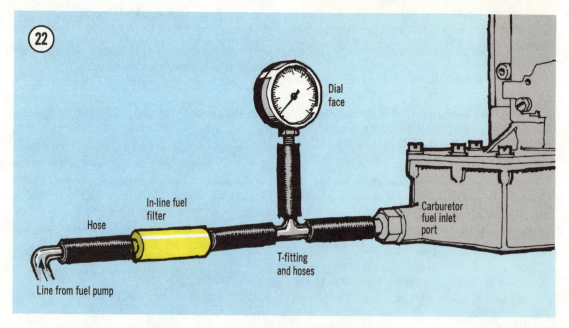

Dial face

In-line fuel filter

Hose

Line from fuel pump

T-fitting and hoses

Carburetor fuel inlet port

Emission control systems vary considerably from model to model. Individual models contain variations of the four systems described here. In addition, they may include other special systems. Use the index to find specific emission control components in other chapters.

Many of the systems and components are factory set and sealed. Without special expensive test equipment, it is impossible to adjust the systems to meet state and federal requirements.

Troubleshooting can also be difficult without special equipment. The procedures described below will help you find emission control parts which have failed, but repairs may have to be entrusted to a dealer or other properly equipped repair shop.

With the proper equipment, you can test the carbon monoxide and hydrocarbon levels.

Figure 23 provides some sources of trouble if the readings are not correct.

Positive Crankcase Ventilation

Fresh air drawn from the air cleaner housing scavenges emissions (e.g., piston blow-by) from the crankcase, then the intake manifold vacuum draws emissions into the intake manifold. They can then be reburned in the normal combustion process. **Figure 24** shows a typical system. **Figure 25** provides a testing procedure.

Thermostatic Air Cleaner

The thermostatically controlled air cleaner maintains incoming air to the engine at a predetermined level, usually about 100°F or higher. It mixes cold air with heated air from the exhaust manifold region. The air cleaner in-

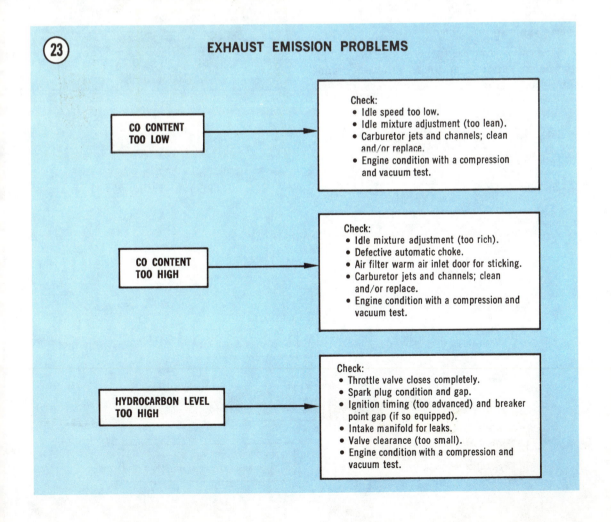

(23) **EXHAUST EMISSION PROBLEMS**

CO CONTENT TOO LOW

Check:
- Idle speed too low.
- Idle mixture adjustment (too lean).
- Carburetor jets and channels; clean and/or replace.
- Engine condition with a compression and vacuum test.

CO CONTENT TOO HIGH

Check:
- Idle mixture adjustment (too rich).
- Defective automatic choke.
- Air filter warm air inlet door for sticking.
- Carburetor jets and channels; clean and/or replace.
- Engine condition with a compression and vacuum test.

HYDROCARBON LEVEL TOO HIGH

Check:
- Throttle valve closes completely.
- Spark plug condition and gap.
- Ignition timing (too advanced) and breaker point gap (if so equipped).
- Intake manifold for leaks.
- Valve clearance (too small).
- Engine condition with a compression and vacuum test.

cludes a temperature sensor, vacuum motor, and a hinged door. See **Figure 26**.

The system is comparatively easy to test. See **Figure 27** for the procedure.

Air Injection Reaction System

The air injection reaction system reduces air pollution by oxidizing hydrocarbons and carbon monoxide as they leave the combustion chamber. See **Figure 28**.

The air injection pump, driven by the engine, compresses filtered air and injects it at the exhaust port of each cylinder. The fresh air mixes with the unburned gases in the exhaust and promotes further burning. A check valve prevents exhaust gases from entering and damaging the air pump if the pump becomes inoperative, e.g., from a fan belt failure.

Figure 29 explains the testing procedure for this system.

Fuel Evaporation Control

Fuel vapor from the fuel tank passes through the liquid/vapor separator to the carbon canister. See **Figure 30**. The carbon absorbs and

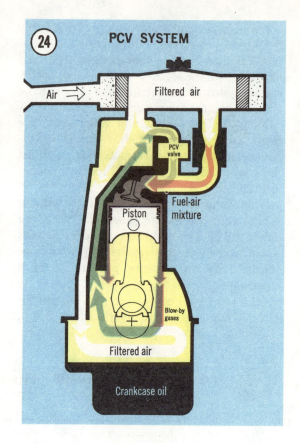

(24) PCV SYSTEM

Air → Filtered air

PCV valve

Fuel-air mixture

Piston

Blow-by gases

Filtered air

Crankcase oil

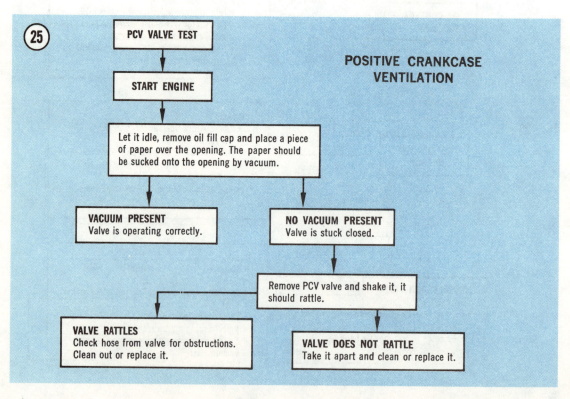

(25) PCV VALVE TEST

POSITIVE CRANKCASE VENTILATION

START ENGINE

Let it idle, remove oil fill cap and place a piece of paper over the opening. The paper should be sucked onto the opening by vacuum.

VACUUM PRESENT
Valve is operating correctly.

NO VACUUM PRESENT
Valve is stuck closed.

Remove PCV valve and shake it, it should rattle.

VALVE RATTLES
Check hose from valve for obstructions. Clean out or replace it.

VALVE DOES NOT RATTLE
Take it apart and clean or replace it.

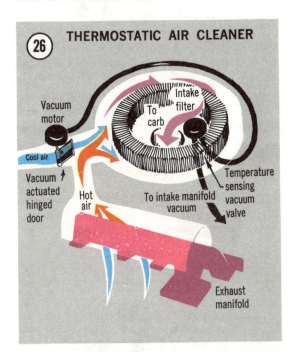

26 THERMOSTATIC AIR CLEANER

Vacuum motor

Intake filter

To carb

Cool air

Vacuum actuated hinged door

Hot air

To intake manifold vacuum

Temperature sensing vacuum valve

Exhaust manifold

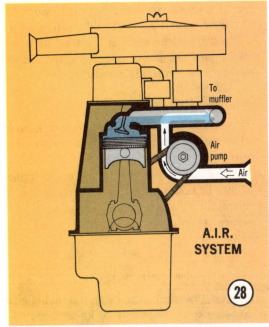

To muffler

Air pump

Air

A.I.R. SYSTEM

28

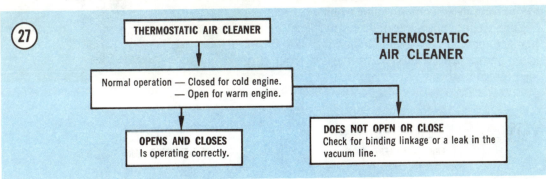

27

THERMOSTATIC AIR CLEANER

**THERMOSTATIC
AIR CLEANER**

Normal operation — Closed for cold engine.
— Open for warm engine.

OPENS AND CLOSES
Is operating correctly.

DOES NOT OPEN OR CLOSE
Check for binding linkage or a leak in the vacuum line.

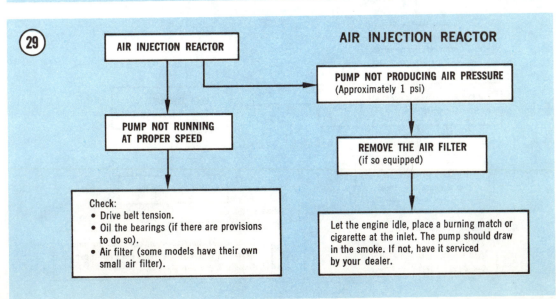

29

AIR INJECTION REACTOR

AIR INJECTION REACTOR

PUMP NOT PRODUCING AIR PRESSURE
(Approximately 1 psi)

**PUMP NOT RUNNING
AT PROPER SPEED**

REMOVE THE AIR FILTER
(if so equipped)

Check:
• Drive belt tension.
• Oil the bearings (if there are provisions to do so).
• Air filter (some models have their own small air filter).

Let the engine idle, place a burning match or cigarette at the inlet. The pump should draw in the smoke. If not, have it serviced by your dealer.

stores the vapor when the engine is stopped. When the engine runs, manifold vacuum draws the vapor from the canister. Instead of being released into the atmosphere, the fuel vapor takes part in the normal combustion process.

Exhaust Gas Recirculation

The exhaust gas recirculation (EGR) system is used to reduce the emission of nitrogen oxides (NOx). Relatively inert exhaust gases are introduced into the combustion process to slightly reduce peak temperatures. This reduction in temperature reduces the formation of NOx.

Figure 31 provides a simple test of this system.

ENGINE NOISES

Often the first evidence of an internal engine trouble is a strange noise. That knocking, clicking, or tapping which you never heard before may be warning you of impending trouble.

While engine noises can indicate problems, they are sometimes difficult to interpret correctly; inexperienced mechanics can be seriously misled by them.

Professional mechanics often use a special stethoscope which looks similar to a doctor's stethoscope for isolating engine noises. You can do nearly as well with a "sounding stick" which can be an ordinary piece of doweling or a section of small hose. By placing one end in contact with the area to which you want to listen and the other end near your ear, you can hear

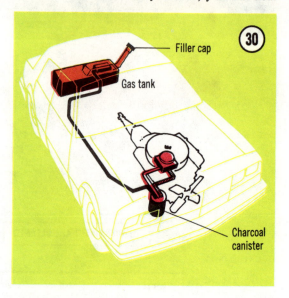

③⓪ Filler cap

Gas tank

Charcoal canister

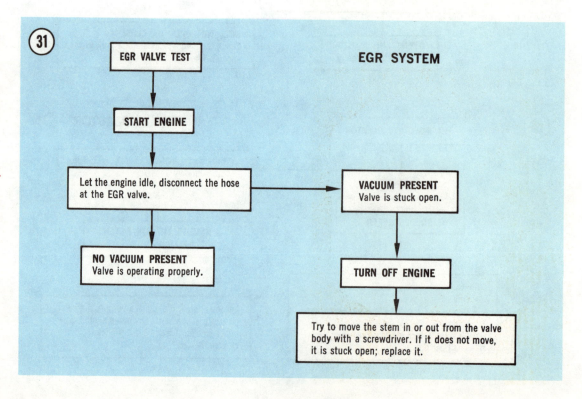

③① EGR VALVE TEST   EGR SYSTEM

START ENGINE

Let the engine idle, disconnect the hose at the EGR valve.

NO VACUUM PRESENT
Valve is operating properly.

VACUUM PRESENT
Valve is stuck open.

TURN OFF ENGINE

Try to move the stem in or out from the valve body with a screwdriver. If it does not move, it is stuck open; replace it.

sounds emanating from that area. The first time you do this, you may be horrified at the strange noises coming from even a normal engine. If you can, have an experienced friend or mechanic help you sort the noises out.

Clicking or Tapping Noises

Clicking or tapping noises usually come from the valve train, and indicate excessive valve clearance.

If your vehicle has adjustable valves, the procedure for adjusting the valve clearance is explained in Chapter Three. If your vehicle has hydraulic lifters, the clearance may not be adjustable. The noise may be coming from a collapsed lifter. These may be cleaned or replaced as described in the engine chapter.

A sticking valve may also sound like a valve with excessive clearance. In addition, excessive wear in valve train components can cause similar engine noises.

Knocking Noises

A heavy, dull knocking is usually caused by a worn main bearing. The noise is loudest when the engine is working hard, i.e., accelerating hard at low speed. You may be able to isolate the trouble to a single bearing by disconnecting

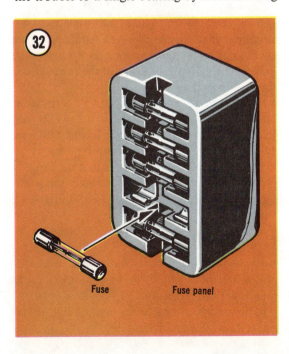

Fuse   Fuse panel

the spark plugs one at a time. When you reach the spark plug nearest the bearing, the knock will be reduced or disappear.

Worn connecting rod bearings may also produce a knock, but the sound is usually more "metallic." As with a main bearing, the noise is worse when accelerating. It may even increase further just as you go from accelerating to coasting. Disconnecting spark plugs will help isolate this knock as well.

A double knock or clicking usually indicates a worn piston pin. Disconnecting spark plugs will isolate this to a particular piston, however, the noise will *increase* when you reach the affected piston.

A loose flywheel and excessive crankshaft end play also produce knocking noises. While similar to main bearing noises, these are usually intermittent, not constant, and they do not change when spark plugs are disconnected.

Some mechanics confuse piston pin noise with piston slap. The double knock will distinguish the piston pin noise. Piston slap is identified by the fact that it is always louder when the engine is cold.

ELECTRICAL ACCESSORIES

Lights and Switches (Interior and Exterior)

1. *Bulb does not light* — Remove the bulb and check for a broken element. Also check the inside of the socket; make sure the contacts are clean and free of corrosion. If the bulb and socket are OK, check to see if a fuse has blown or a circuit breaker has tripped. The fuse panel **(Figure 32)** is usually located under the instrument panel. Replace the blown fuse or reset the circuit breaker. If the fuse blows or the breaker trips again, there is a short in that circuit. Check that circuit all the way to the battery. Look for worn wire insulation or burned wires.

If all the above are all right, check the switch controlling the bulb for continuity with an ohmmeter at the switch terminals. Check the switch contact terminals for loose or dirty electrical connections.

2. *Headlights work but will not switch from either high or low beam* — Check the beam selector switch for continuity with an ohmmeter

at the switch terminals. Check the switch contact terminals for loose or dirty electrical connections.

3. *Brake light switch inoperative* — On mechanically operated switches, usually mounted near the brake pedal arm, adjust the switch to achieve correct mechanical operation. Check the switch for continuity with an ohmmeter at the switch terminals. Check the switch contact terminals for loose or dirty electrical connections.

4. *Back-up lights do not operate* — Check light bulb as described earlier. Locate the switch, normally located near the shift lever. Adjust switch to achieve correct mechanical operation. Check the switch for continuity with an ohmmeter at the switch terminals. Bypass the switch with a jumper wire; if the lights work, replace the switch.

Directional Signals

1. *Directional signals do not operate* — If the indicator light on the instrument panel burns steadily instead of flashing, this usually indicates that one of the exterior lights is burned out. Check all lamps that normally flash. If all are all right, the flasher unit may be defective. Replace it with a good one.

2. *Directional signal indicator light on instrument panel does not light up* — Check the light bulbs as described earlier. Check all electrical connections and check the flasher unit.

3. *Directional signals will not self-cancel* — Check the self-cancelling mechanism located inside the steering column.

4. *Directional signals flash slowly* — Check the condition of the battery and the alternator (or generator) drive belt tension (**Figure 4**). Check the flasher unit and all related electrical connections.

Windshield Wipers

1. *Wipers do not operate* — Check for a blown fuse or circuit breaker that has tripped; replace or reset. Check all related terminals for loose or dirty electrical connections. Check continuity of the control switch with an ohmmeter at the switch terminals. Check the linkage and arms

for loose, broken, or binding parts. Straighten out or replace where necessary.

2. *Wiper motor hums but will not operate* — The motor may be shorted out internally; check and/or replace the motor. Also check for broken or binding linkage and arms.

3. *Wiper arms will not return to the stowed position when turned off* — The motor has a special internal switch for this purpose. Have it inspected by your dealer. Do not attempt this yourself.

Interior Heater

1. *Heater fan does not operate* — Check for a blown fuse or circuit breaker that has tripped. Check the switch for continuity with an ohmmeter at the switch terminals. Check the switch contact terminals for loose or dirty electrical connections.

2. *Heat output is insufficient* — Check the heater hose/engine coolant control valve usually located in the engine compartment; make sure it is in the open position. Ensure that the heater door(s) and cable(s) are operating correctly and are in the open position. Inspect the heat ducts; make sure that they are not crimped or blocked.

COOLING SYSTEM

The temperature gauge or warning light usually signals cooling system troubles before there is any damage. As long as you stop the vehicle at the first indication of trouble, serious damage is unlikely.

In most cases, the trouble will be obvious as soon as you open the hood. If there is coolant or steam leaking, look for a defective radiator, radiator hose, or heater hose. If there is no evidence of leakage, make sure that the fan belt is in good condition. If the trouble is not obvious, refer to **Figures 33 and 34** to help isolate the trouble.

Automotive cooling systems operate under pressure to permit higher operating temperatures without boil-over. The system should be checked periodically to make sure it can withstand normal pressure. **Figure 35** shows the equipment which nearly any service station has for testing the system pressure.

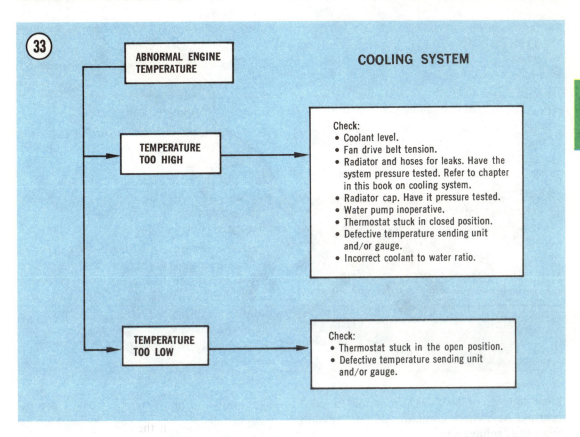

33

ABNORMAL ENGINE
TEMPERATURE

COOLING SYSTEM

2

TEMPERATURE
TOO HIGH

Check:
- Coolant level.
- Fan drive belt tension.
- Radiator and hoses for leaks. Have the system pressure tested. Refer to chapter in this book on cooling system.
- Radiator cap. Have it pressure tested.
- Water pump inoperative.
- Thermostat stuck in closed position.
- Defective temperature sending unit and/or gauge.
- Incorrect coolant to water ratio.

TEMPERATURE
TOO LOW

Check:
- Thermostat stuck in the open position.
- Defective temperature sending unit and/or gauge.

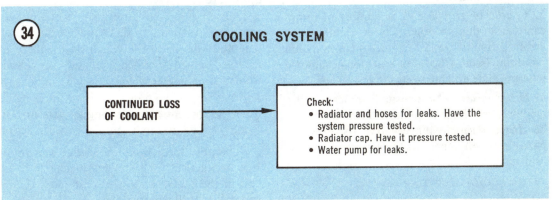

34

COOLING SYSTEM

CONTINUED LOSS
OF COOLANT

Check:
- Radiator and hoses for leaks. Have the system pressure tested.
- Radiator cap. Have it pressure tested.
- Water pump for leaks.

CLUTCH

All clutch troubles except adjustments require transmission removal to identify and cure the problem.

1. *Slippage* — This is most noticeable when accelerating in a high gear at relatively low speed. To check slippage, park the vehicle on a level surface with the handbrake set. Shift to 2nd gear and release the clutch as if driving off. If the clutch is good, the engine will slow and stall. If the clutch slips, continued engine speed will give it away.

Slippage results from insufficient clutch pedal free play, oil or grease on the clutch disc, worn pressure plate, or weak springs.

2. *Drag or failure to release* — This trouble usually causes difficult shifting and gear clash, especially when downshifting. The cause may be excessive clutch pedal free play, warped or bent pressure plate or clutch disc, broken or

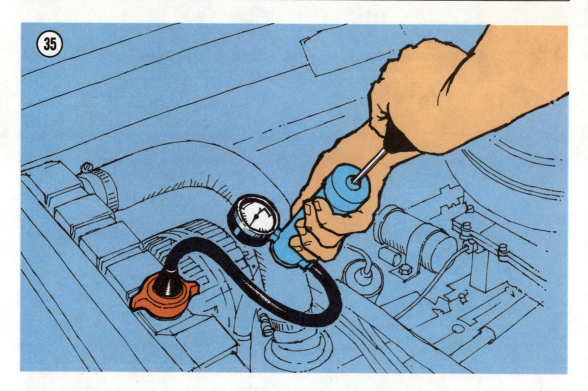

loose linings, or lack of lubrication in pilot bearing. Also check condition of transmission main shaft splines.

3. *Chatter or grabbing* — A number of things can cause this trouble. Check tightness of engine mounts and engine-to-transmission mounting bolts. Check for worn or misaligned pressure plate and misaligned release plate.

4. *Other noises* — Noise usually indicates a dry or defective release or pilot bearing. Check the bearings and replace if necessary. Also check all parts for misalignment and uneven wear.

MANUAL TRANSMISSION/TRANSAXLE

Transmission and transaxle troubles are evident when one or more of the following symptoms appear:

   a. Difficulty changing gears

   b. Gears clash when downshifting

   c. Slipping out of gear

   d. Excessive noise in NEUTRAL

   e. Excessive noise in gear

   f. Oil leaks

Transmission and transaxle repairs are not recommended unless the many special tools required are available.

Transmission and transaxle troubles are sometimes difficult to distinguish from clutch troubles. Eliminate the clutch as a source of trouble before installing a new or rebuilt transmission or transaxle.

AUTOMATIC TRANSMISSION

Most automatic transmission repairs require considerable specialized knowledge and tools. It is impractical for the home mechanic to invest in the tools, since they cost more than a properly rebuilt transmission.

Check fluid level and condition frequently to help prevent future problems. If the fluid is orange or black in color or smells like varnish, it is an indication of some type of damage or failure within the transmission. Have the transmission serviced by your dealer or competent automatic transmission service facility.

BRAKES

Good brakes are vital to the safe operation of the vehicle. Performing the maintenance speci-

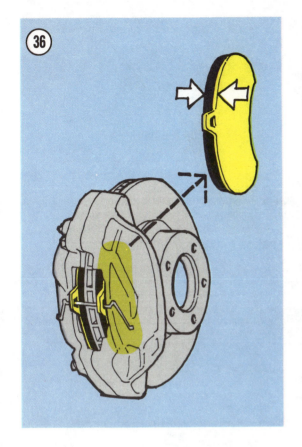

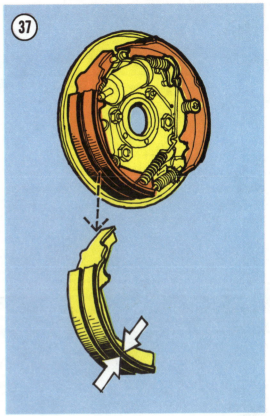

fied in Chapter Three will minimize problems with the brakes. Most importantly, check and maintain the level of fluid in the master cylinder, and check the thickness of the linings on the disc brake pads (**Figure 36**) or drum brake shoes (**Figure 37**).

If trouble develops, **Figures 38 through 40** will help you locate the problem. Refer to the brake chapter for actual repair procedures.

STEERING AND SUSPENSION

Trouble in the suspension or steering is evident when the following occur:

a. Steering is hard
b. Car pulls to one side
c. Car wanders or front wheels wobble
d. Steering has excessive play
e. Tire wear is abnormal

Unusual steering, pulling, or wandering is usually caused by bent or otherwise misaligned suspension parts. This is difficult to check without proper alignment equipment. Refer to the suspension chapter in this book for repairs that you can perform and those that must be left to a dealer or suspension specialist.

If your trouble seems to be excessive play, check wheel bearing adjustment first. This is the most frequent cause. Then check ball-joints as described below. Finally, check tie rod end ball-joints by shaking each tie rod. Also check steering gear, or rack-and-pinion assembly to see that it is securely bolted down.

TIRE WEAR ANALYSIS

Abnormal tire wear should be analyzed to determine its causes. The most common causes are the following:

a. Incorrect tire pressure
b. Improper driving
c. Overloading
d. Bad road surfaces
e. Incorrect wheel alignment

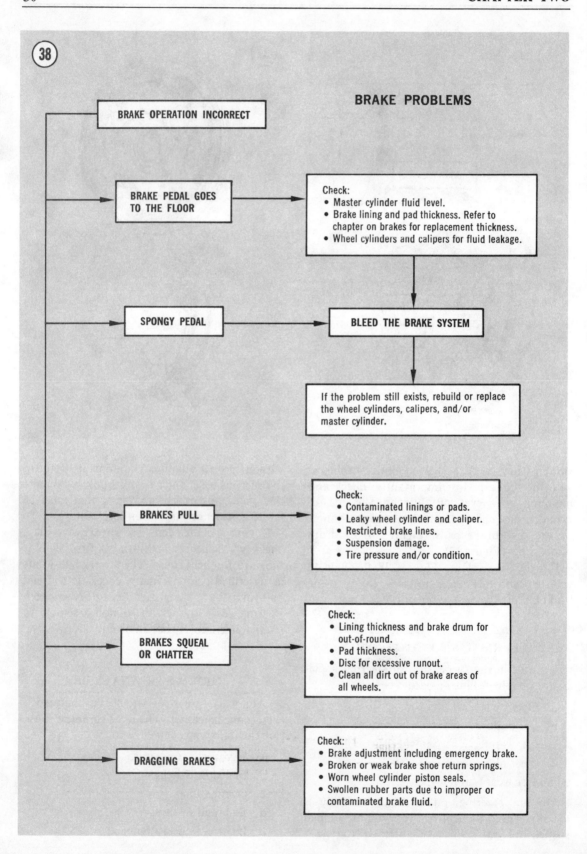

(38)

BRAKE PROBLEMS

BRAKE OPERATION INCORRECT

BRAKE PEDAL GOES TO THE FLOOR

Check:
• Master cylinder fluid level.
• Brake lining and pad thickness. Refer to chapter on brakes for replacement thickness.
• Wheel cylinders and calipers for fluid leakage.

SPONGY PEDAL

BLEED THE BRAKE SYSTEM

If the problem still exists, rebuild or replace the wheel cylinders, calipers, and/or master cylinder.

BRAKES PULL

Check:
• Contaminated linings or pads.
• Leaky wheel cylinder and caliper.
• Restricted brake lines.
• Suspension damage.
• Tire pressure and/or condition.

BRAKES SQUEAL OR CHATTER

Check:
• Lining thickness and brake drum for out-of-round.
• Pad thickness.
• Disc for excessive runout.
• Clean all dirt out of brake areas of all wheels.

DRAGGING BRAKES

Check:
• Brake adjustment including emergency brake.
• Broken or weak brake shoe return springs.
• Worn wheel cylinder piston seals.
• Swollen rubber parts due to improper or contaminated brake fluid.

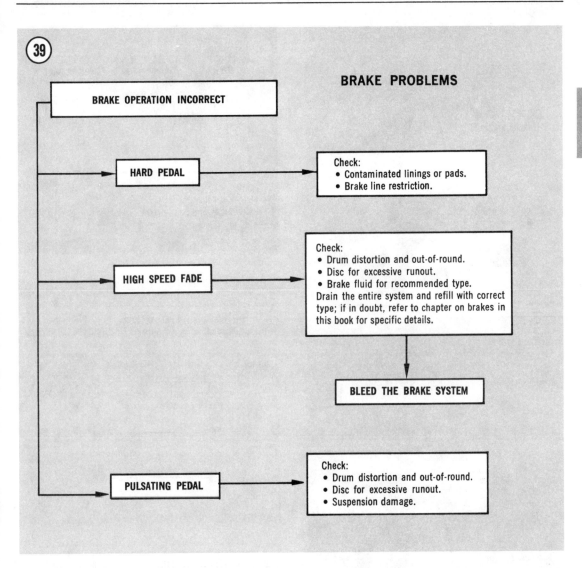

BRAKE PROBLEMS

BRAKE OPERATION INCORRECT

HARD PEDAL

Check:
• Contaminated linings or pads.
• Brake line restriction.

HIGH SPEED FADE

Check:
• Drum distortion and out-of-round.
• Disc for excessive runout.
• Brake fluid for recommended type.
Drain the entire system and refill with correct type; if in doubt, refer to chapter on brakes in this book for specific details.

BLEED THE BRAKE SYSTEM

PULSATING PEDAL

Check:
• Drum distortion and out-of-round.
• Disc for excessive runout.
• Suspension damage.

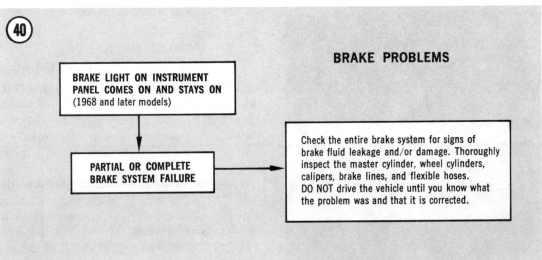

BRAKE PROBLEMS

BRAKE LIGHT ON INSTRUMENT PANEL COMES ON AND STAYS ON
(1968 and later models)

PARTIAL OR COMPLETE BRAKE SYSTEM FAILURE

Check the entire brake system for signs of brake fluid leakage and/or damage. Thoroughly inspect the master cylinder, wheel cylinders, calipers, brake lines, and flexible hoses.
DO NOT drive the vehicle until you know what the problem was and that it is corrected.

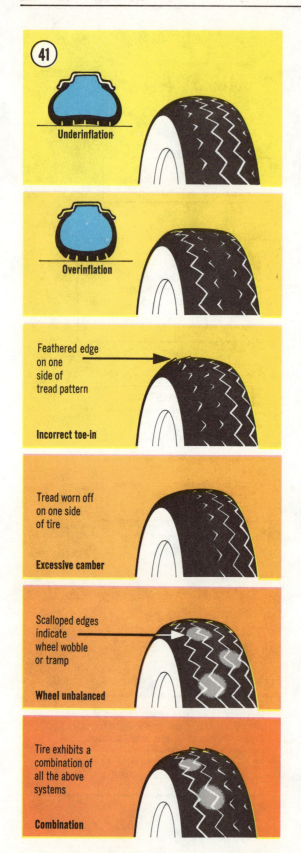

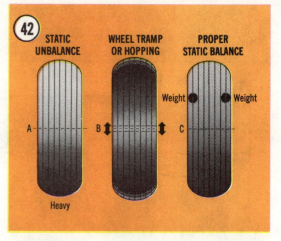

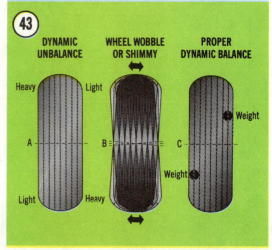

Figure 41 identifies wear patterns and indicates the most probable causes.

WHEEL BALANCING

All four wheels and tires must be in balance along two axes. To be in static balance (**Figure 42**), weight must be evenly distributed around the axis of rotation. (A) shows a statically unbalanced wheel; (B) shows the result — wheel tramp or hopping; (C) shows proper static balance.

To be in dynamic balance (**Figure 43**), the centerline of the weight must coincide with the centerline of the wheel. (A) shows a dynamically unbalanced wheel; (B) shows the result — wheel wobble or shimmy; (C) shows proper dynamic balance.

CHAPTER THREE

LUBRICATION, MAINTENANCE AND TUNE-UP

This chapter deals with the maintenance necessary to keep your truck running properly. **Tables 1-4** list maintenance intervals. (**Tables 1-10** are at the end of the chapter.) Some procedures are done at fuel stops, while others are done at specified intervals of miles or time.

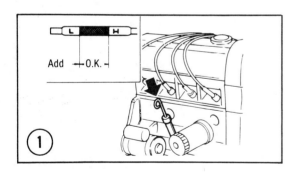

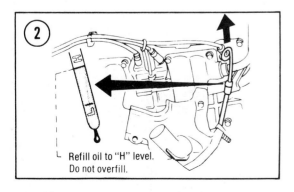

Refill oil to "H" level.
Do not overfill.

The service schedules are intended for trucks given normal use. More frequent service is required under the following conditions:

a. Stop-and-go driving

b. Constant high-speed driving

c. Severe dust

d. Rough or salted roads

e. Very hot, very cold or rainy weather

Some maintenance procedures are included in the *Tune-up* section at the end of the chapter, and detailed instructions will be found there. Other steps are described in various chapters. Chapter references are included with these steps.

FUEL STOP CHECKS

1. With the engine off, pull out the dipstick. See **Figure 1** (1980) or **Figure 2** (1981). Wipe it with a clean rag, insert it and pull it out again. Check oil level. Top up to the "H" mark on the dipstick if necessary, using a grade recommended in **Table 5** and **Table 6**. Add oil through the hole in the rocker arm cover (**Figure 3**).

2. Check coolant level in the reservoir tank (**Figure 4**). It should be between the MIN and MAX marks. Top up as needed. If the tank is empty, check radiator level as well.

> *WARNING*
> *The radiator cap should not be removed when the engine is warm or hot. If this is unavoidable, cover the cap with a thick rag. Turn it slowly counterclockwise against the first stop (about 1/4 turn). Let **all** pressure (hot water and steam) escape. Then press the cap down and turn counterclockwise to remove. If the cap is removed too soon, a fountain of scalding coolant may shoot out of the radiator, bounce off the hood and spray all over you.*

3. Check battery electrolyte level. On translucent batteries, it should be between the marks on the battery case (**Figure 5**). On black batteries, it should be even with the bottom of the filler wells. See **Figure 6**.

4. Check fluid in the windshield washer tank. It should be kept full. Use windshield washer solvent, following the manufacturer's instructions.

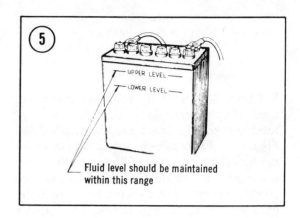

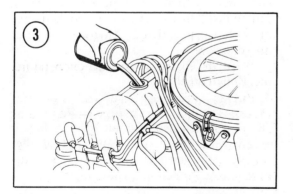

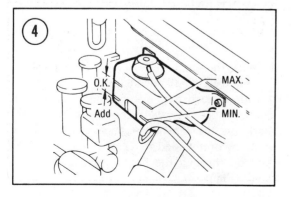

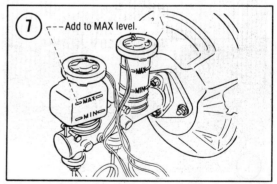

Fluid level should be maintained within this range

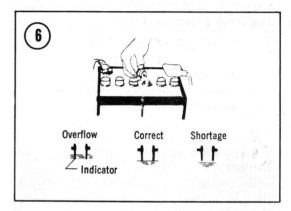

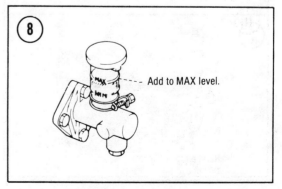

3

CAUTION
Do not use radiator antifreeze in the washer tank. The runoff may damage the truck's paint.

5. Check fluid level in the clutch and brake master cylinders. 1980 models use twin reservoirs for the brake master cylinder. See **Figure 7**. 1981 models use a single brake master cylinder reservoir (**Figure 8**). Since the reservoirs are translucent, this check can be done at a glance. Fluid should be between the lines on the reservoirs. If low, top up with brake fluid marked DOT 3. The same fluid is used for clutch and brakes.

CAUTION
Do not remove reservoir caps unless topping up fluid. Clean the area around the caps before removal.

6. Check tire pressures (**Table 7**). This should be done when the tires are cold (after driving less than one mile). When the tires heat up from driving, the air in them expands and gives false high pressure readings.

SCHEDULED MAINTENANCE

Engine Oil and Filter

If the truck is given normal use, change the oil when recommended in **Tables 2-4**. If it is used for stop-and-go driving, in dusty areas or left idling for long periods, change the oil every 3,000 miles or 3 months.

Use an oil recommended in **Table 5** and **Table 6**. The rating (SE) is usually printed on top of the can (**Figure 9**).

To drain the oil and change the filter, you will need:

  a. Drain pan
  b. Oil can spout or can opener and funnel
  c. Filter wrench
  d. 5 quarts of oil
  e. Oil filter

There are several ways to discard the old oil safely. The easiest is to pour it from the drain pan into a gallon bleach or milk bottle. The oil can be taken to a service station for dumping or, where permitted, thrown in your household trash.

1. Warm the engine to operating temperature, then shut it off.

2. Put the drain pan under the drain plug (**Figure 10**). Remove the plug and let the oil drain for at least 10 minutes.

3. Unscrew the oil filter (**Figure 11**) counterclockwise. Use a filter wrench if the filter is too tight to remove by hand.

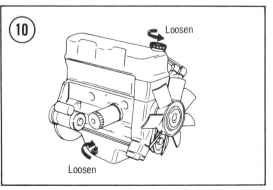

Loosen

Loosen

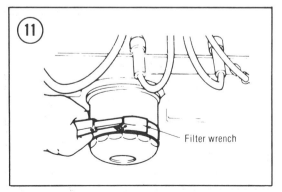

Filter wrench

4. Wipe the gasket surface on the engine block clean with a lint-free cloth.

5. Coat the neoprene gasket on the new filter with clean engine oil. See **Figure 12**.

6. Screw the filter onto the engine *by hand* until the gasket just touches the engine block. At this point, there will be a very slight resistance when turning the filter.

7. Tighten the filter 2/3 turn more *by hand*. If the filter wrench is used, the filter will probably be overtightened. This will cause an oil leak.

8. Install the oil pan drain plug. Tighten it securely.

9. Remove the oil filler cap (**Figure 10**).

10. Pour oil into the engine. Capacity is listed in **Table 8**.

11. Start the engine and let it idle. The instrument panel oil pressure light will remain on for 15-30 seconds, then go out.

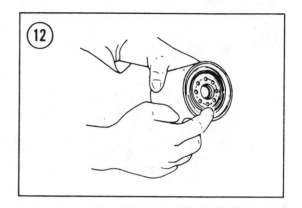

> *CAUTION*
> *Do not rev the engine to make the oil pressure light go out. It takes time for the oil to reach all areas of the engine and revving it could damage dry parts.*

12. While the engine is running, check the drain plug and oil filter for leaks.

13. Turn the engine off. Let the oil settle for several minutes, then check level on the dipstick. See **Figure 13** (1980) or **Figure 14** (1981). Add oil if necessary to bring the level up to the "H" mark, but *do not* overfill.

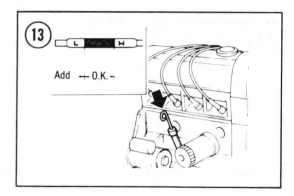

Add ─┼─ O.K. ─

Manual Transmission Oil Level Check

Remove the filler plug from the side of the transmission (**Figure 15**). Make sure oil is up to the bottom of the filler plug threads. Top up if necessary with an oil recommended in **Table 5** and **Table 6**.

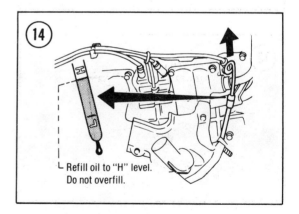

└ Refill oil to "H" level.
  Do not overfill.

Manual Transmission Oil Change

1. Drive the truck several miles to warm the oil. This allows it to drain freely.

2. Place a pan beneath the drain plug (**Figure 16**). Remove the drain plug and let the oil drain for at least 10 minutes.

3. After the oil has drained, install the drain plug. Fill the transmission with an oil recommended in **Tables 5** and **Table 6**. Oil capacity is listed in **Table 8**.

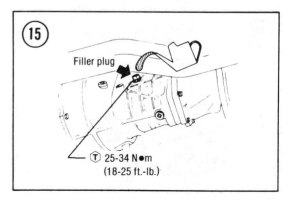

Filler plug

Ⓣ 25-34 N•m
(18-25 ft.-lb.)

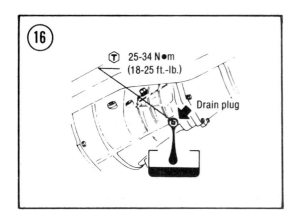

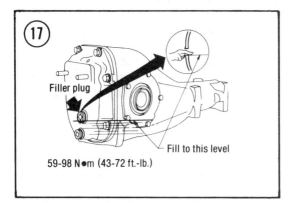

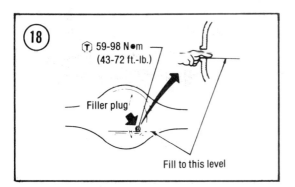

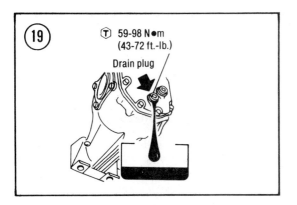

Differential Oil Level Check

Remove the filler plug. See **Figure 17** (front differential) or **Figure 18** (rear differential). Oil should be up to the bottom of the filler plug threads. Top up if necessary with an oil recommended in **Tables 5** and **6**.

Differential Oil Change

1. Drive the truck several miles to warm the oil. This allows it to drain freely.
2. Place a pan beneath the drain plug. See **Figure 19** (front differential) or **Figure 20** (rear differential).
3. Remove the drain plug. Let the oil drain for at least 10 minutes.
4. After the oil has drained, install the drain plug. Fill the transmission with an oil recommended in **Table 5** and **Table 6**. Capacity is listed in **Table 8**.

Transfer Case Oil Level Check

Remove the filler plug (**Figure 21**). Oil level should be up to the bottom of the filler plug threads. If necessary, top up with an oil recommended in **Table 5** and **Table 6**.

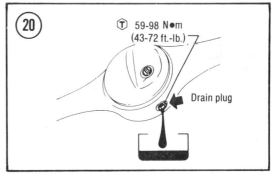

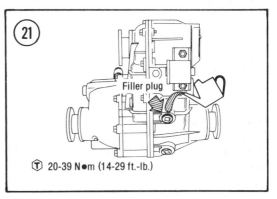

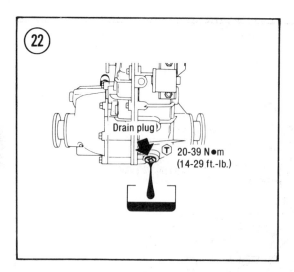

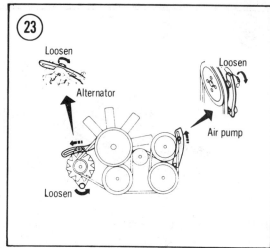

Transfer Case Oil Change

1. Drive the truck several miles to warm the oil. This allows it to drain freely.

2. Place a pan beneath the transfer case. Remove the drain plug (**Figure 22**) and let the oil drain for at least 10 minutes.

3. After the oil has drained, reinstall the drain plug. Fill the transfer case with an oil recommended in **Table 5** and **Table 6**. Capacity is listed in **Table 8**.

Brakes

Check front brake pads for wear. Check pedal free play. Test the brake booster and proportioning valve. See *Brake Booster* and *Proportioning Valve*, Chapter Eleven.

Check rear brake linings for wear and wheel cylinders for fluid leaks. See *Rear Brakes*, Chapter Eleven.

> *NOTE*
> *If the truck is driven on salted roads, inspect front and rear brakes every 3,400 miles or 3 months.*

Leak Inspection

The engine should be checked visually for leaks. Check the oil pan drain plug, oil pan gasket, oil filter, engine front cover and oil pump. Greasy looking dirt at these points may indicate an oil leak. Inspect the radiator and hose connections for coolant residue or rust. Check the fuel connections for signs of gasoline leakage.

Inspect the brake master cylinder, calipers and wheel cylinder for wetness. Do the same for the clutch master and operating cylinders and for all hydraulic line connections.

Drive Belts

To check tension, press on the belts midway between pulleys. All belts should deflect 8-12 mm (1/3-1/2 in.).

To adjust the alternator belt, loosen the alternator mounting and adjusting bolts. See **Figure 23** (1980) or **Figure 24** (1981). Pull or pry the alternator away from the engine to tighten the belt, then tighten the mounting and adjusting bolts. To adjust the air pump belt (1980 only), loosen the air pump mounting and adjusting bolts. See **Figure 23**. Pull or pry the air pump away from the alternator to tighten the belt, then tighten the mounting and adjusting bolts.

To adjust the air conditioning compressor belt, loosen the idler pulley locknut. See **Figure 25** (1980) or **Figure 24** (1981). Turn the adjusting bolt clockwise to tighten the belt or counterclockwise to loosen. Tighten the locknut.

Coolant Hoses and Connections

Inspect all cooling system hoses and connections, including heater hoses. Replace hoses that are cracked, deteriorated or extremely soft. Make sure all clamps are tight.

3

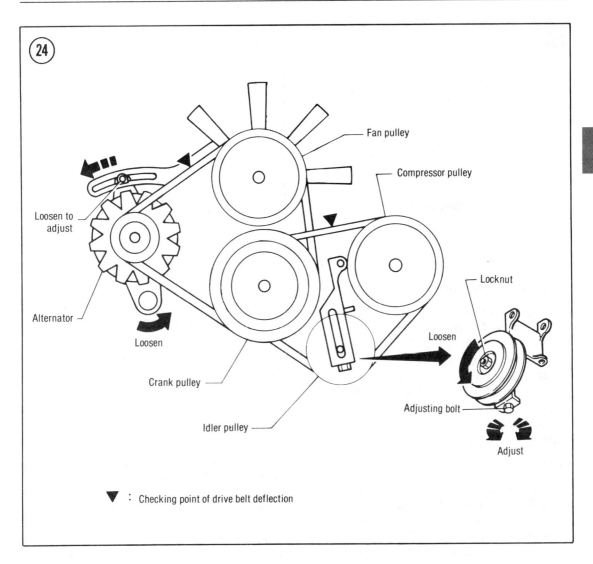

Fan pulley

Compressor pulley

Loosen to
adjust

Locknut

Alternator

Loosen

Loosen

Crank pulley

Adjusting bolt

Idler pulley

Adjust

▼ : Checking point of drive belt deflection

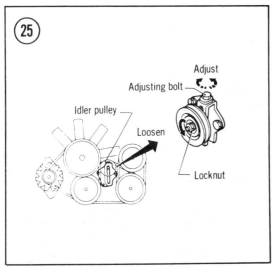

Adjust

Adjusting bolt

Idler pulley

Loosen

Locknut

NOTE
If a hose is in doubtful condition, play it
safe and replace it. Replacing a hose under
roadside working conditions can be a truly
miserable job.

Evaporative Emission Control System

Check the system's hoses for loose
connections, cracks or deterioration. Tighten
or replace as needed.

Brake Fluid

Pump out all the old brake fluid and fill the
hydraulic system with new fluid. See *Brake
Bleeding*, Chapter Eleven.

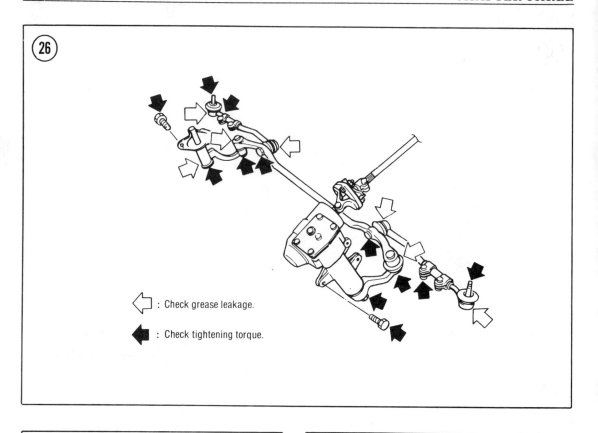

: Check grease leakage.

: Check tightening torque.

: Check fluid leaks.

: Add fluid.

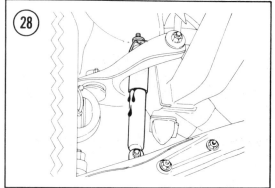

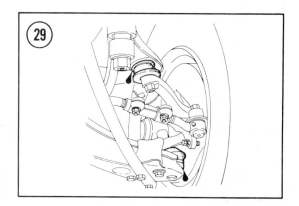

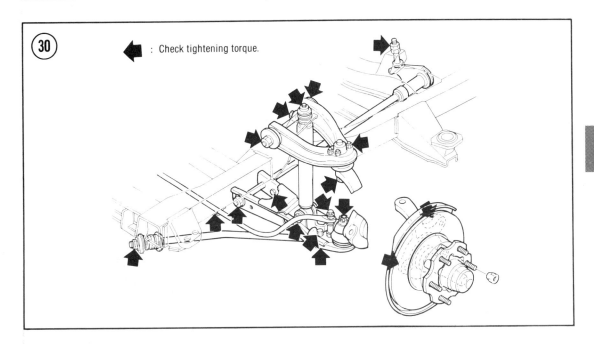

30   : Check tightening torque.

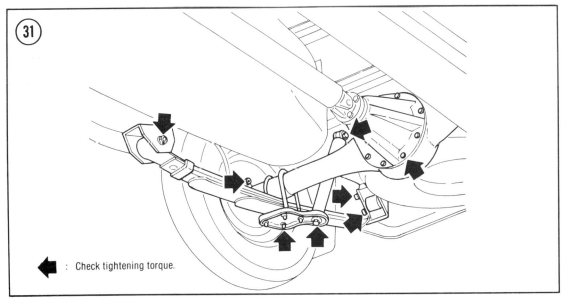

31   : Check tightening torque.

Steering, Suspension and Drive Shafts

1. Check the steering gear box and linkage for loose, missing, worn or damaged parts. See **Figure 26**. Tighten or replace as needed.

2. Check the steering gear for leaks and a low fluid level. See **Figure 27**. Top up if necessary with an oil recommended in **Table 5** and **Table 6**.

3. Check the shock absorbers for fluid leaks (**Figure 28**). Repair or replace as needed.

4. Check front suspension ball-joints for grease leaks or damage. See **Figure 29**. Replace the ball-joints if the dust covers are cracked.

5. Check nuts and bolts in front and rear suspensions for looseness. See **Figure 30** (front suspension) or **Figure 31** (rear suspension).

6. Check the drive shaft for worn universal joints. Shake the drive shaft firmly by hand and look for play. Since the U-joints can't be

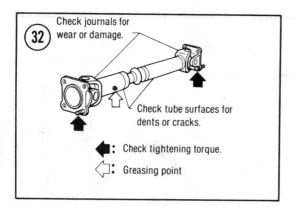

Check journals for wear or damage.

Check tube surfaces for dents or cracks.

◀ : Check tightening torque.

◁ : Greasing point

32

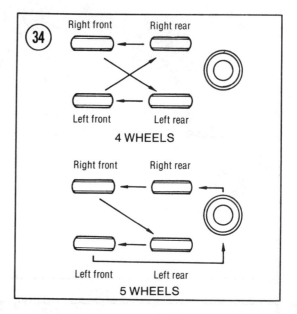

◀ : Check tightening torque

33

repaired, the drive shaft must be replaced if they are defective. Make sure the drive shaft mounting bolts are tight. See **Figure 32**.

Axle Shafts

Check front axle shafts for wear, damage or loose fasteners. See **Figure 33**. Tighten loose fasteners. Replace the axle shaft if wear or damage can be seen.

Wheels and Tires

Have wheel alignment and balance checked by a dealer or front end shop. If the front tires are wearing at a different rate or in a different manner than the rear tires, rotate them. See **Figure 34** (bias or bias belted tires) or **Figure 35** (radial tires).

Hinges, Latches and Locks

Referring to **Figure 36**, lightly grease the hood latch and tailgate release mechanism with multipurpose lithium grease. Apply 1-2 drops of oil to hinges on doors, hood and tailgate. Lubricate striker plates with a non-staining stick lube such as Door-Ease. Lubricate lock tumblers by applying a thin coat of Lubriplate, lock oil or graphite to the key. Insert and work the lock several times. Wipe the key clean.

Coolant

Drain, flush and refill the cooling system. See *Cooling System Flushing*, Chapter Six.

Air Cleaner Element

Replace the air cleaner element as described in the following steps.

34

Right front   Right rear

Left front   Left rear

4 WHEELS

Right front   Right rear

Left front   Left rear

5 WHEELS

35

Right front   Right rear

Left front   Left rear

4 WHEELS

Right frontt   Right rear

Left front   Left rear

5 WHEELS

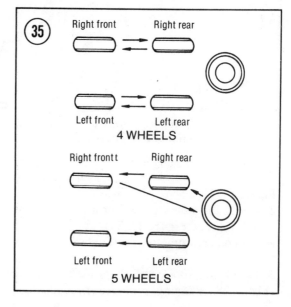

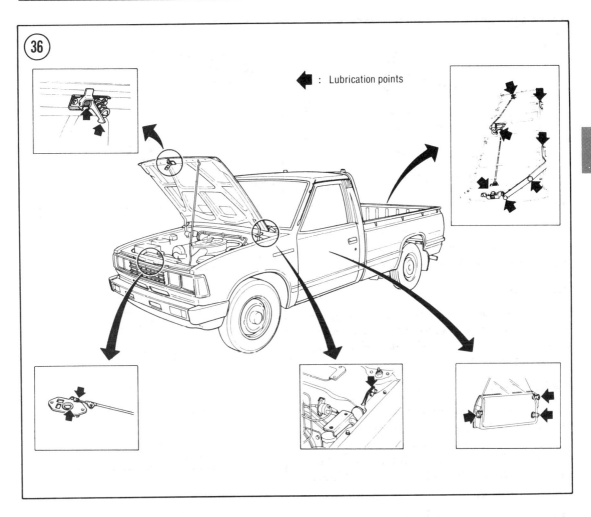

(36)

: Lubrication points

3

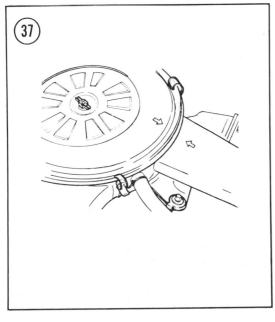

(37)

1. Remove the air cleaner cover.
2. Lift out the filter element and install a new one.
3. Install the air cleaner cover. Align the cover arrows as shown in **Figure 37**.

Air Induction Valve Filter

If equipped with an air induction system, replace the filter. See *Air Induction System*, Chapter Five.

Automatic Temperature Control Air Cleaner

Inspect the ATC air cleaner as described under *Air Cleaner*, Chapter Five.

Positive Crankcase Ventilation System

Inspect the PCV system as described under *Positive Crankcase Ventilation System*, Chapter Five.

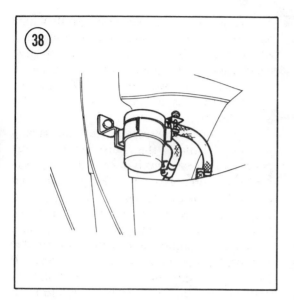

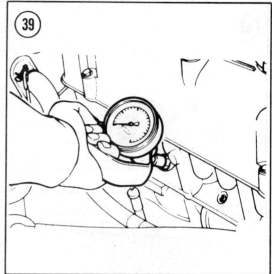

Fuel Filter

Replace the fuel filter if it becomes clogged. This is most likely to happen in very hot or very cold weather.

The filter is mounted near the fuel tank (**Figure 38**). To remove, disconnect the lines and take the filter out. Install a new filter and tighten the line connections.

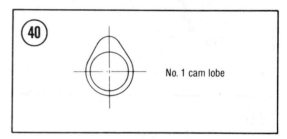

No. 1 cam lobe

Front Wheel Bearings

Remove, clean, adjust and repack the front wheel bearings. See *Wheel Bearings*, Chapter Nine.

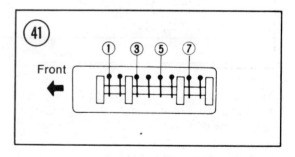

Front

TUNE-UP

Under normal conditions, a tune-up should be done at the intervals specified in **Tables 2-4**. More frequent tune-ups may be needed if the truck is used primarily for stop-and-go driving or is left idling for long periods.

Since different engine systems interact, a tune-up should be done in the following order:

    a. Compression test
    b. Valve adjustment
    c. Ignition system work
    d. Idle adjustment

Compression Test

Although Datsun does not require a compression test as part of their maintenance schedule, you may want to perform this test

before each scheduled tune-up. Record the test results and compare them to previous tests to detect any deterioration in engine mechanical condition.

The compression tester measures the compression pressure built up in each cylinder. Interpretation of compression test results can indicate general cylinder and valve condition. **Figure 39** shows a compression tester in use.

There are 2 types of compression tests: "wet" and "dry." These tests are interpreted together to isolate problems in cylinders and valves. The dry compression test is done first.

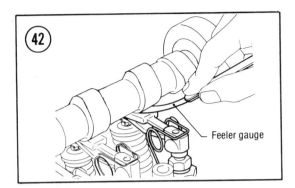

Feeler gauge

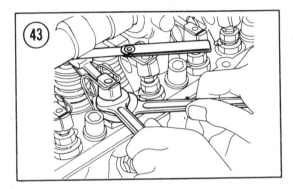

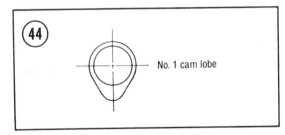

No. 1 cam lobe

To test:

1. Warm the engine to normal operating temperature. Make sure choke is completely open.

2. Remove the spark plugs.

3. Connect the compression tester to one cylinder following the manufacturer's instructions.

4. Have an assistant crank the engine over until there is no further increase in compression. Hold the throttle pedal to the floor while cranking.

5. Remove the tester and record the compression reading.

6. Repeat Steps 3-5 for each cylinder. Compare results with **Table 9**.

When interpreting the results, actual readings are not as important as the difference

in readings. Low readings, although they may be even, are a sign of wear. Low readings in 2 adjacent cylinders may indicate a defective head gasket. A large difference between readings indicates worn or broken rings, leaky or sticking valves, a defective head gasket, or a combination of all.

If the dry compression test indicates a problem, isolate the cause with a wet compression test. This is done in the same way as the dry compression test, except that about one tablespoon of oil is poured down the spark plug hole before performing Steps 3-5. If the wet compression readings are much greater than the dry compression readings, the trouble is probably due to worn or broken rings. If there is little difference between wet and dry readings, the trouble is probably due to leaky or sticking valves. If 2 adjacent cylinders are low, and the wet and dry readings are close, the head gasket may be damaged.

VALVE ADJUSTMENT (1980)

1. Warm the engine to normal operating temperature.

2. Remove the valve cover.

3. Find valve clearance specifications in **Table 10**.

4. Remove the spark plugs. This makes it easier to turn the engine.

NOTE
*Refer to **Spark Plugs** in this chapter for proper removal procedures.*

5. Turn the engine so No. 1 cam lobe points straight up. See **Figure 40**.

6. Check clearance of valves 1, 3, 5 and 7 (**Figure 41**). Measure with a feeler gauge as shown in **Figure 42**.

NOTE
Valves 1 and 5 are exhaust valves; valves 3 and 7 are intake valves.

7. If valve clearance is incorrect, loosen the pivot locknut as shown in **Figure 43**. Turn the pivot to change clearance, then tighten the locknut.

8. Turn the engine until No. 1 cam lobe points straight down. See **Figure 44**.

9. Check the clearances of valves 2, 4, 6, and 8 (**Figure 45**). Adjust if necessary as described in Step 7.

> *NOTE*
> *Valves 2 and 6 are intake valves; valves 4 and 8 are exhaust valves.*

VALVE ADJUSTMENT (1981)

1. Find valve clearance specifications in **Table 10**.
2. Warm the engine to normal operating temperature.
3. Remove the spark plugs. This makes it easier to turn the engine.

> *NOTE*
> *See **Spark Plugs** in this chapter for correct removal procedures.*

4. Remove the rocker arm cover.
5. Turn the engine until No. 1 cam lobe points straight down. See **Figure 46**.
6. Counting from the front of the engine, measure the clearances on valves 1, 4, 6 and 7. See **Figure 47**. Insert a feeler gauge of the specified clearance between valve stem and rocker arm (**Figure 48**). The feeler gauge should move with a very slight drag. If it is too loose or too tight, clearance must be adjusted.

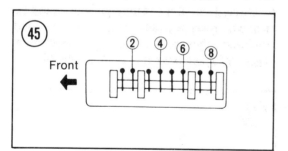

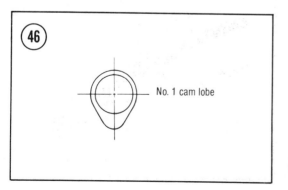

7. To adjust, loosen the rocker pivot locknut (**Figure 49**). Turn the rocker pivot to change clearance, then tighten the nut securely.

> *NOTE*
> *Valves 1 and 4 are intake valves; valves 6 and 7 are exhaust valves.*

8. Turn the engine until No. 1 cam lobe points straight up (**Figure 50**). Check valves 2, 3, 5 and 8 (**Figure 51**).

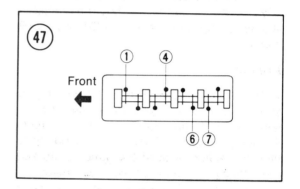

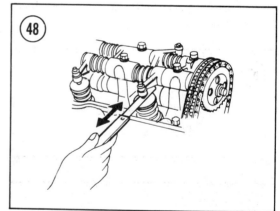

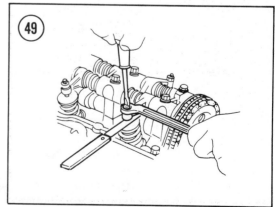

9. If clearance is incorrect, adjust in the same manner as the first 4 valves.

NOTE
Valves 5 and 8 are intake valves; valves 2 and 3 are exhaust valves.

10. Install the rocker arm cover.

SPARK PLUGS

On 1980 Canadian models, spark plugs should be replaced at each tune-up. On all other models, spark plugs should be replaced at alternate tune-ups (every 30,000 miles or 2 years).

Removal

1. Blow out any foreign matter from around spark plugs with compressed air. Use a compressor if you have one. If not, most household vacuum cleaners can be set up to blow air. When most of the outlet is blocked with fingers, enough pressure is created to blow dirt away. Another method is to use a can of compressed inert gas, available from photo stores.

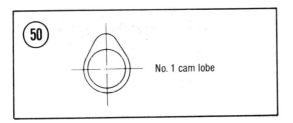

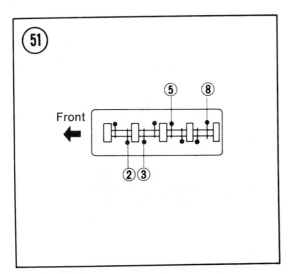

CAUTION
When spark plugs are removed, dirt from around the plugs can fall into the spark plug holes. This can cause expensive engine damage.

2. Mark spark plug wires with the cylinder numbers so you can reconnect them properly. Cylinders are numbered from front to rear of the engine.

NOTE
To make labels, wrap a small strip of masking tape around each wire.

3. Disconnect spark plug wires. Pull off by grasping the connector, *not* the wire. See **Figure 52**. Pulling on the wire may break it.

NOTE
If the boots seem to be stuck, twist them 1/2 turn to break the seal. Do not pull on boots with pliers. The pliers could cut the insulation, causing an electrical short.

4. Remove the plugs with a 13/16 in. spark plug socket. Keep the plugs in order so you know which cylinder they came from.

5. Examine each spark plug. Compare its condition with the illustrations in Chapter Two. Spark plug condition indicates engine condition and can warn of developing trouble.

6. Discard the plugs. Although they could be cleaned, regapped and reused if in good condition, they seldom last very long; new plugs are inexpensive and far more reliable.

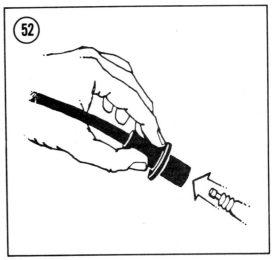

Gapping and Installing the Plugs

New plugs should be carefully gapped to ensure a reliable, consistent spark. Use a special spark plug tool with a wire gauge. See **Figure 53** or **Figure 54**.

1. Remove the plugs from the boxes. See if the small end pieces (**Figure 55**) are screwed on. If not, install them.

2. Find the correct spark plug gap for your truck in **Table 10**. Insert the correct diameter wire gauge between the spark plug electrodes. See **Figure 54**. If the gap is correct, there will be a slight drag as the wire is pulled through. If there is no drag or if the wire won't pull through, bend the side electrode with the gapping tool (**Figure 56**) to change the gap.

3. Put a small drop of oil on the threads of each spark plug.

4. Crank the starter for about 5 seconds to blow away any dirt around the spark plug holes.

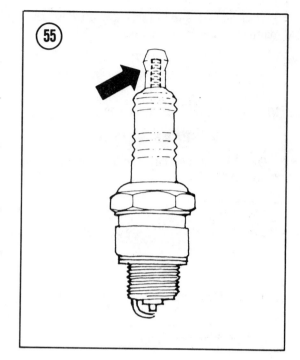

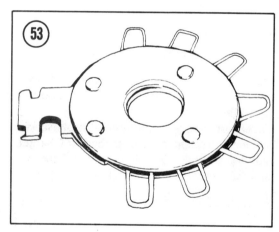

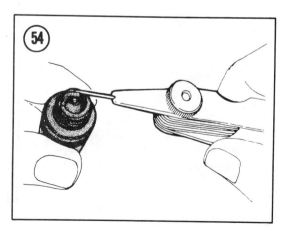

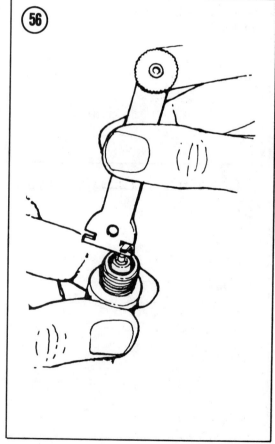

5. Screw each plug in by hand until it seats. Very little effort is required. If force is necessary, the plug is cross-threaded. Unscrew it and try again.

6. Tighten the spark plugs. If you have a torque wrench, tighten to 1.5-2.0 mkg (11-14 ft.-lb.). If not, tighten the plug with fingers, then tighten an additional 1/4-1/2 turn with the plug wrench.

> *CAUTION*
> *Do not overtighten. This prevents the plugs from seating.*

DISTRIBUTOR CAP, WIRES AND ROTOR

On 1980 models, the cap, wires and rotor should be inspected at each tune-up. On all other models, the inspection should be done at alternate tune-ups (every 30,000 miles or 2 years).

1. Pry back the distributor cap clips and remove the cap.

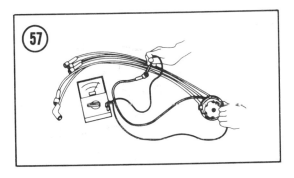

2. If you have an ohmmeter, connect it between each wire end and distributor cap terminal (**Figure 57**). Resistance should be less than 30,000 ohms. If it is higher, remove the wire and test it separately. If resistance is still too high, replace the wire. If not, replace the distributor cap and rotor as a set.

If you don't have an ohmmeter, check the distributor cap terminals for dirt or corrosion. Clean or replace as needed.

Replace the wires if the insulation is melted, brittle or cracked.

3. Check the rotor for burns, cracks or wear. Replace the rotor and cap as a set if these conditions can be seen.

4. Install the rotor. Install the distributor cap and reconnect the wires. Be sure they are connected to the right terminals. Terminals are numbered counterclockwise in the following order: 1, 3, 4, 2. **Figure 58** shows the rotor pointing to No. 1 terminal on 1980 models; **Figure 59** shows the rotor pointing to No. 1 terminal on 1981 models.

IGNITION TIMING

Ignition timing should be checked at each tune-up, except on 1981 models. These do not require periodic timing checks.

Ignition timing requires a stroboscopic timing light of the type described in Chapter One. Connect the light according to manufacturer's instructions.

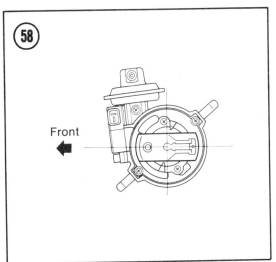

Front

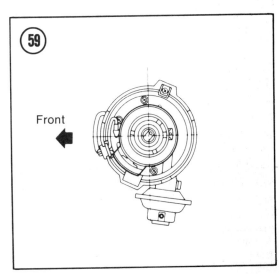

Front

1. Clean the crankshaft pulley and timing marks. See **Figure 60**.

2. Find your engine's timing mark in **Table 10**. Apply white paint to the pulley notch and the appropriate mark on the timing scale.

3. On U.S. models, disconnect and plug the distributor vacuum line (**Figure 61**).

4. Warm up the engine. Connect the timing light and an accurate tune-up tachometer.

5. Start the engine. Compare idle speed to **Table 6**. Adjust if necessary as described under *Idle Speed Adjustment* in this chapter.

6. Point the timing light at the timing marks. If timing is incorrect, shut off the engine. Loosen the distributor lock bolt (**Figure 62**) and rotate the distributor to change timing.

7. Start the engine and check the adjustment. Repeat Step 5 until timing is correct.

> *WARNING*
> *Never touch the distributor wires when the engine is running. This can cause a painful shock, even if the insulation is in perfect condition.*

IDLE SPEED ADJUSTMENT

Idle speed is the only fuel system adjustment practical for home mechanics. Idle mixture is adjustable on 1980 models, but requires a CO meter. If you don't have one, have idle mixture adjusted by a Datsun dealer or other competent shop.

1. Warm the engine to normal operating temperature.

2. After the engine is warm, run the engine at 2,000 rpm for 5 minutes (1980) or 2 minutes (1981) with the hood open.

3. On 1980 models, rev the engine to 1,500-2,000 rpm 2 or 3 times.

4. Check idle speed. Compare with **Table 10**.

5. If necessary, adjust idle speed with the idle speed screw (**Figure 63**).

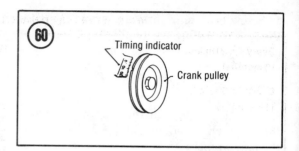
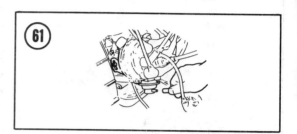
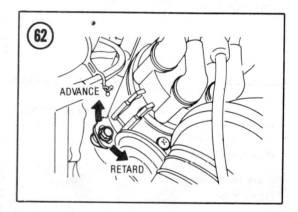

Table 1　FUEL STOP CHECKS

Engine oil	Check level
Coolant	Check reserve tank level
Battery electrolyte	Check level
Windshield washer fluid	Check container level
Brake fluid	Check level
Clutch fluid	Check level
Tire pressures	Check

Table 2   SCHEDULED MAINTENANCE, 1980 U.S. MODELS

Every 7,500 miles (6 months)	Engine oil and filter
Every 15,000 miles (12 months)	Transmission oil level check Differential oil level check Transfer case oil level check Brakes Leak inspection Drive belts Brake fluid Steering, suspension, and drive shafts Front axle shafts Wheels and tires Hinges, latches, locks Tune-up
Every 30,000 miles (24 months)	Coolant Air cleaner element ATC air cleaner Air induction valve filter Evaporative emission control system Front wheel bearings

3

Table 3   SCHEDULED MAINTENANCE, 1980 CANADIAN MODELS

Every 7,500 miles (6 months)	Engine oil and filter
Every 15,000 miles (12 months)	Transmission oil level check Differential oil level check Transfer case oil level check Brakes Leak inspection Coolant hoses and connections Drive belts Brake fluid Steering, suspension, and drive shafts Front axle shafts Wheels and tires
Every 30,000 miles (24 months)	Hinges, latches, locks ATC air cleaner Vacuum lines Tune-up Coolant Air cleaner element PCV valve and filter Air induction valve filter Evaporative emission control system Fuel filter Front wheel bearings

Table 4 SCHEDULED MAINTENANCE (1981)

Every 7,500 miles (6 months)	Engine oil and filter
Every 15,000 miles (12 months)	Transmission oil level check Differential oil level check Transfer case oil level check Brakes Leak inspection Drive belts Brake fluid Steering, suspension, and drive shafts Front axle shafts Wheels and tires Hinges, latches, locks Tune-up
Every 30,000 miles (24 months)	Coolant Air cleaner element Air induction valve filter Evaporative emission control system Front wheel bearings

Table 5 RECOMMENDED LUBRICANTS

Engine oil	API service SE
Transmission, transfer case, and steering gear	API GL-4
Differentials	API GL-5
Multipurpose grease	NLGI no.2
Brake and clutch fluid	DOT 3
Antifreeze	Ethylene glycol base

Table 6   LUBRICANT VISCOSITY

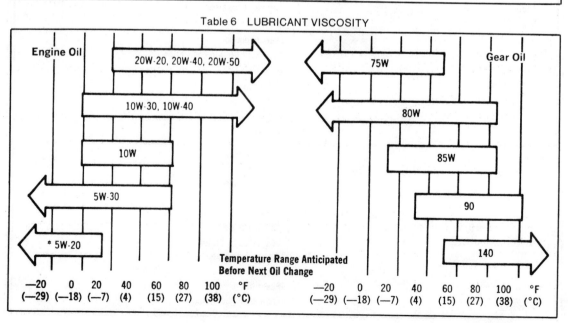

3

Table 7 TIRE PRESSURES

Size	Load range	Pressure (psi)
G 78-15	B	28
G R 78-15	B	28

Table 8 APPROXIMATE REFILL CAPACITIES

Engine oil (including filter)	4.3 liters (4-1/2 qt.)
Transmission oil	
4-speed	1.7 liters (3-5/8 pt.)
5-speed	2.0 liters (4-1/4 pt.)
Transfer case	1.4 liters (3 pt.)
Differential	
Front	1.0 liter (2-1/8 pt.)
Rear	1.25 liters (2-5/8 pt.)
Steering gear	0.33 liters (3/4 pt.)
Cooling system (including reservoir tank)	
1980	8.9 liters (9-3/8 qt.)
1981	10.2 liters (10-3/4 qt.)
Windshield washer tank	
1980	2 liters (2-1/8 qt.)
1981	1.85 liters (2 qt.)
Fuel tank	
1980 short bed	50 liters (13-1/4 gal.)
1980 long bed	64 liters 16-7/8 gal.)
1981 short bed	60 liters (15-7/8 gal.)
1981 long bed	75 liters (16-7/8 gal.)

Table 9 ENGINE COMPRESSION SPECIFICATIONS

Standard compression	171 psi (12 kg/cm^2)
Minimum compression	128 psi (9 kg/cm^2)
Maximum variation between cylinders	Lowest reading within 80 per cent of highest

Table 10   TUNE-UP SPECIFICATIONS

Valve clearance	
1980	
Intake, hot	0.25 mm (0.010 in.)
Exhaust, hot	0.30 mm (0.012 in.)
Intake, cold	0.17 mm (0.007 in.)
Exhaust, cold	0.24 mm (0.009 in.)
1981	
Intake, hot	0.30 mm (0.012 in.)
Exhaust, hot	0.30 mm (0.012 in.)
Intake, cold	0.21 mm (0.008 in.)
Exhaust, cold	0.23 mm (0.009 in.)

Spark plugs (NGK brand)	
Type, 1980	
Standard (U.S.)	BP6ES-11, BPR6ES-11
Hot type (U.S.)	BP4ES-11, BPR4ES-11,
	BP5ES-11, BPR5ES-11
Cold type (U.S.)	BP7ES-11, BPR7ES-11
Standard (Canada)	BPR6ES
Hot type (Canada)	BPR4ES, BPR5ES
Cold Type (Canada)	BPR7ES
Type, 1981	
Standard (U.S.)	BP6ES
Hot type (U.S.)	BP5ES
Cold type (U.S.)	BP7ES
Standard (Canada)	BPR6ES
Hot type (Canada)	BPR5ES
Cold type (Canada)	BPR7ES
Gap	
1980 (U.S.)	1.0-1.1 mm (0.039-0.043 in.)
All others	0.8-0.9 mm (0.031-0.035 in.)

Ignition timing (at idle speed)	
1980 California	12 +/- 2° BTDC
1980 non-California	10 +/- 2° BTDC
1981	5 +/- 2° BTDC

Idle speed	
1980 U.S.	600 +/- 100
1980 Canada	600
1981	800 +/- 100

ENGINE

The 1980 models use the L20B engine. The overhead camshaft, mounted in 4 brackets on top of the cylinder head, operates the valves through finger rockers. The crankshaft, supported by 5 main bearings, drives the camshaft through a double-row chain and 2 sprockets. The lubrication system consists of an external oil pump and full-flow filter.

The 1981 models use the Z22 engine. This engine is similar to the L20B. The main differences are in engine displacement and cylinder head design.

The Z22 engine uses a crossflow cylinder head with hemispherical combustion chambers. The ignition system uses 2 spark plugs per cylinder. This ensures that the fuel mixture will burn, even though a larger than normal percentage of exhaust gas is recirculated. Exhaust gas recirculation is used to control emissions.

Specifications and tightening torques are listed in **Table 1** and **Table 2** at the end of the chapter.

ENGINE REMOVAL

The engine and transmission are removed as a unit, then separated.

1. Disconnect the negative cable from the battery.

2. Remove the hood. See *Hood*, Chapter Twelve.

3. Drain the oil from engine and transmission.

4. Remove the air cleaner. See *Air Cleaner Removal/Installation*, Chapter Five.

5. Disconnect the hoses and wires connecting the engine to the truck. See **Figure 1** (1980) or **Figure 2** (1981).

6. If equipped with air conditioning, loosen the idler pulley locknut (**Figure 3**). Loosen the adjusting bolt, then remove the compressor drive belt. Unbolt the compressor from the engine, then tie it back out of the way. See **Figure 4**.

WARNING
Never disconnect the compressor hoses. The refrigerant can cause frostbite if it touches skin and blindness if it touches the eyes. If discharged near an open flame, the refrigerant forms poisonous gas.

7. Remove the console. See *Console*, Chapter Twelve.

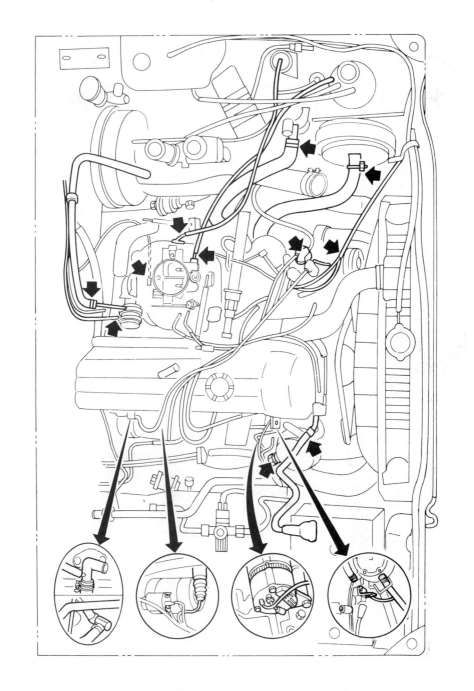

1

1980 ENGINE

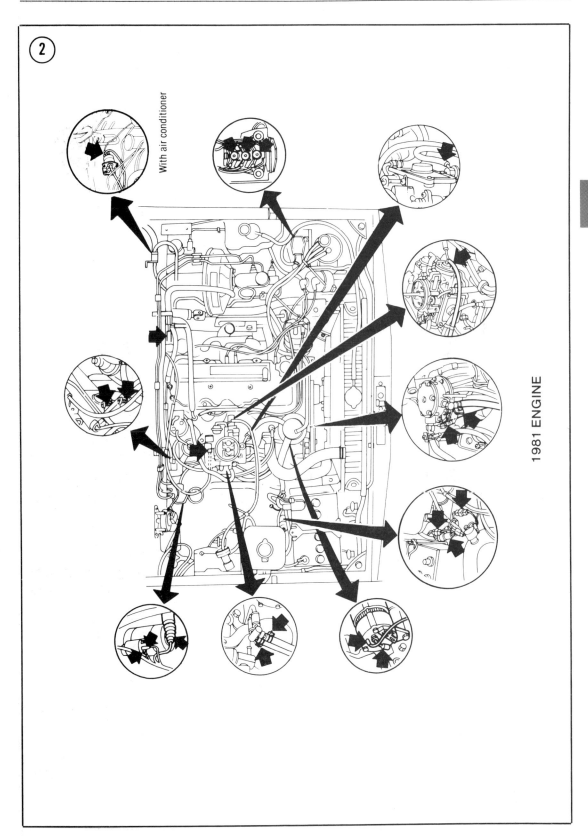

With air conditioner

1981 ENGINE

②

4

8. Remove the snap ring and shift lever pivot pin (**Figure 5**). Take the shift lever out.

9. Drain the cooling system. See *Cooling System Flushing*, Chapter Six.

10. Remove the upper and lower radiator hoses. Remove the radiator and shroud. See *Radiator*, Chapter Six.

11. Disconnect the reverse switch and neutral switch wires from the side of the transmission. See **Figure 6**.

12. Detach the handbrake cables from the balance lever. See *Handbrake*, Chapter Eleven.

13. Disconnect the primary drive shaft and front drive shaft. See *Drive Shafts*, Chapter Ten.

14. Remove the clutch operating cylinder. See *Operating Cylinder, Removal/Installation*, Chapter Eight.

15. Remove the front differential rear mounting bolts (**Figure 7**).

16. Remove the front differential front mounting bolt (**Figure 8**).

17. Remove the front exhaust pipe. See *Exhaust System*, Chapter Five.

18. Attach a hoist to the engine. Hydraulic crane type hoists, available from rental dealers, are the easiest to use.

19. Raise the hoist just enough to remove the weight from the motor mounts.

20. Remove the front differential mounting member (**Figure 9**).

21. Detach the transmission mounting member from the transmission and body. See **Figure 10**.

22. Remove the motor mount nuts and bolts. See **Figure 11** and **Figure 12** (1980) or **Figure 13** and **Figure 14** (1981).

23. Detach the idler arm bracket from the frame. See **Figure 15**. Push the steering cross rod down.

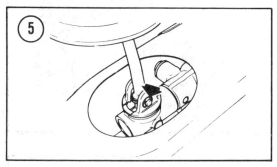

⑤

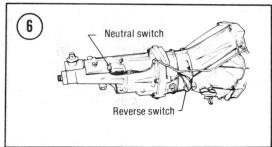

⑥ Neutral switch

Reverse switch

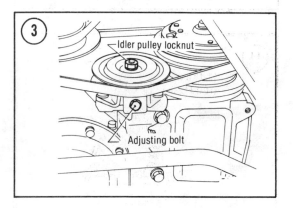

③ Idler pulley locknut

Adjusting bolt

④

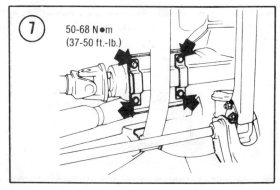

⑦ 50-68 N•m
(37-50 ft.-lb.)

⑧

Ⓣ 71-96 N●m
(52-71 ft.-lb.)

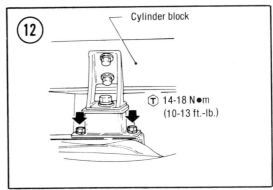

⑫ Cylinder block

Ⓣ 14-18 N●m
(10-13 ft.-lb.)

⑨

Ⓣ 71-96 N●m
(52-71 ft.-lb.)

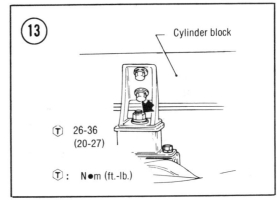

⑬ Cylinder block

Ⓣ 26-36
(20-27)

Ⓣ : N●m (ft.-lb.)

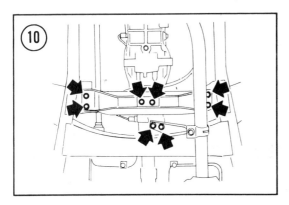

⑩

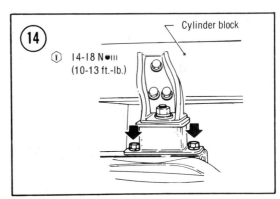

⑭ Cylinder block

Ⓘ 14-18 N●m
(10-13 ft.-lb.)

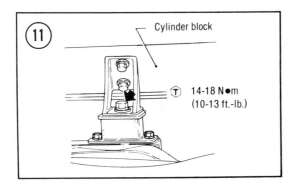

⑪ Cylinder block

Ⓣ 14-18 N●m
(10-13 ft.-lb.)

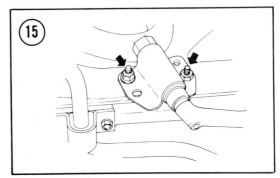

⑮

4

24. At this point, there should be nothing connecting the engine and transmission to the truck. Double-check to be sure.

25. Lift the engine and transmission out of the engine compartment. See **Figure 16**.

CAUTION
Do not let the engine and transmission strike equipment on the engine compartment sidewalls.

ENGINE INSTALLATION

Engine installation is simply the reverse of removal. Fasten the engine and transmission securely to their mounts before tightening anything else. See **Table 2** (end of chapter) for tightening torques. Fill the engine with a 50/50 mixture of antifreeze and water. Fill the engine and transmission with oils recommended in Chapter Three (**Table 5** and **Table 6**).

DISASSEMBLY CHECKLISTS

These checklists tell how much of the engine to remove and disassemble to do a specific type of service (such as a valve job). They will prevent unnecessary work and make sure nothing is left out.

To use the checklists, remove and inspect each part mentioned. Then go through the checklists backwards, installing the parts. Each major part is covered under its own heading in this chapter, unless otherwise noted.

Decarbonizing or Valve Service

1. Remove the intake and exhaust manifolds.
2. Remove the rocker arms and camshaft.
3. Remove the cylinder head.
4. Remove and inspect valves. Inspect valve guides and seats, repairing or replacing as necessary.
5. Assemble by reversing Steps 1-4.

Valve and Ring Service

1. Perform Steps 1-4 for valve service.
2. Remove the oil pan.
3. Remove the pistons together with the connecting rods.
4. Remove the piston rings. It is not necessary to separate the pistons from the connecting rods unless a piston, connecting rod or piston pin needs repair or replacement.

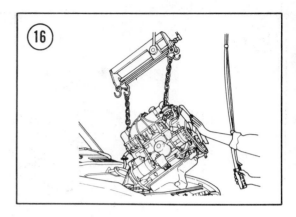

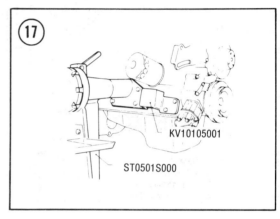

KV10105001

ST0501S000

5. Assemble by reversing Steps 1-4.

General Overhaul

1. Remove the engine and transmission and separate them. Remove the clutch (Chapter Eight) from manual transmission cars.
2. Remove the motor mount bracket, oil filter and oil pressure sender from the right-hand side of the engine.
3. If available, place the engine in a stand. **Figure 17** shows the Datsun stand and adapter. Similar stands are available from rental dealers. The stand isn't absolutely necessary, but will make the job much easier.
4. Check the engine for signs of coolant and oil leaks.
5. Clean the outside of the engine.
6. Remove the distributor. See *Ignition System*, Chapter Seven.
7. Remove the hoses and tubes connected to the engine.
8. Remove the fuel lines.
9. Remove the intake and exhaust manifolds.

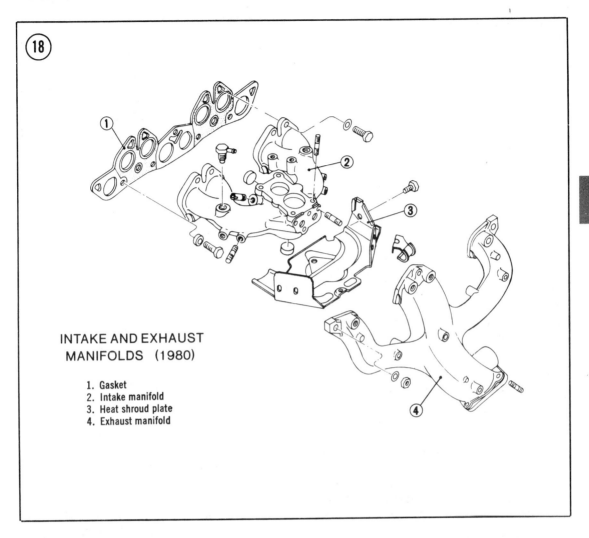

(18)

INTAKE AND EXHAUST
MANIFOLDS (1980)

1. Gasket
2. Intake manifold
3. Heat shroud plate
4. Exhaust manifold

4

10. On 1980 models, remove the thermostat housing, together with the thermostat. See *Thermostat*, Chapter Six.

11. Remove the water pump. See *Water Pump*, Chapter Six.

12. Remove the oil pump.

13. Remove the rocker arms and camshaft.

14. Remove the front cover, timing chain and sprockets.

15. Remove the cylinder head.

16. Remove the oil pan and pickup.

17. Remove the pistons and connecting rods.

18. Remove the flywheel.

19. Remove the crankshaft.

20. Inspect the cylinder block.

21. Assemble by reversing Steps 1-19.

INTAKE AND EXHAUST MANIFOLDS

Manifold Removal/Installation (1980)

Figure 18 shows the 1980 manifolds.

1. If the engine is still in the truck, drain about one gallon of coolant from the radiator. If the coolant is clean, drain it into a clean container and save it for reuse.

2. Remove the air cleaner. See *Air Cleaner, Removal/Installation*, Chapter Five.

3. Disconnect the wires for automatic choke and carburetor solenoid.

4. Disconnect the throttle linkage fom the carburetor. See *Throttle Linkage*, Chapter Five.

5. Disconnect the fuel inlet line. Plug the line so it won't leak gasoline.

6. Disconnect the exhaust pipe from the manifold.

7. Disconnect the EGR tube (**Figure 19**).

8. Remove the back pressure transducer (**Figure 20**).

9. On trucks equipped with air injection systems, disconnect the air injection hose from the check valve. See *Air Injection System*, Chapter Five.

10. On trucks equipped with air induction systems, disconnect the air induction hose from the air gallery. See *Air Induction System*, Chapter Five.

> *CAUTION*
> *The manifolds should come off easily during the next step. If not, check to make sure all fasteners have been removed.*

11. Remove all manifold fasteners, then take the manifolds off.

12. Installation is the reverse of removal. Use a new manifold gasket. Tighten fasteners to specifications (**Table 2**).

Intake Manifold Removal/Installation (1981)

1. If the engine is still in the truck, drain about one gallon of coolant from the radiator. If the coolant is clean, drain it into a clean container and save it for reuse.

2. Remove the air cleaner. See *Air Cleaner, Removal/Installation*, Chapter Five.

3. Disconnect the wires for automatic choke and carburetor solenoid.

4. Disconnect the throttle linkage fom the carburetor. See *Throttle Linkage*, Chapter Five.

5. Disconnect the fuel inlet line. Plug the line so it won't leak gasoline.

6. If carburetor removal is planned, do it now. See *Carburetor, Removal/Installation*, Chapter Five.

7. Disconnect the emission control hoses connecting the manifold to engine and car body. See *Emission Controls*, Chapter Five.

> *CAUTION*
> *The intake manifold should come off easily during the next step. If not, make sure all fasteners have been removed.*

8. Refer to **Figure 21** and detach the manifold from the engine.

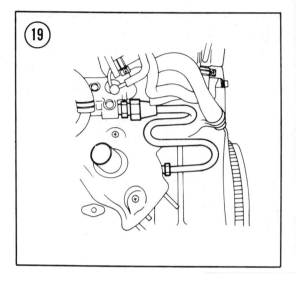

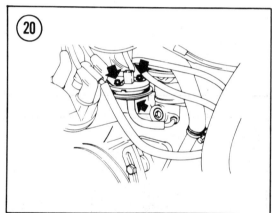

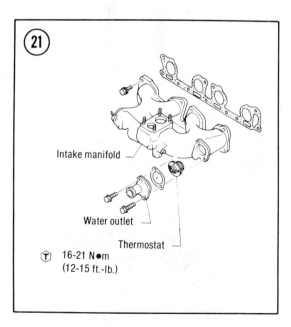

Intake manifold

Water outlet

Thermostat

(T) 16-21 N•m
(12-15 ft.-lb.)

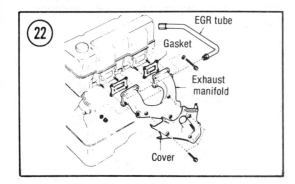

(22)

EGR tube

Gasket

Exhaust
manifold

Cover

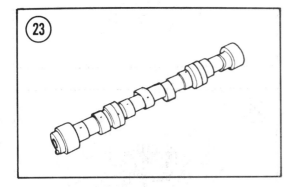

(23)

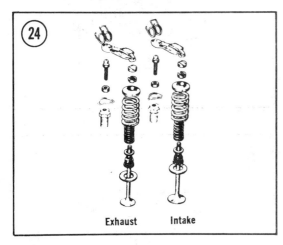

(24)

Exhaust   Intake

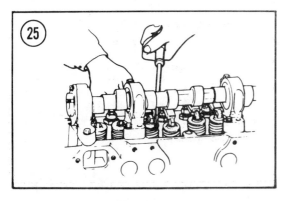

(25)

9. Installation is the reverse of removal. Use a new gasket. Tighten the manifold fasteners to specifications (**Table 2**).

Exhaust Manifold Removal/Installation (1981)

1. Remove the air cleaner. See *Air Cleaner, Removal/Installation*, Chapter Five.
2. Disconnect the exhaust pipe from the manifold.
3. Detach the EGR tube from the manifold. See **Figure 22**.

> *CAUTION*
> *The manifold should come off easily during the next step. If not, make sure all fasteners have been removed.*

4. Detach the manifold from the engine. Remove it together with the cover.
5. If necessary, remove the cover from the manifold.
6. Installation is the reverse of removal. Use new gaskets. Tighten fasteners to specifications (**Table 2**).

ROCKER ARMS AND CAMSHAFT (1980)

Figure 23 shows the camshaft. **Figure 24** shows the rocker arm assembly and related parts.

Rocker Arm Removal

1. Remove the rocker arm cover.
2. Remove the springs looped over the tops of the rocker arms.
3. Loosen the locknut on the rocker arm pivot. Compress the valve spring by using a heavy-bladed screwdriver as a fulcrum. See **Figure 25**.
4. Withdraw the rocker arm while holding the valve springs down with the screwdriver. Be careful not to lose the rocker arm guide located between the rocker arm and the top of the valve stem.
5. If the rocker pivot is visibly worn, unscrew it from the cylinder head, together with its locknut.
6. Install by reversing Steps 1-5.

4

Rocker Arm Inspection

Check the rocker arm for visible wear on its cam contact surface, pivot contact surface and valve contact surface. If wear or any defects can be seen, replace the rocker arm. If the rocker arm pivot is visibly worn, both the pivot and its corresponding rocker arm must be replaced.

Camshaft Removal

1. Remove the rocker arm cover.
2. Remove the fuel pump. See *Fuel Pump, Removal/Installation*, Chapter Five.
3. Check camshaft end play. Position a dial indicator as shown in **Figure 26**. Slide the camshaft back and forth against the dial gauge pointer. The reading on the gauge is camshaft end play. Compare with specifications (**Table 1**). Replace the camshaft locate plate if end play is not within specifications.
4. Turn the engine over by hand until the timing marks on camshaft and timing chain are aligned. See **Figure 27**. This will enable you to position the camshaft correctly during installation.
5. Remove the rocker arms as described in this chapter.
6. Insert a hardwood wedge such as Datsun tool part No. ST17420001 between the sides of the chain. **Figure 27** shows the tool in place; **Figure 28** shows it alone. This tool keeps the timing chain from slipping off the crankshaft sprocket. It also keeps the timing chain tensioner piston from popping out. If the chain slips off or the tensioner pops out, the front cover and oil pan will have to be removed to reinstall them.

> *NOTE*
> *If you make your own tool, use a piece of hardwood about one inch thick. Do not use plywood, since this may leave fragments in the engine. Drill a hole in the top of the tool so it can be pulled out.*

7. Remove the bolt from the front end of the camshaft. Remove the fuel pump lobe and camshaft sprocket. Take the sprocket out of the chain and drape the chain out of the way.
8. Remove 2 bolts and take the camshaft locate plate off the front camshaft bracket.

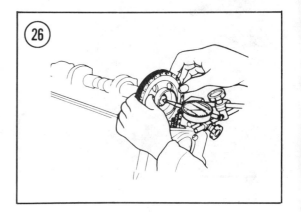

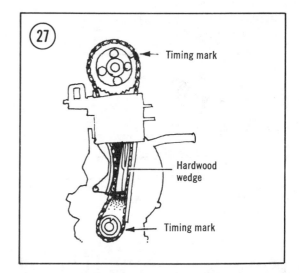

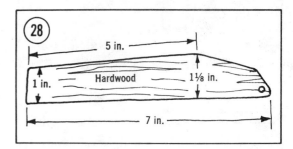

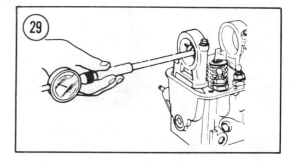

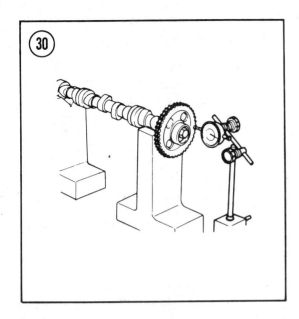

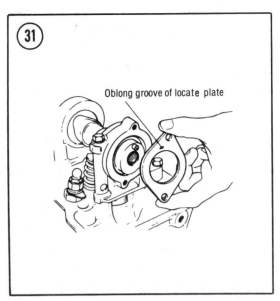

Oblong groove of locate plate

9. Carefully withdraw the camshaft toward the front of the engine. Rotate the camshaft slowly while removing. Be careful not to scratch the camshaft bearing surfaces.

CAUTION
Even though removal looks easy it is difficult to realign brackets correctly. Misaligned brackets will cause a broken camshaft.

Camshaft Inspection

NOTE
If you don't have precision measuring equipment, have inspection done by a machine shop.

1. Measure the inner diameter of the camshaft bearings (**Figure 29**). Compare with specifications (**Table 1**). If any bearings are worn beyond the maximum, replace the entire cylinder head.

2. Measure the outer diameter of the camshaft journals. Subtract these figures from the bearing inner diameters to determine camshaft bearing clearance. If the bearings were within specifications during Step 1 and oil clearance is excessive, the camshaft must be replaced.

3. Measure camshaft bend. Rotate the camshaft between accurate centers (such as

V-blocks or a lathe) with a dial indicator contacting the second and third journals. If camshaft bend (total indicator reading) exceeds specifications (**Table 1**), replace the camshaft.

4. Check the camshaft sprocket for runout. Measure with the sprocket installed on the camshaft, as shown in **Figure 30**. Replace the sprocket if runout exceeds specifications in **Table 1**.

Camshaft Installation

1. Coat the camshaft journals and bearing surface with clean engine oil.

2. Carefully install the camshaft in the brackets. Rotate the camshaft slowly while installing to ease installation.

3. Install the camshaft locate plate and secure it with 2 bolts. The small groove in the locate plate (**Figure 31**) goes on top and faces the front of the engine.

4. Install the rocker arms as described in this chapter.

5. Lift up the timing chain and remove the support tool. Place the camshaft sprocket in the chain.

NOTE
Make sure the timing marks in chain and sprocket are aligned.

6. Slide the sprocket onto the camshaft. Use No. 2 sprocket locating hole (**Figure 32**).

7. Install the fuel pump cam, then the sprocket bolt and lockwasher. Tighten to specifications (**Table 2**).

8. Install the fuel pump. See *Fuel Pump, Removal/Installation*, Chapter Five.

9. Install the rocker arm cover.

ROCKER ARMS AND CAMSHAFT (1981)

Removal

1. Remove the rocker arm cover.

2. Turn the engine until the timing marks on chain and sprocket are aligned. See **Figure 33**.

NOTE
There are 3 dowel holes in the camshaft sprocket. Be sure No. 2 hole (center hole of the 3) is straight up.

3. Remove the camshaft sprocket bolt.

4. Take the sprocket off the camshaft (**Figure 34**). Let it rest on the engine front cover.

5. If the sprocket is to be removed from the timing chain, support the timing chain with a hardwood wedge. **Figure 35** shows the tool; **Figure 36** shows it in use. This tool keeps the timing chain from falling off the crankshaft sprocket. It also keeps the timing chain tensioner from popping out. If the chain slips

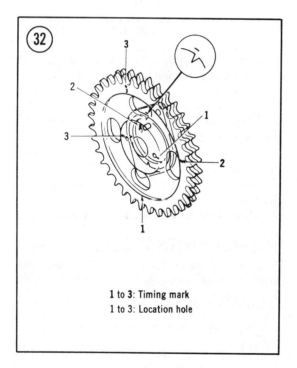

1 to 3: Timing mark
1 to 3: Location hole

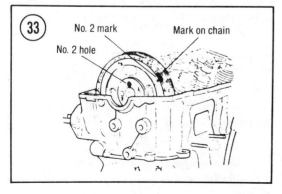

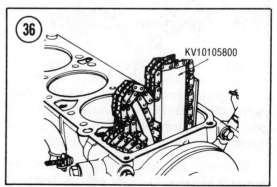

KV10105800

off the sprocket or the tensioner pops out, the front cover and oil pan will have to be removed to put them back.

NOTE

If you make your own tool, use a piece of hardwood about one inch thick. Do not use plywood, since this may leave fragments in the engine. Drill a hole in the top of the tool so it can be pulled out.

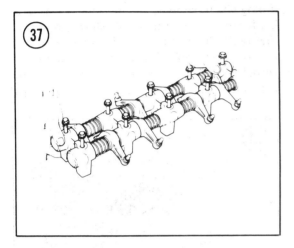

(37)

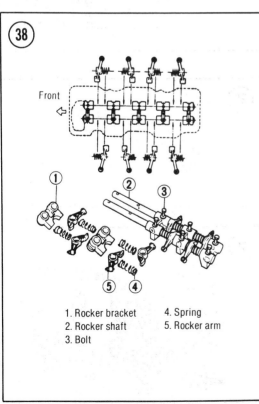

(38)

Front

1. Rocker bracket   4. Spring
2. Rocker shaft   5. Rocker arm
3. Bolt

6. Remove the rocker assembly bolts. Loosen in several stages, starting with the center bolts and working outward.

7. Lift the rocker assembly off the cylinder head. See **Figure 37**.

8. Lift the camshaft out of the cylinder head.

9. Installation is the reverse of removal. Tighten the rocker bracket bolts to specifications (**Table 2**). Tighten in several stages, working inward from the front and rear rocker brackets.

Rocker Assembly Inspection

1. Remove the rocker arms, springs and brackets. See **Figure 38**.

NOTE

The front and rear bolts hold the rocker brackets onto the shafts. When these bolts are removed, spring pressure will push the end rocker brackets off. Slide the brackets off slowly, so the springs don't fly off and get lost.

2. Check rocker arms for visible wear on the cam contact surface, pivot surface and valve contact surface. Replace worn or damaged rocker arms.

3. Check rocker shafts for wear or damage. Replace as needed.

4. Make sure rocker bracket oil passages are clear.

5. Replace worn or deformed rocker springs.

6. Assemble the rocker assembly. Be sure rocker stand letter marks (**Figure 39**) correspond with the marks on the cylinder

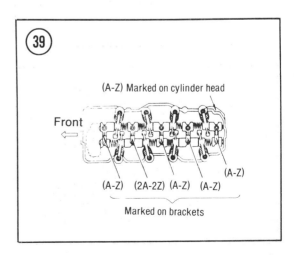

(39)

(A-Z) Marked on cylinder head

Front

(A-Z)

(A-Z) (2A-2Z) (A-Z) (A-Z)

Marked on brackets

4

head. Be sure rocker shafts are positioned with their punch marks toward the front (**Figure 40**). The intake rocker shaft has slits as shown.

NOTE
Rocker arms for cylinders 1 and 3 (counting from the front of the engine) are interchangeable. These rocker arms are stamped with the number "1". Rocker arms for cylinders 2 and 4 are also interchangeable and are stamped with the number "2".

Camshaft Inspection

If you don't have the necessary precision measuring equipment, the next steps can be done inexpensively by a machine shop.
1. Reinstall the rocker brackets. Measure inner diameter with a bore gauge (**Figure 41**). If excessive, replace the cylinder head.
2. Measure outer diameter of the camshaft journals with a micrometer. If worn to less than the minimum, replace the camshaft.
3. Measure camshaft lobe height. Compare with specifications (**Table 1**). If the lobes are worn to 0.25 mm (0.010 in.) less than specified, replace the camshaft.
4. Place the camshaft between accurate centers, such as V-blocks or a lathe. Rotate the camshaft one full turn and measure bend with a dial indicator. See **Figure 42**. Maximum bend (total indicator reading) is 0.1 mm (0.004 in.). If excessive, replace the camshaft.
5. Place the camshaft in the brackets. Measure end play with a dial indicator (**Figure 43**). If it exceeds 0.2 mm (0.008 in.), replace the camshaft or cylinder head, whichever is worn.

Installation

1. Liberally coat the camshaft bearing surfaces with clean engine oil.

CAUTION
The camshaft dowel must be up during the next step. Otherwise valves may strike the piston tops.

2. Lay the camshaft in the saddles with the dowel upward. See **Figure 44**.
3. Install the rocker assembly (**Figure 45**). Tighten to specifications (**Table 2**). Tighten in 2 or 3 stages, working outward from the center bolts.

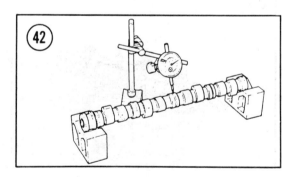

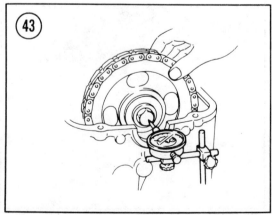

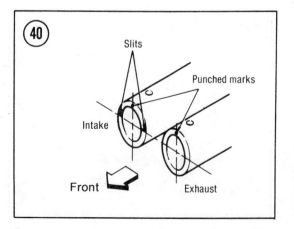

CAUTION
*If the cylinder head is off the engine, place it on blocks so the valves aren't pushed into the workbench. See **Figure 45**.*

4. Install the camshaft sprocket in the timing chain (if it was removed). Be sure the chain and sprocket timing marks are aligned (**Figure 46**).

5. Bolt the sprocket to the camshaft. Be sure the camshaft dowel is in No. 2 sprocket dowel hole (**Figure 46**).

6. Apply gasket sealer to the end seal saddles (**Figure 47**), then install the rocker arm cover.

OIL PAN AND PUMP

Oil Pan Removal/Installation

1. Set the handbrake. Place the transmission in FIRST.

2. Jack up the front end of the truck and place it on jackstands.

3. Remove the front differential. See *Differential*, Chapter Ten.

4. Remove the transmission-to-engine stiffener braces.

5. Unbolt the oil pan and take it off. Tap gently with a rubber mallet if necessary to break the gasket seal.

6. Unbolt the oil strainer and take it off.

7. Clean the oil pan and strainer thoroughly. If difficult to clean, have the pan and strainer boiled out by a machine shop.

8. Check for cracks, dents, bent gasket surfaces and damaged drain hole threads. Replace the oil pan if damage is serious.

9. Install by reversing Steps 1-6. Remove all traces of old gasket and sealer fom the oil pan and cylinder block. Use new gaskets, coated on both sides with gasket sealer. Tighten the oil pan bolts evenly, a little at a time, to prevent warping the oil pan.

Oil Pump Removal/Installation

1. Remove the distributor cap. Turn the engine so No. 1 piston is at top dead center on its compression stroke. When this occurs, the

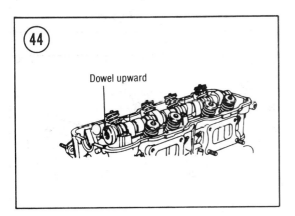

(44)
Dowel upward

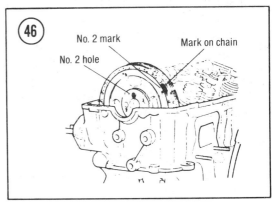

(46)
No. 2 mark
Mark on chain
No. 2 hole

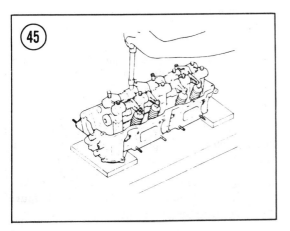

(45)

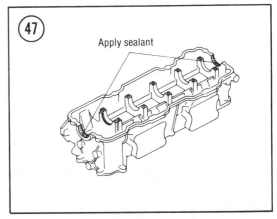

(47)
Apply sealant

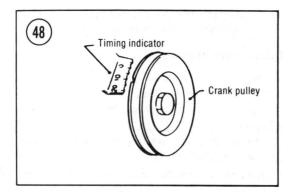

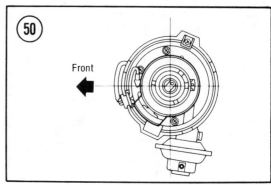

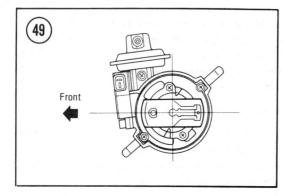

0 degree mark on the timing scale will align with the crankshaft pulley notch (**Figure 48**). In addition, the rotor will point to No. 1 terminal in the distributor cap. See **Figure 49** (1980) or **Figure 50** (1981 models).

> *NOTE*
> *Be sure to check rotor position as well as the timing marks. The timing marks also line up when No. 1 piston is at TDC on its exhaust stroke.*

2. Drain the engine oil.

> *NOTE*
> *It is possible to remove the oil pump without draining the oil. However, if an oil pump problem is suspected, the oil should be changed as a matter of good practice.*

3. Remove the pump mounting bolts, then take the pump off. See **Figure 51**.

4. Installation is the reverse of removal. Make sure the punch mark on the distributor driving spindle lines up with the oil hole in the oil pump drive shaft (**Figure 52**). Make sure the drive spindle fits securely in the base of the distributor. Tighten the oil pump mounting bolts to specifications (**Table 2**).

Disassembly/Inspection/Assembly

1. Remove the oil pump cover and gasket. See **Figure 53**.

2. Lift out the inner and outer pump rotors. Remove the regulator valve parts.

3. Clean all parts in solvent. Check the distributor drive spindle and pump rotors for wear, scoring or damage. Check oil pump clearances (**Figure 54**) and compare with specifications at the end of the chapter. Replace the pump if any clearances are excessive.

4. Lay a straightedge across the pump body and rotors (**Figure 55**). Measure the gap between rotors and straightedge, or pump body and straightedge, with a feeler gauge. If the gap exceeds specifications (end of chapter), replace the oil pump.

5. Check the regulator valve and spring for wear or damage. Replace the valve assembly if any parts are defective.

6. Reassemble the pump, using a new gasket. The chamfered side of the outer rotor (**Figure 56**) faces into the oil pump.

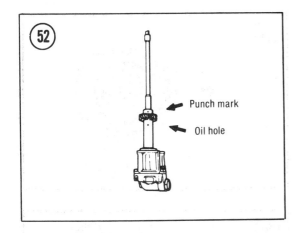

52

Punch mark

Oil hole

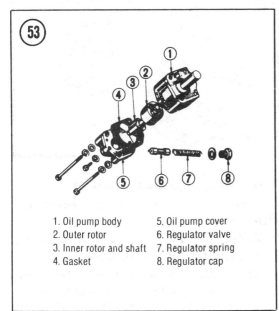

53

1. Oil pump body
2. Outer rotor
3. Inner rotor and shaft
4. Gasket
5. Oil pump cover
6. Regulator valve
7. Regulator spring
8. Regulator cap

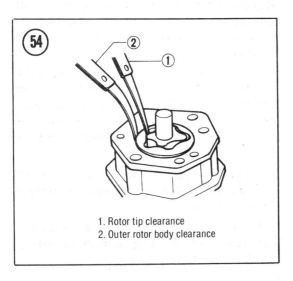

54

1. Rotor tip clearance
2. Outer rotor body clearance

FRONT COVER, TIMING CHAIN AND SPROCKETS

Front Cover Removal

1. Remove the radiator and fan. See *Radiator Removal/Installation*, Chapter Six.
2. Remove the drive belts. See *Drive Belts*, Chapter Three.
3. Remove the distributor. See *Ignition System*, Chapter Seven.
4. Remove the oil pan, oil pump and oil pump driving spindle as described under *Oil Pan and Pump* in this chapter.
5. Remove the crankshaft pulley.
6. Unbolt the front cover from the engine block and cylinder head. Remove it by pulling forward and down (the water pump comes off with the cover).

Front Oil Seal Replacement

1. Remove the front cover as described in the preceding section.
2. Carefully pry out the old oil seal. Do not gouge the aluminum front cover.
3. Tap in a new oil seal. Coat the lip of the seal with multipurpose grease.

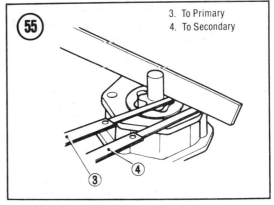

55

3. To Primary
4. To Secondary

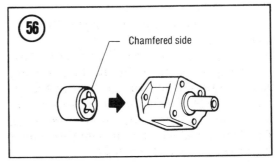

56

Chamfered side

4

Sprocket and Chain Removal

1. Remove the front cover as described earlier.

2. Remove the valve rocker cover.

3. Install the crankshaft pulley bolt in the crankshaft. Put a wrench on the bolt and turn the engine over until the timing marks on chain and sprockets are aligned. See **Figure 57**.

4. Unbolt the chain tensioner and guides from the block. See **Figure 58**.

5. Unbolt the camshaft sprocket from the camshaft.

6. Remove the timing chain from the crankshaft sprocket.

7. Remove the oil thrower, oil pump drive gear and crankshaft sprocket from the front of the crankshaft. If the sprocket is difficult to remove, use a puller as shown in **Figure 59**. These are available from rental dealers.

> *CAUTION*
> *Do not rotate the crankshaft and camshaft separately or the valves will be forced against the piston tops.*

Inspection

1. Thoroughly clean all parts in solvent before inspection.

2. Check the chain tensioner assembly and chain guides for wear or damage. Replace if these are evident.

3. Check the sprockets, oil pump drive gear and oil thrower for wear or damage. Replace as needed.

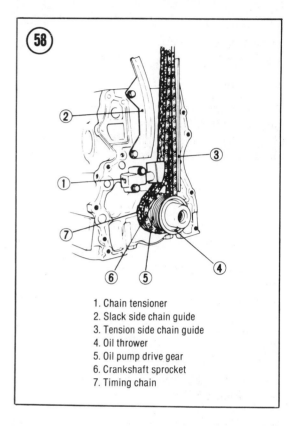

1. Chain tensioner
2. Slack side chain guide
3. Tension side chain guide
4. Oil thrower
5. Oil pump drive gear
6. Crankshaft sprocket
7. Timing chain

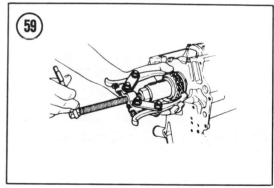

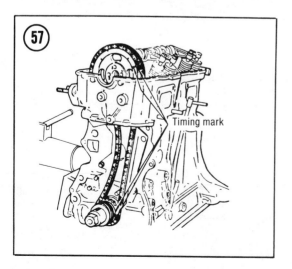

Timing mark

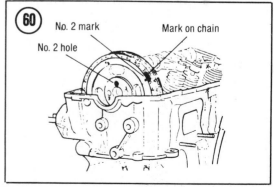

No. 2 mark   Mark on chain
No. 2 hole

4. Check the chain for wear, damage or stretching of the roller links. Replace if these can be seen.

Chain and Sprocket Installation

1. Install the Woodruff keys in the crankshaft keyways if they have been removed.
2. Install the crankshaft sprocket, oil pump drive gear and oil thrower.

NOTE
The crankshaft sprocket timing mark faces forward. The side of the oil pump drive gear with the large inner chamfer faces rearward.

3. Install the chain guides on the cylinder block.
4. Install the timing chain on the crankshaft sprocket. Be sure the timing mark on the chain is aligned with the mark on the sprocket. See **Figure 57**.
5. Install the camshaft sprocket in the chain. Be sure the chain and sprocket timing marks align (**Figure 57**).

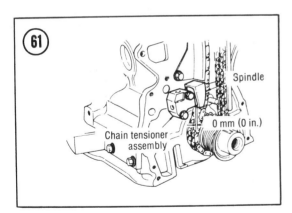
Spindle
0 mm (0 in.)
Chain tensioner assembly

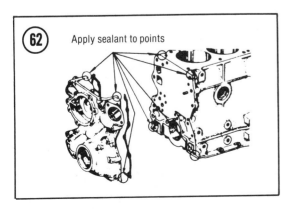
Apply sealant to points

6. Slide the camshaft sprocket onto the camshaft. Be sure the camshaft dowel is straight up. Align No. 2 dowel hole (center hole of the 3) with the camshaft dowel. See **Figure 60**.
7. Install the camshaft sprocket bolt. Tighten to specifications (**Table 1**).
8. Push the chain tensioner piston all the way into the tensioner. Install the tensioner on the engine.
9. Position the slack side chain guide so the tensioner piston is held all the way in. See **Figure 61**.
10. Make sure the chain and sprocket timing marks are aligned.

Front Cover Installation

Installation is the reverse of removal, plus the following.
1. Use new left and right cover gaskets, coated on both sides with gasket sealer. Apply small amounts of sealer to the corners of the front cover. See **Figure 62**.
2. Take care not to bend the front portion of the head gasket when installing the cover. Be sure to install the cylinder head-to-cover bolts.
3. Fill the engine with oil and the radiator with coolant. See Chapter Three for types and quantities.

CYLINDER HEAD

Cylinder Head Removal

1. Completely drain the cooling system. See *Cooling System Flushing*, Chapter Six.
2. Remove all spark plugs.
3. Remove the air cleaner. See *Air Cleaner*, Chapter Five.
4. Remove the valve rocker cover.
5. Remove the intake and exhaust manifolds. See *Intake and Exhaust Manifolds* in this chapter.
6. Turn the camshaft so its sprocket locating pin is straight up. This provides a reference point for later installation.
7. Remove the camshaft sprocket as described under *Camshaft and Rocker Arms* in this chapter.
8. Remove the small bolts attaching the cylinder head to the engine front cover.

9. Remove the cylinder head bolts. To prevent warping the head, loosen the bolts in several stages. Follow the order shown in **Figure 63** (1980) or **Figure 64** (1981).

10. Once the head bolts are removed, lift the cylinder head off the engine. If the head is difficult to remove, tap it gently with a rubber mallet. Under no circumstances should you pry the head off.

Cylinder Head Inspection

1. Check the cylinder head for water leaks before cleaning.

2. Clean the cylinder head thoroughly in solvent. While cleaning, check for cracks or other visible damage. Look for corrosion or foreign material in oil or water passages. Clean the passages with a stiff spiral wire brush, then blow them out with compressed air.

3. Check the cylinder head bottom (block mating) surface for flatness. Place an accurate straightedge along its surface (**Figure 65**). If there is any gap, measure it with a feeler gauge. Measure along the 6 lines shown. If the gap exceeds specifications, have the head resurfaced by a machine shop.

NOTE
Total material milled from head and block must not be more than 0.2 mm (0.008 in).

4. Check studs in the cylinder head for damage. Replace damaged studs.

Decarbonizing

1. Without removing valves, remove all deposits from the combustion chambers, intake ports and exhaust ports. Use a wire brush dipped in solvent or make a scraper out of hardwood. Be careful not to scratch or gouge the combustion chambers.

2. After all carbon is removed from the combustion chambers and ports, clean the entire head in solvent.

3. Clean away all carbon on the piston tops. Do not remove the carbon ridge at the top of the cylinder bore.

Cylinder Head Installation

1. Be sure the cylinder head, block and cylinder bores are clean. Check all visible oil passages for cleanliness.

2. Install the camshaft and rocker arms in the cylinder head. Turn the camshaft so its

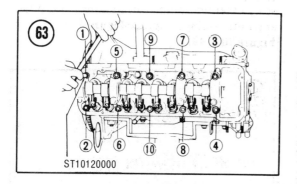

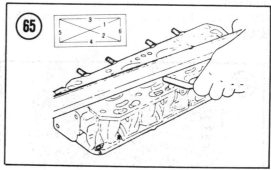

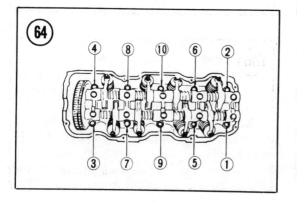

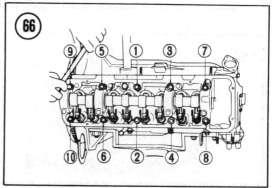

sprocket locating dowel is straight up. This must be done before the cylinder head is installed to prevent the valves from striking the piston tops.

3. Install a new cylinder head gasket. Never reuse an old head gasket. Do *not* use gasket sealer on the head gasket.

NOTE
During the next step, look at the valves and make sure none of them are open far enough to strike the piston tops.

4. Position the cylinder head on the block. Install the cylinder head bolts.

5. With the engine cool, tighten the head bolts. Follow the sequence in **Figure 66** (1980) or **Figure 67** (1981). Tighten a little at a time, in several stages, to prevent warping the cylinder head. Correct final torque is 69-78 N•m (51-58 ft.-lb.).

6. Install the timing chain and camshaft sprocket as described under *Rocker Arms and Camshaft, Installation*, in this chapter.

7. Install the intake and exhaust manifolds.

8. Install the spark plugs and rocker arm cover.

9. Fill the cooling system with a 50/50 mixture of ethylene glycol-based antifreeze and water.

10. Change the oil. See *Engine Oil and Filter*, Chapter Three.

11. Run the engine for several minutes, let it cool, then recheck head bolt tightness.

VALVES AND VALVE SEATS

Some of the following procedures must be done by a dealer or machine shop, since they require special knowledge and expensive machine tools. Others, while possible for the home mechanic, are difficult or time-consuming. A general practice among those who do their own service is to remove the cylinder head, perform all disassembly except valve removal and take the head to a machine shop for inspection and service. Since the cost is low in relation to the required effort and equipment, this is usually the best approach, even for experienced mechanics.

Valve Removal

1. Remove the cylinder head as described under *Cylinder Head* in this chapter.

2. If you haven't already done so, remove the camshaft and rocker arms from the head.

3. Compress each valve spring with a compressor like the one shown in **Figure 68**. Remove the valve keepers and release the spring tension. Remove the spring washer, oil seal, inner and outer valve springs and inner and outer spring seats. See **Figure 69** (1980) or **Figure 70** (1981).

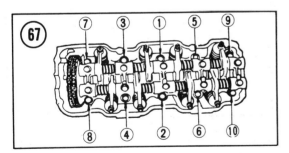

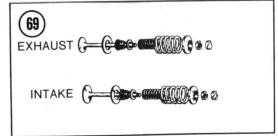

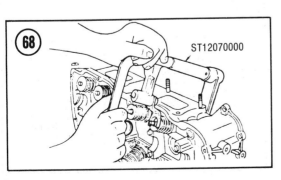

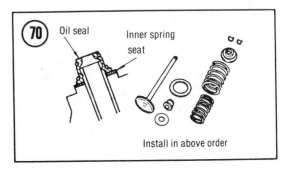

CAUTION
Remove any burrs from valve stem grooves before removing the valves. Otherwise the valve guides will be damaged.

Valve and Valve Guide Inspection

1. Clean the valves with a wire brush and solvent. Discard cracked, warped or burned valves.

2. Measure valve stems at top, center and bottom for wear. A machine shop can do this when the valves are ground. Also measure the length of each valve and the diameter of each valve head.

3. The valve faces and stem ends should be resurfaced when the valves are ground. No more than 0.5 mm (0.020 in.) may be removed from valve stem ends. Valve faces may not be ground thinner than 0.5 mm (0.020 in.).

4. Remove all carbon and varnish from valve guides with a stiff spiral wire brush.

NOTE
The next step assumes that all valve stems have been measured and are within specifications. Replace valves with worn stems before performing this step.

5. Insert each valve into the guide from which it was removed. Hold the valve just slightly off its seat and rock it back and forth in a direction parallel with the rocker arms (**Figure 71**). This is the direction in which the greatest wear normally occurs. If the valve stem rocks more than approximately 0.2 mm (0.008 in.), the valve guide is probably worn.

6. If there is any doubt about valve guide condition after performing Step 5, measure the valve guide at top, center and bottom with a bore gauge. See **Figure 72** (1980) or **Figure 73** (1981). Replace worn guides.

7. Measure valve spring free length and compare with specifications. Replace springs that are too long or too short. Measure spring bend with a square. Replace springs bent beyond specifications.

8. Test the valve springs under load on a spring tester. Replace weak springs.

9. Inspect valve seat inserts. If worn or burned, they must be reconditioned. This is a job for a dealer or machine shop, although the procedure is described later in this section.

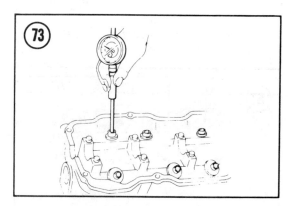

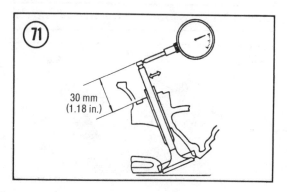

30 mm
(1.18 in.)

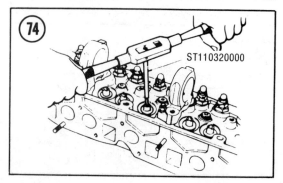

ST110320000

Valve Guide Replacement

This procedure requires a press and reaming tools. If you do not have the necessary equipment, take the job to a dealer or machine shop.

1. Remove worn guides with a press and suitable drift. This can be done at room temperature, but will be easier if the head is heated first.
2. Ream the guide holes in the cylinder head to specifications (end of chapter).
3. Heat the cylinder head to 150-200° C (302-392° F).
4. Press the guides in from the top of the cylinder head until their snap rings contact the head.
5. Measure valve guide bores. Ream to specifications. See **Figure 74** (1980) or **Figure 75** (1981).

Valve Seat Inserts

The valve seats are cut into inserts. Replacement requires precision machine tools and special skills. Take the job to a dealer or qualified machine shop.

1. Remove the old valve seat by boring it out until it collapses. Be sure not to cut the cylinder head during boring.
2. Select a valve seat insert and check its outside diameter. Compare with specifications (end of chapter).
3. Machine the cylinder head recess diameter to fit the valve seat insert, using the valve guide as an axis.
4. Heat the cylinder head to 150-200° C (302-392° F).
5. Press the valve seat insert into place. Be sure it beds securely on the cylinder head. Stake the insert at 4 or more places.
6. Grind the valve seats as described in the following procedure.

Valve Seat Reconditioning

1. Cut the valve seats to specified dimensions, using a cutter or special stone. See **Figure 76** (1980 intake), **Figure 77** (1980 exhaust), **Figure 78** (1981 intake) or **Figure 79** (1981 exhaust).

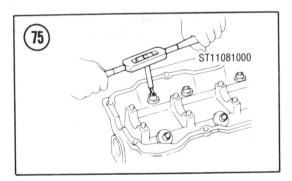

⑦⑤
ST11081000

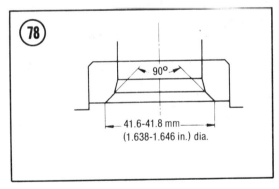

⑦⑧
90°
41.6-41.8 mm
(1.638-1.646 in.) dia.

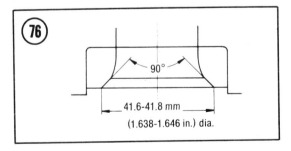

⑦⑥
90°
41.6-41.8 mm
(1.638-1.646 in.) dia.

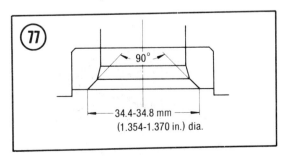

⑦⑦
90°
34.4-34.8 mm
(1.354-1.370 in.) dia.

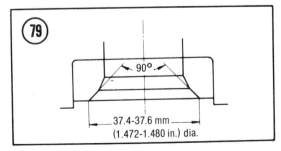

⑦⑨
90°
37.4-37.6 mm
(1.472-1.480 in.) dia.

2. Coat the corresponding valve face with Prussian blue dye.
3. Insert the valve into the valve guide.
4. Rotate the valve under light pressure approximately 1/4 turn.
5. Lift the valve out. If it seats properly, the dye will transfer evenly to the valve face.

Valve Installation

1. Coat the valves with oil and install them in the cylinder head.
2. Install the valve spring seats, oil seals, springs and spring washers. Compress the valve springs and install the keepers.

PISTON/CONNECTING ROD ASSEMBLY

Piston Removal

1. Remove the cylinder head and oil pan as described under *Cylinder Head* and *Oil Pan and Pump* in this chapter.
2. Remove the carbon ridge at the top of the cylinder bores with a ridge reamer. These are available from rental dealers.
3. Rotate the crankshaft so the connecting rod is centered in the bore.

> *NOTE*
> *Check for cylinder numbers stamped on connecting rod and cap (**Figure 80**). If they aren't visible, make your own.*

4. Remove the nuts securing the connecting rod cap. Lift off the cap, together with the lower bearing half.
5. Push the piston and connecting rod out of the bore with a wooden hammer handle (**Figure 81**).
6. Remove the piston rings with a ring remover (**Figure 82**).

Piston Pin Removal/Installation

The pistons are press-fitted to the connecting rods and hand-fitted to the pistons. Removal requires a press and support stand. This is a job for a dealer or machine shop, which is equipped to fit the pistons to the pins, ream the pin bushings to the correct diameter and install the pistons on the connecting rods.

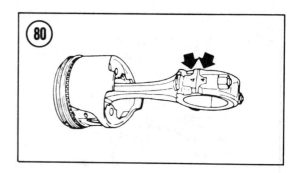

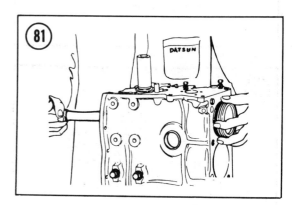

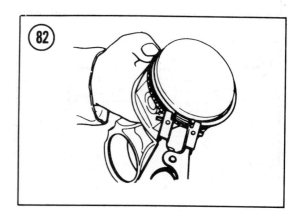

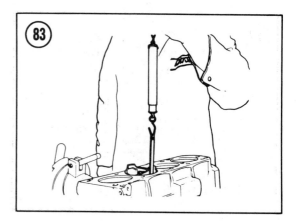

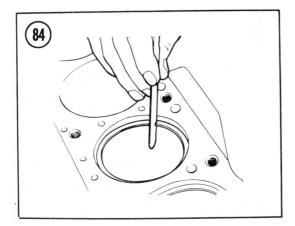

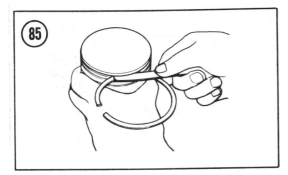

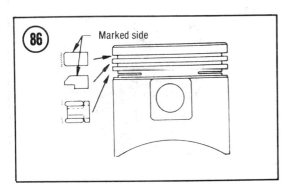

Marked side

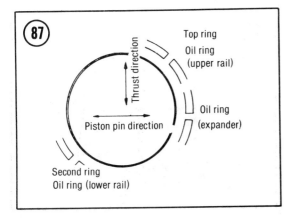

Thrust direction

Top ring
Oil ring
(upper rail)

Oil ring
(expander)

Piston pin direction

Second ring
Oil ring (lower rail)

Piston Clearance Check

This procedure should be done at room temperature. The cylinder walls must be clean and dry.

1. Referring to **Figure 83**, insert the piston without rings upside down in the cylinder bore. Insert a 0.04 mm (0.0016 in.) feeler gauge between piston and cylinder wall and attach a spring scale as shown.

2. Pull on the spring scale. Note the amount of force required to pull the feeler gauge out of the cylinder. This should range from 0.2-1.5 kg (0.4-3.3 lb.). If the required pull is greater than specified, piston clearance is less than it should be. If the pull is less, piston clearance is greater.

3. Repeat the procedure for all 4 cylinders and pistons.

Piston Ring Fit/Installation

1. Check the ring gap of each piston ring. To do this, position the ring at the top or bottom of the ring travel area and square it by tapping gently with an inverted piston.

NOTE
If the cylinders have not been rebored, check the gap at the bottom of the ring travel, where the cylinder is least worn.

2. Measure ring gap with a feeler gauge as shown in **Figure 84**. Compare with specifications at the end of the chapter.

3. Check side clearance of the rings as shown in **Figure 85**. Place the feeler gauge alongside the ring all the way into the groove. Specifications are listed in **Table 1**.

4. Using a ring expander tool, carefully install the oil control ring, then the compression rings. Oil rings consist of 3 segments. The wavy segment goes between the flat segments to act as a spacer. Upper and lower flat segments are interchangeable. The second compression ring is tapered (**Figure 86**). On 1981 models, the second ring is undercut as well as tapered. The top compression ring has a chrome plated friction surface. The top sides of both compression rings are marked and must be up.

5. Position the ring gaps as shown in **Figure 87**.

Connecting Rod Inspection

1. Have connecting rod straightness checked by a dealer or machine shop. Compare with specifications for bend and twist (**Table 1**).

2. Install the connecting rods and bearings on the crankshaft. Insert a feeler gauge between the connecting rod big end and crankshaft and measure the clearance (**Figure 88**). Replace the connecting rod if clearance exceeds specifications (end of chapter).

3. If any connecting rods are replaced, make sure new ones are within 7 grams (0.25 oz.) of the old ones.

Measuring Bearing Clearance

1. Place connecting rods and upper bearing halves on the proper crankpins (connecting rod journals).

2. Cut a piece of Plastigage (**Figure 89**) the width of the bearing. Place the Plastigage on the crankpin, then install the lower bearing half and cap.

> *NOTE*
> *Do not place Plastigage over the crankpin oil hole.*

3. Tighten connecting rod cap to specifications (end of chapter). Do not rotate the crankshaft while the Plastigage is in place.

4. Remove the connecting rod cap. Bearing clearance is determined by comparing the width of the flattened Plastigage to the markings on the envelope (**Figure 90**). If clearance is excessive, the crankshaft must be reground and undersize bearings installed.

Installing Piston/Connecting Rod Assembly

1. Make sure the pistons are correctly installed on the connecting rods. The notch in the piston goes toward the front of the engine. The oil hole in the connecting rod big end goes toward the right-hand side of the engine. See **Figure 91**.

2. Be sure ring gaps are positioned correctly.

3. Immerse the entire piston in clean engine oil. Coat the cylinder wall with oil.

4. Slide a ring compressor over the rings. Compress the rings into the grooves.

5. Install the piston/connecting rod assembly in its cylinder as shown in **Figure 92**. Tap

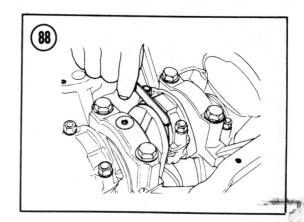

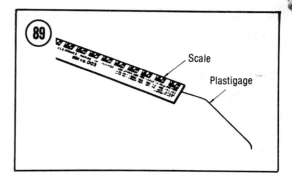

Scale

Plastigage

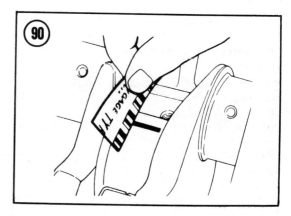

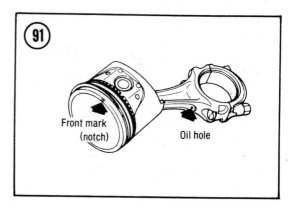

Front mark (notch)

Oil hole

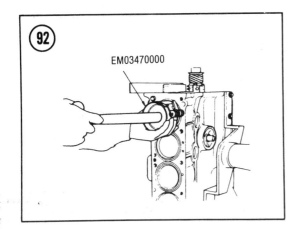

EM03470000

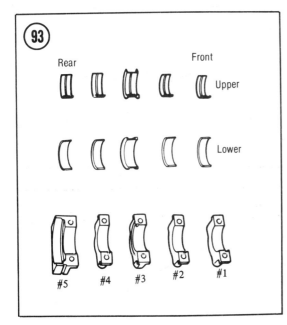

Rear   Front

Upper

Lower

#5   #4   #3   #2   #1

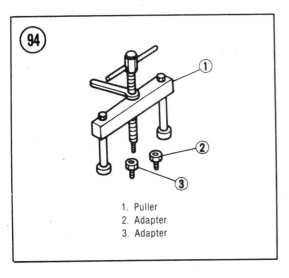

1. Puller
2. Adapter
3. Adapter

lightly with a wooden hammer handle to insert the piston. Be sure the connecting rod number corresponds to the cylinder number (counting from the front of the engine).

CAUTION
Use extreme care not to let the connecting rod nick the crankshaft journal.

6. Clean the connecting rod bearings carefully, including the back sides. Coat the crankpins and bearings with clean engine oil. Place the bearings in the connecting rod and cap.

7. Install the connecting rod cap. Make sure the cylinder numbers on the rod and cap are on the same side. Tighten the cap nuts to specifications (end of chapter).

8. Check connecting rod big end play as described under *Connecting Rod Inspection*, Step 2.

CRANKSHAFT

Removal

1. Unbolt the main bearing caps. Place the caps in order on a clean workbench (**Figure 93**). A puller (Datsun part No. KV101041S0; Kent-Moore No. J25647) may be necessary to remove the center and rear caps. See **Figure 94**. If you do not have such a tool, take the engine to a dealer for cap removal.

2. Remove 2 side oil seals, then take the rear oil seal off the crankshaft (**Figure 95**).

3. Lift the crankshaft out of the engine. Lay the crankshaft, main bearings and bearing caps in order on a clean workbench.

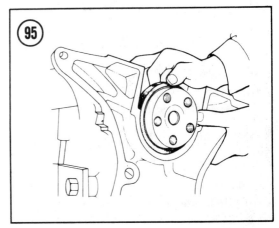

Inspection

1. Clean the crankshaft thoroughly with solvent. Blow out the oil passages with compressed air.

> *NOTE*
> *If you do not have precision measuring equipment, have a machine shop perform Steps 2 and 3.*

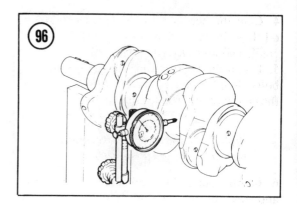

2. Check crankpins and main bearing journals for wear, scoring and cracks. Check all journals against specifications (end of chapter) for out-of-roundness, taper and wear. If necessary, have the crankshaft reground.

3. Check the crankshaft for bending. Mount the crankshaft between accurate centers (such as V-blocks or a lathe) and rotate it one full turn with a dial indicator contacting the center journal. See **Figure 96**. The crankshaft must be reground if bent beyond specifications.

4. Measure crankshaft end play. Install the crankshaft in the block. Pry the crankshaft to front or rear with a hammer handle (**Figure 97**). Insert a feeler gauge between the crankshaft and the center bearing flange. Replace the center bearing if end play exceeds specifications (end of chapter).

Measuring Main Bearing Clearance

Main bearing clearance is measured in the same manner as connecting rod bearing clearance, described earlier in this chapter. Excessive clearance requires that the bearings be replaced, the crankshaft be reground or both.

Installation

1. Thoroughly clean bearings, including the back sides.

2. Install the bearings in the cylinder block and bearing caps. Bearings 1 and 5 (counting from the front of the engine) are interchangeable. Bearings 2 and 4 are interchangeable. Bearing 3 is flanged.

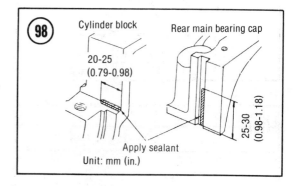

> *NOTE*
> *Upper bearing halves have oil grooves; lower bearing halves do not.*

3. Make sure the bearing locating tangs are correctly positioned in the cylinder block and bearing cap grooves.

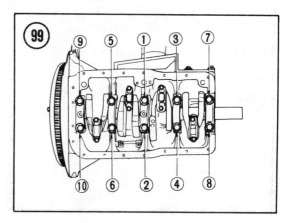

4. Coat the bearings freely with clean engine oil. Lay the crankshaft in the block. Coat the crankshaft journals with engine oil.

5. Install the bearing caps and tighten the cap bolts slightly. Make sure the arrow marks on the caps face the front of the engine.

NOTE
*Apply small amounts of gasket sealer to the rear bearing cap (**Figure 98**).*

6. Gently push the crankshaft toward front and rear of the engine to verify that the bearings and caps are properly aligned and seated.

7. Tighten the cap bolts to specifications (end of chapter). Tighten gradually in 2 or 3 stages, in the order shown in **Figure 99**. Rotate the crankshaft during tightening to make sure it isn't binding. If the crankshaft becomes hard to turn, stop and find out why before continuing. Check for foreign material on bearings and journals. Make absolutely certain that bearings are the correct size, especially if the crankshaft has been reground. Never use undersize bearings if the crankshaft has not been reground.

8. Recheck crankshaft end play (**Figure 97**).

9. Tap the rear side seals into place (**Figure 100**). Install the rear seal with a drift such as Datsun part No. KV10105500 (Kent-Moore No. J25640-01). See **Figure 101**. If the tool is not available, use a piece of pipe the same diameter as the seal.

Pilot Bushing

The pilot bushing, located inside the rear end of the crankshaft, supports the transmission input shaft.

1. Check the bushing for visible wear and damage. If wear or damage can be seen, remove the bushing with a puller such as Datsun tool part No. ST16610001 (Kent-Moore No. J23907). See **Figure 102**.

NOTE
Pilot bushing pullers are usually available from rental dealers. If you can't find one, another method is to fill the bushing with grease, then tap a clutch pilot tool into the bushing hole. The hydraulic force should push the bushing out.

2. Tap a new bushing in to a depth of 4 mm (0.157 in.). See **Figure 103**.

CAUTION
Do not tap hard enough to damage the bushing. Do not drive the bushing in too far.

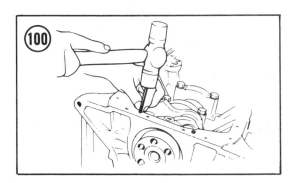

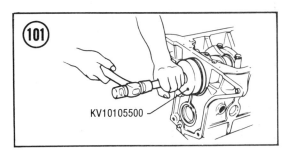

KV10105500

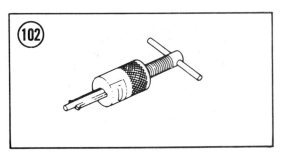

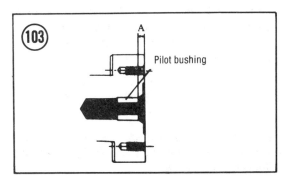

Pilot bushing

CYLINDER BLOCK INSPECTION

1. Remove the crankcase oil separator prior to inspection. See **Figure 104**.

2. Clean the block thoroughly with solvent and check all freeze plugs for leaks. Replace any freeze plugs that are suspect. It is a good idea to replace all of them. While cleaning, check oil and water passages for sludge, dirt and corrosion. If the passages are very dirty, the block should be boiled out by a machine shop.

> *NOTE*
> *Block boiling necessitates replacement of all freeze plugs. However, a block dirty enough to need boiling almost certainly needs these parts replaced anyway.*

3. Examine the block for cracks.

4. Check flatness of the cylinder block's top surface. Use an accurate straightedge as shown in **Figure 105**. Have the block resurfaced if it is warped more than 0.1 mm (0.004 in.).

> *NOTE*
> *Total material removed from block and cylinder head must not be more than 0.2 mm (0.008 in.).*

5. Measure the cylinder bores for out-of-roundness or excessive wear with a bore gauge (**Figure 106**). Measure the bores at top, center, and bottom, in front-to-rear and side-to-side directions. Compare measurements to specifications at the end of the chapter. If the cylinders exceed maximum tolerances, they must be rebored. Reboring is also necessary if the cylinder walls are badly scuffed or scored.

> *NOTE*
> *Before boring, install all main bearing caps and tighten to specifications. Bore in the following order: 2-4-1-3.*

FLYWHEEL

Removal/Installation

1. Remove the engine. Separate the engine and transmission.

2. Remove the clutch from the flywheel. See *Clutch Removal*, Chapter Eight.

3. Unbolt the flywheel from the crankshaft (**Figure 107**).

4. Installation is the reverse of removal. Tighten flywheel bolts to specifications (end of chapter). Tighten gradually in a diagonal pattern.

Inspection

1. Check the flywheel for scoring and wear. If the surface is glazed or slightly scratched, have it resurfaced by a machine shop. Replace the flywheel if damage is severe.

2. Measure flywheel runout with a dial indicator (**Figure 108**). Replace or resurface the flywheel if runout is excessive.

3. Inspect the flywheel ring gear teeth. If the teeth are chipped, broken or excessively worn, have a new ring gear shrunk onto the flywheel by a machine shop.

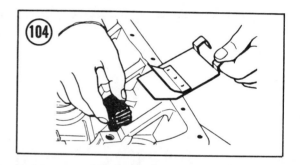

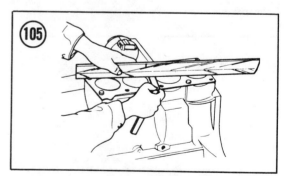

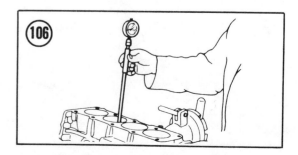

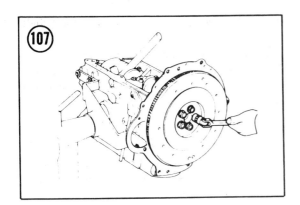

Tables are on the following pages.

Table 1   ENGINE SPECIFICATIONS

Cylinder head	
Maximum surface warp	0.1 mm (0.004 in.)
Valve face angle	45°

Valves	
Head diameter	
Intake	42.0-42.2 mm (1.654-1.661 in.)
Exhaust, 1980	35.0-35.2 mm (1.378-1.386 in.)
Exhaust, 1981	38.0-38.2 mm (1.496-1.504 in.)
Stem diameter	
Intake	7.965-7.980 mm (0.3136-0.3142 in.)
Exhaust	7.945-7.960 mm (0.3128-0.3134 in.)
Valve length, 1980	
Intake	114.9-115.2 mm (4.524-4.535 in.)
Exhaust	115.7-116.0 mm (4.555-4.567 in.)
Valve length, 1981	
Intake	122.8-123.1 mm (4.835-4.846 in.)
Exhaust	123.6-123.9 mm (4.866-4.878 in.)
Valve face angle	45° 30'
Head edge thickness, standard	
Intake	1.3 mm (0.051 in.)
Exhaust	1.5 mm (0.059 in.)
Head edge thickness, minimum	0.5 mm (0.020 in.)

Valve springs, 1980	
Free length	
Inner	44.85 mm (1.7657 in.)
Outer	49.98 mm (1.9677 in.)
Loaded length, standard	
Inner	35 mm @ 12.3 kg (1.378 in. @ 27.1 lb.)
Outer	40 mm @ 21.3 kg (1.575 in. @ 47 lb.)
Loaded length, minimum	
Inner	35 mm @ 10 kg (1.3783 in. @ 22.1 lb.)
Outer	40 mm @ 17.8 kg (1.575 in. @ 39.2 lb).
Bend, maximum	
Inner	1.9 mm (0.075 in.)
Outer	2.2 mm (0.087 in.)

(continued)

Table 1 ENGINE SPECIFICATIONS (continued)

Valve springs, 1981	
Free length	
Inner	44.1 mm (1.7362 in.)
Outer	49.77 mm (1.9594 in.)
Loaded length, standard	
Inner	35 mm @ 11 kg (1.3783 in. @ 24.3 lb.)
Outer	40 mm @ 23 kg (1.575 in. @ 50.7 lb.)
Loaded length, minimum	
Inner	35 mm @ 9.8 kg (1.3783 in. @ 19.6 lb.)
Outer	40 mm @ 19.3 kg (1.575 in. @ 42.6 lb).
Bend, maximum	
Inner	1.9 mm (0.075 in.)
Outer	2.2 mm (0.08i in.)

Valve Guides	
Valve stem-to-guide clearance, standard	
Intake	0.020-0.053 mm (0.0008-0.0021 in.)
Exhaust	0.040-0.073 mm (0.0016-0.0029 in.)
Valve stem-to-guide clearance, maximum	0.1 mm (0.004 in.)
Guide inner diameter	8.000-8.018 mm (0.3150-0.3157 in.)
Guide hole diameter	
Standard	11.985-11.996 mm (0.4718-0.4723 in.)
Oversize	12.185-12.196 mm (0.4797-0.4802 in.)

Rocker arms (1981 only)	
Rocker arm to shaft clearance	0.007-0.049 mm (0.0003-0.00019 in.)

Camshaft	
End play, maximum	0.2 mm (0.008 in.)
Lobe height	38.477-38.527 mm (1.5148-1.5168 in.)
Lobe wear, maximum	0.25 mm (0.0098 in.)
Journal diameter	32.935-32.955 mm (1.2967-1.2974 in.)
Bend, maximum (total indicator reading)	
1980	0.05 mm (0.002 in.)
1981	0.2 mm (0.008 in.)
Bearing inner diameter	
1980	48.000-48.016 mm (1.88981.8904 in.)
1981	33.000-33.025 mm (1.2992-1.3002 in.)
Journal-to-bearing clearance, 1980	
Standard	0.038-0.067 mm (0.0015-0.002 in.)
Maximum	0.1 mm (0.004 in.)
Journal-to-bearing clearance, 1981	
Standard	0.045-0.090 mm (0.0018-0.0028 in.)
Maximum	0.1 mm (0.004 in.)

(continued)

Table 1   ENGINE SPECIFICATIONS (continued)

Oil pump	
Outer rotor to body clearance	
Standard	0.15-0.21 mm (80.006-0.008 in.)
Maximum	0.5 mm (0.020 in.)
Rotor tip clearance	
Standard	0.12 mm (0.005 in.) or less
Maximum	0.2 mm (0.008 in.)
Rotor to straightedge clearance	0.06 mm (0.002 in.) or less
Pump body to straightedge clearance	0.03 mm (0.001 in.) or less
Connecting rods	
Big end play	
Standard	0.2-0.3 mm (0.008-0.012 mm)
Maximum	0.6 mm (0.024 in.)
Bearing clearance	
Standard	0.025-0.055 mm (0.0010-0.0022 in.)
Maximum	0.12 mm (0.005 in.)
Bend or twist per 100 mm (3.94 in.) of connecting rod length	
Standard	0.03 mm (0.0012 in.)
Maximum	0.05 mm (0.002 in.)
Pistons	
Ring gap, standard	
Top ring	0.25-0.40 mm (0.010-0.016 in.)
Second ring	0.15-0.30 mm (0.006-0.012 in.)
Oil ring	0.30-0.90 mm (0.012-0.036 in.)
Maximum gap, all rings	1 mm (0.039 in.)
Side clearance, standard	
Top ring	0.040-0.073 mm (0.0016-0.0029 in.)
Second ring	0.030-0.063 mm (0.0012-0.0025 in.)
Oil ring	None
Side clearance, maximum	
Top and second rings	0.1 mm (0.004 in.)
Oil ring	None
Piston diameter	
Standard	84.985-85.035 mm (3.3459-3.3478 in.)
0.5 mm (0.020 in.) oversize	84.465-85.515 mm (3.3648-3.3667 in.)
1.0 mm (0.039 in. oversize	95.965-86.015 mm (3.3844-3.3864 in.)
Crankshaft	
Main bearing clearance	
Standard	0.020-0.062 mm (0.0008-0.0024 in.)
Maximum	0.12 mm (0.005 in.)
Journal diameter	54.942-54.955 mm (2.1631-2.1636 in.)
Crankpin diameter	49.961-49.974 mm (1.9670-1.9675 in.)
Journal and crankpin out-of-round and taper	
Standard	Less than 0.01 mm (0.0004 in.)
Maximum	0.03 mm (0.0012 in.)
Crankshaft bend (total indicator reading)	
1980 standard	Less than 0.05 mm (0.002 in.)
1980 maximum	0.1 mm (0.004 in.)
1981 standard	Less than 0.025 mm (0.001 in.)
1981 maximum	0.05 mm (0.002 in.)
Crankshaft end play	
Standard	0.05-0.18 mm (0.002-0.007 in.)
Maximum	0.3 mm (0.012 in.)

Table 2   TIGHTENING TORQUES

Fastener	N•m	Ft.-lb.
A/C compressor bracket	44-54	33-40
Alternator bracket	35-59	29-43
Alternator to adjusting bar	20-29	14-22
Camshaft sprocket bolt	118-157	87-116
Chain guides	5.9-9.8	4.5-7
Chain tensioner	5.9-9.8	4.5-7
Connecting rod caps	44-54	33-40
Crankshaft pulley bolt	118-157	87-116
Cylinder head to block		
1980	69-83	51-61
1981	69-78	51-58
Cylinder head to front cover	3.9-7.8	3-6
Exhaust manifold		
1980	12-16	9-12
1981	16-21	12-15
Flywheel to crankshaft	137-157	101-116
Front cover bolts		
M8 (large)	10-16	7-12
M6 (small)	3.9-9.8	3-7
Intake manifold		
1980	12-16	9-12
1981	16-21	12-15
Main bearing caps	44-54	33-40
Motor mounts		
Brackets to engine	25-35	19-26
Brackets to insulator, 1980	25-35	19-26
Brackets to insulator, 1981	26-36	20-27
Left insulator to body	45-60	33-44
Right insulator to body	14-18	10-13
Insulator to transmission, 1980	31-36	23-27
Insulator to transmission, 1981	42-49	31-36
Transmission member to insulator, 1980	16-22	12-16
Transmission member to insulator, 1981	31-35	23-26
Transmission member to body	31-42	23-31
Oil pan		
1980	5.9-9.8	4.5-7
1981	5-7	3.5-5
Oil pan drain plug	20-29	14-22
Oil pump	11-15	8-11
Oil strainer	10-16	7-12
Rocker arm locknuts (1981 only)	16-22	12-16
Rocker cover		
1980	10-16	7-12
1981	8-10	6-7
Rocker pivot locknuts (1981 only)	49-59	36-43
Rocker shaft brackets (1981 only)	15-25	11-18
Spark plugs	15-20	11-14
Water inlet and outlet	10-16	7-12
Water pump		
M8 (large)	10-16	7-12
M6 (small)	3.9-9.8	3-7

(continued)

Table 2   TIGHTENING TORQUES (continued)

Fastener	N•m	Ft.-lb.
Shock absorber upper nut	30-40	22-30
Shock absorber lower nut	16-22	12-16
Spring U-bolt nuts	88-98	65-72
Spring front pin nut	50-68	37-50
Spring shackle	50-68	37-50
Backing plate bolts	53-63	39-46
Wheel bearing locknut	147-196	108-145
Differential mounting nuts	17-25	12-18
Differential drain and filler plugs	59-98	43-72
Rebound bumpers	16-22	12-16
Drive shaft to differential	24-32	17-24

FUEL, EXHAUST, AND EMISSION
CONTROL SYSTEMS

5

This chapter includes service procedures for the air cleaner, carburetor, fuel pumps, exhaust system, fuel tank, throttle linkage and emission controls. **Tables 1-2** are at the end of the chapter.

AIR CLEANER

The air cleaner uses a viscous paper element, which should be replaced at intervals specified in Chapter Three. The air cleaner also incorporates several emission control devices. Refer to the following illustrations:

a. **Figure 1**—1980 California models
b. **Figure 2**—1980 49-state models
c. **Figure 3**—all 1981 trucks

Automatic Temperature Control System

This system regulates the temperature of air entering the engine. When the engine is cold, the vacuum motor closes the air control valve. Hot air is then drawn from around the exhaust manifold. As the engine warms up, the valve opens and the air cleaner draws air through the fresh air duct. Inspect as follows.

1. Make sure vacuum hoses are properly connected and in good condition. See **Figure 1**, **Figure 2** or **Figure 3**.

2. With the engine cold, disconnect the fresh air duct from the air cleaner.

3. Look down the air cleaner inlet with a mirror (**Figure 4**). The valve should be blocking the hot air duct. When the engine is started, the valve should move to block the fresh air duct.

4. Warm the engine to normal operating temperature. The valve should move to block the hot air duct. In very cold weather, the valve may take a long time to do this.

5. If the valve doesn't work properly, disconnect the hose from the vacuum motor. See **Figure 5**. Start the engine. There should be vacuum at the end of the hose. If not, check for damaged or disconnected hoses. Replace or connect as needed.

6. If the hoses are good, connect a length of hose to the vacuum motor and suck on it. The valve should move to block the fresh air intake. If it doesn't, check the vacuum motor linkage for binding. If the linkage isn't binding, replace the vacuum motor.

7. If the flap valve does move to close the fresh air intake and the hoses are good, replace the temperature sensor.

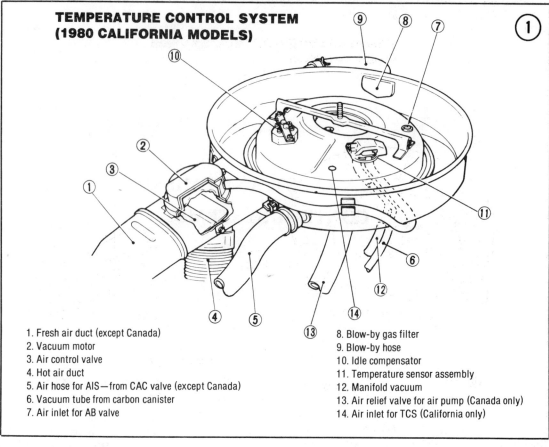

TEMPERATURE CONTROL SYSTEM (1980 CALIFORNIA MODELS)

1. Fresh air duct (except Canada)
2. Vacuum motor
3. Air control valve
4. Hot air duct
5. Air hose for AIS—from CAC valve (except Canada)
6. Vacuum tube from carbon canister
7. Air inlet for AB valve
8. Blow-by gas filter
9. Blow-by hose
10. Idle compensator
11. Temperature sensor assembly
12. Manifold vacuum
13. Air relief valve for air pump (Canada only)
14. Air inlet for TCS (California only)

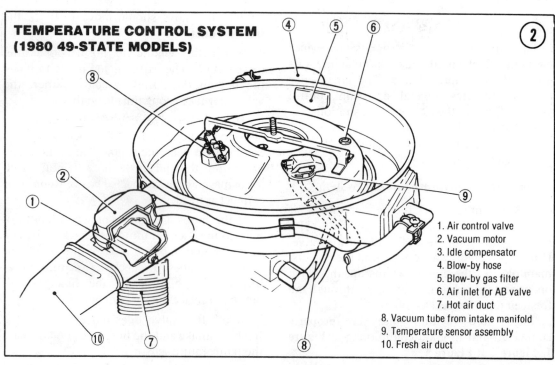

TEMPERATURE CONTROL SYSTEM (1980 49-STATE MODELS)

1. Air control valve
2. Vacuum motor
3. Idle compensator
4. Blow-by hose
5. Blow-by gas filter
6. Air inlet for AB valve
7. Hot air duct
8. Vacuum tube from intake manifold
9. Temperature sensor assembly
10. Fresh air duct

③

TEMPERATURE CONTROL SYSTEM
(1981 TRUCKS)

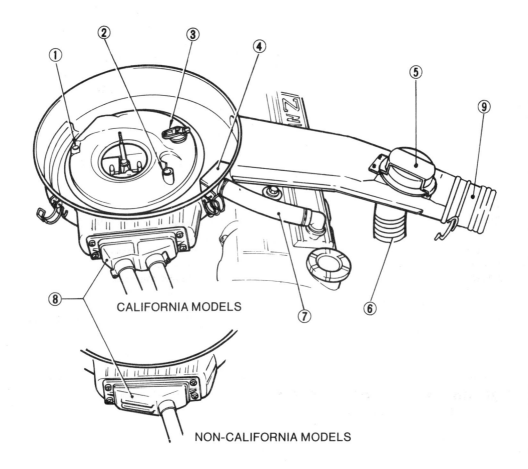

CALIFORNIA MODELS

NON-CALIFORNIA MODELS

5

1. Air hole for TCS and EGR system
2. Air inlet for AB valve
3. Temperature sensor
4. Blow-by gas filter
5. Vacuum motor
6. Hot air duct
7. Blow-by hose
8. Air induction valve case
9. Fresh air duct

Idle Compensator (1980 Only)

The idle compensator (**Figure 1** or **Figure 2**) is a double thermostatic valve operated by underhood temperature. It prevents overrich fuel mixture during hot idle conditions by admitting extra air to the intake manifold. One valve opens at 60-70° C (140-158° F); the other opens at 70-90° C (158-194° F). Test as follows.

1. Remove the air cleaner cover.
2. Remove 2 idle compensator securing screws. Detach the air hose and take the idle compensator out.
3. Connect a tube to the bottom of the idle compensator. Block one side of the idle compensator with a finger (**Figure 6**) and suck on the tube. It should be extremely difficult or impossible to suck air through the tube at temperatures below 60° C (140° F).
4. Place the idle compensator in water with a thermometer (**Figure 7**). Heat the water and watch the valves. The valve marked "9" should open between 60 and 70° C (140-158° F). The valve marked "10" should open between 70 and 90° C (158-194° F). Replace

the idle compensator if a valve fails to open or opens at the wrong temperature.

Air Cleaner Removal/Installation

Refer to **Figure 1**, **Figure 2** or **Figure 3** for this procedure.
1. Unbolt the air cleaner from its bracket.
2. On 1981 models, detach the air induction valve case from the side of the air cleaner.
3. Loosen the air cleaner base bolt.
4. Remove the air cleaner cover nut.
5. Disconnect the fresh air duct, hot air duct and hoses.
6. Lift the air cleaner off.
7. Installation is the reverse of removal.

CARBURETOR

All models use a 2-barrel downdraft carburetor. The carburetor includes an anti-dieseling solenoid and electrically heated automatic choke. The anti-dieseling solenoid blocks the carburetor slow circuit when the engine is turned off. This prevents the engine from running with the ignition off. The choke heater causes the choke to open quickly and at a precise rate.

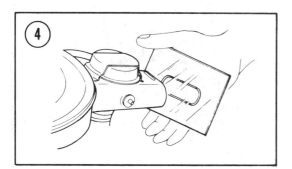

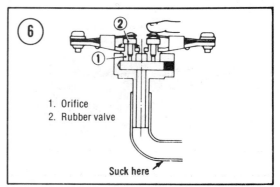

1. Orifice
2. Rubber valve

Suck here

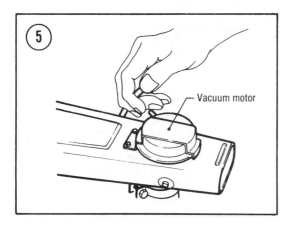

Vacuum motor

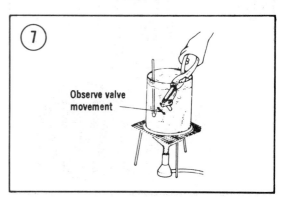

Observe valve movement

Automatic Choke Inspection

1. Remove the air cleaner as described in this chapter.

2. Move the choke plate by hand and check for binding. If the plate does not move smoothly, clean or repair the linkage as needed.

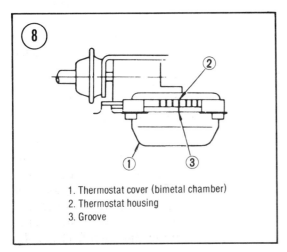

1. Thermostat cover (bimetal chamber)
2. Thermostat housing
3. Groove

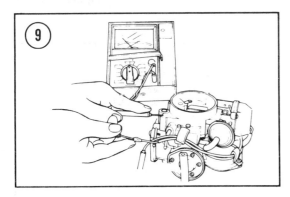

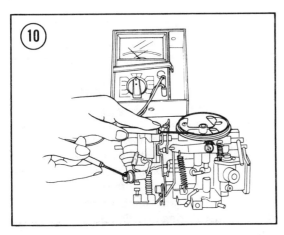

3. On 1980 models, make sure the choke cover groove aligns with the center mark on the thermostat housing. See **Figure 8**.

4. Connect an ohmmeter between the choke heater terminal and carburetor body. See **Figure 9** (1980) or **Figure 10** (1981). Resistance should be 3.7-8.9 ohms. If not, replace the choke cover (1980) or choke chamber assembly (1981).

CAUTION
During the next steps, connect the ohmmeter only between the terminals indicated.

5. Disconnect the function test connector (**Figure 11**). With the engine off, connect an ohmmeter between terminals A and B. The ohmmeter should indicate continuity (little or no resistance). If not, check the wiring for breaks or bad connections. Refer to the wiring diagrams at the end of this manual.

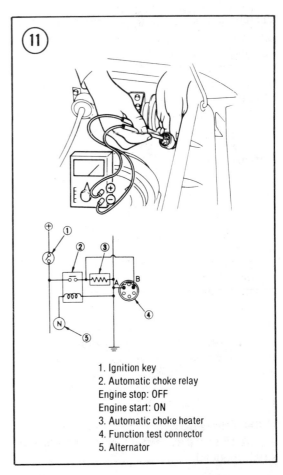

1. Ignition key
2. Automatic choke relay
Engine stop: OFF
Engine start: ON
3. Automatic choke heater
4. Function test connector
5. Alternator

6. Start the engine and let it idle. Connect a voltmeter between terminals A and B (**Figure 11**). It should indicate approximately 12 volts. If it indicates zero, check the wiring for breaks or bad connections. Refer to the wiring diagrams at the end of this manual. If the wiring is good, test the choke relay as described in this chapter.

Choke Relay Test

1. Remove the relay from the relay bracket near the hood release handle. See **Figure 12**.
2. Connect an ohmmeter between terminals 4 and 5 (**Figure 13**). The ohmmeter should indicate little or no resistance. If not, replace the relay.
3. Connect the ohmmeter between terminals 1 and 2. Again, there should be little or no resistance. If not, replace the relay.
4. Connect the ohmmeter between terminals 1 and 3. The ohmmeter should indicate no continuity (infinite resistance). If not, replace the relay.
5. Connect a 12-volt battery between terminals 4 and 5 with 2 lengths of wire. An ohmmeter connected between terminals 1 and 3 should show little or no resistance; an ohmmeter connected between terminals 1 and 2 should show infinite resistance. If not, replace the relay.

Carburetor Removal/Installation

1. Remove the air cleaner as described in this chapter.
2. Label and disconnect the fuel and vacuum lines. Plug the fuel lines so they won't leak gasoline.
3. Disconnect the wires for choke heater and anti-dieseling solenoid.
4. Disconnect the throttle linkage.
5. Remove the carburetor mounting nuts. Lift the carburetor off the intake manifold.
6. Installation is the reverse of removal. Use a new gasket. Tighten the mounting nuts to 12-18 N•m (9-13 ft.-lb.).

Carburetor Disassembly

Refer to **Figure 14** (1980 U.S. models), **Figure 15** (1980 Canadian trucks) or **Figure 16** (1981 models).

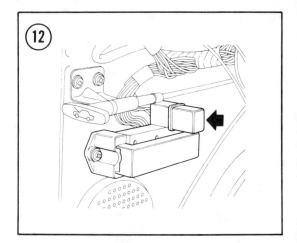

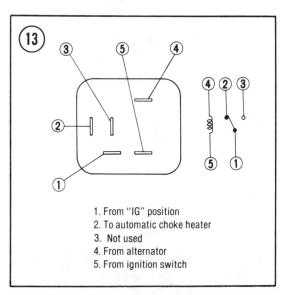

1. From "IG" position
2. To automatic choke heater
3. Not used
4. From alternator
5. From ignition switch

1. When removing jets, note their locations and the number stamped in each jet.
2. Make sure wrenches and screwdrivers fit exactly.
3. Lay all parts in order to ease reassembly.
4. On 1980 models, do not remove parts marked with an asterisk in **Figure 14** or **Figure 15**.
5. Do not remove linkage parts from the throttle shafts unless they are bent or otherwise damaged. Be sure replacement parts are available before removing.
6. On 1980 models, remove the limiter cap from the idle mixture screw. Count the number of turns required to remove the screw to the nearest 1/8 turn and write this number down for use during installation.

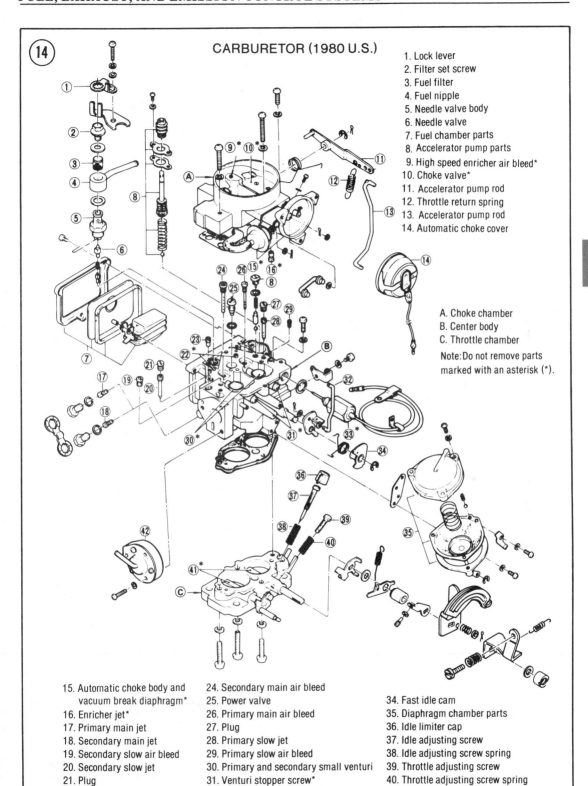

CARBURETOR (1980 U.S.)

1. Lock lever
2. Filter set screw
3. Fuel filter
4. Fuel nipple
5. Needle valve body
6. Needle valve
7. Fuel chamber parts
8. Accelerator pump parts
9. High speed enricher air bleed*
10. Choke valve*
11. Accelerator pump rod
12. Throttle return spring
13. Accelerator pump rod
14. Automatic choke cover

A. Choke chamber
B. Center body
C. Throttle chamber
Note: Do not remove parts marked with an asterisk (*).

5

15. Automatic choke body and vacuum break diaphragm*
16. Enricher jet*
17. Primary main jet
18. Secondary main jet
19. Secondary slow air bleed
20. Secondary slow jet
21. Plug
22. Air bleed*
23. Coasting jet
24. Secondary main air bleed
25. Power valve
26. Primary main air bleed
27. Plug
28. Primary slow jet
29. Primary slow air bleed
30. Primary and secondary small venturi
31. Venturi stopper screw*
32. Choke connecting rod
33. Anti-dieseling solenoid valve
34. Fast idle cam
35. Diaphragm chamber parts
36. Idle limiter cap
37. Idle adjusting screw
38. Idle adjusting screw spring
39. Throttle adjusting screw
40. Throttle adjusting screw spring
41. Primary and secondary throttle valves*
42. By-pass air control unit

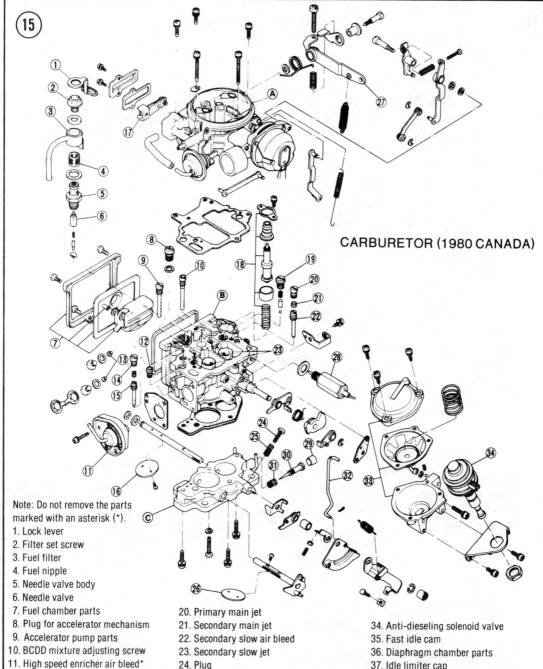

CARBURETOR (1980 CANADA)

Note: Do not remove the parts marked with an asterisk (*).

1. Lock lever
2. Filter set screw
3. Fuel filter
4. Fuel nipple
5. Needle valve body
6. Needle valve
7. Fuel chamber parts
8. Plug for accelerator mechanism
9. Accelerator pump parts
10. BCDD mixture adjusting screw
11. High speed enricher air bleed*
12. Choke valve*
13. Accelerator pump lever
14. Throttle return spring
15. Accelerator pump rod
16. Automatic choke cover
17. Automatic choke body and
    vacuum break diaphragm
18. Enricher jet*
19. Coasting air bleed I*

20. Primary main jet
21. Secondary main jet
22. Secondary slow air bleed
23. Secondary slow jet
24. Plug
25. Coasting jet
26. Secondary main air bleed
27. Power valve
28. Primary main air bleed
29. Plug
30. Primary slow air jet
31. Primary slow air bleed
32. Primary and secondary small venturi
33. Choke connecting rod

34. Anti-dieseling solenoid valve
35. Fast idle cam
36. Diaphragm chamber parts
37. Idle limiter cap
38. Idle adjusting screw
39. Idle adjusting screw spring
40. Throttle adjusting screw
41. Throttle adjusting screw spring
42. Primary and secondary throttle valve
43. BCDD (for Canada)
 A. Choke chamber
 B. Center body
 C. Throttle chamber

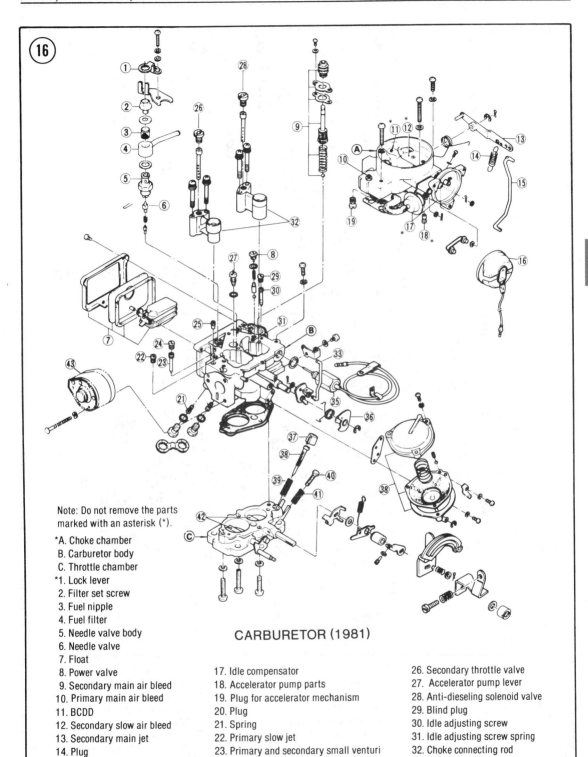

CARBURETOR (1981)

Note: Do not remove the parts marked with an asterisk (*).

*A. Choke chamber
B. Carburetor body
C. Throttle chamber
*1. Lock lever
2. Filter set screw
3. Fuel nipple
4. Fuel filter
5. Needle valve body
6. Needle valve
7. Float
8. Power valve
9. Secondary main air bleed
10. Primary main air bleed
11. BCDD
12. Secondary slow air bleed
13. Secondary main jet
14. Plug
15. Secondary slow jet
16. Primary throttle valve

17. Idle compensator
18. Accelerator pump parts
19. Plug for accelerator mechanism
20. Plug
21. Spring
22. Primary slow jet
23. Primary and secondary small venturi
24. Throttle adjusting screw
25. Throttle adjusting screw spring

26. Secondary throttle valve
27. Accelerator pump lever
28. Anti-dieseling solenoid valve
29. Blind plug
30. Idle adjusting screw
31. Idle adjusting screw spring
32. Choke connecting rod
33. Diaphragm chamber parts
34. Dashpot

7. On 1981 models, drill out the idle mixture screw seal (**Figure 17**). Pry the seal out, then remove the screw. Write down the number of turns required to remove the screw (to the nearest 1/8 turn).

Carburetor Inspection

1. Thoroughly clean all metal parts (except BCDD and solenoid) in solvent or carburetor cleaner. The secondary throttle diaphragm should be replaced if it is included in the repair kit. If not, clean it with a lint-free cloth.

> *CAUTION*
> *Do not insert objects such as drill bits or pieces of wire into jets and passages while cleaning them. These openings are carefully calibrated and scratching them may seriously affect carburetor performance.*

2. If jets and passages are difficult to clean, blow them out with compressed air. If a compressor is not available, use a spray carburetor cleaner. These usually come with plastic tubes which fit into the can's nozzle, making it easy to spray the cleaner into jets and passages.

3. Check the needle valve and seat for wear. Replace as needed. If a new needle valve and seat are included in the repair kit, install them no matter what the old parts look like.

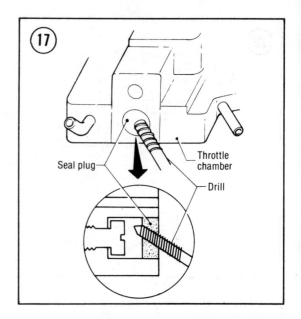

Seal plug · Throttle chamber · Drill

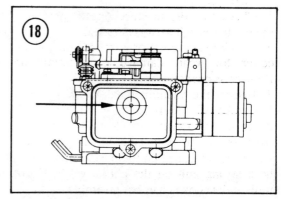

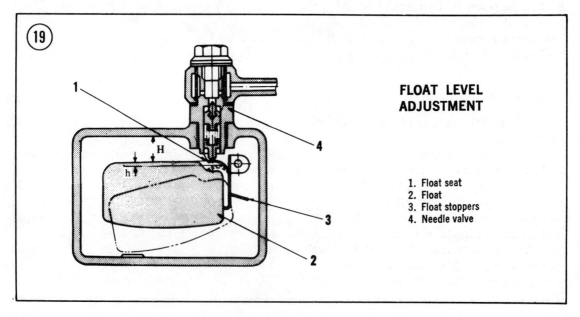

FLOAT LEVEL ADJUSTMENT

1. Float seat
2. Float
3. Float stoppers
4. Needle valve

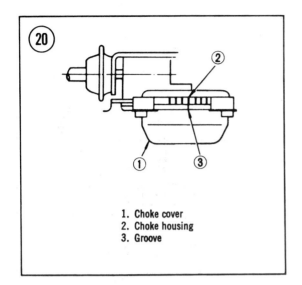

1. Choke cover
2. Choke housing
3. Groove

4. Check all castings for cracks. Replace cracked castings.
5. Check the idle mixture screw for wear at the tip. Replace if wear is detected.
6. Check the accelerator pump piston seal and cover for wear, damage or deterioration. Replace as needed.
7. Inspect the vacuum break diaphragm (15, **Figure 14**; 17, **Figure 15**; or 44, **Figure 16**). To do this, disconnect the vacuum break hose from the carburetor body. Hold the choke valve shut and suck on the hose. There should be a strong pull on the choke valve. If not, replace the choke chamber assembly.
8. Test the solenoid. Connect a 12-volt battery between the solenoid body and solenoid wire. The solenoid should click each time current is applied. If not, replace it.

Carburetor Assembly

Assembly is the reverse of disassembly, plus the following.
1. Use new gaskets and seals.
2. When assembling the center body and throttle chamber, note that the center bottom screw has a hole in it for the power valve. Be sure this screw goes in the center hole.
3. Be sure the main jets and air bleeds are installed in the correct holes. Refer to the numbers written down during disassembly. If you didn't write the numbers down, refer to **Table 1**.

4. Screw in the idle mixture screw the same number of turns required for removal.
5. After assembly, adjust float level, fast idle and choke cover (1980 only) as described in this chapter. If you have a CO meter, check idle mixture. If not, have this done by a dealer.

Float Level Adjustment

This adjustment can be made with the carburetor on or off the engine.
1. If the carburetor is on the engine, check fuel level at idle speed. It should be approximately halfway up the sight glass (**Figure 18**). If not, adjust float level.

WARNING
Let the engine cool before the next step. It may be impossible to avoid spilling gasoline. Place a fire extinguisher nearby.

2. If the carburetor is on the engine, place a container beneath it to catch dripping fuel, then remove the float chamber cover.
3. Raise the float all the way. Measure the gap between float and float chamber (dimension "H," **Figure 19**). It should be 7.2 mm (0.238 in.). If not, slide the float off its pivot and bend the float seat to change dimension "H".
4. Let the float hang down. Raise the needle valve with a knife blade or similar tool. Measure the gap between needle valve and float seat (dimension "h," **Figure 19**) with a gauge rod or drill bit. It should be 1.3-1.7 mm (0.051-0.067 in.).
Adjust if necessary by bending the float stopper.
5. Reinstall the float chamber cover.

Choke Cover Adjustment (1980 Only)

1. Have an assistant floor the throttle pedal. The choke valve should close. It should open without binding when pushed with a finger. If not, check the choke linkage for worn, damaged, disconnected or missing parts. Replace or reconnect as needed.
2. Align the groove on the choke cover with the center mark on the choke housing. See **Figure 20**. Then tighten the choke cover screws.

5

Fast Idle Adjustment (1980)

Fast idle is the speed at which the engine idles when it is cold and the choke is operating. As the engine warms, idle speed gradually returns to normal.

The adjustment is made with the carburetor on the engine.

1. Warm the engine to normal operating temperature. Connect a tune-up tachometer to the engine.
2. Place the fast idle screw on the first step of the fast idle cam. See **Figure 21** and **Figure 22**.
3. Check fast idle speed. It should be 1,900-2,800 rpm. To adjust, loosen the nut (2, **Figure 22**) and turn the fast idle screw (3). When clearance is correct, tighten the nut.

Fast Idle Adjustment (1981)

Fast idle is the speed at which the engine operates when it is cold and the choke is operating. As the engine warms, idle speed gradually returns to normal.

The adjustment is made with the carburetor off the engine.

1. Place the fast idle screw on the first step of the fast idle cam. See **Figure 21** and **Figure 22**.
2. Measure clearance between primary throttle plate and bore (A, **Figure 23**) with a gauge rod or drill bit. It should be 0.81-0.95 mm (0.032-0.037 in.). If incorrect, loosen the nut (2, **Figure 22**) and turn the fast idle screw (3). When speed is correct, tighten the nut.

FUEL PUMP

1980 models use a mechanical fuel pump, mounted on the front of the engine and driven by an eccentric lobe on the camshaft. 1981 models use an electric fuel pump mounted next to the fuel tank. Fuel pump testing is covered in Chapter Two, under *Fuel System Troubleshooting*. Refer to **Table 2** for performance specifications.

Removal/Installation (Mechanical Pump)

1. Disconnect the fuel inlet and outlet lines from the pump. Plug the lines to stop fuel leakage.
2. Remove the fuel pump nuts and take the pump off. See **Figure 24**.

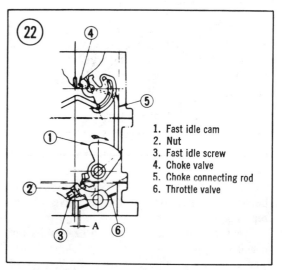

1. Fast idle cam
2. Nut
3. Fast idle screw
4. Choke valve
5. Choke connecting rod
6. Throttle valve

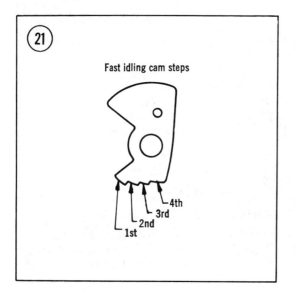

Fast idling cam steps

4th
3rd
2nd
1st

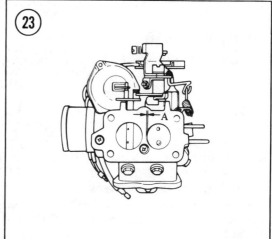

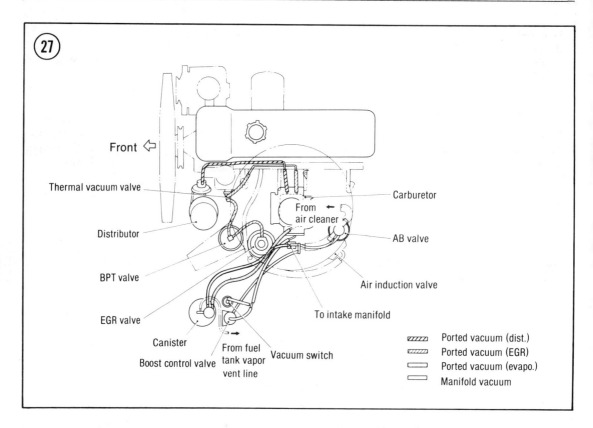

(27)

Front ⇐

Thermal vacuum valve

Distributor

BPT valve

EGR valve

Canister

Boost control valve

From fuel tank vapor vent line

Vacuum switch

From air cleaner

Carburetor

AB valve

Air induction valve

To intake manifold

	Ported vacuum (dist.)
	Ported vacuum (EGR)
	Ported vacuum (evapo.)
	Manifold vacuum

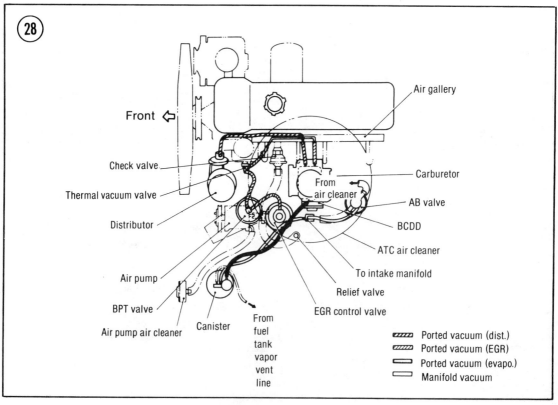

(28)

Front ⇐

Check valve

Thermal vacuum valve

Distributor

Air pump

BPT valve

Air pump air cleaner

Canister

From fuel tank vapor vent line

Air gallery

From air cleaner

Carburetor

AB valve

BCDD

ATC air cleaner

To intake manifold

Relief valve

EGR control valve

	Ported vacuum (dist.)
	Ported vacuum (EGR)
	Ported vacuum (evapo.)
	Manifold vacuum

c. **Figure 27** — 1980 49-state models
d. **Figure 28** — 1980 Canadian models
e. **Figure 29** — 1981 California models
f. **Figure 30** — 1981 non-California models

POSITIVE CRANKCASE VENTILATION

The PCV system, used on all models, routes crankcase fumes into the combustion chambers for burning. The system doesn't require periodic service, except on 1980 Canadian models.

System Inspection

Refer to **Figure 31** (1980) or **Figure 32** (1981).

1. Remove the air cleaner cover. Take out the PCV filter and install a new one.
2. Remove the PCV valve. Hold it next to your ear and shake it. If the valve rattles, it is okay. If not, replace it. On 1980 Canadian models, replace the valve every 30,000 miles or 2 years, whether it seems good or not.
3. Check the PCV hoses for clogging, cracks or deterioration. Clean or replace as needed.

5

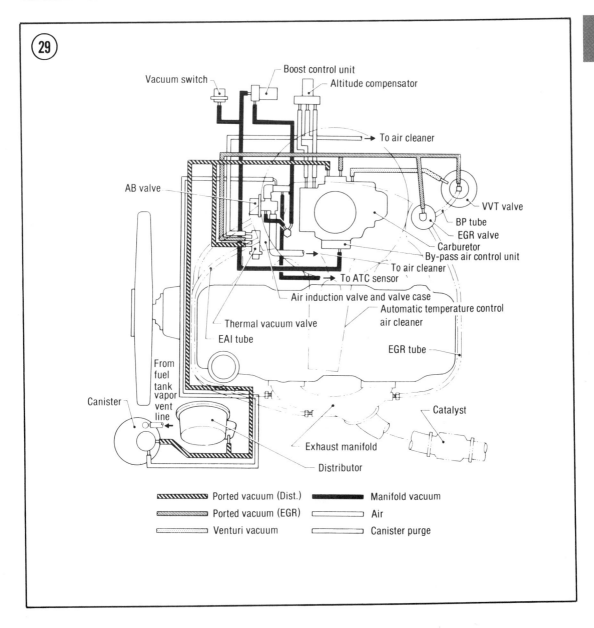

(29)

Vacuum switch
Boost control unit
Altitude compensator
To air cleaner
AB valve
VVT valve
BP tube
EGR valve
Carburetor
By-pass air control unit
To air cleaner
To ATC sensor
Air induction valve and valve case
Automatic temperature control air cleaner
Thermal vacuum valve
EAI tube
EGR tube
From fuel tank vapor vent line
Canister
Catalyst
Exhaust manifold
Distributor

Ported vacuum (Dist.)		Manifold vacuum	
Ported vacuum (EGR)		Air	
Venturi vacuum		Canister purge	

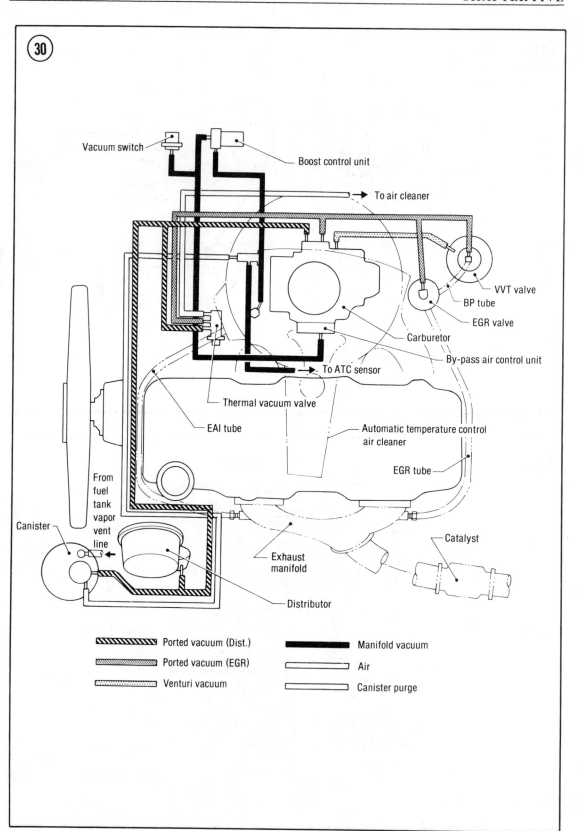

30

Vacuum switch

Boost control unit

To air cleaner

VVT valve

BP tube

EGR valve

Carburetor

By-pass air control unit

To ATC sensor

Thermal vacuum valve

EAI tube

Automatic temperature control air cleaner

EGR tube

From fuel tank vapor vent line

Canister

Catalyst

Exhaust manifold

Distributor

▨▨▨ Ported vacuum (Dist.)	■■■	Manifold vacuum
▨▨▨ Ported vacuum (EGR)	▭▭▭	Air
⋯⋯⋯ Venturi vacuum	▭▭▭	Canister purge

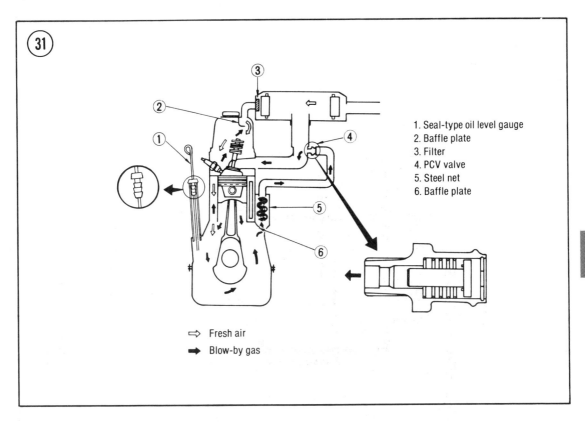

31

1. Seal-type oil level gauge
2. Baffle plate
3. Filter
4. PCV valve
5. Steel net
6. Baffle plate

⇨ Fresh air
➡ Blow-by gas

5

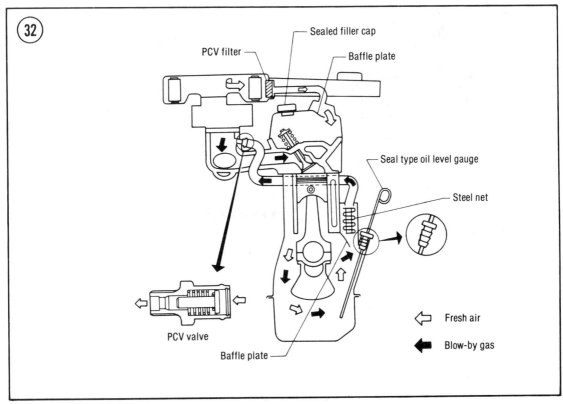

32

Sealed filler cap

PCV filter

Baffle plate

Seal type oil level gauge

Steel net

PCV valve

Baffle plate

⇦ Fresh air
➡ Blow-by gas

EXHAUST GAS RECIRCULATION

This system, used on all models, recirculates part of the exhaust gas into the combustion chambers. This lowers combustion temperature, reducing the emission of oxides of nitrogen.

The system doesn't require periodic service. If it develops a problem, however, it may cause a rough idle. If a problem is suspected, test as described in the following section.

System Inspection

Refer to **Figure 33** (1980) or **Figure 34** (1981). Start with the engine cold. Coolant temperature must be below 50° C (122° F) on 1980 models and 15° C (59° F) on 1981 trucks.
1. Check the system for wear and damage. If necessary, clean the engine so parts are easy to see.
2. Replace any cracked or broken hoses.
3. Reach beneath the EGR valve. Lift the diaphragm. It should move smoothly, without sticking or binding.

4. Start the engine. Raise engine speed to 3,000-3,500 rpm (1980) or 2,000-2,500 rpm (1981). Make sure the EGR valve does not move.

5. Warm the engine above the temperature specified in Step 1. Again, raise engine speed to 3,000-3,500 rpm (1980) or 2,000-2,500 rpm (1981). This time, the EGR valve should move.

6. If the system has performed properly so far, it is okay. If not, perform the next steps to find the cause.

7. Disconnect the EGR valve vacuum hose. Place a finger over the hose end.

8. Start the engine. Raise engine speed to 3,000-3,500 rpm. There should be vacuum at the hose end. If there is no vacuum, replace the thermal vacuum valve. If there is vacuum, replace the EGR valve. If you aren't sure, have the system tested further by a dealer or mechanic familiar with Datsun emission controls.

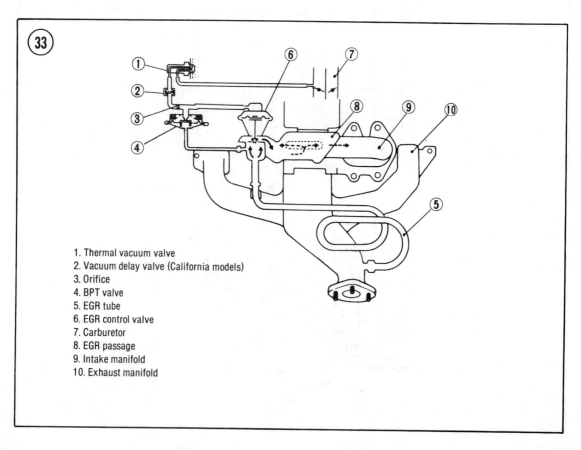

1. Thermal vacuum valve
2. Vacuum delay valve (California models)
3. Orifice
4. BPT valve
5. EGR tube
6. EGR control valve
7. Carburetor
8. EGR passage
9. Intake manifold
10. Exhaust manifold

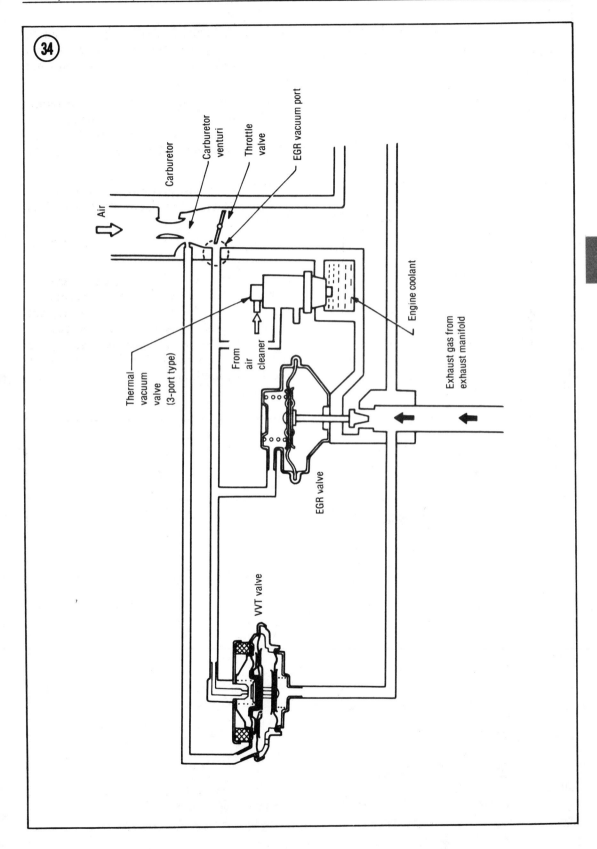

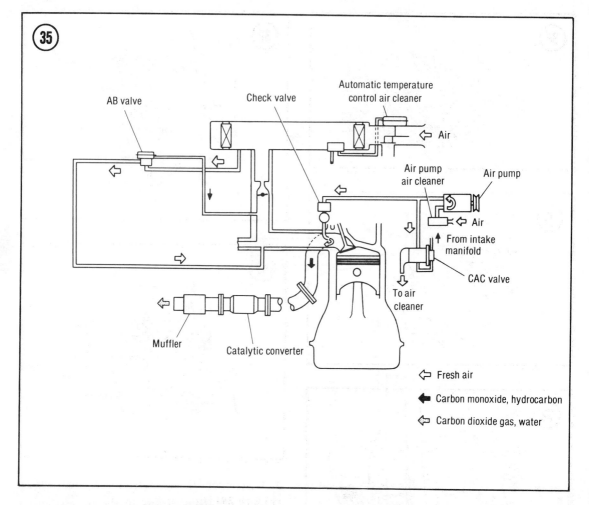

(35)

AB valve

Check valve

Automatic temperature
control air cleaner

Air

Air pump
air cleaner

Air pump

Air

From intake
manifold

CAC valve

To air
cleaner

Muffler

Catalytic converter

⇦ Fresh air

◀ Carbon monoxide, hydrocarbon

⇦ Carbon dioxide gas, water

AIR INJECTION SYSTEM

An air injection system (**Figure 35**) is used on 1980 California trucks. The system uses a pump to force air under pressure into the exhaust ports. This allows combustion to continue for a longer time to reduce carbon monoxide and unburned hydrocarbons in the exhaust.

Air pump repair requires special tools and should be left to a dealer or other competent shop. None of the other components is repairable.

Air Pump Air Cleaner

The air pump air cleaner element should be replaced at intervals specified in Chapter Three.

1. Detach the air pump air cleaner from its bracket.

2. Remove the filter element and lower body (**Figure 36**).

3. Install a new filter element and lower body. Attach the air cleaner to its bracket.

Anti-backfire Valve Test

1. Warm the engine to normal operating temperature.

2. Disconnect the anti-backfire valve hose from the air cleaner and place a thumb on the hose end. See **Figure 37**.

3. With the engine idling, there should not be any suction at the hose end. If there is, replace the anti-backfire valve.

4. Raise engine speed to 3,000-3,500 rpm, then release the throttle quickly. There should be suction at the hose end. If not, replace the anti-backfire valve.

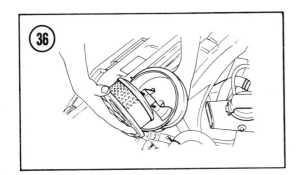

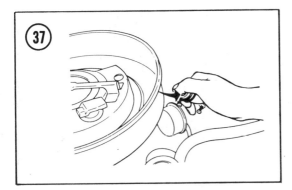

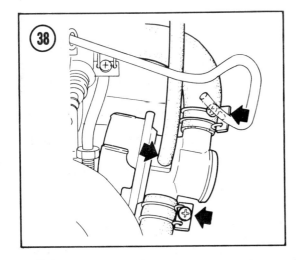

Anti-backfire Valve Removal/Installation

1. Disconnect the hoses and vacuum tube (**Figure 38**). Take the anti-backfire valve out.
2. Installation is the reverse of removal.

Check Valve Test

1. Warm the engine to normal operating temperature.
2. Check the air injection hoses for leaks. Tighten or replace as needed.

3. Disconnect the hose from the check valve (**Figure 39**). Look inside the valve. The valve plate should be against its seat (toward you, away from the engine). Push the valve plate in. It should return to its seat without binding.
4. With the hose disconnected, start the engine and watch the valve plate. Slight flutter at idle is permissible. Raise engine speed to 1,500 rpm. There should be no exhaust gas leakage past the plate. If there is, replace the check valve.

Check Valve Removal/Installation

1. Remove the air cleaner as described in this chapter.
2. Unscrew the check valve (**Figure 40**).

CAUTION
Use 2 wrenches as shown to prevent bending the air injection tubes.

3. Installation is the reverse of removal.

Air Pump Removal/Installation

1. Disconnect the hoses from the air pump.

2. Loosen the air pump mounting and adjusting bolts (**Figure 41**). Push the air pump toward the engine to loosen the drive belt, then take the drive belt off.

3. Remove the air pump mounting and adjusting bolts, then take the air pump off.

4. Installation is the reverse of removal. Adjust the air pump drive belt as described under *Drive Belts*, Chapter Three.

AIR INDUCTION SYSTEM

This system uses exhaust gas pulses to draw air into the exhaust ports. The extra air allows combustion to continue for a longer time, reducing carbon monoxide and unburned hydrocarbons in the exhaust.

Refer to the following illustrations:
a. **Figure 42** — 1980 non-California
b. **Figure 43** — 1981 California
c. **Figure 44** — 1981 non-California

System Inspection

1. Check the system for visible damage. Check the hoses for cracks or loose connections. Replace or tighten as needed.

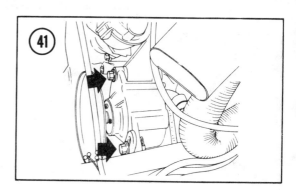

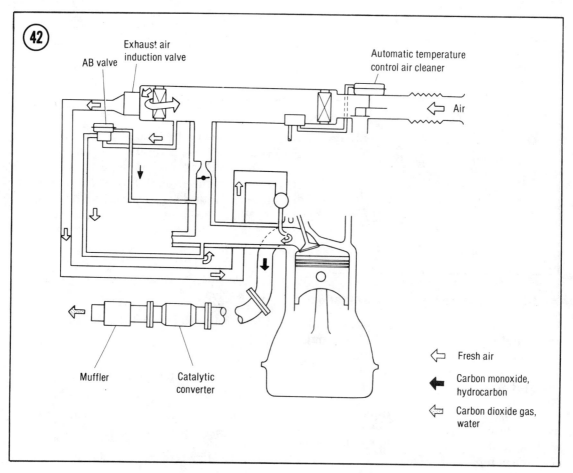

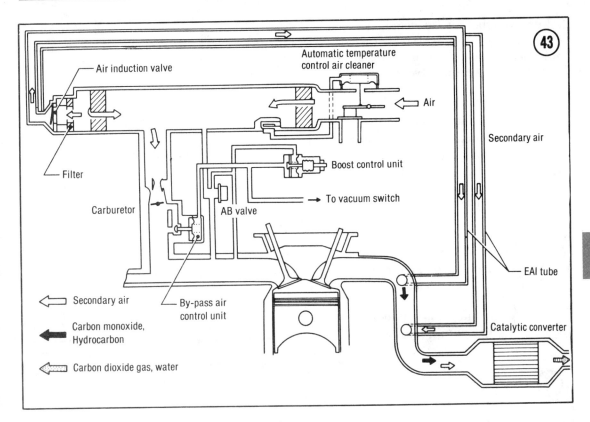

Air induction valve

Automatic temperature control air cleaner

Air

Filter

Boost control unit

Carburetor

To vacuum switch

AB valve

Secondary air

EAI tube

⟸ Secondary air

By-pass air control unit

Catalytic converter

⬅ Carbon monoxide, Hydrocarbon

⟸ Carbon dioxide gas, water

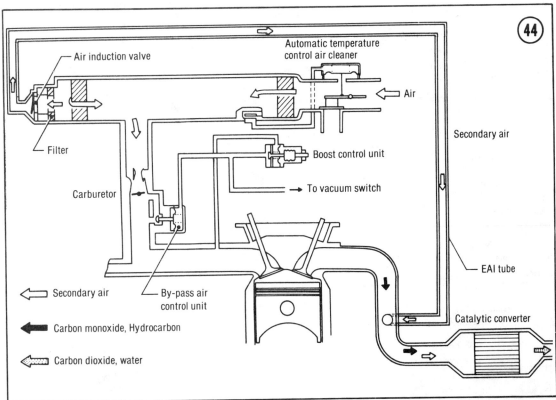

Air induction valve

Automatic temperature control air cleaner

Air

Filter

Boost control unit

Carburetor

To vacuum switch

Secondary air

EAI tube

⟸ Secondary air

By-pass air control unit

Catalytic converter

⬅ Carbon monoxide, Hydrocarbon

⟸ Carbon dioxide, water

2. Remove the air induction valve case
(**Figure 45**) from the air cleaner. Take out the
air induction valve and filter. Install a new
filter, then reinstall the valve and case.

EVAPORATIVE EMISSION CONTROL SYSTEM

This system, used on all models, is designed
to prevent gasoline vapor from escaping into
the atmosphere. The system should be
inspected, and the carbon canister filter
replaced, at intervals specified in Chapter
Three.

Inspection

1. Check the vapor lines (**Figure 46**) for loose
connections or damage. Tighten or replace as
needed.
2. Remove the filter from the bottom of the
carbon canister (**Figure 47**). Install a new one.

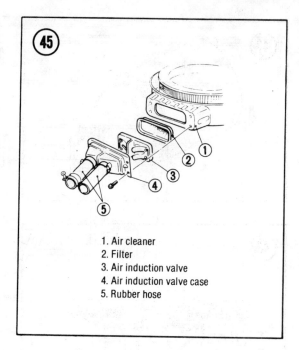

1. Air cleaner
2. Filter
3. Air induction valve
4. Air induction valve case
5. Rubber hose

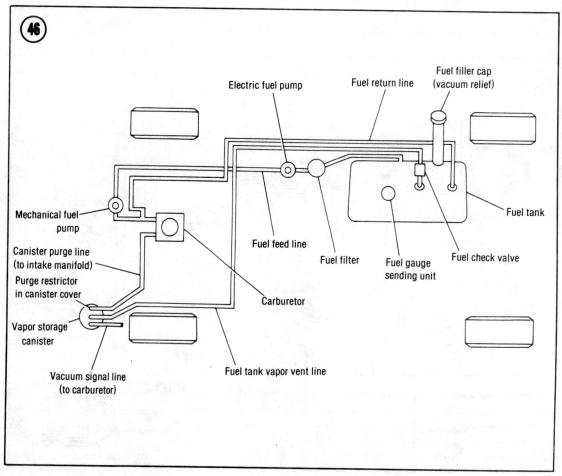

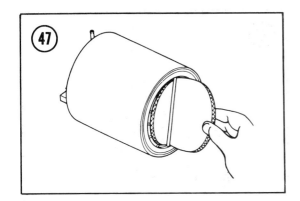

3. Remove the fuel filler cap and wipe the inside of it clean. Suck on the cap's valve (**Figure 48**). There should be resistance, then the valve should click and air should flow into the valve. If there is no resistance or if air can't be sucked through the valve, replace the fuel filler cap.

SPARK TIMING CONTROL SYSTEM

This system, used on 1980 California models and all 1981 trucks, retards ignition timing under specified driving conditions.

On 1980 California models, the system consists of a vacuum switching valve and top gear detecting switch. See **Figure 49**. When the transmission is in any gear but fourth (or fifth if so equipped), the vacuum switching valve opens the vacuum advance line to air. This weakens the vacuum signal to the distributor and retards ignition timing. In fourth or fifth gear, the vacuum switching valve closes. The full vacuum signal then reaches the distributor and ignition timing is advanced.

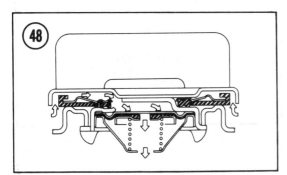

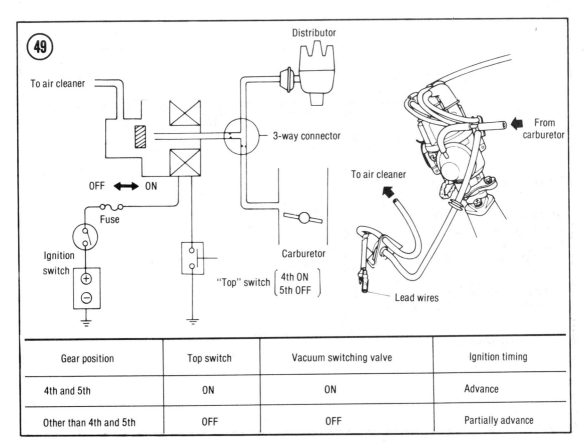

Gear position	Top switch	Vacuum switching valve	Ignition timing
4th and 5th	ON	ON	Advance
Other than 4th and 5th	OFF	OFF	Partially advance

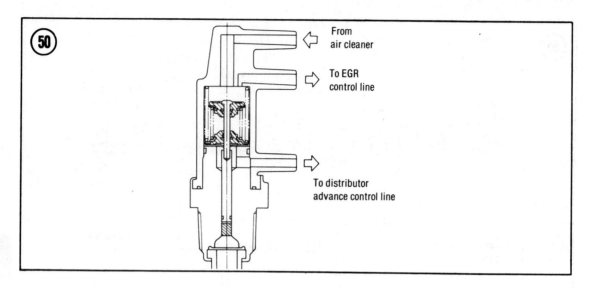

On 1981 models, the system consists of a thermal vacuum valve (**Figure 50**) and related hoses. With the engine cold, the thermal vacuum valve closes to allow full vacuum to the distributor. As the engine warms up, the valve opens to expose the distributor vacuum line to air. This blocks the vacuum signal and retards ignition timing.

System Test (1980)

This procedure requires 2 people.
1. Make sure all wires and hoses are properly connected and in good condition. Tighten or replace as needed.
2. Connect a timing light to the engine.
3. Run the engine at approximately 2,000 rpm. Have an assistant move the shift lever to all gear positions and note ignition timing. It should be more advanced in fourth gear (and fifth, if so equipped) than in the other gears. If not, have the system tested further by a dealer or mechanic familiar with Datsun emission controls.

System Test (1981)

This procedure requires 2 people.
1. Connect a timing light to the engine.

> *NOTE*
> *If air temperature is above 15°C (59°F), cool the thermal vacuum valve (mounted on the water outlet elbow) with ice.*

2. Start the engine and let it idle. Note ignition timing.

3. Warm the engine until the coolant temperature needle is in the center of the gauge, then recheck ignition timing. It should be more advanced than it was with the engine cold. If not, have the system tested further by a dealer or mechanic familiar with Datsun emission controls.

FUEL SHUTOFF SYSTEM

This system (**Figure 51**) shuts off fuel flow to the carburetor slow circuit during deceleration. The system does not need periodic inspection. System testing should be left to a dealer or mechanic familiar with Datsun emission controls.

INTAKE MANIFOLD VACUUM CONTROL SYSTEM

This system, used on 1981 models, reduces engine oil consumption by reducing intake manifold vacuum during hard deceleration. It consists of a boost control unit (**Figure 52**) and bypass air control valve (**Figure 53**). When intake manifold vacuum reaches high levels, the boost control valve signals the bypass air control valve to admit additional air to the intake manifold.

The system doesn't need periodic inspection. Testing and adjustment should be left to a dealer or mechanic familiar with Datsun emission controls.

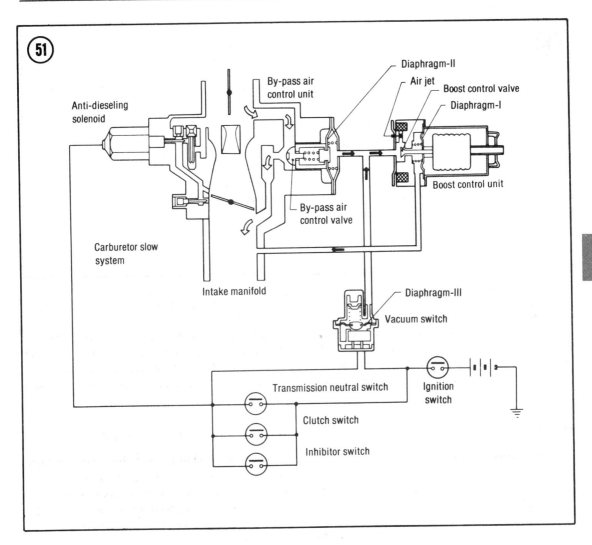

51

Anti-dieseling solenoid

By-pass air control unit

Diaphragm-II

Air jet

Boost control valve

Diaphragm-I

Boost control unit

By-pass air control valve

Carburetor slow system

Intake manifold

Diaphragm-III

Vacuum switch

Transmission neutral switch

Ignition switch

Clutch switch

Inhibitor switch

5

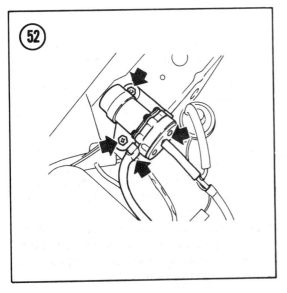

52

53

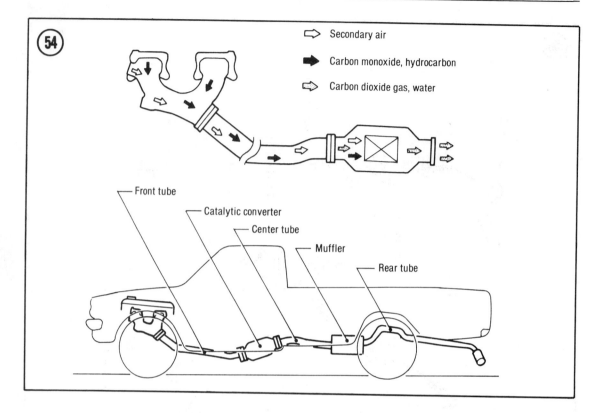

➪ Secondary air

➡ Carbon monoxide, hydrocarbon

➪ Carbon dioxide gas, water

Front tube

Catalytic converter

Center tube

Muffler

Rear tube

CATALYTIC CONVERTER

A catalytic converter is used on all except 1980 Canadian trucks. The converter (**Figure 54**) is mounted in the exhaust line and resembles a muffler. It uses a platinum or palladium catalyst to convert unburned hydrocarbons and carbon monoxide into carbon dioxide and water. No periodic service is needed.

ALTITUDE COMPENSATOR

This device, used on California models, admits additional air to the carburetor at high altitudes. This compensates for the overrich fuel mixture caused by thin ambient air.

Testing

To test, disconnect the carburetor end of each carburetor-to-compensator line. See **Figure 55**. Try to blow air through each line into the compensator. This should be impossible at altitudes below 600 m (2,000 ft.). Above that altitude, it should be possible. If the compensator doesn't perform properly, replace it.

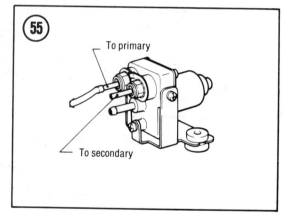

To primary

To secondary

EXHAUST SYSTEM

The exhaust system consists of a catalytic converter, muffler and connecting pipes. See **Figure 56** (1980) or **Figure 57** (1981).

Removal/Installation

1. Prior to removal, soak all nuts, bolts and pipe joints with penetrating oil such as WD-40.
2. Undo the necessary clamps and hanger brackets, referring to the appropriate illustrations.

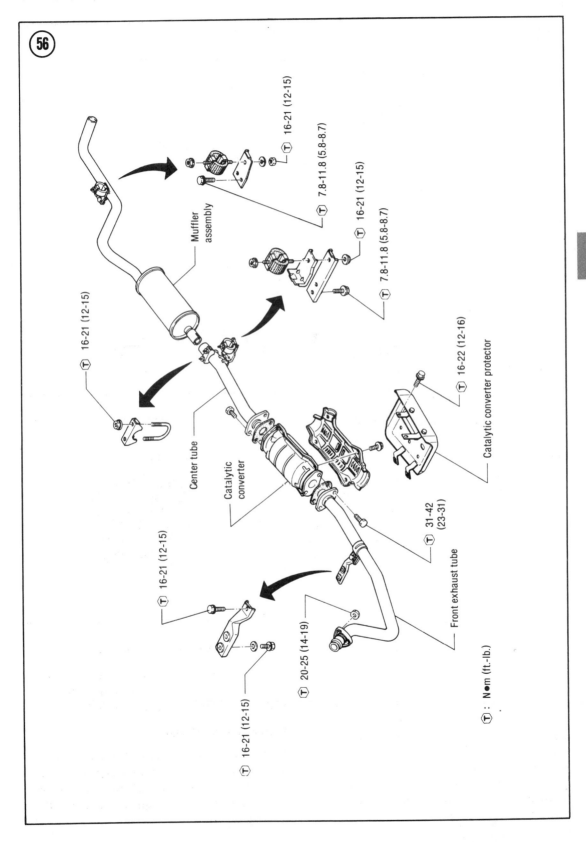

56

16-21 (12-15)

7.8-11.8 (5.8-8.7)

16-21 (12-15)

7.8-11.8 (5.8-8.7)

Muffler assembly

16-21 (12-15)

16-22 (12-16)

Catalytic converter protector

Center tube

Catalytic converter

16-21 (12-15)

31-42 (23-31)

Front exhaust tube

16-21 (12-15)

20-25 (14-19)

T : N•m (ft.-lb.)

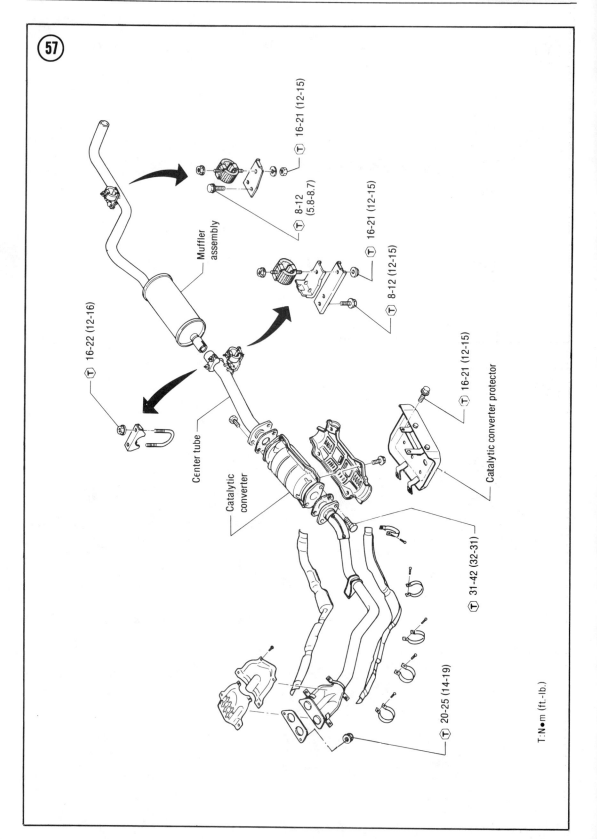

(57)

16-21 (12-15)

8-12
(5.8-8.7)

16-21 (12-15)

Muffler
assembly

16-21 (12-15)

8-12 (12-15)

16-22 (12-16)

16-21 (12-15)

Catalytic converter protector

Center tube

Catalytic
converter

31-42 (32-31)

20-25 (14-19)

T:N●m (ft.-lb.)

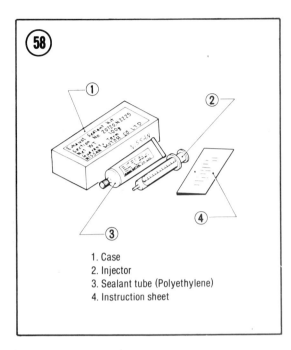

1. Case
2. Injector
3. Sealant tube (Polyethylene)
4. Instruction sheet

NOTE
*An injected sealer is used at the front end of the muffler. See **Figure 58**. To remove, break the seal by tapping the joint with a metal hammer. Twist the muffler back and forth, then tap it off with a rubber mallet.*

3. Check removed parts for excessive rust and for impact damage. Check rubber mounts for melting, cracks or deterioration. Replace as needed.

4. Installation is the reverse of removal. Inject sealer into the muffler front connection with a Datsun sealer kit (**Figure 59**). Let the engine idle for 10 minutes to cure the sealer. Do not accelerate sharply for 20-30 minutes.

FUEL TANK

Removal/Installation

Refer to **Figure 60** for this procedure.

1. Disconnect the negative cable from the battery.
2. Drain the fuel from the tank.

WARNING
Do not store the fuel in an open container, since it represents an extreme fire hazard. Store it in a sealed metal container, away from heat, flames or sparks.

3. Disconnect the tank hoses (**Figure 61**).
4. Remove the tank protector.
5. Detach the tank from the truck and take it out.
6. Installation is the reverse of removal. Make sure all connections are tight. Check for leaks after adding gasoline to the tank.

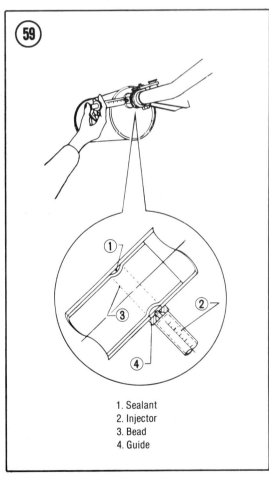

1. Sealant
2. Injector
3. Bead
4. Guide

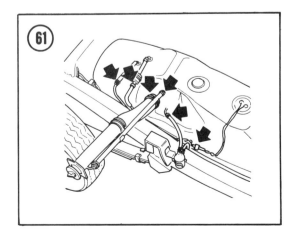

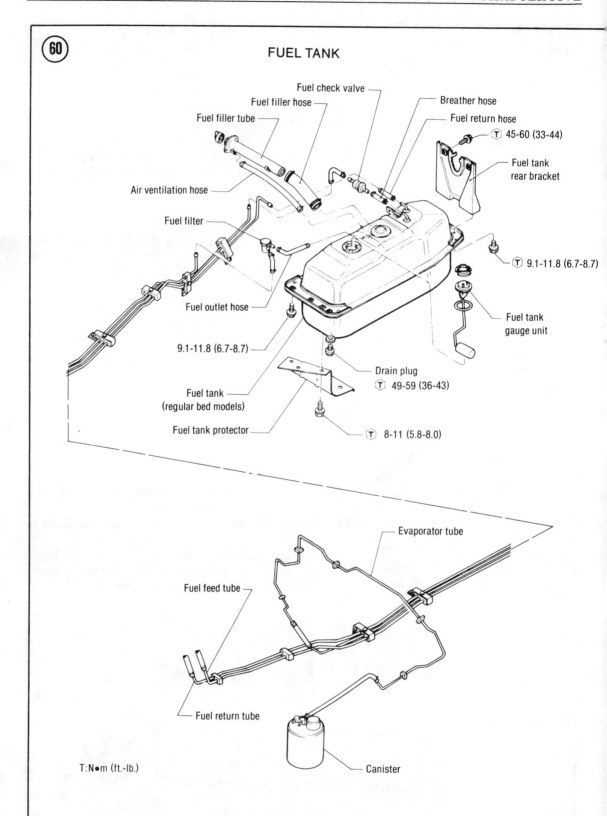

FUEL TANK

Fuel check valve

Fuel filler hose

Fuel filler tube

Breather hose

Fuel return hose

Ⓣ 45-60 (33-44)

Fuel tank
rear bracket

Air ventilation hose

Fuel filter

Ⓣ 9.1-11.8 (6.7-8.7)

Fuel outlet hose

Fuel tank
gauge unit

9.1-11.8 (6.7-8.7)

Drain plug
Ⓣ 49-59 (36-43)

Fuel tank
(regular bed models)

Fuel tank protector

Ⓣ 8-11 (5.8-8.0)

Evaporator tube

Fuel feed tube

Fuel return tube

Canister

T:N•m (ft.-lb.)

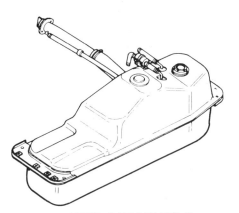

KING CAB MODELS

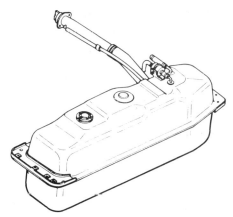

LONG BED MODELS

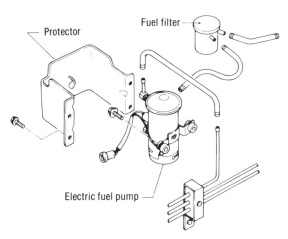

ELECTRIC FUEL PUMP EQUIPPED MODEL

5

Repairing Leaks

WARNING
A fuel tank is capable of exploding and killing anyone nearby. Always observe the following precautions when repairing a tank.

1. Have the tank steam cleaned inside and outside.

2. Fill the tank with inert gas such as carbon dioxide or nitrogen or fill the tank completely with water. Highly explosive vapor can form if any air space is left in the tank.

3. Set a fire extinguisher nearby. After the repair is made, pour the water out (if used). Put about a quart of gasoline in the tank and slosh it around. Pour the gasoline out, blow the tank dry and install it in the truck.

THROTTLE LINKAGE ADJUSTMENTS

Figure 62 shows the 1980 throttle linkage. **Figure 63** shows the 1981 design.

1. Check pedal height (**Figure 64**). If incorrect, loosen the pedal stopper locknut. Turn the pedal stopper bolt to change height, then tighten the locknut.

2. Remove the air cleaner as described in this chapter. Open the choke plate by hand, pull the throttle lever up, then release the choke plate.

3. Let the throttle close completely.

4. On 1980 models, loosen the clamp (**Figure 65**). Pull the cable in direction "A" until the throttle lever is just about to move. Then move the cable back 1.0-1.5 mm (0.039-0.059 in.) and tighten the clamp.

5. On 1981 models, loosen the locknut (**Figure 66**). Tighten the adjusting nut until the throttle lever is just about to move. Loosen the adjusting nut one or two turns so throttle cable play is 1.0-2.5 mm (0.039-0.098 in.). Tighten the locknut.

6. Floor the accelerator and measure distance "T" (**Figure 64**). If incorrect, adjust with the pedal stopper bolt.

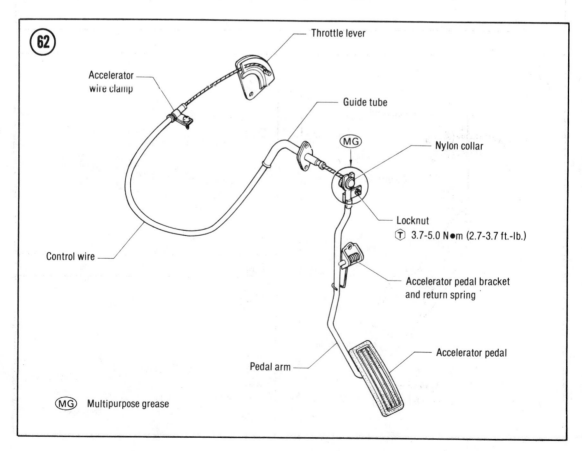

62

Throttle lever

Accelerator wire clamp

Guide tube

MG

Nylon collar

Locknut
Ⓣ 3.7-5.0 N•m (2.7-3.7 ft.-lb.)

Control wire

Accelerator pedal bracket and return spring

Accelerator pedal

Pedal arm

MG Multipurpose grease

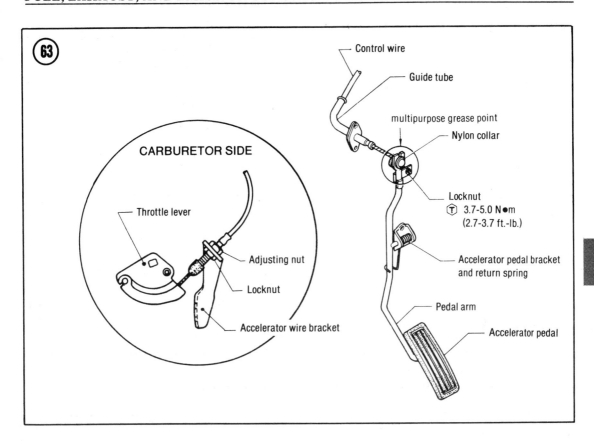

63

Control wire

Guide tube

multipurpose grease point

Nylon collar

Locknut
Ⓣ 3.7-5.0 N●m
(2.7-3.7 ft.-lb.)

Accelerator pedal bracket
and return spring

Pedal arm

Accelerator pedal

CARBURETOR SIDE

Throttle lever

Adjusting nut

Locknut

Accelerator wire bracket

5

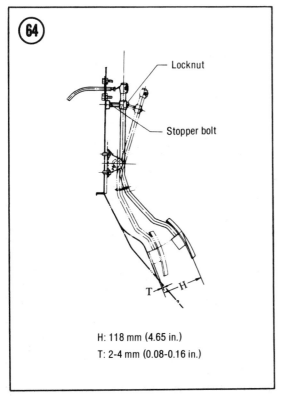

64

Locknut

Stopper bolt

T ⊢ H

H: 118 mm (4.65 in.)
T: 2-4 mm (0.08-0.16 in.)

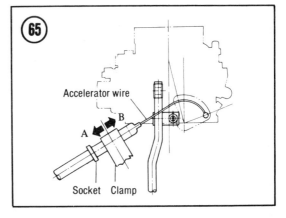

65

Accelerator wire

B

A

Socket   Clamp

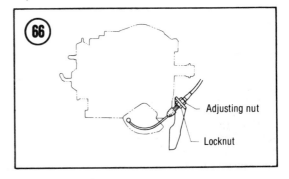

66

Adjusting nut

Locknut

Table 1   CARBURETOR SPECIFICATIONS

1980	
Primary main jet	
California	104
Non-California	105
Secondary main jet	
California	170
Non-California	165
Primary main air bleed	
California	70
Non-California	60
Secondary main air bleed	60
Primary slow jet	48
Secondary slow jet	70
Power valve	35
1981	
Primary main jet	
California	110
Non-California	105
Secondary main jet	155
Primary main air bleed	
California	90
Non-California	80
Secondary main air bleed	60
Primary slow jet	47
Secondary slow jet	100
Power valve	
California	35
Non-California	40

Table 2   FUEL PUMP SPECIFICATIONS

Mechanical fuel pump	
Static pressure	
1980	3.0-3.9 psi
1981	3.0-3.8 psi
Capacity at 1,000 rpm	
1980	More than 1 liter (34 fl. oz.) per minute
1981	More than 1.7 liters (58 fl. oz.) per minute
Electric fuel pump	
Static pressure	3.1-3.8 psi
Capacity	More than 1.4 liters (47 fl. oz.) per minute

CHAPTER SIX

COOLING, HEATING, AND AIR CONDITIONING SYSTEMS

All models use a centrifugal water pump to propel coolant through the radiator, engine and heater. A thermostat controls coolant flow.

A fluid-drive fan conserves power and reduces engine noise at high speeds. The heater is a hot water type which circulates coolant through a small radiator (heater core) under the dash.

This chapter includes service procedures for the thermostat, water pump, radiator, heater and air conditioner. Cooling system flushing procedures are also described.

COOLING SYSTEM FLUSHING

Refer to **Figure 1** (1980) or **Figure 2** (1981). The recommended coolant is a 50/50 mixture of ethylene glycol-based antifreeze and water. This protects the system from freezing to approximately -36° C (-32° F). Higher antifreeze concentrations may be used in colder areas.

The system should be drained, flushed and refilled at intervals specified in Chapter Three. If desired, a chemical flushing agent may be used prior to the flushing method described here.

1. Coolant can stain concrete and harm plants. Park the truck over a gutter or similar area.

2. Place the heater temperature lever on the instrument panel in the HOT position.

3. Open the tap at the bottom of the radiator (**Figure 3**). Remove the engine drain plug. See **Figure 4** (1980) or **Figure 5** (1981).

4. After the engine has finished draining, install the plug and close the tap.

5. Remove the thermostat as described under *Thermostat* in this chapter. Temporarily reinstall the water outlet elbow.

6. Disconnect the top radiator hose from the radiator. Disconnect the bottom hose from the engine.

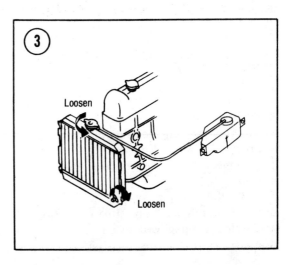

3 Loosen Loosen

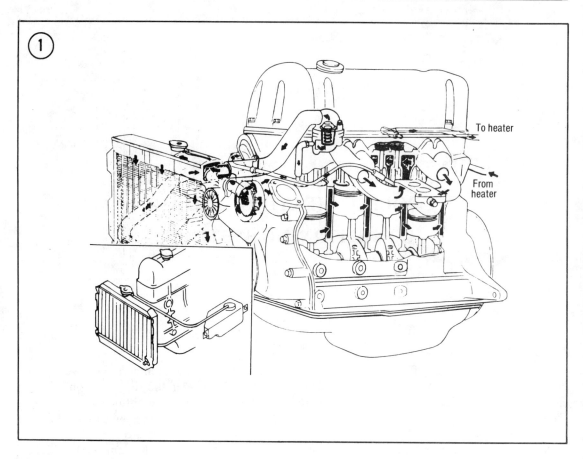

7. Disconnect the heater hoses from the engine.

8. Connect a garden hose to one heater hose. This does not have to be a positive fit, as long as most of the water enters the heater hose. Run water into the heater hose until clear water flows from the other heater hose.

9. Insert the garden hose into the top radiator hose. Run water into the hose until clear water flows from the bottom hose.

10. Insert the garden hose into the hose fitting at the bottom of the radiator. Run water into the radiator until clear water flows from the top fitting.

11. Turn off the water.

12. Remove the engine drain plug and let out any remaining water. Reinstall the drain plug.

13. Connect the hoses to the engine and radiator.

14. Fill the cooling system with a 50/50 mixture of ethylene glycol-based antifreeze and water, even if you live in an area that doesn't require this degree of freeze protection. The antifreeze makes a good corrosion inhibitor. Cooling system capacity is listed in **Table 1** at the end of the chapter.

15. Run the engine for several minutes and check for leaks. Recheck coolant level and top off as needed.

THERMOSTAT

The thermostat blocks water flow to the radiator when the engine is cold. As the engine warms up, the thermostat gradually opens, allowing water to circulate through the radiator.

Removal and Testing

1. Make sure the engine is cool.

2. Drain about one gallon of coolant from the radiator. If the coolant is clean, save it for reuse.

3. Detach the hose from the water outlet elbow.

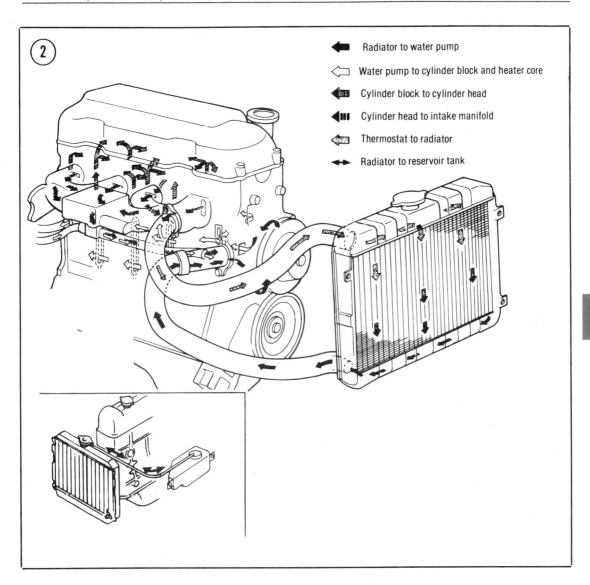

Radiator to water pump

Water pump to cylinder block and heater core

Cylinder block to cylinder head

Cylinder head to intake manifold

Thermostat to radiator

Radiator to reservoir tank

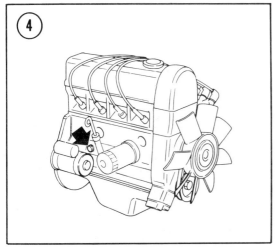

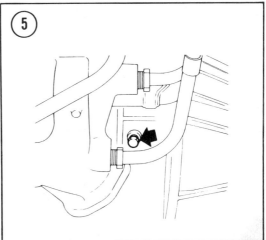

4. Unbolt the outlet elbow from the engine and lift it off. Lift out the thermostat. See **Figure 6** (1980) or **Figure 7** (1981).

5. Submerge the thermostat in water with a thermometer (**Figure 8**).

NOTE
Support the thermostat with wire so it doesn't touch the sides or bottom of the pan.

6. Heat the water until the thermostat just begins to open, then check the water temperature (**Table 1**). If the valve opens at the wrong temperature or fails to open, replace the thermostat.

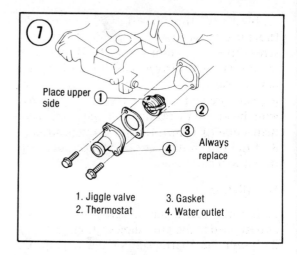

Place upper side

Always replace

1. Jiggle valve   3. Gasket
2. Thermostat   4. Water outlet

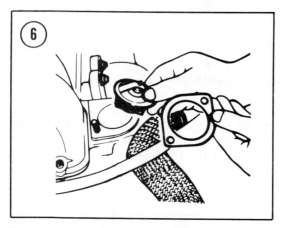

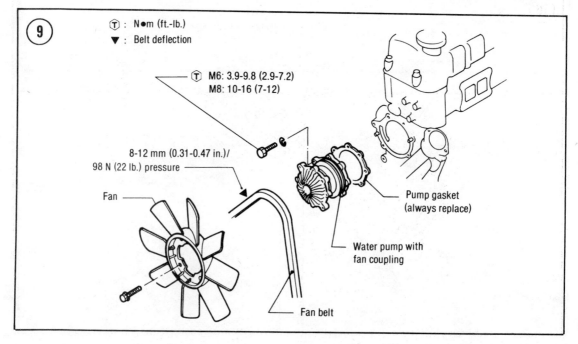

⊤ : N●m (ft.-lb.)
▼ : Belt deflection

⊤ M6: 3.9-9.8 (2.9-7.2)
M8: 10-16 (7-12)

8-12 mm (0.31-0.47 in.)/
98 N (22 lb.) pressure

Fan

Pump gasket
(always replace)

Water pump with
fan coupling

Fan belt

7. Measure the maximum lift of the thermostat valve. To do this, mark a screwdriver at a point 8 mm (0.31 in.) from the tip. The screwdriver is used as a measuring device. Heat the water to specified opening temperature and measure the lift of the valve with the marked screwdriver. If valve lift is less than 8 mm (0.31 in.), replace the thermostat.

8. Let the water cool. Make sure the thermostat closes.

Installation

1. If a new thermostat is being installed, test as described in the preceding section.

2. Install the thermostat in the engine. On 1981 models, make sure the jiggle valve (**Figure 7**) is toward the top when the thermostat is installed.

3. Install the water outlet elbow. Use a new gasket, coated on both sides with gasket sealer.

4. Tighten the outlet elbow, then reconnect the hose.

RADIATOR

Removal/Installation

1. Make sure the engine is cool enough to touch.

2. Coolant can stain concrete and harm plants. Park the car over a gutter or similar area.

3. Open the drain tap at the bottom of the radiator (**Figure 3**). Let the coolant drain.

4. Disconnect the radiator and reservoir tank hoses.

5. Detach the fan shroud from the radiator. Lay it back over the fan.

6. Remove the radiator mounting bolts and lift the radiator out.

7. Installation is the reverse of removal. Fill the engine with a 50/50 mixture of ethylene glycol-based antifreeze and water. Run the engine and check for leaks.

FAN

Removal/Installation

1. Remove the radiator and shroud as described in the preceding section.

2. Loosen the alternator mounting and adjusting bolts. Push the alternator toward the engine to loosen the fan belt, then take the belt off.

3. Detach the fan from the water pump. See **Figure 9** (1980) or **Figure 10** (1981). Take the fan out.

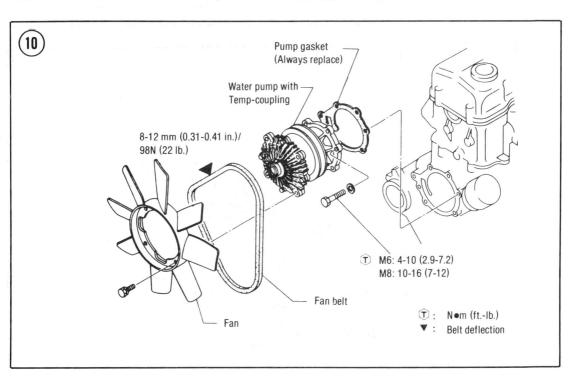

(10)

Pump gasket (Always replace)

Water pump with Temp-coupling

8-12 mm (0.31-0.41 in.)/ 98N (22 lb.)

M6: 4-10 (2.9-7.2)
M8: 10-16 (7-12)

Fan belt

Fan

T : N●m (ft.-lb.)
▼ : Belt deflection

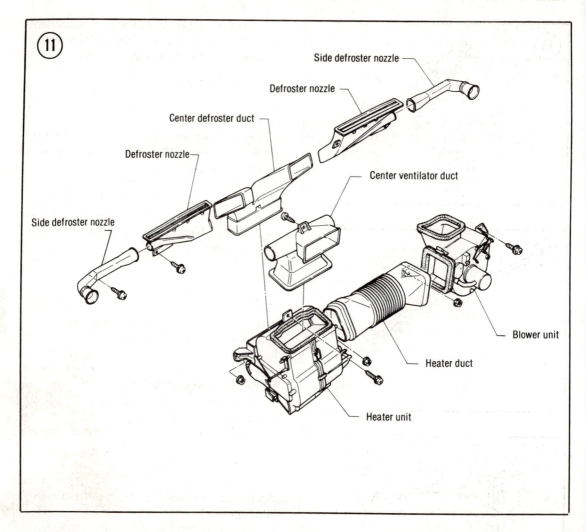

(11)

Side defroster nozzle

Defroster nozzle

Center defroster duct

Defroster nozzle

Side defroster nozzle

Center ventilator duct

Blower unit

Heater duct

Heater unit

4. Installation is the reverse of removal. Fill the cooling system with a 50/50 mixture of ethylene glycol-based antifreeze and water. Run the engine and check for leaks.

Inspection

1. Check the fan for obvious damage such as broken blades. Replace as needed.
2. Check the fan coupling for damage or oil leaks. Replace if these are found. Since the fan coupling and water pump are a single unit, the water pump must be replaced if the fan coupling is defective.

WATER PUMP

The water pump and fan coupling are combined into a single unit. If one or the other is defective, both must be replaced.

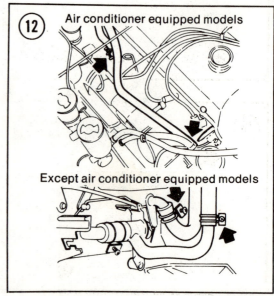

(12) **Air conditioner equipped models**

Except air conditioner equipped models

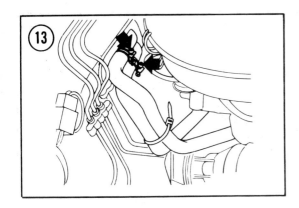

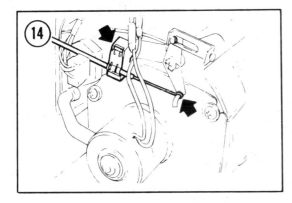

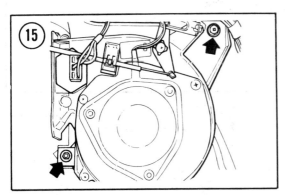

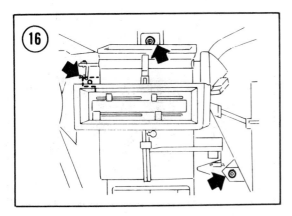

A water pump may warn of impending failure by making noise. If the seal is defective, coolant may leak from behind the fan.

Removal/Installation

1. Remove the fan as described in the preceding section.
2. Remove the water pump bolts. See **Figure 9** (1980) or **Figure 10** (1981). Take the water pump off the engine.
3. Installation is the reverse of removal. Use a new gasket, coated on both sides with gasket sealer. Tighten the thin bolts to 3.9-9.8 N•m (3-7 ft.-lb.) Tighten the thick bolts to 10-16 N•m (7-12 ft.-lb.).

HEATER

Heater Removal/Installation

Refer to **Figure 11** for this procedure.
1. Disconnect the negative cable from the battery.
2. Drain the cooling system. See *Cooling System Flushing* in this chapter.
3. Place a plastic sheet, such as a painting dropcloth, on the floor of the truck.
4. On 1980 trucks without air conditioning, remove the heater duct, then disconnect the heater hoses. See **Figure 12**.
5. On 1980 trucks with air conditioning, disconnect the heater hoses from the engine. See **Figure 12**.
6. On 1981 trucks, disconnect the heater hoses at the firewall. See **Figure 13**.
7. Remove the console and instrument panel as described in Chapter Twelve.
8. Disconnect the air intake cable from the heater blower unit. See **Figure 14**.
9. If equipped with air conditioning, remove the heater blower unit (**Figure 15**). Remove the air conditioner mounting nuts and bolts, but do not take the air conditioner out.
10. Remove the heater fasteners (**Figure 16**), then take the heater out.
11. Installation is the reverse of removal. Adjust the heater cables as described in this chapter. Fill the cooling system as described under *Cooling System Flushing*. Turn the temperature control lever to HOT and run the engine for several minutes. Recheck coolant level and top up as needed.

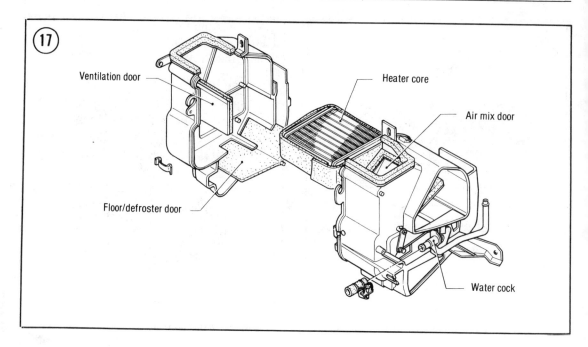

(17) Ventilation door — Heater core — Air mix door — Floor/defroster door — Water cock

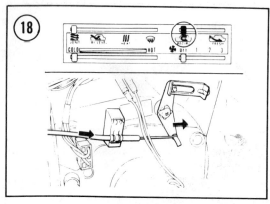

(18)

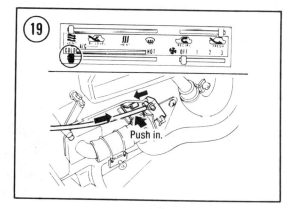

(19) Push in.

Heater Core Removal/Installation

1. Remove the heater as described in this chapter.

2. Disassemble the heater case, referring to **Figure 17**. Take the core out.

3. Installation is the reverse of removal.

Cable Adjustment

1. To adjust the air intake door cable, set the air intake lever in the RECIRC position. Loosen the cable clamp (**Figure 18**). Push the cable and lever in the direction shown in **Figure 18**, then tighten the clamp.

2. To adjust the air mix door and water valve cable, set the control lever in the COLD position. Loosen the clamp (**Figure 19**). Push the cable and water valve lever in the directions shown, then tighten the clamp.

3. Move the air control lever all the way to the right. Loosen the cable clamp (**Figure 20**). Move the side link in the direction shown, then tighten the clamp.

Control Assembly Removal/Installation

1. Remove the package tray.

2. Place the temperature lever in the COLD position.

3. Disconnect the heater and blower cables. See **Figure 21**.

4. Pull off the control knobs. See **Figure 22**.

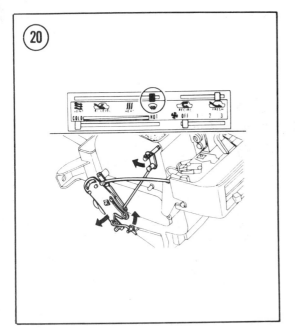

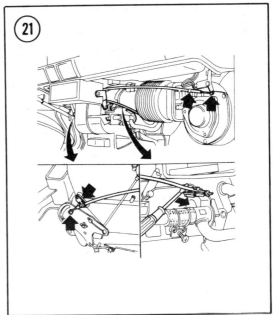

6

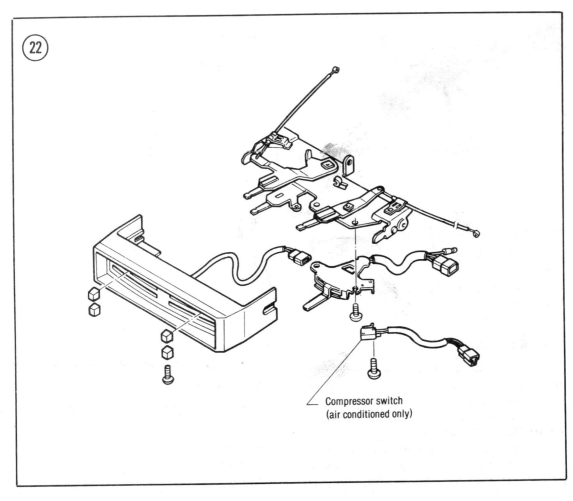

Compressor switch
(air conditioned only)

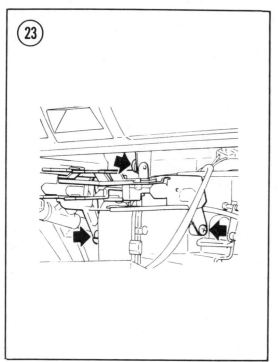

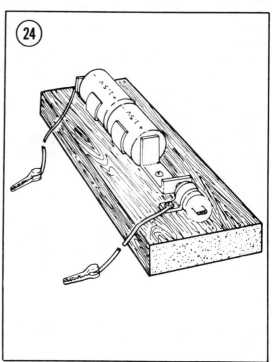

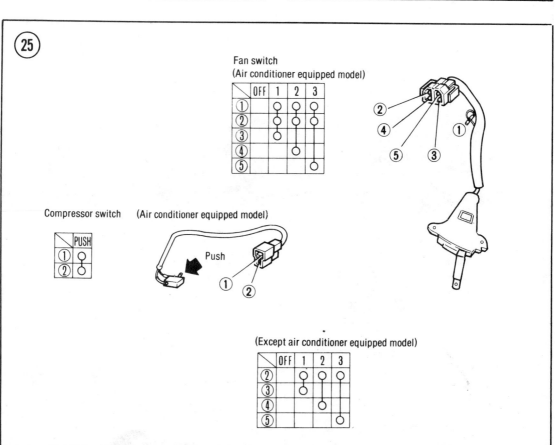

Fan switch
(Air conditioner equipped model)

	OFF	1	2	3
①		O	O	O
②		O	O	O
③		O		
④			O	O
⑤				O

Compressor switch (Air conditioner equipped model)

		PUSH
①		O
②		O

Push

(Except air conditioner equipped model)

	OFF	1	2	3
②		O	O	O
③		O		
④			O	O
⑤				O

6. Detach the control assembly (**Figure 23**) and take it out.

7. Installation is the reverse of removal. Adjust the heater cables as described in this chapter.

Fan Switch Testing

The fan switch can be tested with an ohmmeter or battery powered test lamp like the one shown in **Figure 24**. To test, remove the control assembly and identify the terminals. See **Figure 25** (1980) or **Figure 26** (1981).

With the switch off, there should not be continuity between any of the terminals. An ohmmeter connected between any terminals should show infinite resistance and a test lamp should stay out.

With the switch in the first position, there should be continuity between terminals 1 and 2 (without air conditioning) or terminals 1, 2 and 3 (with air conditioning). An ohmmeter connected between these terminals should show little or no resistance. A test lamp should light.

Move the switch to the remaining positions. Make sure there is continuity between the terminals indicated in **Figure 25** (1980) or **Figure 26** (1981).

AIR CONDITIONING

This section covers the maintenance and minor repairs that can prevent or correct most air conditioning problems. Major repairs require special training and tools and should be left to a dealer or air conditioning shop.

6

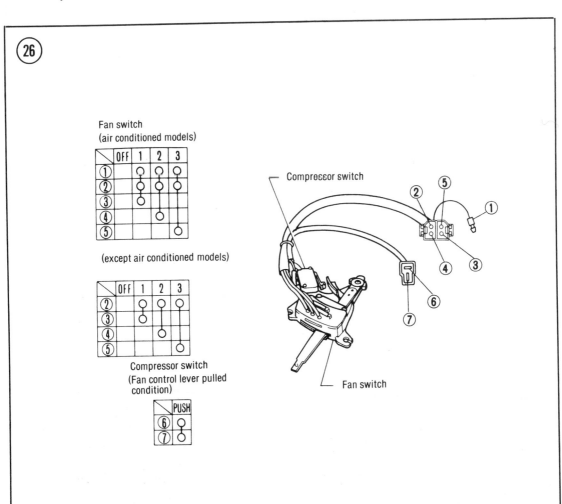

(26)

Fan switch
(air conditioned models)

(except air conditioned models)

Compressor switch
(Fan control lever pulled condition)

Compressor switch

Fan switch

SYSTEM OPERATION

A schematic of the air conditioning system is shown in **Figure 27**. These 5 basic components are common to all air conditioning systems:

a. Compressor
b. Condenser
c. Receiver/drier
d. Expansion valve
e. Evaporator

WARNING
*The components, connected with high-pressure hoses and tubes, form a closed loop. The refrigerant in the system is under very high pressure. It can cause frostbite if it touches skin and blindness if it touches the eyes. If discharged near a flame, the refrigerant creates poisonous gas. If the refrigerant can is hooked up wrong, it can explode. For these reasons, **read this entire section** before working on the system.*

For practical purposes, the cycle begins at the compressor. The refrigerant, in a warm, low-pressure vapor state, enters the low-pressure side of the compressor. It is compressed to a high-pressure hot vapor and pumped out of the high-pressure side to the condenser.

Air flow through the condenser removes heat from the refrigerant and transfers the heat to the outside air. As the heat is removed, the refrigerant condenses to a warm, high- pressure liquid.

The refrigerant then flows to the receiver/drier where moisture is removed and impurities are filtered out. The refrigerant is stored in the receiver/drier until it is needed. The receiver/drier incorporates a sight glass that permits visual monitoring of the condition of the refrigerant as it flows. From the receiver/drier, the refrigerant then flows to the expansion valve. The expansion valve is thermostatically controlled and meters refrigerant to the evaporator. As the refrigerant leaves the expansion valve it changes from a warm, high-pressure liquid to a cold, low-pressure liquid.

In the evaporator, the refrigerant removes heat from the passenger compartment air that is blown across the evaporator's fins and tubes. In the process, the refrigerant changes from a cold, low-pressure liquid to a warm, high-pressure vapor. The vapor flows back to the compressor, where the cycle begins again.

GET TO KNOW YOUR VEHICLE'S SYSTEM

Locate each of the following components in turn:
a. Compressor
b. Condenser
c. Receiver/drier
d. Expansion valve
e. Evaporator

Compressor

The compressor (**Figure 28**) is located on the front of the engine, like the alternator, and is driven by a V-belt. The large pulley on the front of the compressor contains an electromagnetic clutch. This activates and operates the compressor when the air conditioning is switched on.

Condenser

The condenser is mounted in front of the radiator (**Figure 28**). Air passing through the fins and tubes removes heat from the refrigerant in the same manner it removes heat from the engine coolant as it passes through the radiator.

Receiver/Drier

The receiver/drier (**Figure 29**) is a small tank-like unit, usually mounted to one of the wheel wells. It incorporates a sight glass through which refrigerant flow can be seen. The refrigerant's appearance is used to troubleshoot the system.

Expansion Valve

The expansion valve (**Figure 30**) is located between the receiver/drier and the evaporator. It is mounted on the evaporator housing.

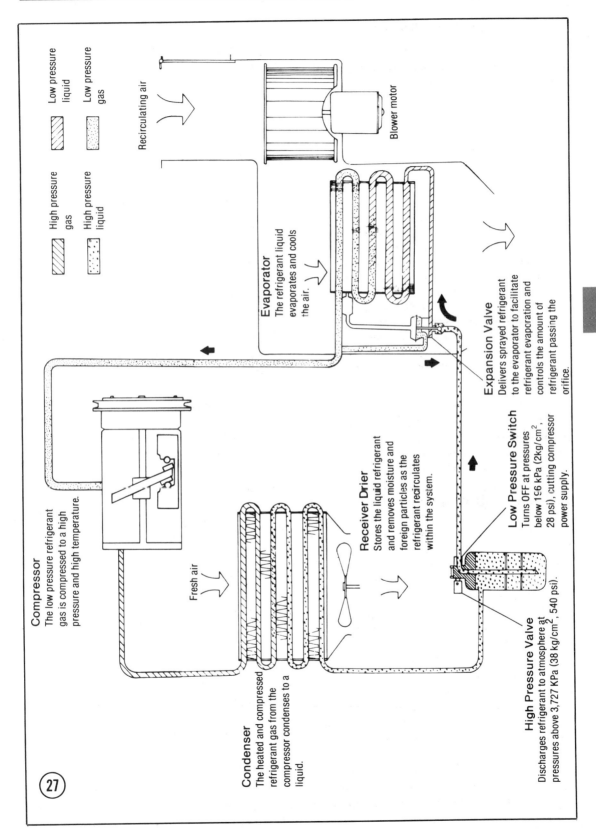

Low pressure liquid

Low pressure gas

High pressure gas

High pressure liquid

Recirculating air

Blower motor

Evaporator
The refrigerant liquid evaporates and cools the air.

Expansion Valve
Delivers sprayed refrigerant to the evaporator to facilitate refrigerant evapcration and controls the amount of refrigerant passing the orifice.

Compressor
The low pressure refrigerant gas is compressed to a high pressure and high temperature.

Fresh air

Receiver Drier
Stores the liquid refrigerant and removes moisture and foreign particles as the refrigerant recirculates within the system.

Low Pressure Switch
Turns OFF at pressures below 196 kPa (2kg/cm², 28 psi), cutting compressor power supply.

Condenser
The heated and compressed refrigerant gas from the compressor condenses to a liquid.

High Pressure Valve
Discharges refrigerant to atmosphere at pressures above 3,727 KPa (38 kg/cm², 540 psi).

27

6

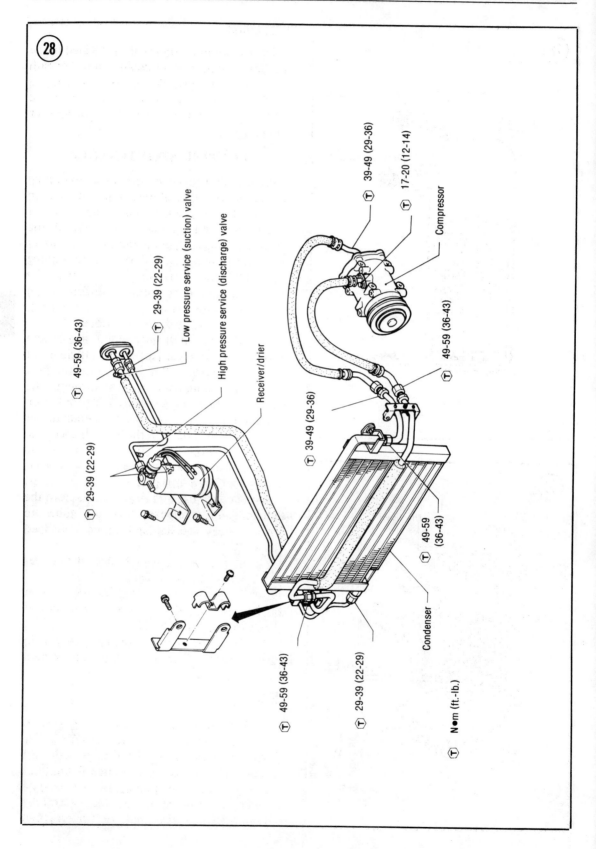

(28)

49-59 (36-43) T

29-39 (22-29) T

Low pressure service (suction) valve

High pressure service (discharge) valve

39-49 (29-36) T

17-20 (12-14) T

Compressor

Receiver/drier

49-59 (36-43) T

29-39 (22-29) T

39-49 (29-36) T

49-59 (36-43) T

Condenser

49-59 (36-43) T

29-39 (22-29) T

N•m (ft.-lb.)

T

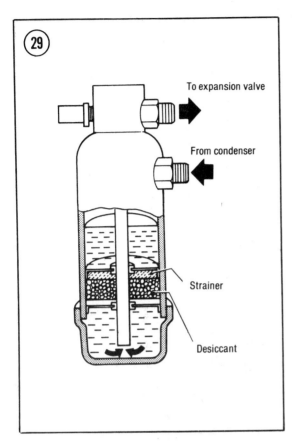

(29)

To expansion valve

From condenser

Strainer

Desiccant

Evaporator

The evaporator (**Figure 30**) is located in the passenger compartment cooling unit, beneath the instrument panel. Warm air is blown across the fins and tubes, where it is cooled and dried and then ducted into the passenger compartment.

ROUTINE MAINTENANCE

Basic maintenance of the air conditioning system is easy; at least once a month, even in cold weather, start your engine, turn on the air conditioner and operate it at each of the control settings. Operate the air conditioner for about 10 minutes, with the engine running at 1,500 rpm. This will ensure that the compressor seal does not deform from sitting in the same position for a long period of time. If this occurs, the seal is likely to leak.

The efficiency of the air conditioning system also depends in great part on the efficiency of the cooling system. This is because the heat from the condenser passes through the radiator. If the cooling system is dirty or low on coolant, it may be impossible to operate the air conditioner without overheating. Inspect the coolant. If necessary, flush and refill the cooling system as described under *Cooling System Flushing* in this chapter.

With an air hose and a soft brush, clean the radiator and condenser fins and tubes to remove bugs, leaves and other imbedded debris.

Check drive belt tension as described under *Drive Belts*, Chapter Three.

If the condition of the cooling system thermostat is in doubt, test it as described under *Thermostat* in this chapter.

Once you are sure the cooling system is in good condition, the air conditioning system can be inspected.

Inspection

1. Clean all lines, fittings and system components with solvent and a clean rag. Pay particular attention to the fittings; oily dirt around connections almost certainly indicates a leak. Oil from the compressor will migrate through the system to the leak. Carefully tighten the connection, but don't overtighten

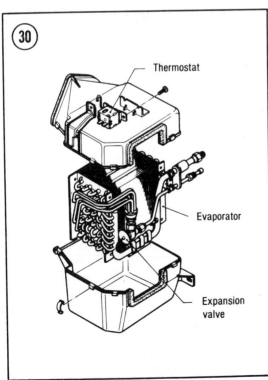

(30)

Thermostat

Evaporator

Expansion valve

6

and strip the threads. If the leak persists, it will soon be apparent once again as oily dirt accumulates. Clean the sight glass with a clean, dry cloth.

2. Clean the condenser fins and tubes with a soft brush and an air hose or with a high-pressure stream of water from a garden hose. Remove bugs, leaves and other imbedded debris. Carefully straighten any bent fins with a screwdriver, taking care not to puncture or dent the tubes.

3. Start the engine and check the operation of the blower motor and the compressor clutch by turning the controls on and off. If either the blower or the clutch fails to operate, shut off the engine and check the fuses and fusible links. If they are burned out, replace them. If the fuses are good, remove them and clean the fuse holder contacts. Then check the clutch and blower operation again.

Testing

1. Place the transmission in NEUTRAL. Set the parking brake.
2. Start the engine and run it at a fast idle.
3. Set the temperature control to its coldest setting and the blower to high. Allow the system to operate for 10 minutes with the doors and windows open. Then shut them and set the blower on its lowest setting.
4. Check air temperature at the outlet. It should be noticeably colder than the surrounding air. If not, the refrigerant level is probably low. Check the sight glass as described in the following step.
5. Run the engine at a fast idle and switch on the air conditioning. Look at the sight glass (**Figure 31**) and check for the following:
   a. Bubbles—the refrigerant level is low.
   b. Oily or cloudy—the system is contaminated. Have it serviced by a dealer or air conditioning shop.
   c. Clear glass—either there is enough refrigerant, too much or the system is so close to empty it can't make bubbles. If there is no difference between the inlet and outlet air temperatures, the system is probably near empty. If the system does blow cold air, it either has the right amount of refrigerant or too much. To

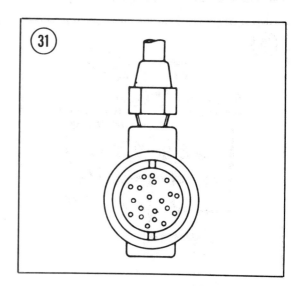

tell which, turn off the air conditioner while watching the sight glass. If the refrigerant foams, then clears up, the amount is correct. If it doesn't foam, but stays clear, there is too much.

REFRIGERANT

The air conditioning system uses a refrigerant called dichlorodifluoromethane, or R-12.

> *WARNING*
> *R-12 creates freezing temperatures when it evaporates. This can cause frostbite if it touches skin and blindness if it touches the eyes. If discharged near an open flame, R-12 creates poisonous gas. If the refrigerant can is hooked up to the pressure side of the compressor, it may explode. Always wear safety goggles when working with R-12.*

Charging

This section applies to partially discharged or empty air conditioning systems. If a hose has been disconnected or any internal part of the system exposed to air, the system should be evacuated and recharged by a dealer or air conditioning shop.

Recharge kits are available from auto parts stores. Be sure the kit includes a gauge set.

1. Carefully read and understand the gauge manufacturer's instructions before charging the system.

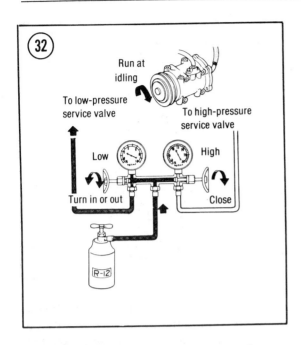

Run at idling

To low-pressure service valve

To high-pressure service valve

Low

High

Turn in or out

Close

R-12

2. Place the refrigerant can in a pan of *warm* water, *not hot.*

WARNING
Water temperature must not exceed 40° C (104° F). If it does, the can may explode.

3. Turn the handle of the refrigerant can tap valve all the way counterclockwise to retract the needle.
4. Turn the disc on the can tap valve all the way counterclockwise. Install the valve on the can.
5. Connect the center hose to the can tap valve.
6. Make sure the gauge valves are closed.
7. Turn the can tap valve clockwise to make a hole in the can.
8. Turn the handle all the way counterclockwise to fill the center hose with air.
9. Slowly loosen the nut connecting the center hose to the gauge set, until hissing can be heard. Let this continue for a few seconds to purge air from the hose, then tighten the nut.

CAUTION
During the next steps, the refrigerant can must remain upright. If it is turned upside down, refrigerant will enter the system as a liquid, which may damage the compressor.

10. Open the low pressure valve (**Figure 32**). Adjust the valve so the gauge reads no more than 2.8 kg/cm^2 (40 psi).

CAUTION
Leave the high pressure valve closed at all times.

11. Run the engine at idle (below 1,500 rpm) and turn on the air conditioner. Let the system charge until the sight glass is free of air bubbles. See **Figure 31**.

NOTE
If the system is nearly empty, another can of refrigerant will be needed. Attach it as described in the following steps.

12. Close the low pressure valve.
13. Remove the can tap valve and attach a new can. Don't make a hole in the new can yet.
14. Slightly loosen the can tap valve disc. Barely open the low pressure valve for a few seconds to purge air from the hose. Close the low pressure valve, then tighten the can tap valve disc.
15. Turn the can tap valve handle clockwise to make a hole in the can. Let the system charge until the sight glass is free of air bubbles.
16. Once the system is fully charged, close the low pressure valve.
17. Close the can tap valve. Very slowly loosen the charge line to allow any remaining refrigerant to escape.

WARNING
Wear gloves and safety goggles to prevent frostbite and blindness. Do not allow any open flame near the refrigerant or poisonous gas may be formed.

18. Turn off the engine. Cover the compressor service valve fittings with a shop rag, then quickly disconnect them.
19. Install the caps on the service valves.

TROUBLESHOOTING

If the air conditioner fails to blow cold air, the following steps will help locate the problem.
1. First, stop the truck and look at the control settings. One of the most common air conditioning problems occurs when the temperature is set for maximum cold and the

blower is set on low. This promotes ice buildup on the evaporator fins and tubes, particularly in humid weather. Eventually, the evaporator will ice over completely and restrict air flow. Turn the blower on high and place a hand over an air outlet. If the blower is running but there is little or no air flowing through the outlet, the evaporator is probably iced up. Leave the blower on high and turn the temperature control off or to its warmest setting and wait. It will take 10-15 minutes for the ice to start melting.

2. If the blower is not running, the fuse or fusible link may be blown, there may be a loose wiring connection or the motor may be burned out. First, check the fuse block for a blown or incorrectly seated fuse. Check for a burned out fusible link. Then check the wiring for loose connections.

3. Shut off the engine and inspect the compressor drive belt. If loose or worn, tighten or replace. See *Drive Belts*, Chapter Three.

4. Start the engine. Check the compressor clutch by turning the air conditioner on and off. If the clutch does not activate, its fuse or fusible link may be blown or the evaporator temperature-limiting switches may be defective. If the fuse or fusible link is defective, replace it. If not, have the system checked by a dealer or air conditioning shop.

5. If the system checks out okay to this point, start the engine, turn on the air conditioner and watch the refrigerant through the sight glass. If it fills with bubbles after a few seconds, the refrigerant level is low. If the sight glass is oily or cloudy, the system is contaminated and should be serviced by a shop as soon as possible. Corrosion and deterioration occur very quickly and if not taken care of at once will result in a very expensive repair job.

6. If the system still appears to be operating as it should but air flow into the passenger compartment is not cold, check the condenser and cooling system radiator for debris that could block air flow. Recheck the cooling system as described under *Inspection*.

7. If the preceding steps have not solved the problem, take the car to a dealer or air conditioning shop for service.

Table 1   COOLING SYSTEM SPECIFICATIONS

Cooling system capacity (including reservoir tank)	
1980	8.9 liters (9-3/8 qt.)
1981	10.2 liters (10-3/4 qt.)
Thermostat opening temperature*	
Standard type	82° C (180° F)
Cold area type	88° C (190° F)
Hot area type	76.5° C (170° F)
Thermostat valve lift	
Standard type	8 mm (5/16 in.) @ 95° C (203° F)
Cold area type	8 mm (5/16 in.) @ 100° C (212° F)
Hot area type	8 mm (5/16 in.) @ 90° C (104° F)

*Actual opening temperature may vary slightly. This does not   indicate a defective thermostat.

ELECTRICAL SYSTEM

7

This chapter provides service procedures for the battery, charging system, starter lights, switches, horn, windshield washers, fuses and fusible links, turn signals, and ignition system. Wiring diagrams are included at the end of the book. **Table 1** and **Table 2** are at the end of the chapter.

BATTERY

Care and Inspection

1. Disconnect both battery cables and remove the battery.
2. Clean the top of the battery with a baking soda and water solution. Scrub it with a stiff bristle brush. Wipe battery clean with a cloth moistened in ammonia or baking soda solution.

CAUTION
Keep cleaning solution out of battery cells or the electrolyte will be seriously weakened.

3. Clean battery terminals with a stiff wire brush or one of the many tools made for this purpose.

4. Check entire battery case for cracks.
5. Install the battery and reconnect the battery cables.

CAUTION
Be sure the battery cables are connected to the proper terminals. Connecting the battery backwards can damage the alternator.

6. Coat the battery connections with Vaseline or light mineral grease after tightening.
7. If the battery has removable filler caps, check electrolyte level. Top up with distilled water if necessary.

Testing

This procedure applies to batteries with removable filler caps. Testing sealed maintenance-free batteries requires special equipment, but a service station can make the test for a nominal fee.

Hydrometer testing is the best way to check battery condition. Use a hydrometer with numbered graduations from 1.100-1.300 rather than one with just color-coded bands.

To use the hydrometer, squeeze the rubber ball, insert the tip in the cell and release the ball (**Figure 1**).

Draw enough electrolyte to float the weighted float inside the hydrometer. Note the number in line with the surface of the electrolyte. This is the specific gravity for the cell. Return the electrolyte to the cell from which it came.

The specific gravity of the electrolyte in each battery cell is an excellent indicator of that cell's condition. A fully charged cell will read 1.260 or more at 20° C (68° F). If the cells test below 1.200, the battery must be recharged. Charging is also necessary if the specific gravity of the cell varies more than 0.025 from cell to cell.

NOTE
Specific gravity varies with electrolyte temperature. For every 6° below 25° C (80° F), subtract 0.004 from the reading. For every 6° above 25° C (80° F), add 0.004 to the reading.

Charging

The battery need not be removed from the car for charging. Just make certain that the area is well-ventilated and that there is no chance of sparks or flames occurring near the battery.

WARNING
Charging batteries give off highly explosive hydrogen gas. If this explodes, it may spray battery acid over a wide area.

Disconnect the cables from the battery. On fillable batteries, make sure the electrolyte is fully topped up.

Connect the charger to the battery— negative to negative, positive to positive. If the charger output is variable, select a low setting (5-10 amps), set the voltage selector to 12 volts and plug the charger in. If the battery is severely discharged, allow it to charge for at least 8 hours. Batteries that aren't as badly discharged require less charging time. **Table 1** gives approximate charge rates. On fillable batteries, check charging progress with the hydrometer.

Charging System Test

On all models, refer to **Figure 2** for this procedure. On 1980 models, refer to **Figure 3** as well; on 1981 models, refer to **Figure 4**.

CHARGING SYSTEM

The charging system consists of the battery, alternator, voltage regulator and wiring. The regulator is an integrated circuit type, built into the alternator.

Alternator repair is not practical for home mechanics. If test procedures indicate a defective alternator, replace it with a new or rebuilt unit.

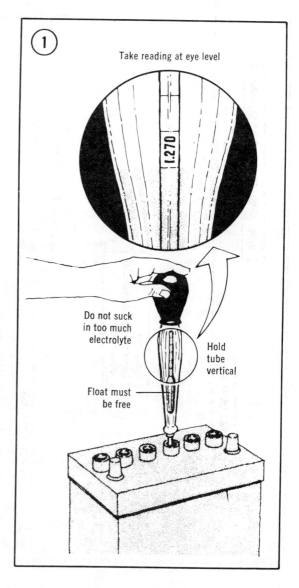

Take reading at eye level

1.270

Do not suck in too much electrolyte

Hold tube vertical

Float must be free

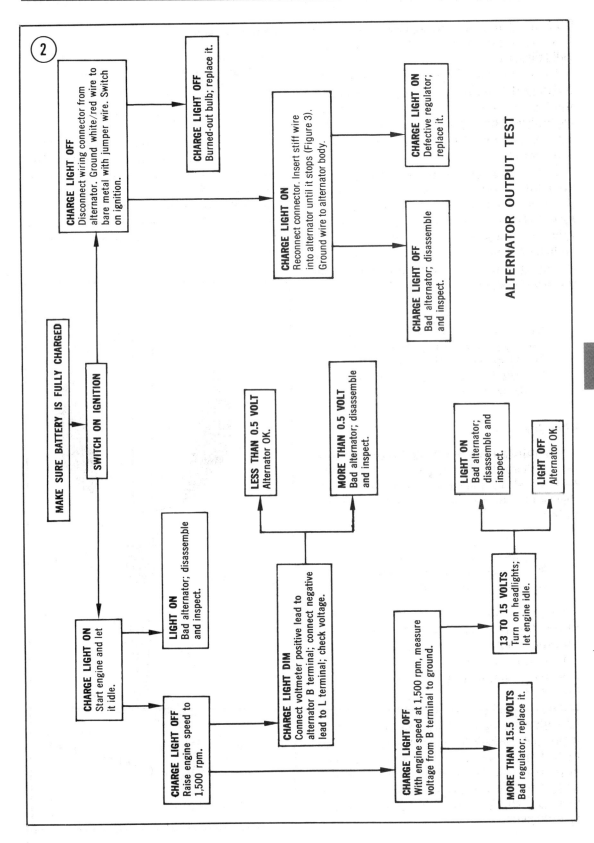

②

CHARGE LIGHT OFF
Disconnect wiring connector from alternator. Ground white/red wire to bare metal with jumper wire. Switch on ignition.

CHARGE LIGHT OFF
Burned-out bulb; replace it.

CHARGE LIGHT ON
Reconnect connector. Insert stiff wire into alternator until it stops (Figure 3). Ground wire to alternator body.

CHARGE LIGHT ON
Defective regulator; replace it.

CHARGE LIGHT OFF
Bad alternator; disassemble and inspect.

ALTERNATOR OUTPUT TEST

MAKE SURE BATTERY IS FULLY CHARGED

SWITCH ON IGNITION

7

LESS THAN 0.5 VOLT
Alternator OK.

MORE THAN 0.5 VOLT
Bad alternator; disassemble and inspect.

LIGHT ON
Bad alternator; disassemble and inspect.

LIGHT OFF
Alternator OK.

CHARGE LIGHT ON
Start engine and let it idle.

LIGHT ON
Bad alternator; disassemble and inspect.

CHARGE LIGHT DIM
Connect voltmeter positive lead to alternator B terminal; connect negative lead to L terminal; check voltage.

CHARGE LIGHT OFF
With engine speed at 1,500 rpm, measure voltage from B terminal to ground.

13 TO 15 VOLTS
Turn on headlights; let engine idle.

CHARGE LIGHT OFF
Raise engine speed to 1,500 rpm.

MORE THAN 15.5 VOLTS
Bad regulator; replace it.

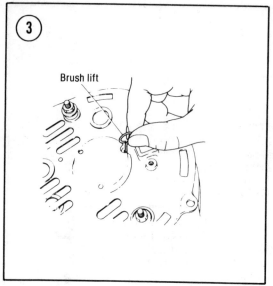

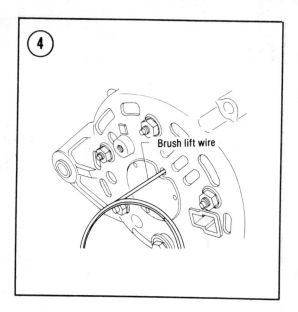

Alternator Removal/Installation

1. Disconnect the negative cable from the battery.
2. Disconnect the wires from the alternator.
3. Loosen and remove the alternator drive belt. See *Drive Belts*, Chapter Three.
4. Remove the alternator mounting and adjusting bolts. Lift the alternator out.
5. Installation is the reverse of removal. Adjust alternator belt tension as described under *Drive Belts*, Chapter Three.

Regulator Replacement

This procedure requires partial disassembly of the alternator. If test procedures indicate a defective regulator, the regulator can be replaced by a dealer or electrical shop. However, the cost of replacement should be compared to the price of a rebuilt alternator.

STARTER

All models use a conventional starter (**Figure 5**). Canadian models use a reduction gear starter (**Figure 6**).

Starter overhaul is not practical for home mechanics. If test procedures indicate a problem other than with solenoid or brushes, replace the starter with a new or rebuilt unit.

Starter Testing

Refer to **Figure 7** for this procedure.

Starter Removal/Installation

1. Disconnect the negative cable from the battery.
2. Disconnect the thin black-yellow or black-red wire and thick black cable from the solenoid. Do not disconnect the wire running from solenoid to starter body.
3. Remove the starter mounting bolts. Pull the starter forward, then take it out.
4. Installation is the reverse of removal. Tighten the starter mounting bolts to 29-39 N•m (22-29 ft.-lb.).

Solenoid Replacement

1. Remove the starter as described in this chapter.
2. Disconnect the wire running from solenoid to starter.
3. Remove the solenoid attaching bolts.
4. Unhook the solenoid plunger from the shift lever inside the starter. Lift the solenoid off.
5. Installation is the reverse of removal.

Brush Replacement (Conventional Starter)

1. Remove the starter as described earlier.
2. Remove the dust cover, snap ring and thrust washer(s) from the front end of the starter. See **Figure 5**.

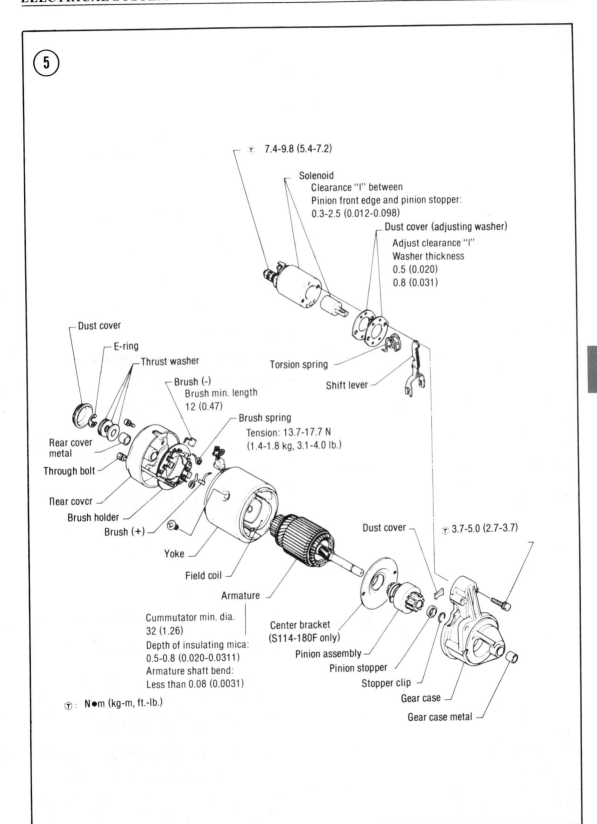

⑤

ⓣ 7.4-9.8 (5.4-7.2)

Solenoid
Clearance "I" between
Pinion front edge and pinion stopper:
0.3-2.5 (0.012-0.098)
Dust cover (adjusting washer)
Adjust clearance "I"
Washer thickness
0.5 (0.020)
0.8 (0.031)

Dust cover
E-ring
Thrust washer
Brush (-)
Brush min. length
12 (0.47)
Brush spring
Tension: 13.7-17.7 N
(1.4-1.8 kg, 3.1-4.0 lb.)

Torsion spring
Shift lever

Rear cover metal
Through bolt
Rear cover
Brush holder
Brush (+)
Yoke
Field coil
Armature

Cummutator min. dia.
32 (1.26)
Depth of insulating mica:
0.5-0.8 (0.020-0.0311)
Armature shaft bend:
Less than 0.08 (0.0031)

Dust cover
ⓣ 3.7-5.0 (2.7-3.7)

Center bracket
(S114-180F only)
Pinion assembly
Pinion stopper
Stopper clip
Gear case
Gear case metal

ⓣ: N●m (kg-m, ft.-lb.)

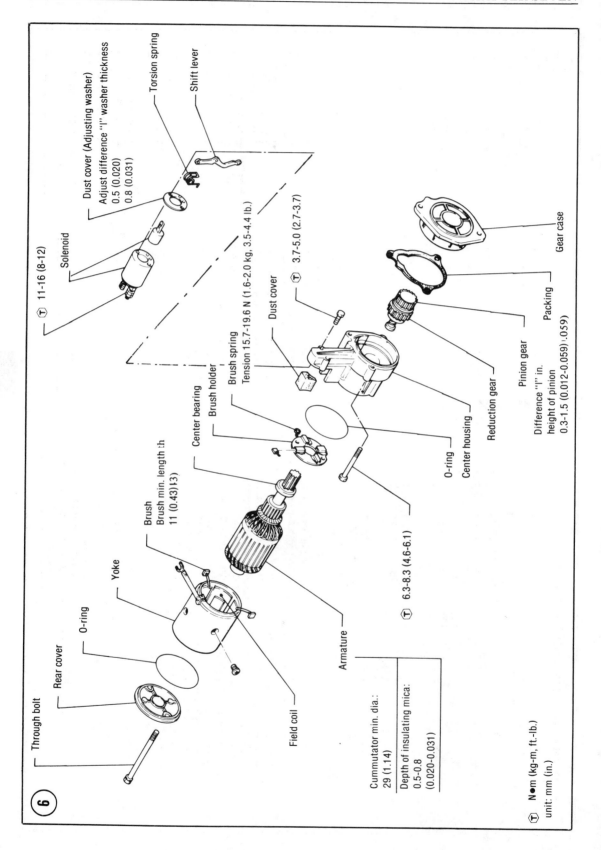

Through bolt

Rear cover

O-ring

Yoke

Brush
Brush min. length th
11 (0.43)├3

Center bearing

Brush holder

Brush spring
Tension 15.7-19.6 N (1.6-2.0 kg, 3.5-4.4 lb.)

Dust cover

Solenoid

Dust cover (Adjusting washer)
Adjust difference "l" washer thickness
0.5 (0.020)
0.8 (0.031)

Torsion spring

Shift lever

Ⓣ 11-16 (8-12)

Ⓣ 3.7-5.0 (2.7-3.7)

Gear case

Packing

Pinion gear

Difference "l" in.
height of pinion
0.3-1.5 (0.012-0.059) .059)

Reduction gear

Center housing

O-ring

Ⓣ 6.3-8.3 (4.6-6.1)

Armature

Field coil

Cummutator min. dia.:
29 (1.14)

Depth of insulating mica:
0.5-0.8
(0.020-0.031)

Ⓣ N●m (kg-m, ft.-lb.)
unit: mm (in.)

⑥

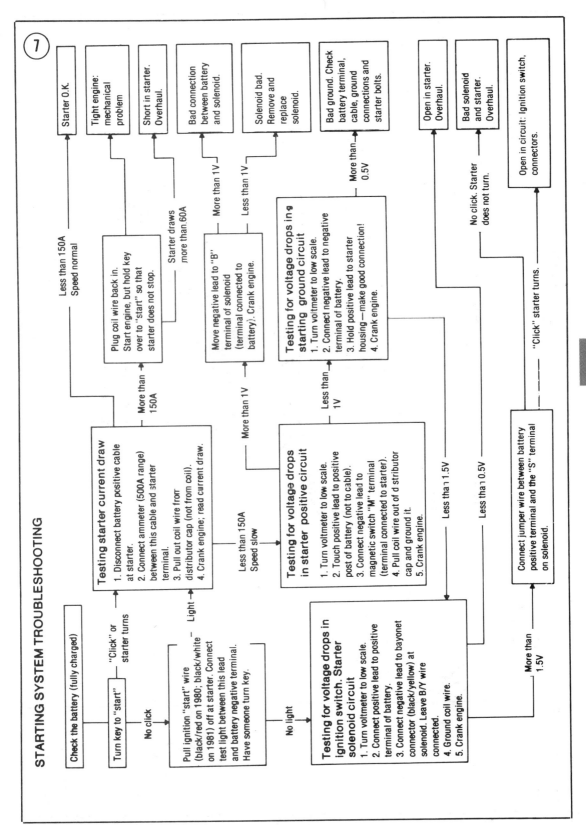

STARTING SYSTEM TROUBLESHOOTING

⑦

Check the battery (fully charged)

Turn key to "start"

No click ———

Pull ignition "start" wire (black/red on 1980; black/white on 1981) off at starter. Connect test light between this lead and battery negative terminal. Have someone turn key.

No light ———

Testing for voltage drops in ignition switch. Starter solenoid circuit
1. Turn voltmeter to low scale.
2. Connect positive lead to positive terminal of battery.
3. Connect negative lead to bayonet connector (black/yellow) at solenoid. Leave B/Y wire connected.
4. Ground coil wire.
5. Crank engine.

"Click" or starter turns

— Light —

Testing starter current draw
1. Disconnect battery positive cable at starter.
2. Connect ammeter (500A range) between this cable and starter terminal.
3. Pull out coil wire from distributor cap (not from coil).
4. Crank engine; read current draw.

Less than 150A
Speed slow

Testing for voltage drops in starter positive circuit
1. Turn voltmeter to low scale.
2. Touch positive lead to positive post of battery (not to cable).
3. Connect negative lead to magnetic switch "M" terminal (terminal connected to starter).
4. Pull coil wire out of distributor cap and ground it.
5. Crank engine.

Connect jumper wire between battery positive terminal and the "S" terminal on solenoid.

More than 150A

Plug coil wire back in. Start engine, but hold key over to "start" so that starter does not stop.

Starter draws more than 60A

More than 1V ———

Move negative lead to "B" terminal of solenoid (terminal connected to battery). Crank engine.

Less than 1V ———

Testing for voltage drops in starting ground circuit
1. Turn voltmeter to low scale.
2. Connect negative lead to negative terminal of battery.
3. Hold positive lead to starter housing—make good connection!
4. Crank engine.

More than 0.5V

Less than 1V ———

Less than 1.5V ———

Less than 0.5V ———

More than 1.5V

Less than 150A
Speed normal

Starter O.K.

Tight engine: mechanical problem

Short in starter. Overhaul.

Bad connection between battery and solenoid.

Solenoid bad. Remove and replace solenoid.

Bad ground. Check battery terminal, cable, ground connections and starter bolts.

Open in starter. Overhaul.

Bad solenoid and starter. Overhaul.

No click. Starter does not turn.

"Click" starter turns.

Open in circuit: Ignition switch, connectors.

7

3. Remove the through bolts and setscrews. Take the end cover off the starter. See **Figure 8**.

4. Make a wire hook and pull back the brush springs (**Figure 9**). Slide the brushes out of their slots.

5. Measure brush length. It should be more than 12 mm (1/2 in.). Replace worn brushes.

6. Check brush movement in the slots. Clean the slots and brushes if movement is not smooth. Examine brush springs. It should take a pull of 1.4-1.8 kg (3.1-4.0 lb.) to bend the springs. Replace weak springs.

7. Check the brush holder for shorts to ground. Use an ohmmeter or a continuity tester such as the one shown in **Figure 10**.

Touch one tester lead to the brush holder and the other to the positive brush slots. These are the 2 slots with insulating material under them. If the ohmmeter shows continuity (test lamp lights), a short circuit exists. Replace the brush holder.

8. Install brushes by reversing Steps 1-4.

CAUTION
Use resin core solder when soldering brush leads. Do not use acid core solder.

Brush Replacement (Reduction Gear Starter)

1. Remove the through-bolts and front cover from the starter.

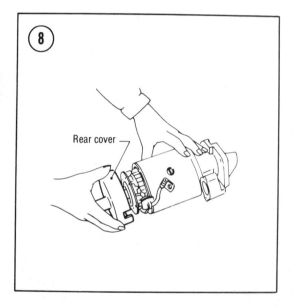

Rear cover

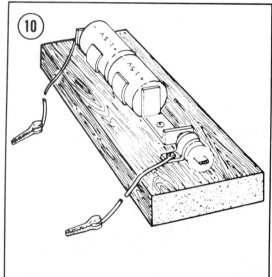

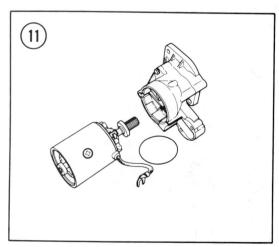

2. Separate the yoke from the center housing. See **Figure 11**.

3. Make a wire hook and pull back the positive brush springs. See **Figure 12**. Pull the positive brushes out of their slots.

> *NOTE*
> *The positive brushes are attached to the field coil, not to the brush holder.*

4. Slide the brush holder off of the commutator. Remove the negative brushes from their slots.

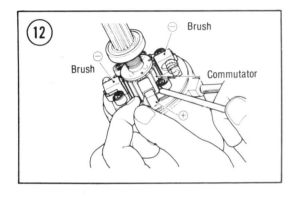

5. Measure brush length. Minimum brush length is 11 mm (7/16 in.). Replace the brushes if any are shorter than the minimum.

6. Check brush movement in the slots. Clean the slots and brushes if movement is not smooth. Examine brush springs. Replace if weak or damaged.

7. Check the brush holder for shorts to ground. Use an ohmmeter or a continuity tester like the one shown in **Figure 10**. Touch one probe to the brush holder and the other to the positive (insulated) brush slots. If the ohmmeter shows continuity (test lamp lights), replace the brush holder.

LIGHTING SYSTEM

Table 2 lists bulb specifications.

Headlight Replacement

1. Turn the grille fasteners to release them (**Figure 13**), then take the grille out.

2. Remove the headlight retaining screws (**Figure 14**). Take the bulb out.

> *NOTE*
> *Do not turn the aiming screws.*

3. Installation is the reverse of removal. If necessary, have headlight aim adjusted by a dealer or service station.

Other Bulbs

All bulbs except the headlights and instrument panel bulbs are type A, B or C (**Figure 15**). To replace a type A bulb, press it into its socket and turn counterclockwise to remove. To replace type B or C bulbs, pull the bulb out.

7

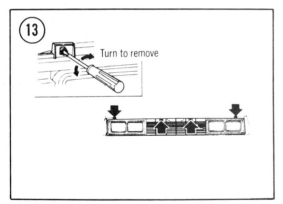

Turn to remove

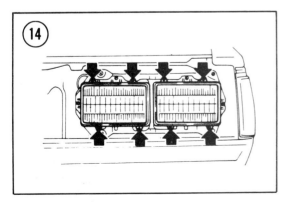

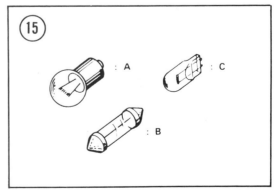

Refer to the following illustrations:

a. Front parking/turn signal lights—**Figure 16**

b. Front side marker lights—**Figure 17**

c. Rear side marker, brake, tail and back-up lights—**Figure 18**

d. License plate lights—**Figure 19**

e. Interior light—**Figure 20**

To replace instrument panel bulbs, remove the instrument cluster. See *Instruments* in this chapter.

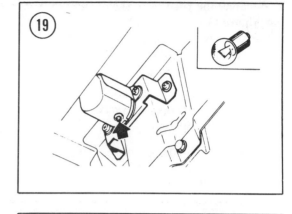

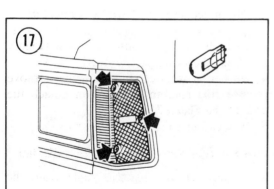

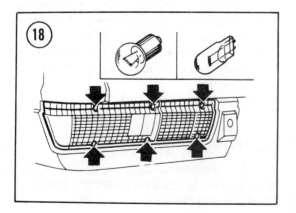

EXCEPT KING CAB   KING CAB

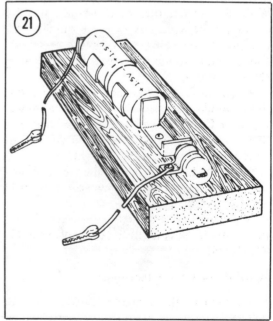

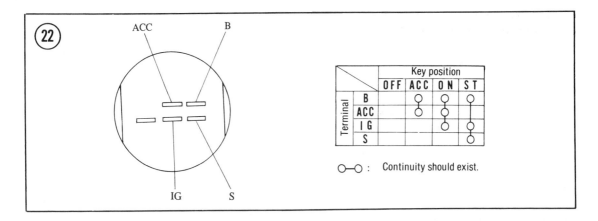

		OFF	ACC	ON	ST
		Key position			
Terminal	B		○	○	
	ACC		○	○	
	IG			○	○
	S				○

○—○ : Continuity should exist.

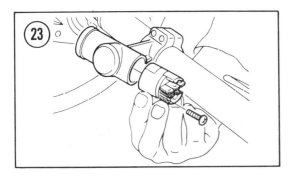

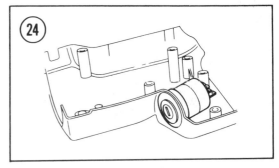

7

SWITCHES

Switches can be tested with an ohmmeter or continuity tester like the one shown in **Figure 21**. To test the ignition switch, for example, disconnect its wiring connector. See **Figure 22**. With the switch off, there should not be continuity between any of the terminals. An ohmmeter connected between the terminals should show infinite resistance and a test lamp should stay out.

When the key is turned to the ACC position, there should be continuity between terminals B and ACC. An ohmmeter connected between these terminals should show little or no resistance. A test lamp should light.

When the key is turned to the ON position, there should be continuity between terminals B, ACC and IG.

When the key is turned to the ST position, there should be continuity between terminals ST, IG and S.

Ignition Switch Replacement

1. Disconnect the negative cable from the battery.

2. Disconnect the switch wiring connector.
3. On trucks equipped with steering locks, remove the switch mounting screw (**Figure 23**). Take the switch off the steering lock.
4. On trucks without steering locks, remove the steering column cover, then detach the switch. See **Figure 24**.
5. Installation is the reverse of removal.

Combination Switch Removal/Installation

1. Disconnect the negative cable from the battery.
2. Remove the steering wheel. See *Steering Wheel Removal/Installation*, Chapter Nine.
3. Remove the steering column shell.
4. Disconnect the switch wiring connectors.
5. Detach the switch from the steering column and take it off.
6. Installation is the reverse of removal.

Combination Switch Test

The combination switch is tested in the same manner as the ignition switch, described in this chapter.

1. To test the lighting switch, refer to **Figure 25** (1980) or **Figure 26** (1981).
2. To test the turn signal or horn switch, refer to **Figure 27**.
3. To test the wiper/washer switch, refer to **Figure 28**.

INSTRUMENTS

Cluster Removal/Installation

Refer to **Figure 29** for this procedure.
1. Disconnect the negative cable from the battery.
2. Reach behind the instrument panel. Disconnect the speedometer cable and gauge wiring.
3. Remove the cluster cover screws (**Figure 30**).
4. Remove the cluster screws (**Figure 31**) and take the cluster out.
5. To replace individual gauges, disassemble the cluster, referring to **Figure 29**.
6. To replace bulbs, refer to **Figure 32** (1980) or **Figure 33** (1981).

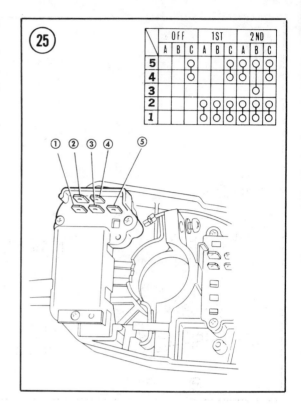

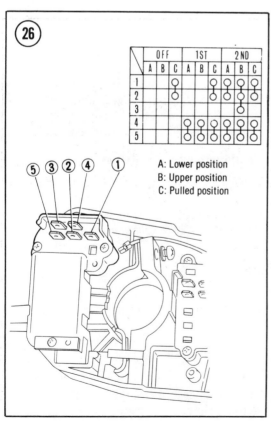

A: Lower position
B: Upper position
C: Pulled position

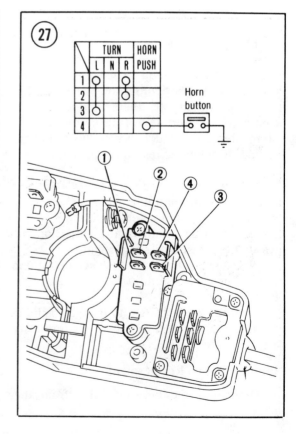

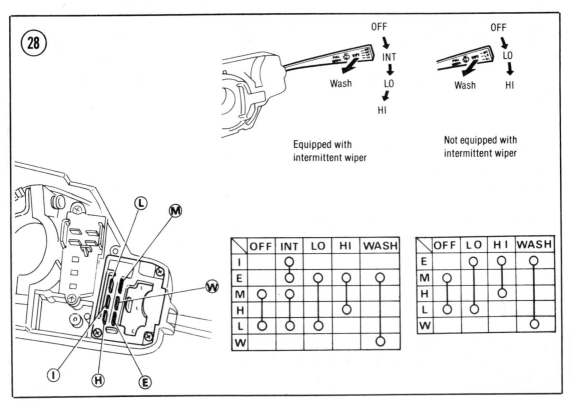

	OFF	INT	LO	HI	WASH
I		○			
E		○	○	○	○
M	○	○			
H				○	
L	○	○	○		
W					○

	OFF	LO	HI	WASH
E		○	○	○
M	○			
H			○	
L	○	○		
W				○

Equipped with intermittent wiper

Not equipped with intermittent wiper

7

INSTRUMENT PANEL

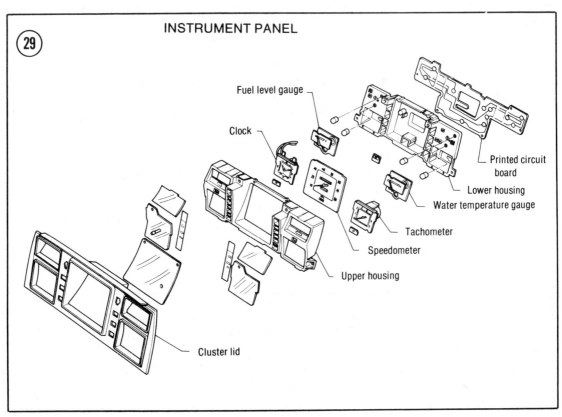

Fuel level gauge

Clock

Printed circuit board

Lower housing

Water temperature gauge

Tachometer

Speedometer

Upper housing

Cluster lid

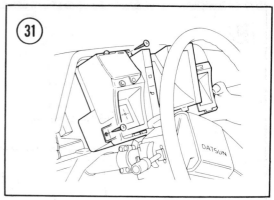

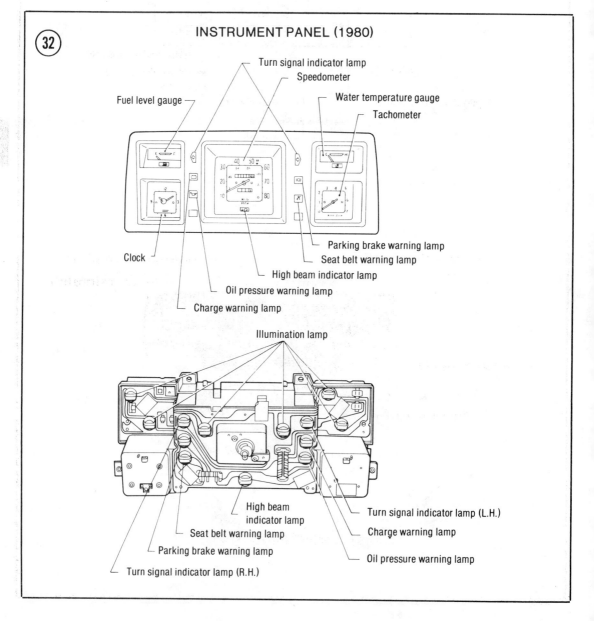

INSTRUMENT PANEL (1980)

Turn signal indicator lamp

Speedometer

Fuel level gauge

Water temperature gauge

Tachometer

Parking brake warning lamp

Seat belt warning lamp

High beam indicator lamp

Clock

Oil pressure warning lamp

Charge warning lamp

Illumination lamp

High beam indicator lamp

Turn signal indicator lamp (L.H.)

Seat belt warning lamp

Charge warning lamp

Parking brake warning lamp

Oil pressure warning lamp

Turn signal indicator lamp (R.H.)

(33)

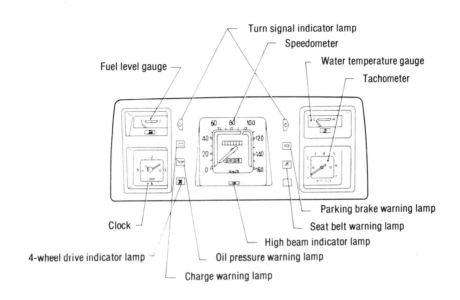

Turn signal indicator lamp
Speedometer
Water temperature gauge
Tachometer
Fuel level gauge

Parking brake warning lamp
Seat belt warning lamp
Clock
High beam indicator lamp
4-wheel drive indicator lamp
Oil pressure warning lamp
Charge warning lamp

7

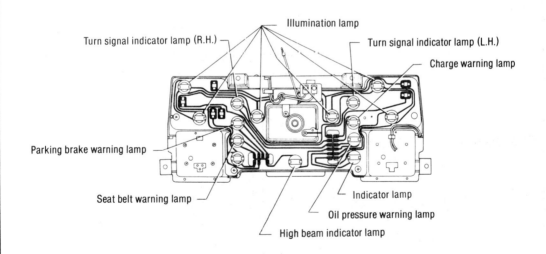

Illumination lamp
Turn signal indicator lamp (R.H.)
Turn signal indicator lamp (L.H.)
Charge warning lamp

Parking brake warning lamp

Seat belt warning lamp
Indicator lamp
Oil pressure warning lamp
High beam indicator lamp

INSTRUMENT PANEL (1981)

HORN

There are 2 horns, mounted at the front of the engine compartment.

Testing

1. If the horns work, but are not loud enough, make sure the wires are making good contact and the horns are properly grounded to the body.
2. If only one horn works, check the wiring to the non-working horn. If the horn is receiving current and is grounded properly, it is probably defective.
3. If neither horn works, check the horn fuse, then the battery as described in this chapter.
4. If the horn fuse and battery are good, remove the horn relay. This is mounted near the steering column (**Figure 34**).
5. Connect an ohmmeter or battery powered test lamp between the relay terminals shown in **Figure 35**. The ohmmeter should indicate infinite resistance (test lamp should stay out). If not, replace the relay.

NOTE
For the next step, use an ohmmeter or non-powered test lamp. Do not use a battery powered test lamp.

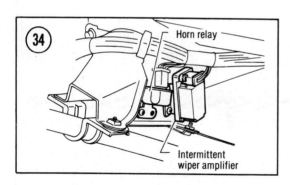

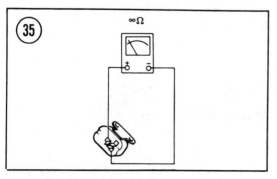

6. Set up the test circuit shown in **Figure 36**. The test lamp should light or ohmmeter should show continuity. If not, replace the relay.
7. If the horn relay is good, test the horn switch. This is part of the combination switch, described under *Switches* in this chapter.

Horn Removal/Installation

1. Disconnect the negative cable from the battery.
2. Remove the front parking/turn signal lamp assembly (**Figure 37**).
3. Disconnect the horn wires. Detach the horn and take it out.
4. Installation is the reverse of removal.

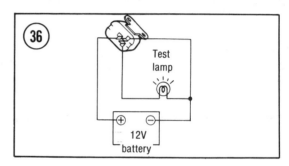

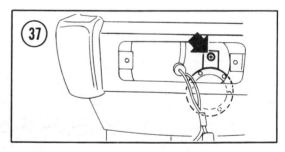

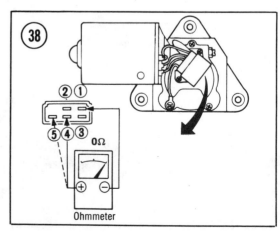

WINDSHIELD WIPERS
AND WASHERS

Wiper Motor Test

1. Disconnect the wiper motor wiring connector.

2. Identify the motor terminals, referring to **Figure 38**. There should be continuity between terminals 1 and 4 and between terminals 1 and 5. An ohmmeter connected between these terminals should indicate little or no resistance. A battery powered test lamp connected between the terminals should light. If not, replace the motor.

3. Connect a 12-volt battery between the terminals shown in **Figure 39**. The motor should run at low speed. If not, replace it.

4. With the motor still running, connect an ohmmeter or test lamp between the terminals shown in **Figure 40**. The ohmmeter should cycle from continuity to no continuity. The test lamp should light, then go out. If not, replace the motor.

Wiper Motor Removal/Installation

1. Disconnect the negative cable from the battery.

2. Disconnect the wiper motor wiring connector.

3. Detach the motor mounting bracket. See **Figure 41**.

4. Remove the nut securing the wiper motor to the linkage. Take the motor out.

5. Installation is the reverse of removal.

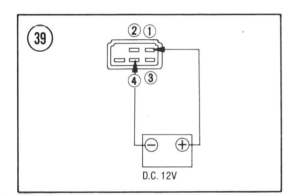

D.C. 12V

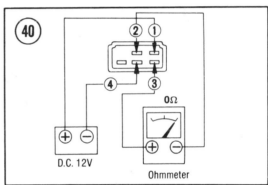

D.C. 12V

Ohmmeter

7

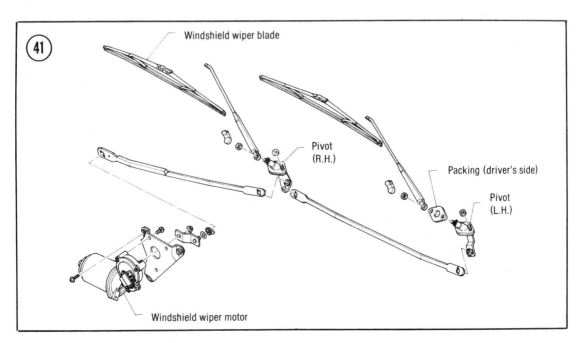

Windshield wiper blade

Pivot (R.H.)

Packing (driver's side)

Pivot (L.H.)

Windshield wiper motor

Washer Motor and Tank Removal/Installation

The windshield washer motor is mounted on the washer fluid tank. To remove, disconnect the motor wires and fluid hose. Take out the tank and detach the motor from it. Installation is the reverse of removal.

FUSES AND FUSIBLE LINKS

Fuse Replacement

The fuse block is located under the passenger side of the instrument panel (**Figure 42**). **Figure 43** identifies 1980 fuses. **Figure 44** identifies 1981 fuses.

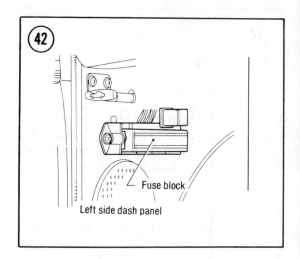

④		Fuse block
	Left side dash panel		

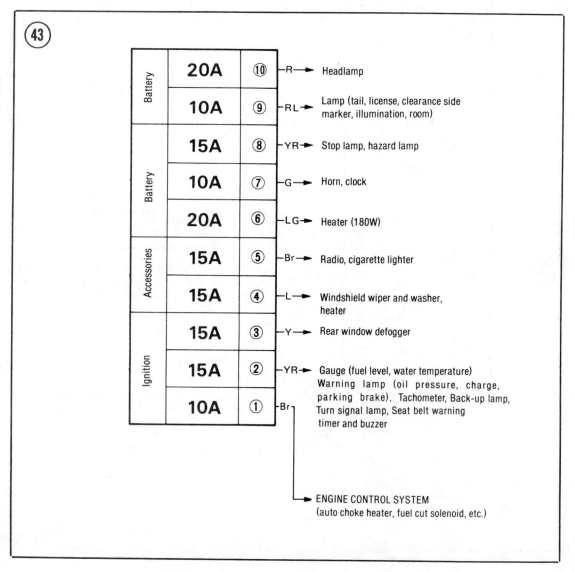

④

Battery	**20A**	⑩	R →	Headlamp
	10A	⑨	RL →	Lamp (tail, license, clearance side marker, illumination, room)
Battery	**15A**	⑧	YR →	Stop lamp, hazard lamp
	10A	⑦	G →	Horn, clock
	20A	⑥	LG →	Heater (180W)
Accessories	**15A**	⑤	Br →	Radio, cigarette lighter
	15A	④	L →	Windshield wiper and washer, heater
Ignition	**15A**	③	Y →	Rear window defogger
	15A	②	YR →	Gauge (fuel level, water temperature) Warning lamp (oil pressure, charge, parking brake), Tachometer, Back-up lamp, Turn signal lamp, Seat belt warning timer and buzzer
	10A	①	Br →	

ENGINE CONTROL SYSTEM (auto choke heater, fuel cut solenoid, etc.)

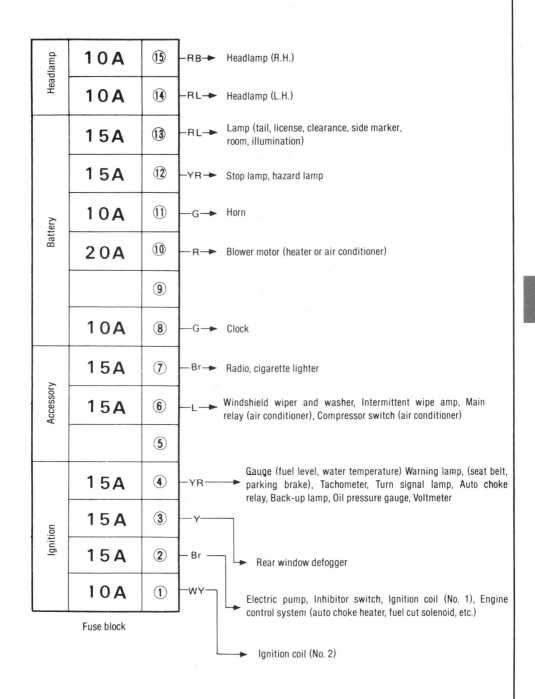

Headlamp	**10A**	⑮	─RB➤	Headlamp (R.H.)
	10A	⑭	─RL➤	Headlamp (L.H.)
Battery	**15A**	⑬	─RL➤	Lamp (tail, license, clearance, side marker, room, illumination)
	15A	⑫	─YR➤	Stop lamp, hazard lamp
	10A	⑪	─G➤	Horn
	20A	⑩	─R➤	Blower motor (heater or air conditioner)
		⑨		
	10A	⑧	─G➤	Clock
Accessory	**15A**	⑦	─Br➤	Radio, cigarette lighter
	15A	⑥	─L➤	Windshield wiper and washer, Intermittent wipe amp, Main relay (air conditioner), Compressor switch (air conditioner)
		⑤		
Ignition	**15A**	④	─YR─	Gauge (fuel level, water temperature) Warning lamp, (seat belt, parking brake), Tachometer, Turn signal lamp, Auto choke relay, Back-up lamp, Oil pressure gauge, Voltmeter
	15A	③	─Y─	
	15A	②	─Br─	Rear window defogger
	10A	①	─WY─	Electric pump, Inhibitor switch, Ignition coil (No. 1), Engine control system (auto choke heater, fuel cut solenoid, etc.)

Fuse block

Ignition coil (No. 2)

7

To replace, pull out the old fuse. If the fuse holder is corroded, sand it clean. Be sure the new fuse has the same amperage rating as the old one.

Whenever a fuse blows, find out the cause before replacing. Usually the trouble is a short circuit in the wiring. This may be caused by worn-through insulation or by a wire that works its way loose and touches metal. Carry several spare fuses in the glove compartment.

CAUTION
Never substitute tinfoil or wire for a fuse. An overload could cause a fire and complete loss of the truck.

Fusible Link Replacement

Fusible links are short sections of thin wire in a thicker wire. They are intended to burn out if an overload occurs, thus protecting the wiring harnesses.

The fusible links are located next to the battery (**Figure 45**). Burned-out fusible links can usually be detected by melted or burned insulation. They may smoke before burning out. Suspect links with no apparent damage can be checked for continuity with an ohmmeter or self-powered test lamp. If a link burns out, unplug it and plug in a new one.

TURN SIGNALS AND HAZARD FLASHERS

Inspection

1. *Turn signals don't work, but hazard flashers do*: Check the fuse. On 1980 models, check the red fusible link. On 1981 models, check the green fusible link. See *Fuses and Fusible Links* in this chapter.

If the fuse and fusible link are good, check the wiring. Wiring diagrams are at the end of the book.

If the wiring is good, test the turn signal switch. See *Switches* in this chapter.

If the turn signal switch is good, disconnect the wiring connector from the hazard switch. Identify terminals 1 and 2, referring to **Figure 46**. Connect a test lead (wire and 15-amp fuse) between the corresponding terminals in the wiring harness. If the turn signals operate, replace the hazard flasher switch.

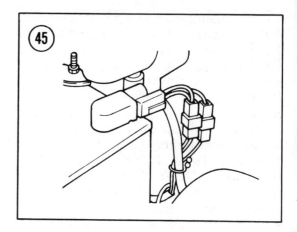

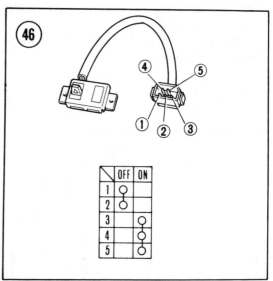

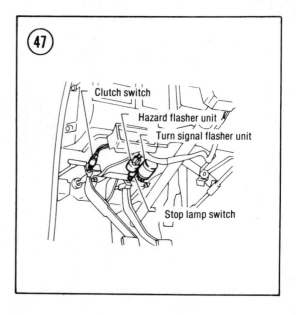

If the hazard flasher switch is good, replace the turn signal flasher unit. See **Figure 47**.

2. *Hazard lamps don't work, but turn signals do*: Check the fuse. If the fuse is good, check the red fusible link (1980) or black fusible link (1981). See *Fuses and Fusible Links* in this chapter.

If the fuse and fusible links are good, test the hazard switch. Identify terminals 3, 4, and 5 referring to **Figure 46**. Connect a test lead (wire and 15-amp fuse) between the corresponding terminals in the wiring harness. If the left lamps operate when terminals 3 and 4 are connected and the right lamps operate when terminals 3 and 5 are connected replace the hazard flasher switch.

If the switch is good, replace the hazard flasher unit (**Figure 47**).

3. *Turn signals flash too slowly or too fast*. Check for burned out bulbs. Replace as needed.

If all bulbs work, make sure the right bulbs are being used. See **Table 2**.

If the right bulbs are being used, check the wiring for loose or dirty connections. Wiring diagrams are at the end of the book.

If the wiring is good, replace the turn signal flasher unit (**Figure 47**).

4. *Turn signals flash irregularly.* Check for burned out bulbs. Replace as needed.

If all bulbs work, make sure the right bulbs are being used. See **Table 2**.

If the right bulbs are being used, check the wiring for loose or dirty connections. Wiring diagrams are at the end of the book.

IGNITION SYSTEM

All models use an integrated circuit, magnetic pulse controlled ignition system. 1981 models use 2 spark plugs per cylinder. **Figure 48** is a schematic of the 1980 system; **Figure 49** shows the 1981 system.

7

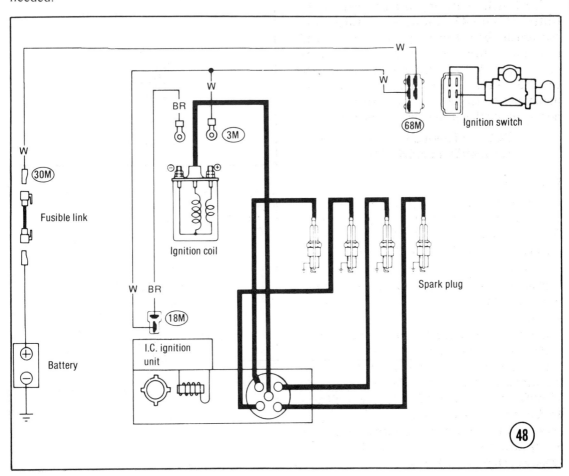

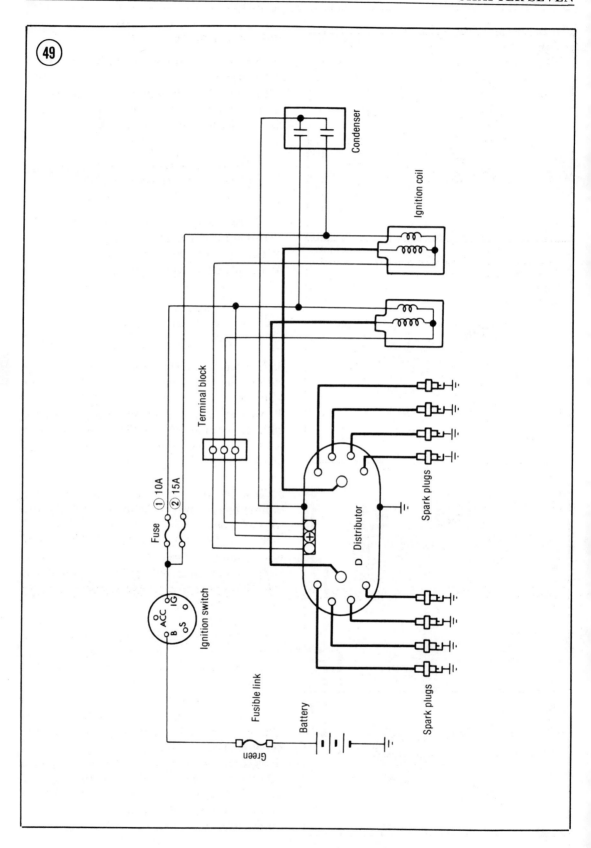

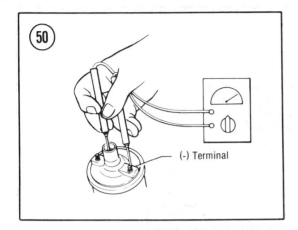

(-) Terminal

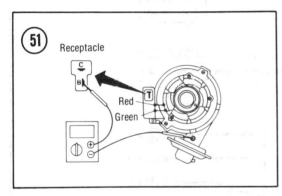

Receptacle

Red

Green

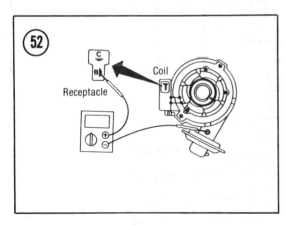

Coil

Receptacle

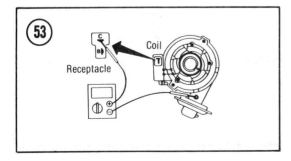

Coil

Receptacle

Ignition System Test (1980)

This test requires a voltmeter and ohmmeter.

1. Connect the voltmeter between the battery terminals and note the reading. This is battery voltage. Write it down for later use.

NOTE
The reading should be at least 11.5 volts. If not, inspect the battery and charging system as described in this chapter.

2. Disconnect the thick wire from the distributor cap. Crank the starter and note the voltage reading between battery terminals. Again, write the reading down.

NOTE
Voltage while cranking should be at least 9.6 volts. If not, inspect the battery and charging system.

3. Inspect the distributor cap and ignition wiring. See the *Tune-up* section of Chapter Three.

4. Measure ignition coil secondary resistance with the ohmmeter. See **Figure 50**. It should be 8,200-12,400 ohms. If resistance is not within the specified range, replace the ignition coil.

5. Test the power supply circuit. Connect a voltmeter as shown in **Figure 51**. Turn the key to ON, but don't start the engine. The voltmeter should indicate 11.5-12.5 volts. If it is less than this, check the wiring from ignition switch to the integrated circuit (IC) unit on the side of the distributor. Wiring diagrams are at the end of the book.

6. Disconnect the thick wire from the distributor cap. Ground the wire by connecting it to bare metal. Connect the voltmeter as shown in **Figure 52** and crank the starter. The voltage reading should be within 1 volt of battery cranking voltage (written down in Step 2). It should be at least 8.6 volts. If not, check the ignition switch and the wiring to the integrated circuit unit.

7. Connect the voltmeter as shown in **Figure 53**. Turn the key to ON, but don't start the engine. Voltage should be 11.5-12.5 volts. If so, skip the next step. If less than 11.5 volts, perform the next step.

8. Test the coil primary circuit. Connect the ohmmeter as shown in **Figure 54**. Resistance should be 0.84-1.02 ohms. If not within this range, replace the ignition coil. If resistance is correct, check the ignition switch. See *Switches* in this chapter. Also check the wiring from ignition switch to the integrated circuit (IC) unit on the side of the distributor.

9. Connect the voltmeter as shown in **Figure 55**. Disconnect the thick wire from the distributor cap and ground it to bare metal. Crank the starter and note the voltmeter reading. It should be 0.5 volts or less. If not, make sure the distributor is properly grounded to the engine. Check the wiring from chassis ground to the battery. Make sure the battery connections are clean and tight.

> *NOTE*
> *The engine should be at normal operating temperature for Steps 10 and 11. The thick coil wire should remain grounded.*

10. With the key off, connect the ohmmeter as shown in **Figure 56**. The reading should be approximately 400 ohms. If much above or below 400 ohms, check the pickup coil (Step 11) and its wiring.

11. Set the voltmeter to the low scale (0-5 volts preferred). Connect the voltmeter to the distributor as shown in **Figure 57**. Turn the key to START and watch the voltmeter needle. If it holds steady, go to Step 12. If it wavers, hold the disconnected wire about 1/4 inch from bare metal, crank the starter and check for spark.

> *WARNING*
> *Hold the wire with a heavily insulated tool. The wire can cause a painful shock, even if the insulation is in perfect condition and you don't touch the end of the wire.*

If there is no spark, replace the integrated circuit unit on the side of the distributor.

12. Remove the distributor cap. Check the pickup coil and reluctor for damage. Replace the distributor if these are found. If the pickup coil and reluctor are good, check the wiring from pickup coil to IC unit. Tighten or replace as needed.

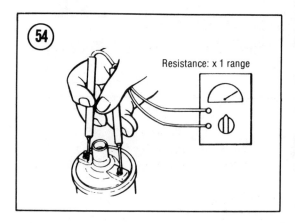

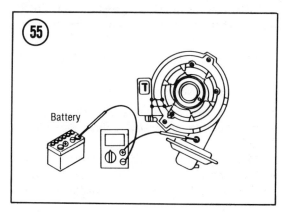

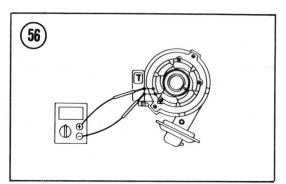

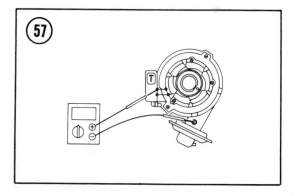

Ignition System Test (1981)

This test requires a voltmeter and ohmmeter.

1. Connect the voltmeter between the battery terminals and note the reading. This is battery voltage. Write it down for later use.

NOTE

The reading should be at least 11.5 volts. If not, inspect the battery and charging system as described under in this chapter.

2. Disconnect the thick wire from the distributor cap. Crank the starter and note the voltage reading between battery terminals. Again, write the reading down.

NOTE

Voltage while cranking should be at least 9.6 volts. If not, inspect the battery and charging system.

3. Inspect the distributor cap and ignition wiring. See the *Tune-up* section of Chapter Three.

4. Measure ignition coil secondary resistance with the ohmmeter. See **Figure 58**. It should be 7,300-11,000 ohms. If resistance is not within the specified range, replace the ignition coil.

NOTE

Test both ignition coils.

5. Test the power supply circuit. Connect a voltmeter as shown in **Figure 59**. Turn the key to ON, but don't start the engine. The voltmeter should indicate 11.5-12.5 volts. If it is less than this, check the wiring from ignition switch to integrated circuit (IC) unit on the side of the distributor. Wiring diagrams are at the end of this manual.

6. Disconnect the thick wire from the distributor cap. Ground the wire by connecting it to bare metal. Connect the voltmeter as shown in **Figure 59** and crank the starter. The voltage reading should be within 1 volt of battery cranking voltage (written down in Step 2). It should be at least 8.6 volts. If not, check the ignition switch and the wiring to the integrated circuit unit.

7. Connect the voltmeter as shown in **Figure 60**. Turn the key to ON, but don't start the engine. Voltage should be 11.5-12.5 volts. If so, skip the next step. If less than 11.5 volts, perform the next step.

8. Connect the voltmeter as shown in **Figure 61**. With the key in the ON position, but the engine not running, voltage should be 11.5-12.5 volts. If it is, skip the next step. If less than 11.5 volts, perform the next step.

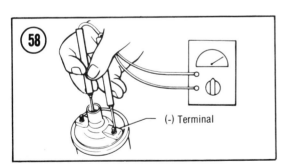

(58) (-) Terminal

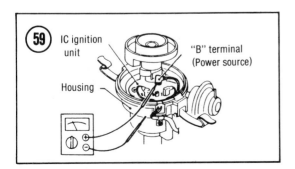

(59) IC ignition unit

"B" terminal (Power source)

Housing

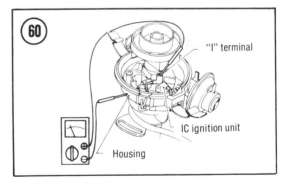

(60) "I" terminal

IC ignition unit

Housing

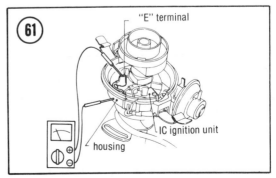

(61) "E" terminal

IC ignition unit

housing

9. Test the coil primary circuit. Connect the ohmmeter as shown in **Figure 62**. Resistance should be 1.04-1.27 ohms. If not within this range, replace the ignition coil.

NOTE
Test both ignition coils.

10. If resistance is correct, check the ignition switch. See *Switches* in this chapter. Also check the wiring from ignition switch to the integrated circuit (IC) unit on the side of the distributor.

11. Connect the voltmeter as shown in **Figure 63**. Disconnect the thick wire from the distributor cap and ground it to bare metal. Crank the starter and note the voltmeter reading. It should be 0.5 volts or less. If not, make sure the distributor is properly grounded to the engine. Check the wiring from chassis ground to the battery. Make sure the connections are clean and tight, including the battery cable connections.

12. If the distributor is properly grounded and wiring connections are good, the integrated circuit unit is defective. Replacement requires partial disassembly of the distributor. This should be done by a dealer or automotive electrical shop.

Distributor Removal/Installation

1. Remove the distributor cap clips and take off the cap.

2. Disconnect the thin wires from the side of the distributor.

3. Disconnect the distributor vacuum line from the vacuum advance unit on the distributor.

4. Turn the engine over until No. 1 piston is at top dead center on its compression stroke. When this occurs, the timing notch in the crankshaft pulley will align with the 0 degree mark on the timing indicator. See **Figure 64**. In addition, the distributor rotor will point to No. 1 plug wire terminal(s) in the distributor cap. See **Figure 65** (1980) or **Figure 66** (1981).

NOTE
Check rotor position as well as the timing marks. The timing marks also line up when No. 1 piston is at TDC on its exhaust stroke.

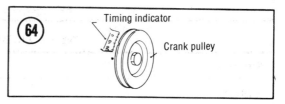

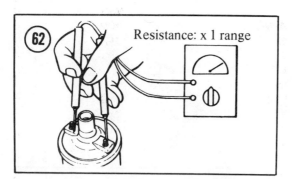

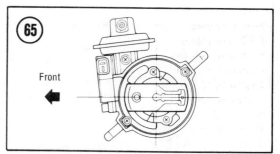

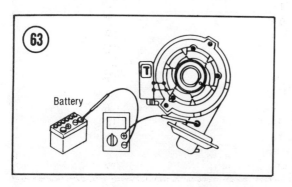

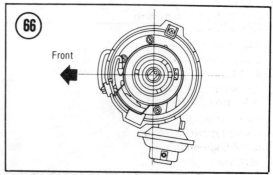

5. To simplify installation, make alignment marks on the distributor body and engine.

6. Remove the distributor body setscrews. Lift the distributor out of the engine.

Distributor Installation

1. If the engine was turned with the distributor out, place No. 1 piston at top dead center on its compression stroke. See *Distributor Removal*, Step 4.

2. Insert the distributor so it engages the driving spindle. Make sure the rotor points to No. 1 terminal in the distributor cap. Align the marks on engine and distributor body.

3. Install the body setscrews and distributor cap. Connect the thin wires and vacuum line to the distributor.

4. Adjust ignition timing as described in the *Tune-up* section of Chapter Three.

Table 1   BATTERY CHARGE PERCENTAGE

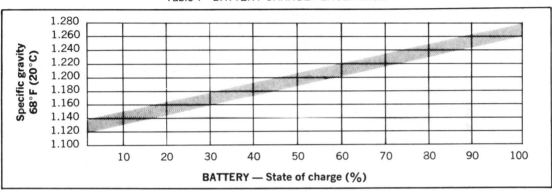

Table 2   BULB SPECIFICATIONS

Application	Wattage	Trade number
Headlights		
Inner	50	4651
Outer	40/60	4652
Front turn signals	27	1156
Front parking lights	5	—
Front side marker lights	5	—
Rear side marker lights	3.8	—
Stop/tail lights	27/8	1157
Rear turn signals	27	1156
Back-up lights	27	1156
License plate lights	10	—
Interior light		
Standard cab	5	—
King Cab	10	—
Oil pressure gauge illumination	3.4	158
Voltmeter illumination	3.4	158
4wd indicator illumination	3.4	158
Other gauge illumination	1.7	—
Warning lamps	3.4	158
Cigarette lighter illumination	1.4	—
Heater A/C illumination	3.4	158
Radio illumination	3.4	158
Rear defogger indicator lamp	1.4	—
Rear defogger switch		
Illumination	3.4	158

CHAPTER EIGHT

CLUTCH AND TRANSMISSION

Datsun 4-wheel drive pickups use a single dry plate hydraulic clutch and a 4-speed or 5-speed manual transmission.

Tables 1-6 are at the end of the chapter.

CLUTCH PART IDENTIFICATION

Many clutch parts have 2 or more names. To prevent confusion, the following list gives part names used in this chapter and common synonyms.

    a. Withdrawal lever—release lever, throw-out arm
    b. Release bearing—throw-out bearing
    c. Operating cylinder—slave cylinder
    d. Pressure plate—pressure plate assembly, clutch cover assembly
    e. Disc—driven plate

CLUTCH ADJUSTMENT

1. Measure pedal height (dimension H, **Figure 1**). It should be 171-177 mm (6.73-6.97 in.). If necessary, loosen the pedal stopper locknut and rotate the pedal stopper to change pedal height.

2. Push the pedal by hand and check free play (dimension A, **Figure 1**). This should be 1-5 mm (0.04-0.20 in.). To adjust, loosen the pushrod locknut and rotate the pushrod to change its effective length.

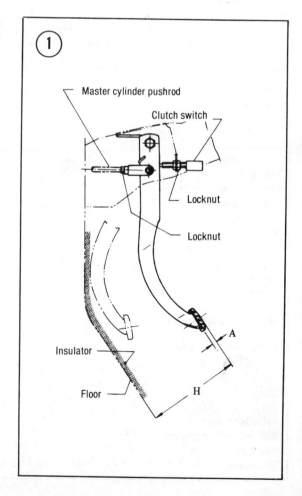

Master cylinder pushrod
Clutch switch
Locknut
Locknut
Insulator
Floor
A
H

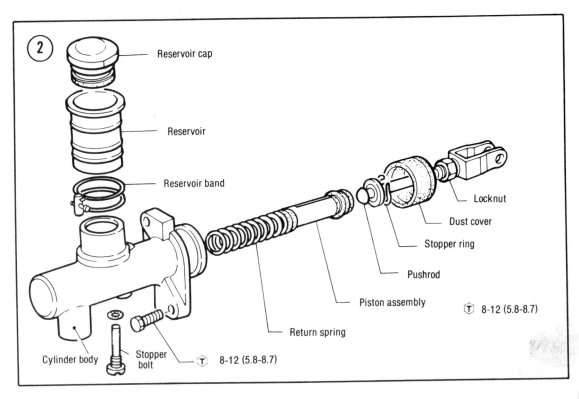

② Reservoir cap

Reservoir

Reservoir band

Cylinder body

Stopper bolt

Ⓣ 8-12 (5.8-8.7)

Return spring

Piston assembly

Ⓣ 8-12 (5.8-8.7)

Pushrod

Stopper ring

Dust cover

Locknut

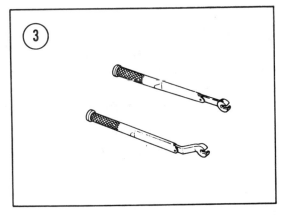

③

MASTER CYLINDER

Figure 2 shows the master cylinder.

Removal/Installation

1. Remove the clevis pin attaching the master cylinder pushrod to the clutch pedal.
2. With a container handy to catch dripping hydraulic fluid, disconnect the hydraulic line from the master cylinder. The factory recommends a flare nut wrench such as Datsun part No. GG94310000 (**Figure 3**). Do not use an adjustable wrench.

CAUTION
Hydraulic fluid will damage paint. Wipe up any spilled fluid immediately, then wash the area with soap and water.

3. Detach the master cylinder from the firewall, then lift it out.
4. Installation is the reverse of removal. Check pedal height as described under *Adjustments* in this chapter. Bleed the clutch as described under *Clutch Bleeding* in this chapter.

Disassembly

Refer to **Figure 2**.
1. Remove the filler cap from the fluid reservoir. Pour the fluid from the cylinder.
2. Pull back the dust cover and remove the stopper ring.
3. Take the stopper out of the cylinder. Remove the pushrod, then the piston assembly.
4. Take the piston cup off the piston and discard it.

NOTE
Do not remove the fluid reservoir unless a new one is being installed.

8

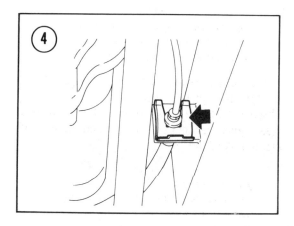

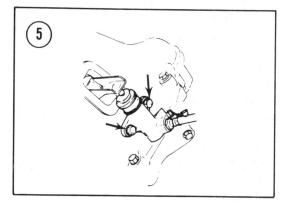

1. Pushrod
2. Dust cover
3. Piston spring
4. Piston
5. Piston cup
6. Operating cylinder
7. Bleeder screw

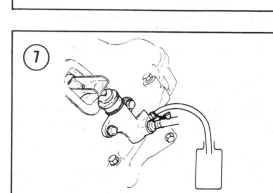

Inspection

1. Thoroughly clean all parts in clean brake fluid before inspection. Do not clean with gasoline, kerosene, or solvent. These leave residues which can cause rubber parts to soften and swell.

2. Check the piston for excessive or uneven wear, scoring, cracks or corrosion. Replace the piston if any of these defects is found.

3. Check the cylinder bore for wear, cracks, scoring, or corrosion. Replace the cylinder if defects are visible.

4. Check the dust cover for wear, cracks, or signs of deterioration. Replace if these are detected. Check the fluid reservoir, filler cap and hydraulic line for wear or damage. Replace as needed.

Assembly

1. Coat the cylinder bore with hydraulic fluid.
2. Install the piston return spring assembly.
3. Soak the piston cups with hydraulic fluid, then install them on the piston. The lips (wide sides) of the cups face into the cylinder bore.

4. Coat the piston with hydraulic fluid and insert it into the cylinder. Be careful not to bend back the lips of the piston cups.

5. Place the dust cover on the pushrod. Insert the pushrod and stopper into the cylinder. Install the stopper ring and push the lip of the dust cover over the cylinder.

OPERATING CYLINDER

Removal/Installation

1. With a container handy to catch dripping hydraulic fluid, diconnect the flexible clutch line from the metal tube. See **Figure 4**.

2. Disconnect the fluid hose from the operating cylinder.

3. Remove 2 cylinder mounting bolts (**Figure 5**). Separate the pushrod from the clutch withdrawal lever. Take the cylinder out.

4. Installation is the reverse of removal. Bleed the clutch as described under *Clutch Bleeding* in this chapter.

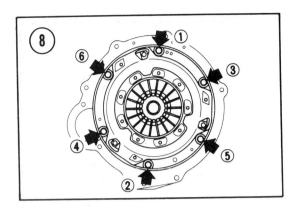

Disassembly and Inspection

Figure 6 shows the operating cylinder.
1. Remove the dust cover.
2. Remove the piston and cup. Discard the cup.
3. Remove the internal spring.
4. Remove the bleed valve.
5. Thoroughly clean all parts in brake fluid. Do not clean with gasoline, kerosene or solvent. These leave residues which can cause rubber parts to soften and swell.
6. Check the piston for excessive or uneven wear, cracks, scoring or corrosion. Replace the piston if these conditions are found.
7. Check the cylinder bore for the defects described in Step 6. Replace the entire cylinder if any of these are found.

Assembly

Assembly is the reverse of the disassembly procedure, plus the following:
1. Soak the piston cup in brake fluid before installation. Make sure the lip of the cup faces into the cylinder when installed.
2. Assemble the spring to the piston before installing the spring and piston.
3. Coat the cylinder bore and piston with brake fluid before installing the piston.

CLUTCH BLEEDING

Bleeding the clutch hydraulic system is necessary whenever air enters it. This occurs when the clutch hydraulic line is disconnected. It can also result from a very low fluid level in the master cylinder or from defective master or slave cylinders. Air in the system can make shifting gears very difficult.

NOTE
This procedure requires 2 people, one to operate the clutch pedal and the other to open and close the bleed valve.

1. Remove the dust cap from the bleed valve.
2. Attach a plastic tube to the bleed valve (**Figure 7**). Place the other end of the tube in a clean glass jar containing several inches of clean brake fluid.

NOTE
Do not allow the end of the tube to slip out of the brake fluid during bleeding. If this happens, air may enter the system and the bleeding procedure will have to be repeated.

3. Top up the clutch master cylinder reservoir with fluid.
4. Pump the pedal 2 or 3 times, then hold it to the floor.
5. While the pedal is down, open the bleed valve 1/3 to 1/2 turn. Let the mixed air and fluid escape. Close the bleed valve while the pedal is still down, then let the pedal up.
6. Repeat Steps 4 and 5 until the fluid entering the jar is free of bubbles. Close the bleed valve, remove the tube and top up the master cylinder.

NOTE
Keep an eye on the master cylinder fluid level during bleeding. If the level is allowed to drop too low, air will be sucked into the system and the bleeding procedure will have to be repeated.

CLUTCH REMOVAL

The engine and transmission must be separated to remove the clutch. This can be done by removing the engine and transmission and separating them (Chapter Four) or by removing just the transmission as described in this chapter. If only clutch work is planned, it will be easier to remove just the transmission.

Once the engine and transmission have been separated, do the following:
1. Mark the edges of the pressure plate and flywheel so they can be reassembled in their same relative positions.
2. Remove the clutch cover bolts gradually in a diagonal pattern to prevent warping the pressure plate. See **Figure 8**.

8

CLUTCH INSPECTION

Clutch Disc

Check the clutch disc for the following:
a. Oil or grease on the facings
b. Glazed facings
c. Warped facings
d. Loose or missing rivets
e. Facings worn to within 0.3 mm (0.012 in.) of any rivet
f. Broken springs
g. Loose fit or rough movement on transmission input shaft splines. Light surface stains may be sanded off the disc. If oil or grease has soaked beneath the surface, the disc must be replaced. The disc must also be replaced if any of the other defects is present or if facings are worn and a new pressure plate is being installed.

Pressure Plate

Check the pressure plate for:
a. Scoring
b. Burn marks (blue-tinted areas)
c. Cracks

Replace the pressure plate if these are evident. If the clutch trouble is still not apparent, take the disc and pressure plate to a competent garage. Have the disc and pressure plate checked for runout and the diaphragm spring for incorrect finger height. Do not attempt to dismantle the disc and pressure plate or readjust the fingers without proper tools and experience.

CLUTCH INSTALLATION

1. Be sure your hands are clean.
2. Inspect the disc facings, pressure plate and flywheel to be sure they are free of grease, oil or other foreign material.
3. Inspect the clutch pilot bushing, located inside the rear end of the crankshaft. If worn or damaged, replace the bushing as described under *Crankshaft*, Chapter Four.
4. Place the clutch disc and pressure plate in position on the flywheel. The long side of the disc hub faces the rear of the car.
5. If reinstalling the original pressure plate, line up the alignment marks made before removal.
6. Center the disc and pressure plate with a pilot shaft such as Datsun part No. KV30100100 (**Figure 9**). Inexpensive pilot shafts are available from some imported car parts stores. Some tool rental dealers carry universal pilot shafts which can be adapted. An input shaft from a junk transmission makes an excellent pilot shaft.
7. Install the clutch cover bolts, tightening gradually in a diagonal pattern (**Figure 8**). Tighten to 1.6-2.1 mkg (12-15 ft.-lb.).

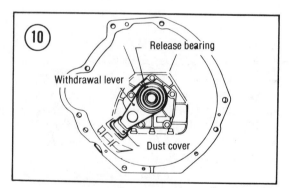

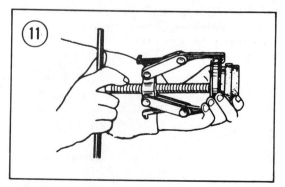

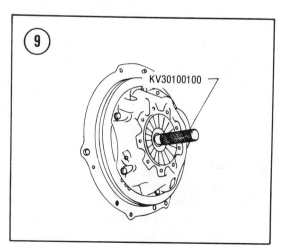

RELEASE MECHANISM

Removal

The release mechanism is mounted in the clutch housing (front part of the transmission case). As with the clutch, the engine and transmission must be separated to remove the release mechanism.

Disassembly

1. Referring to **Figure 10**, remove the dust cover from the clutch housing.
2. Remove the holder spring. Take out the release bearing and sleeve.
3. Detach the retainer spring from the withdrawal lever. Remove the withdrawal lever from its ball pin.

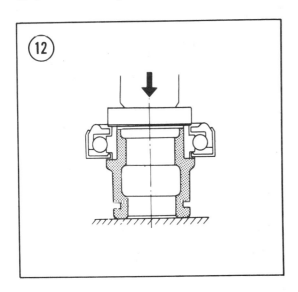

4. Remove the release bearing from its sleeve with a puller (**Figure 11**). The bearing is a press fit on the sleeve.

Inspection

Check release mechanism for the following:
a. Wear at the contact point of withdrawal lever and release bearing sleeve. Replace the sleeve if worn.
b. Grease leaking from the release bearing. Replace the bearing if this is evident.

CAUTION
Do not clean the release bearing in solvent, since it is prelubricated at the factory. Clean with a lint-free cloth.

c. A worn release bearing. To check, hold the inner race with fingers and rotate the outer race while applying light pressure to it. If the bearing feels rough or makes noise, replace it.

Assembly

1. Press the release bearing onto the sleeve (**Figure 12**). When it is in place, rotate the bearing to make sure it operates smoothly.
2. Referring to **Figure 13**, apply a *light* coat of multipurpose grease to the following:
   a. Contact points of withdrawal lever and release bearing sleeve
   b. Contact points of withdrawal lever and ball pin
   c. Contact points of release bearing sleeve and transmission front cover
3. Pack the recess inside the bearing sleeve with multipurpose grease. See **Figure 14**.

8

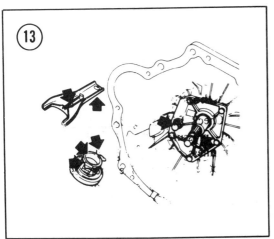

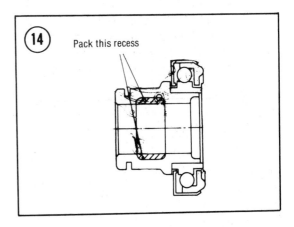

Pack this recess

4. Apply a small amount of molybdenum disulphide grease to the transmission input shaft splines.

5. Place the withdrawal lever in position over the transmission input shaft, with the operating cylinder end through the hole in the clutch housing.

6. Position the release bearing and sleeve on the withdrawal lever. Position the holder spring.

7. Install the dust cover in the clutch housing.

8. Install the transmission as described under *Transmission Removal/Installation* in this chapter.

9. Bleed the clutch as described under *Clutch Bleeding.* Check pedal height as described under *Adjustment.*

TRANSMISSION

Transmission overhaul is not the best starting point for a beginning mechanic. However, it doesn't require special training and the special tools shown in this chapter can easily be duplicated.

Overhaul does require patience and the ability to concentrate. The work area must be clean, free of distractions and inaccessible to pets and small children.

Before starting work, read all parts of this chapter that apply to your transmission. Obtain the necessary tools or substitutes. Check parts availability with local suppliers.

Removal/Installation

1. Disconnect the negative cable from the battery.

2. Disconnect the throttle cable.

3. Remove the center console and shift lever boot. See *Console*, Chapter Twelve.

4. Place the shift lever in NEUTRAL.

5. Remove the pin from the base of the shift lever (**Figure 15**), then lift the lever out.

6. Jack up both ends of the truck and place jackstands at all 4 corners. Be sure the jackstands are securely positioned.

7. Remove the drive shafts. See *Drive Shafts, Removal/Installation*, Chapter Ten.

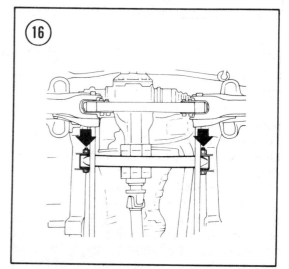

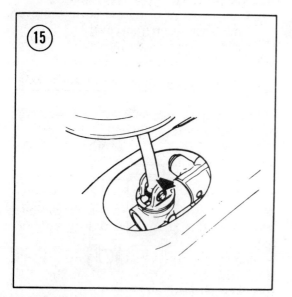

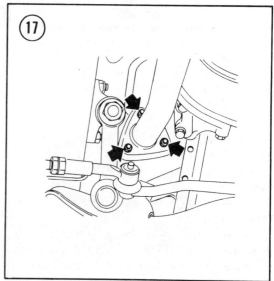

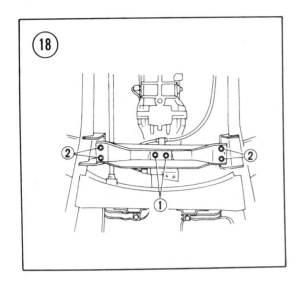

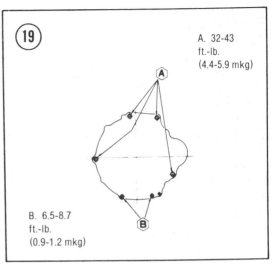

8. Remove the front differential crossmember (**Figure 16**).
9. Disconnect the front exhaust pipe (**Figure 17**).
10. Disconnect the wires from the transmission electrical switches.
11. Unbolt the clutch operating cylinder. See *Operating Cylinder, Removal/Installation* in this chapter.
12. Drain the oil from the transmission.
13. Place a jack beneath the engine to support it. Use a block of wood between jack and oil pan so the pan won't collapse.
14. Remove the starter. See *Starter Removal/Installation*, Chapter Seven.

> *WARNING*
> *In the next step, be sure to use a transmission jack. This type of jack has a cradle which will keep the transmission from falling during removal. Transmission jacks are available from tool rental dealers.*

15. Place a transmission jack beneath the transmission. Unbolt the transmission mount from the transmission, then from the car. See **Figure 18**.
16. Remove the transmission-to-engine bolts (**Figure 19**).
17. Lower the jacks beneath engine and transmission to provide removal clearance. Remove the transmission downward and to the rear.

> *CAUTION*
> *Do not remove the transmission partway. If the transmission's weight is allowed to hang on the input shaft for any length of time, the input shaft and its bearing may be damaged.*

18. Installation is the reverse of removal. Make sure engine and transmission mating surfaces are clean. Tighten all nuts and bolts to specifications (**Table 1**). Fill the transmission with an oil recommended in Chapter Three.

Disassembly (Four-speed Transmission)

All 4-speed models use the F4W71B transmission. Refer to **Figures 20-22** for the following procedures.

1. Clean the outside of the transmission with solvent.
2. Remove the clutch release mechanism. See *Release Mechanism, Removal*, in this chapter.
3. Unscrew the electrical switches from the side of the transmission.
4. Make sure the transmission is still in neutral. It should be possible to turn the rear end of the main shaft with one hand while holding the input shaft from turning with the other.
5. Remove the speedometer pinion clamp bolt from the rear extension, then take the speedometer pinion out.

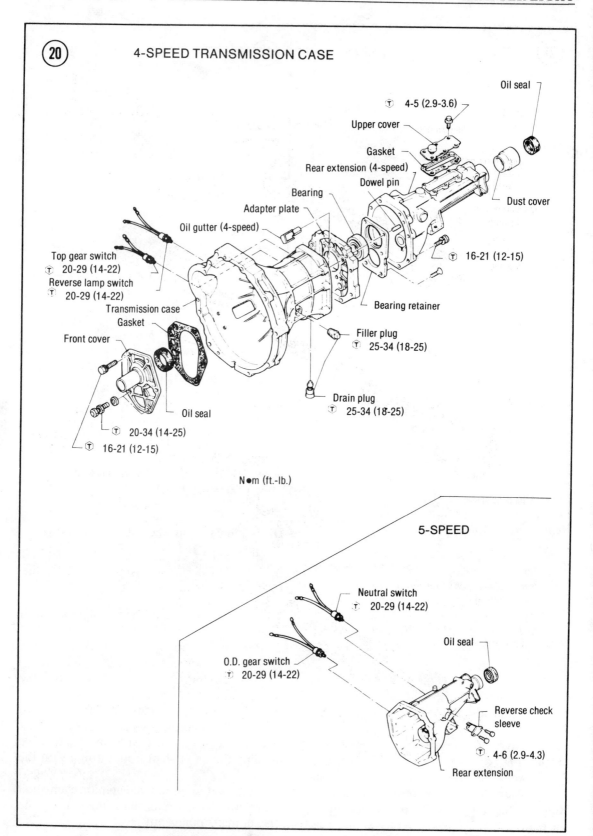

(20) 4-SPEED TRANSMISSION CASE

Oil seal

4-5 (2.9-3.6)

Upper cover

Gasket

Rear extension (4-speed)

Dowel pin

Dust cover

Bearing

Adapter plate

Oil gutter (4-speed)

16-21 (12-15)

Top gear switch
20-29 (14-22)

Reverse lamp switch
20-29 (14-22)

Transmission case

Bearing retainer

Gasket

Front cover

Filler plug
25-34 (18-25)

Oil seal

Drain plug
25-34 (18-25)

20-34 (14-25)

16-21 (12-15)

N•m (ft.-lb.)

5-SPEED

Neutral switch
20-29 (14-22)

Oil seal

O.D. gear switch
20-29 (14-22)

Reverse check
sleeve

4-6 (2.9-4.3)

Rear extension

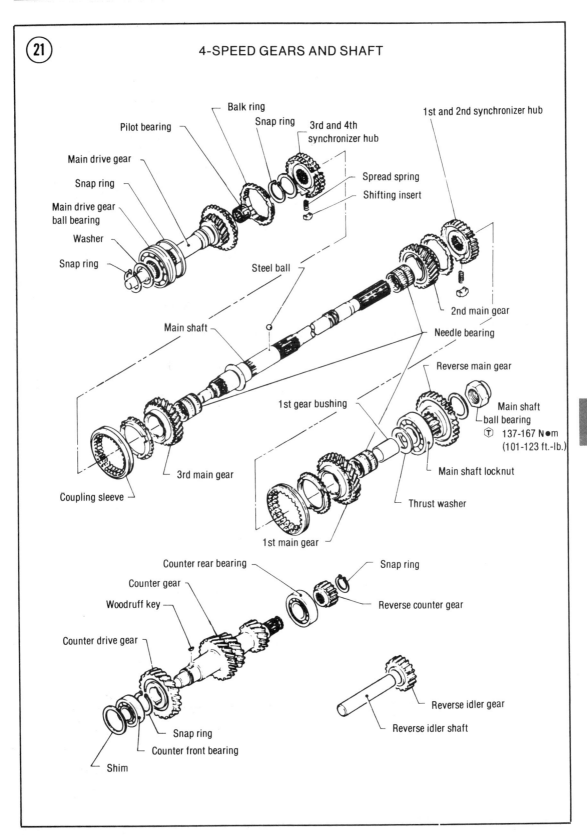

4-SPEED GEARS AND SHAFT

Balk ring
Snap ring
Pilot bearing
3rd and 4th synchronizer hub
1st and 2nd synchronizer hub
Main drive gear
Spread spring
Snap ring
Shifting insert
Main drive gear ball bearing
Washer
Snap ring
Steel ball
2nd main gear
Main shaft
Needle bearing
Reverse main gear
1st gear bushing
Main shaft ball bearing
Ⓣ 137-167 N●m
(101-123 ft.-lb.)
3rd main gear
Main shaft locknut
Coupling sleeve
Thrust washer
1st main gear
Counter rear bearing
Snap ring
Counter gear
Woodruff key
Reverse counter gear
Counter drive gear
Snap ring
Reverse idler gear
Counter front bearing
Reverse idler shaft
Shim

8

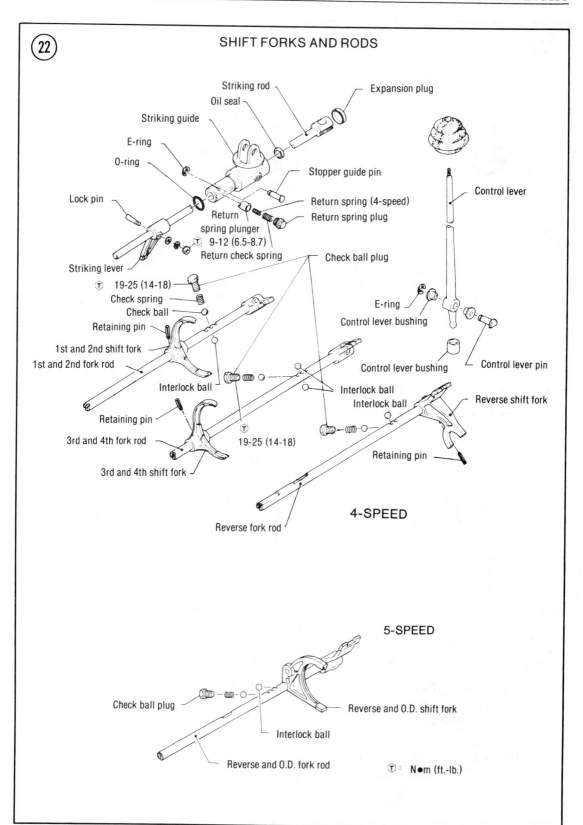

(22) SHIFT FORKS AND RODS

Striking rod

Expansion plug

Oil seal

Striking guide

E-ring

O-ring

Stopper guide pin

Return spring (4-speed)

Return spring plug

Lock pin

Return spring plunger
9-12 (6.5-8.7)

Return check spring

Check ball plug

Striking lever

19-25 (14-18)

Check spring

E-ring

Check ball

Control lever bushing

Retaining pin

1st and 2nd shift fork

1st and 2nd fork rod

Interlock ball

Control lever bushing

Control lever pin

Interlock ball

Retaining pin

Interlock ball

Reverse shift fork

3rd and 4th fork rod

19-25 (14-18)

3rd and 4th shift fork

Retaining pin

Control lever

Reverse fork rod

4-SPEED

5-SPEED

Check ball plug

Reverse and O.D. shift fork

Interlock ball

Reverse and O.D. fork rod

(T): N●m (ft.-lb.)

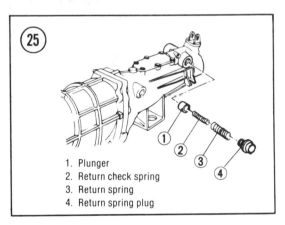

1. Plunger
2. Return check spring
3. Return spring
4. Return spring plug

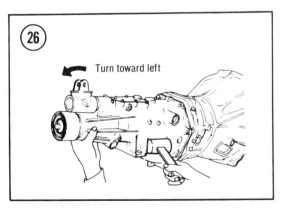

Turn toward left

6. Remove the snap ring and pin from the striking rod. See **Figure 23**.

7. Unscrew the return spring plug (**Figure 24**).

8. Take out the return check spring, return spring and return spring plunger. See **Figure 25**.

9. Turn the striking guide (**Figure 26**) counterclockwise (viewed from the rear of the transmission). Referring to **Figure 20**, unbolt the rear extension from the adapter plate and transmission case. Tap the rear extension loose with a soft-faced mallet, then remove it.

10. Unbolt the front cover from the transmission case. Remove the input shaft bearing shim, then remove the snap ring with snap ring pliers. See **Figure 27**.

11. Tap the transmission case with a soft-faced mallet to free it from the adapter plate. Then take the transmission case off.

12. Position the gear assembly in a holding fixture such as Datsun tool part No. ST23810000 (**Figure 28**). **Figure 29** gives dimensions of the tool, which can easily be made from plywood.

8

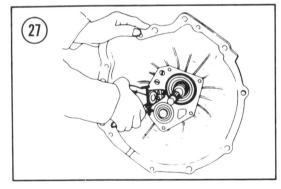

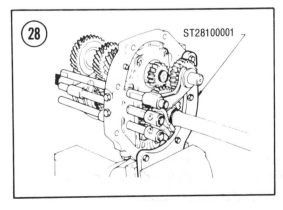

ST28100001

13. Referring to **Figure 21**, drive the roll pins out of the shift forks.

14. Remove all 3 check ball plugs. **Figure 30** is a cross-section view of the adapter plate which shows the check ball plugs, check and interlock balls and shift rods.

15. Tap the shift fork rods out of the adapter plate, then remove the check and interlock balls.

> *NOTE*
> *Perform the following inspection step before continuing with disassembly.*

16. Measure gear end play with a feeler gauge (**Figure 31**). Compare with **Table 2**. Excessive end play can be corrected with thicker snap rings. The main shaft thrust washers should also be checked closely for wear.

> *NOTE*
> *Continue with disassembly as follows.*

17. Engage 2 gears at once. To do this, slide each synchronizer sleeve over the small teeth on one of the gears next to it. This locks the main shaft and gears so they won't turn.

18. Remove the countershaft gear front bearing with a gear puller (**Figure 32**). These are available from tool rental dealers.

19. Remove the countershaft drive gear snap ring.

20. Pull off the countershaft drive gear with a gear puller. Remove the input shaft at the same time. See **Figure 33**.

> *CAUTION*
> *Do not let the needle roller bearing fall out of the input shaft onto the floor.*

21. Carefully file away the lip of the main shaft nut where it is punched into the main shaft. Remove the nut with a 38 mm (1-1/2 in.) wrench and throw it away. See **Figure 34**.

> *NOTE*
> *The nut is tightened to 14-17 mkg (101-123 ft.-lb.). If you don't have the correct wrench, take the gear assembly to a dealer to have the nut removed.*

22. Remove the snap ring from the rear end of the countershaft, then remove the countershaft reverse gear.

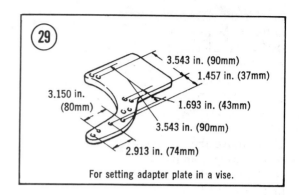

(29)

3.543 in. (90mm)
1.457 in. (37mm)
3.150 in. (80mm)
1.693 in. (43mm)
3.543 in. (90mm)
2.913 in. (74mm)

For setting adapter plate in a vise.

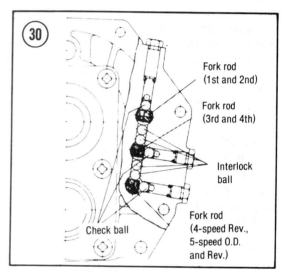

(30)

Fork rod (1st and 2nd)
Fork rod (3rd and 4th)
Interlock ball
Fork rod (4-speed Rev., 5-speed O.D. and Rev.)
Check ball

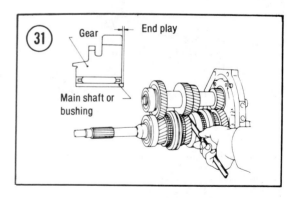

(31)

Gear
End play
Main shaft or bushing

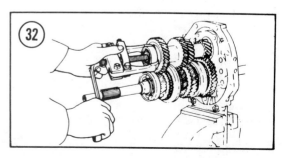

(32)

23. Tap the main shaft with a soft-faced mallet to free it (**Figure 35**). Then remove the main shaft and countershaft from the adapter plate.

24. Remove the machine screws securing the bearing retainer to the adapter plate. These screws have been peened in place, so an impact screwdriver is necessary to remove them.

25. Remove the reverse idler shaft and main shaft bearing from the adapter plate.

26. Remove the thrust washer, its steel ball, first gear and first gear's needle bearing from the rear end of the main shaft.

27. Have the first gear bushing, first-second gear synchronizer and second gear pressed off the main shaft by a machine shop.

Inspection

1. Thoroughly clean all parts in solvent. Remove all traces of old gasket and sealer. Inspect all parts while cleaning and replace any with obvious wear or damage.

2. Check the transmission case and rear extension for cracks. Check all gasket surfaces for gouges or roughness which could cause an oil leak. Small burrs can be removed from gasket surfaces with an oilstone; small gouges can be filled with gasket sealer during assembly. Replace parts with serious damage.

3. Check all bearings for wear or damage. Hold the outer race with one hand and rotate the inner race with the other. See **Figure 36**. Check for noise, roughness and wear. Replace any suspect bearings.

NOTE
If the input shaft bearing or countershaft bearing needs to be replaced, have the old one pressed off and a new one pressed on by a machine shop.

4. Since needle roller bearing wear is hard to see, the needle roller bearings should be replaced whenever the transmission is overhauled.

5. Inspect the bushing at the back of the rear extension. If worn or damaged, the rear extension must be replaced.

6. Carefully pry the oil seal out of the rear extension. Tap in a new one. Use a block of wood to spread the hammer's force, so the seal won't tip sideways and jam. Coat the seal lip and rear extension bushing with gear oil.

8

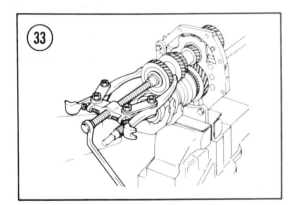

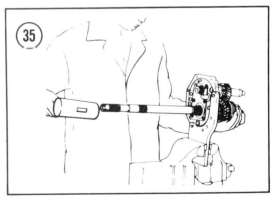

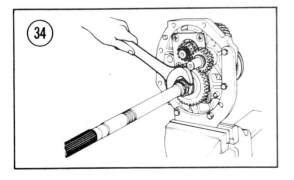

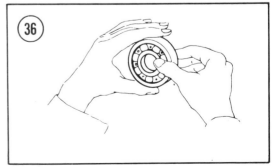

NOTE
The lip of the seal faces into the transmission. See **Figure 37.**

7. Replace the front cover oil seal in the same manner as the rear extension oil seal.
8. Check the main shaft for bending, twisting, cracks or other damage. Check the splines for the types of wear and damage shown in **Figure 38.** Replace if any of these conditions is found.
9. Check gears for chipped, broken or badly worn teeth. Replace gears that show these conditions.
10. Slip a balk ring onto the cones of first, second, third and input shaft gears. Measure the gap between balk ring and the small teeth on the gear (**Figure 39**). Standard gap is 1.2-1.6 mm (0.047-0.063 in.). Minimum is 0.8 mm (0.031 in.). Replace balk rings if gap is less than the minimum.

Assembly (Four-speed Transmission)

Transmission assembly should be done in a dust-free area.

NOTE
Dip each gear, bearing and synchronizer in new gear oil just before assembly.

1. If the oil gutter was removed from the adapter plate, install it as shown in **Figure 40.**
2. If the main shaft bearing was removed from the adapter plate, tap it into position with a soft-faced mallet.
3. Install the reverse idler shaft in the adapter plate. Make sure the cutout in the shaft faces toward the center of the adapter plate.
4. Install the bearing retainer. Make sure the cutout in the reverse idler shaft lines up with the notch in the bearing retainer. Tighten the

adapter plate screws to specifications (**Table 1**). Peen each screw at 2 points with a hammer and punch. See **Figure 41**.
5. Install the following parts in order from the rear end of the mainshaft: needle bearing, second gear, balk ring, first-second gear synchronizer, balk ring, first gear bushing, needle bearing and first gear.
6. Coat the steel ball with grease and install it next to first gear (**Figure 42**). Slip the thrust washer over it.

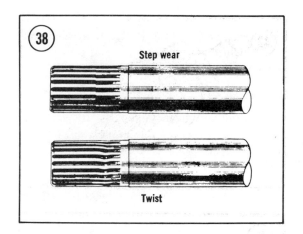

38

Step wear

Twist

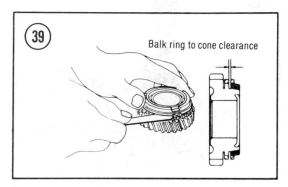

39

Balk ring to cone clearance

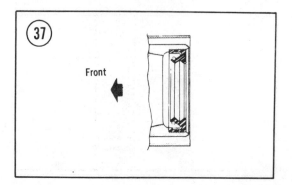

37

Front

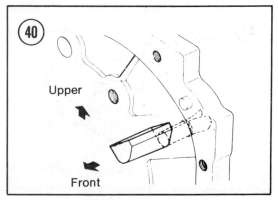

40

Upper

Front

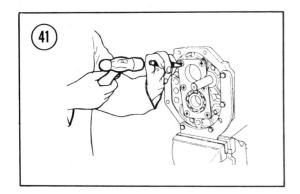

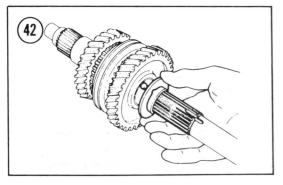

7. Have the main shaft pressed into the adapter plate by a machine shop. A support tool such as Datsun part No. KV31100400 (**Figure 43**) is necessary to prevent damage to the adapter plate.

8. Install new Woodruff keys in the countershaft gear. Tap the keys in gently with a soft-faced mallet. See **Figure 44**.

9. Have the countershaft gear pressed into the adapter plate by a machine shop. See **Figure 45**. A support stand such as Datsun part No. KV31100401 is necessary to prevent damage to the adapter plate.

10. Install the following parts in order from the front end of the main shaft: needle bearing, third gear, balk ring and third-fourth gear synchronizer.

NOTE
*The third-fourth gear synchronizer is offset toward the rear of the main shaft (**Figure 46**). The first-second synchronizer hub is not offset.*

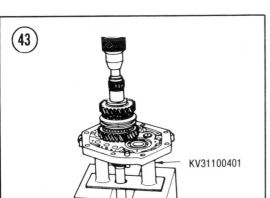

KV31100401

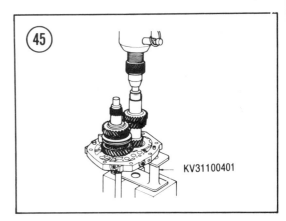

KV31100401

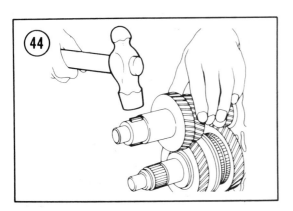

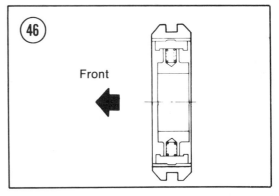

Front

11. Place a thrust washer against the synchronizer, then secure it with a snap ring. Use the thickest snap ring that will fit in the groove. Snap rings are available in several thicknesses.

12. Place a balk ring on the third-fourth gear synchronizer.

13. Place the input shaft pilot bearing on the end of the main shaft.

14. Mesh the countershaft drive gear with the input shaft gear.

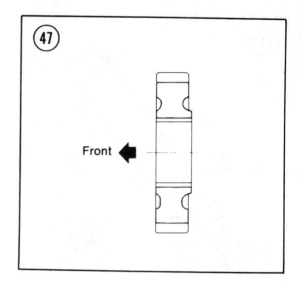

NOTE
*The flat side of the gear hub faces the front of the transmission. See **Figure 47**.*

15. Position the gears as shown in **Figure 48**, then have the countershaft drive gear pressed onto the countershaft by a machine shop. The input shaft is installed at the same time as the countershaft drive gear.

16. Secure the countershaft drive gear with the thickest snap ring that will fit in the groove. Snap rings are available in several thicknesses.

17. Have the countershaft front bearing pressed onto the countershaft, next to the countershaft drive gear. See **Figure 49**.

18. Install reverse main gear on the main shaft. Install the plain washer next to the gear, then install the main shaft nut. Don't torque the nut yet.

19. Install countershaft reverse gear on the rear end of the countershaft. Secure with the thickest snap ring that will fit in the groove. Snap rings are available in several thicknesses.

20. Install reverse idler gear on the reverse idler shaft.

21. Slide the third-fourth gear synchronizer sleeve over the small teeth on third gear. Slide the first-second synchronizer sleeve over the small teeth on first or second gear. This engages 2 gears at once, so the main shaft won't turn.

22. Tighten the main shaft nut to 12-17 mkg (101-123 ft.-lb). If you are near a Datsun dealer, the easiest way to do this is to take the gear assembly to a dealer and have the nut tightened. If not, you will need a 38 mm (1-1/2 in.) box wrench and a piece of pipe large enough to fit over it. The pipe should be about 3 ft. long.

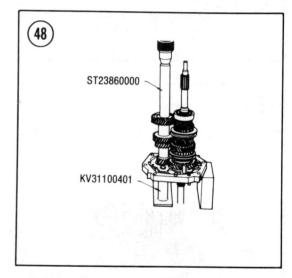

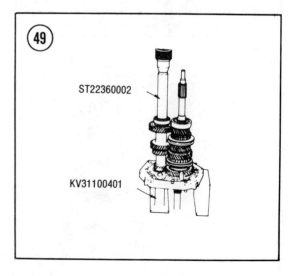

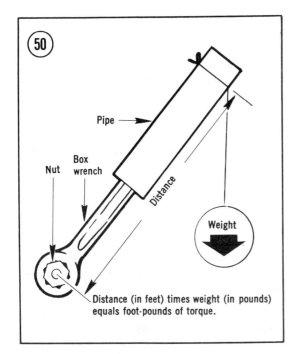

Distance (in feet) times weight (in pounds) equals foot-pounds of torque.

To tighten, place the box wrench over the nut and slip the pipe over the wrench. Measure 2 ft. out from the center of the main shaft and mark this point on the pipe. See **Figure 50**. Hang a 55 lb. weight on the pipe at this point and let it turn the wrench as far as it will go. The distance (2 ft.) times the weight (55 lb.) equals 110 ft.-lb. This is within the specified range of 101-123 ft.-lb.

23. Once the main shaft nut is tightened, punch its lip into the groove in the main shaft. See **Figure 51**.

24. Place the first-second gear shifting fork in its groove on the first-second gear synchronizer. This is the synchronizer closest to the adapter plate.

25. Place the third-fourth gear shifting fork on the third-fourth gear synchronizer sleeve. The longer leg faces away from the countershaft gear.

26. Slide the first-second gear shift rod through the adapter plate into the first-second gear shifting fork. Secure the rod to the fork with a new roll pin.

27. Coat the threads of the longest check ball plug with gasket sealer. Install a check ball, spring and the plug in the adapter plate. See **Figure 52**.

28. Install 2 interlock balls in the adapter plate, on top of the first-second shift rod. See **Figure 53**.

8

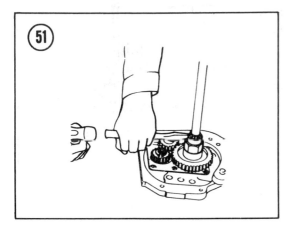

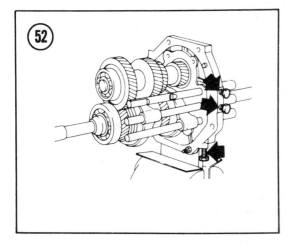

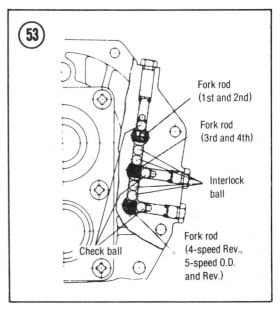

Fork rod (1st and 2nd)

Fork rod (3rd and 4th)

Interlock ball

Check ball

Fork rod (4-speed Rev., 5-speed O.D. and Rev.)

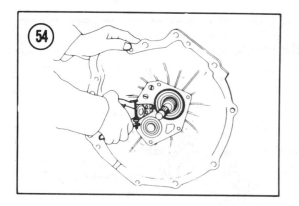

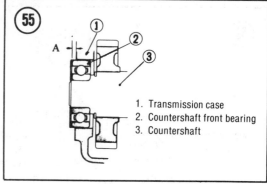

1. Transmission case
2. Countershaft front bearing
3. Countershaft

29. Slide the third-fourth gear shift rod through the adapter plate into the third-fourth gear shifting fork. Secure with a new roll pin.

30. Apply gasket sealer to the threads of one of the check ball plugs. Install a check ball, spring and the plug. See **Figure 52**.

31. Install 2 more interlock balls in the adapter plate (**Figure 53**).

32. Position the reverse shifting fork on the reverse idler gear. Install the reverse shift rod, check ball, spring and check ball plug. See **Figure 53**. Once again, use gasket sealer on the plug threads.

33. Tighten the check ball plugs to specifications (**Table 1**).

34. Make sure the transmission is in neutral. The synchronizer sleeves should be midway between the small teeth on the gears. Reverse idler gear should be disengaged from reverse main gear and counter reverse gear.

35. Make sure all bearings, gears, synchronizers and shift rods are coated with gear oil.

36. Apply gasket sealer to the mating surfaces of transmission case and adapter plate.

37. Install the transmission case on the adapter plate. Tap it into position with a soft-faced mallet.

38. Make sure the main shaft and input shaft rotate freely. Secure the input shaft bearing with a snap ring (**Figure 54**).

39. Apply gasket sealer to the mating surfaces of adapter plate and rear extension. Install the rear extension on the adapter plate. Make sure the striking lever engages the shift rod brackets.

40. Tighten the rear extension bolts to specifications (**Table 1**).

41. Select a shim for the countershaft front bearing. Measure bearing protrusion from the front of the transmission case (distance A, **Figure 55**) and select a shim according to **Table 3**.

42. Stick the shim to the front cover with multipurpose grease.

43. Install the front cover on the transmission case. Use a new gasket, coated on both sides with gasket sealer. Smear gasket sealer on the bolt threads. Tighten the front cover bolts to specifications (**Table 1**).

44. Install the speedometer pinion in the rear extension.

45. Coat the electrical switch threads with gasket sealer. Intall the switches and tighten to specifications (**Table 1**).

46. Install the clutch release mechanism. See *Release Mechanism, Installation* in this chapter.

47. Temporarily install the shift lever. Move it through the gear positions. Turn the input shaft at each position and make sure the main shaft turns smoothly. In neutral, it should be possible to hold the main shaft from turning while turning the input shaft.

48. Install the drain plug. Use gel-type gasket sealer on the plug threads.

Disassembly (Five-speed Transmission)

The model FS5W71B 5-speed transmission is very similar to the F4W71B 4-speed. The main differences are in the gear assembly (**Figure 56**). Procedures not covered in this section will be found under *Disassembly (Four-speed Transmission)* in this chapter.

(56) **5-SPEED TRANSMISSION**

3rd main gear

Snap ring — Pilot bearing

Main drive gear ball bearing

Washer — Coupling sleeve

Balk ring

Snap ring — Washer

Needle bearing

Snap ring

3rd and 4th synchronizer hub

Spread spring

Shifting insert

Main drive gear

Steel ball

Main shaft ball bearing

1st main gear

Main shaft

1st gear bushing

Thrust washer

Overdrive main shaft bearing

Speedometer drive gear

1st and 2nd synchronizer hub

2nd main gear

Washer

Snap ring

Main shaft locknut

① 137-167

(101-123)

O.D. (5th)
main gear

Overdrive
gear bushing

Balk ring

Countershaft locknut
① 98-127 (72-94)

Shifting insert

Countershaft rear
end bearing

Spread spring

Overdrive counter gear

Spread spring
Shifting insert

Needle bearing

Reverse main gear

Reverse counter gear

Insert retainer

Woodruff key

Counter rear
bearing

Snap ring

Reverse idler
thrust washer

O.D. (5th) synchronizer hub

Counter rear
bearing

Reverse counter
gear spacer

Reverse idler gear

Counter gear

Reverse idler gear bearing

Reverse idler thrust washer

Woodruff key

Reverse idler shaft

Shim

Counter drive gear

Counter front bearing

① : N•m (ft.-lb.)

8

1. Before disassembling, check gear end play and backlash. Refer to *Disassembly (Four-speed Transmission)* in this chapter.

2. When removing the transmission case, use a gear puller (**Figure 57**). These are available from tool rental dealers.

3. Remove the front bearing and snap ring from the countershaft gear.

4. Remove the countershaft drive gear and input shaft simultaneously.

5. Slide the third-fourth gear synchronizer sleeve over the small teeth on third gear. Slide the first-second synchronizer sleeve over the small teeth on one of the gears next to it. This engages 2 gears at once to prevent the main shaft from turning.

6. Carefully file away the punched portions of the main shaft nut and countershaft gear nut. Loosen both nuts with a 38 mm (1-1/2 in.) wrench. See **Figure 58**. Take the countershaft gear nut off. Leave the main shaft nut on for now.

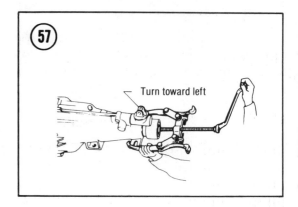

Turn toward left

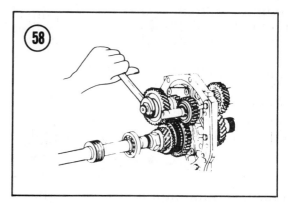

NOTE
If you don't have the correct wrench, take the gear assembly to a Datsun dealer and have the nuts loosened.

7. Remove the countershaft overdrive gear and bearing with a gear puller (**Figure 59**).

8. Remove reverse countershaft gear and its spacer.

9. Remove the snap ring from the reverse idler shaft, then remove reverse idler gear.

10. Remove a snap ring, the speedometer gear and 2 more snap rings from the rear end of the main shaft.

11. Have the main shaft rear bearing pressed off by a machine shop.

12. Remove the following parts in order from the rear end of the main shaft: nut, thrust washer, reverse main gear, overdrive synchronizer and overdrive (fifth) gear.

13. Tap the main shaft loose from the adapter plate with a soft-faced mallet. Remove the main shaft and countershaft simultaneously.

14. Remove the following parts in order from the front end of the main shaft: snap ring, thrust washer, balk ring, third-fourth gear synchronizer, balk ring, third gear and needle bearing.

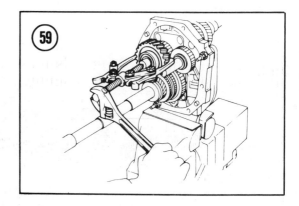

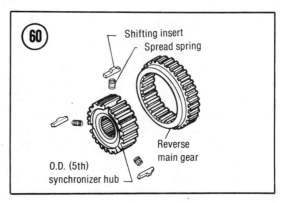

Shifting insert
Spread spring
Reverse main gear
O.D. (5th) synchronizer hub

Inspection (Five-speed)

This is the same as for 4-speed transmissions, described in this chapter.

Assembly (Five-Speed)

Assembly is the reverse of disassembly, plus the following:

1. Dip all gears, bearings and synchronizers in new gear oil before installing.

2. Assemble the overdrive (fifth) gear and its synchronizer as shown in **Figure 60**.

3. Install the overdrive (fifth) gear synchronizer with its hub offset as shown in **Figure 61**.

4. Assemble the reverse idler gear and shaft as shown in **Figure 62**.

5. Tighten the countershaft and main shaft locknuts. Refer to Step 21, *Assembly, Four-speed* in this chapter. Since specified torque for the countershaft nut is 10-13 mkg (72-94 ft.-lb.), use a 45 lb. weight. This gives a torque of 90 ft.-lb., which is within the specified range.

6. After tightening the nuts, peen them into position with a hammer and punch. See **Figure 63**.

TRANSFER CASE

Removal/Installation

1. Disconnect the negative cable from the battery.

2. Jack up all 4 corners of the truck. Support the truck securely with jackstands.

3. Remove the transfer case skid plate (**Figure 64**).

4. Make match marks on the flanges of primary (short) drive shaft and transfer case. Then remove the nuts and bolts securing the primary drive shaft to the transfer case.

5. Remove the front and rear drive shafts. See *Drive Shafts, Removal/Installation*, Chapter Ten.

6. Disconnect the 4-wheel drive switch wires.

7. Unscrew the speedometer cable.

8. Remove the exhaust tube. See *Exhaust System*, Chapter Five.

WARNING
Use a transmission jack for the next steps. This type of jack, available from rental dealers, has a cradle that will prevent the transfer case from falling during removal.

8

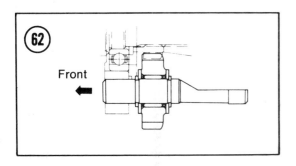

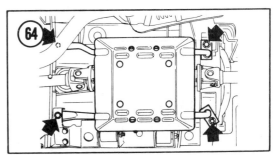

9. Loosen but do not remove the transfer case mounting insulator nuts. See **Figure 65**.

10. Separate the transfer case lever boot from the floor. See **Figure 66**.

11. Remove the transfer case mounting nuts (**Figure 67**). Lower the transfer unit away from the truck, then take it out.

12. Installation is the reverse of removal. If the oil was drained, fill the transfer case with an oil recommended in Chapter Three. Apply gasket sealer to the filler plug threads, then tighten the plug to 20-39 N•m (14-29 ft.-lb.).

Disassembly

Refer to **Figures 68-70** for the following procedures.

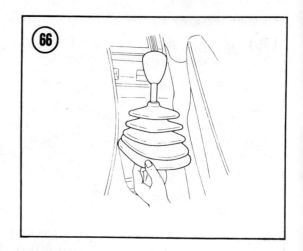

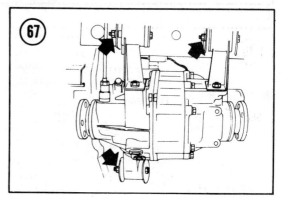

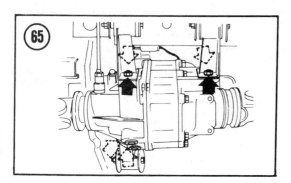

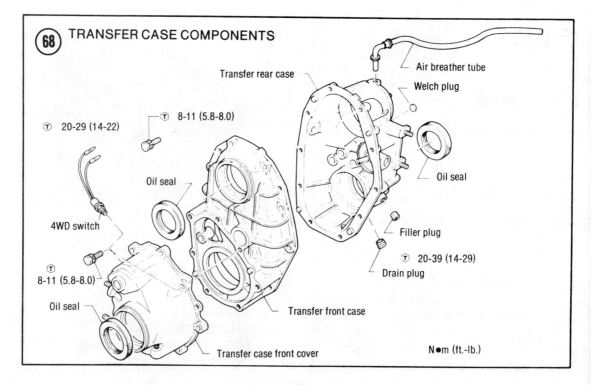

68 TRANSFER CASE COMPONENTS

Transfer rear case

Air breather tube

Welch plug

8-11 (5.8-8.0)

20-29 (14-22)

Oil seal

Oil seal

4WD switch

Filler plug

20-39 (14-29)

8-11 (5.8-8.0)

Drain plug

Oil seal

Transfer front case

Transfer case front cover

N•m (ft.-lb.)

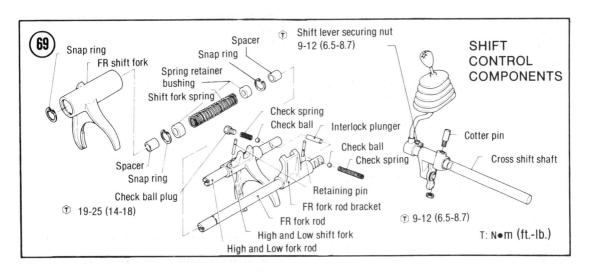

(69)

Snap ring
FR shift fork
Spring retainer bushing
Shift fork spring
Spacer
Snap ring
Spacer
Snap ring
Check ball plug

(T) 19-25 (14-18)

Shift lever securing nut
9-12 (6.5-8.7)

Check spring
Check ball
Interlock plunger
Check ball
Check spring
Retaining pin
FR fork rod bracket
FR fork rod
High and Low shift fork
High and Low fork rod

Cotter pin
Cross shift shaft

(T) 9-12 (6.5-8.7)

SHIFT CONTROL COMPONENTS

T: N●m (ft.-lb.)

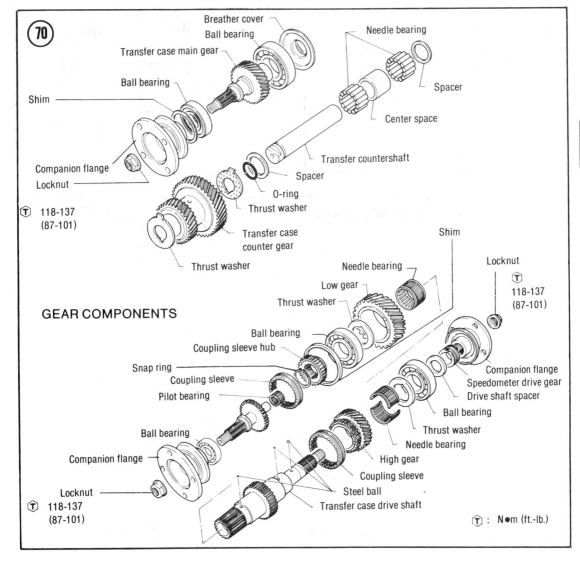

(70)

Breather cover
Ball bearing
Transfer case main gear
Ball bearing
Shim
Companion flange
Locknut

(T) 118-137 (87-101)

Needle bearing
Spacer
Center space
Transfer countershaft
Spacer
O-ring
Thrust washer

Transfer case counter gear
Thrust washer

GEAR COMPONENTS

Ball bearing
Coupling sleeve hub
Snap ring
Coupling sleeve
Pilot bearing
Ball bearing
Companion flange
Locknut

(T) 118-137 (87-101)

Needle bearing
Low gear
Thrust washer

Shim
Locknut
(T) 118-137 (87-101)

Companion flange
Speedometer drive gear
Drive shaft spacer
Ball bearing
Thrust washer
Needle bearing
High gear
Coupling sleeve
Steel ball
Transfer case drive shaft

(T) : N●m (ft.-lb.)

8

1. Clean the outside of the transfer case with solvent.

2. If you haven't already done so, drain the transfer case oil.

3. Hold the transfer case flanges with Datsun tool No. ST3153000 (if available). See **Figure 71**.

> *NOTE*
> *If the special tool is not available, drill 2 holes in a length of angle iron, then bolt it to 2 of the flange bolt holes.*

4. Remove the flange nuts as shown in **Figure 71**, then pull the flanges off.

> *NOTE*
> *If the flanges are difficult to remove, use a gear puller.*

5. Remove the 4-wheel drive switch (**Figure 72**).

6. Unbolt the transfer case front cover from the transfer front case. Then tap the front cover loose with a soft-faced mallet. See **Figure 73**.

7. Remove the front-rear drive shaft and needle bearing. See **Figure 74**.

8. Remove the snap ring securing the front-rear shift fork. See **Figure 75**. Pull out the shift fork and spacer assembly, together with the coupling sleeve.

9. Remove the snap ring that secures the coupling sleeve hub. See **Figure 76**.

10. Pull out the coupling sleeve hub (**Figure 77**).

11. Remove the transfer front case bolts (**Figure 78**). Tap the case loose with a soft-faced mallet.

> *CAUTION*
> *Do not pry the case loose. This will damage the gasket surfaces and cause an oil leak.*

12. Remove the taper pin nut, then tap the taper pin out. See **Figure 79**.

13. Pull out the cross shift shaft (**Figure 80**).

14. Remove the shift lever (**Figure 81**).

15. Remove the check ball plug, spring and check ball. See **Figure 82**.

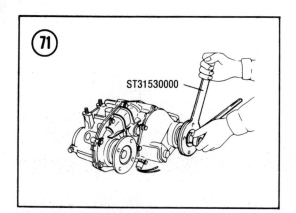

(71) ST31530000

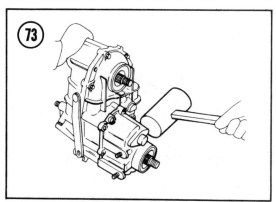

(73)

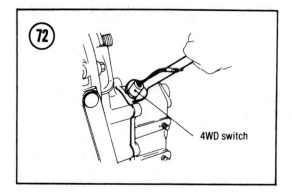

(72) 4WD switch

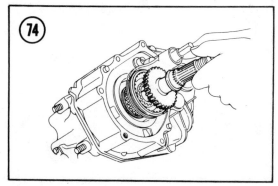

(74)

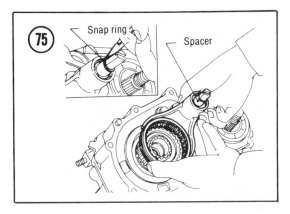

75 Snap ring   Spacer

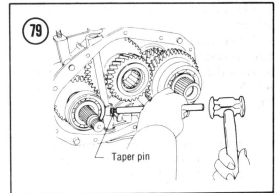

79   Taper pin

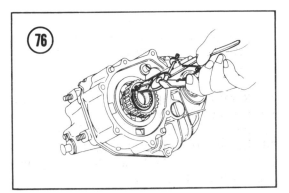

76

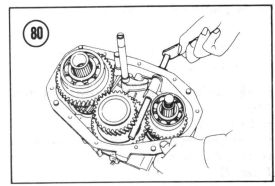

80

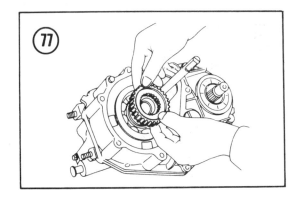

77

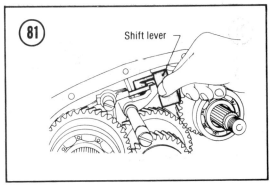

81 Shift lever

78

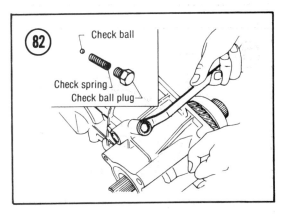

82 Check ball
Check spring
Check ball plug

8

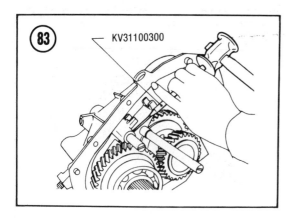

83 KV31100300

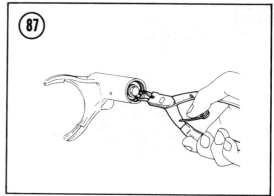

87

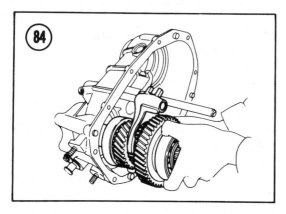

84

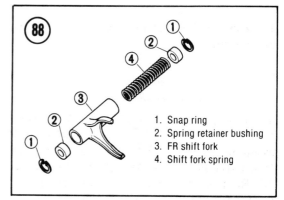

88

1. Snap ring
2. Spring retainer bushing
3. FR shift fork
4. Shift fork spring

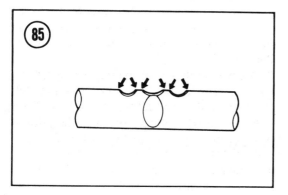

85

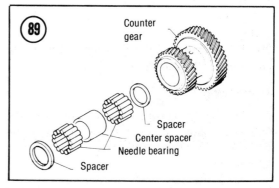

89

Counter gear

Spacer
Center spacer
Needle bearing
Spacer

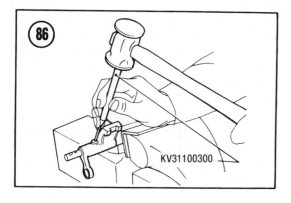

86 KV31100300

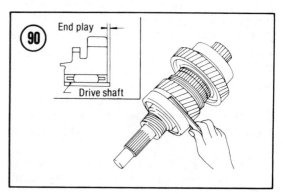

90

End play

Drive shaft

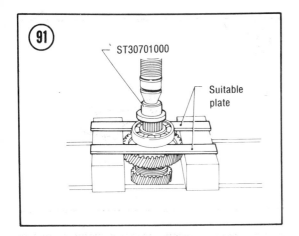

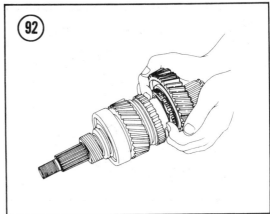

16. Tap out the high-low shift fork retaining pin. See **Figure 83**.

NOTE
During the next step, take care not to drop the counter gear needle bearings.

17. Tap the transfer case drive shaft assembly loose from the case. Pull out the drive shaft assembly, together with the high-low shift fork and counter gear assembly. See **Figure 84**.
18. Remove the transfer case shim. Be sure to save the shim for use during assembly.
19. Remove the high-low and front-rear fork rods, interlock plunger, steel ball and check spring.
20. Take the transfer main gear and breather cover out of the transfer case.

Inspection

1. Thoroughly clean all parts in solvent. While cleaning, check for obvious wear or damage. Replace parts that show these conditions.
2. Check the fork rod notches for wear or damage. See **Figure 85**. Replace the fork rods if wear or damage can be seen.
3. If the front-rear fork rod or bracket is to be replaced, drive out the retaining pin (**Figure 86**). Install the new fork or bracket, then secure it with a new retaining pin.
4. Thread an M8 bolt into the front-rear shift fork (**Figure 87**). Tighten the bolt to compress the spring, then remove the snap ring as shown.
5. Take the spring and its retainer bushings out of the front-rear shift fork. See **Figure 88**.

Check the spring and bushings for wear or damage and replace parts that show these conditions.
6. Reinstall the spring and bushings in the front-rear shift fork.
7. Check the ball bearing at each end of the transfer case main gear for looseness, rough movement or excessive noise. If these conditions are found, have the bearings pressed off and new ones pressed on by a machine shop.
8. Remove the spacers and needle bearings from the counter gear. See **Figure 89**. Since needle bearing wear is hard to see, replace the needle bearings whenever the transfer case is disassembled.
9. Measure end play of the transfer case drive shaft gears with a feeler gauge. See **Figure 90**. Compare with specifications in **Table 4**. If not within specifications, replace the thrust washers or gears, whichever is worn. Refer to Steps 10-15 for replacement procedures.
10. Have the front ball bearing pressed off the transfer case drive shaft by a machine shop. See **Figure 91**.
11. Remove the thrust washer and steel ball, then take off low gear and its needle bearing. See **Figure 92**. The needle bearing should be replaced whenever the transfer case is disassembled. The gear should be replaced if it is worn or damaged.
12. Coat a new needle bearing with gear oil. Install the needle bearing, low gear, steel ball and thrust washer on the transfer case drive shaft. Then have the ball bearing pressed onto the shaft.

8

13. Have the speedometer drive gear and spacer pressed off the transfer case drive shaft. See **Figure 93**.

14. Remove the thrust washer and steel ball from the transfer case drive shaft, then have the ball bearing pressed off. See **Figure 94**.

15. Remove another thrust washer and steel ball. Take off high gear, its needle bearing and its coupling sleeve.

16. Coat a new needle bearing with gear oil and install it. Replace the thrust washers and high gear if worn or damaged. If the ball bearing is loose, rough or noisy, have a new one pressed on. Otherwise, the old one may be used.

17. Carefully pry out the oil seals as shown in **Figure 95**. Tap new seals in with their lips facing into the transfer case. Use a block of wood to spread the hammer's force so the seals won't tip sideways and jam.

18. Check the front cover bearing for looseness, rough movement or excessive noise. If these conditions are found, remove the bearing snap ring (**Figure 96**). Have the bearing pressed out and a new one pressed in by a machine shop.

Assembly

1. If any of the following parts was replaced, new shims may be needed. Perform Steps 2-7 to determine shim thickness. If none of the parts was replaced, the old shims may be used.

    a. Ball bearings
    b. Transfer case drive shaft
    c. Transfer case main gear
    d. Front or rear case

2. Measure the depth of both front case bearing recesses with a vernier caliper. See **Figure 97**. Write down the transfer main gear depth (A, **Figure 98**) and transfer drive shaft depth (B).

3. Measure the depth of both rear case bearing recesses. See **Figure 99**. Write down the transfer main gear depth (C, **Figure 100**) and transfer drive shaft depth (D).

NOTE
*Transfer drive shaft recess depth (D) is measured with the breather cover installed. See **Figure 101**.*

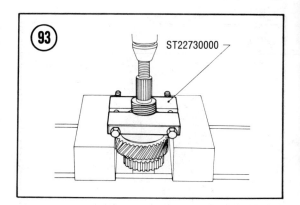

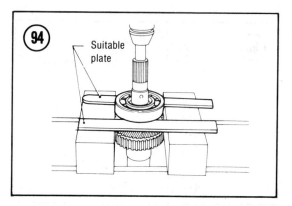

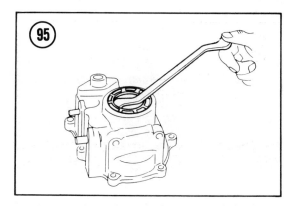

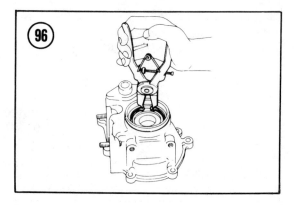

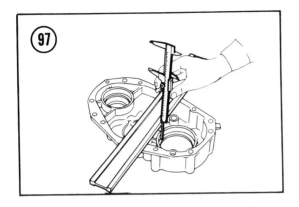

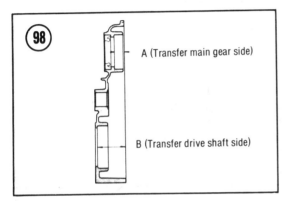

A (Transfer main gear side)

B (Transfer drive shaft side)

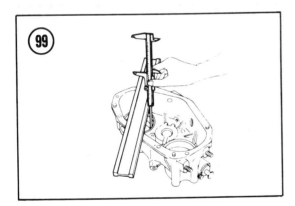

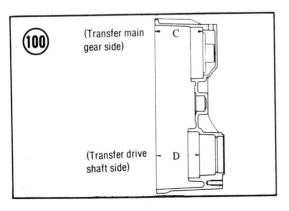

(Transfer main gear side)   C

(Transfer drive shaft side)   D

4. Measure the main gear's assembled length. See **Figure 102**. Write this figure down and call it "E."

5. To select a shim for the main gear, add measurement "A" to measurement "C." Subtract measurement "E" from the total of "A" and "C." Write down the result and call it "L1." Refer to **Table 5** for shim selection.

6. Measure the transfer drive shaft's assembled length. Write this down and call it "F."

7. To select a shim for the transfer drive shaft, add measurement "B" to measurement "D." Subtract measurement "F" from the total of "B" and "D." Write this down and call it "L2." Refer to **Table 6** for shim selection.

8. Install the breather cover and transfer main gear assembly. See **Figure 101**.

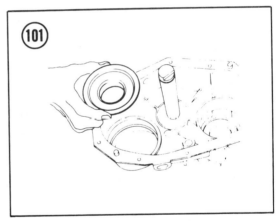

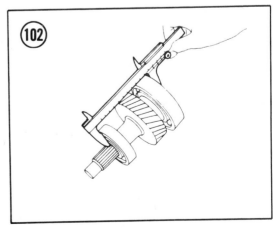

8

9. Tap out the front-rear shift fork plug. See **Figure 103**.

10. Install the check spring and steel ball in their hole in the rear case. Secure them with a rod such as Datsun tool part No. ST23620000 (**Figure 104**).

11. Install the high-low shift fork on the coupling sleeve.

12. Install the front-rear fork rod (**Figure 105**). Push the special tool out as the rod is installed.

13. Secure the front-rear fork rod bracket to the fork rod with a new retaining pin.

14. Coat a new countershaft O-ring with gear oil, then install it on the countershaft. Install the countershaft in the rear case.

15. Install the counter gear thrust washer, then install the counter gear assembly.

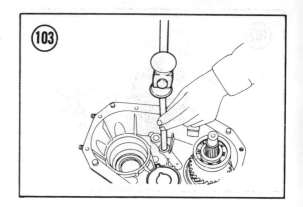

CAUTION
Do not leave the thrust washer out.

16. Lift the counter gear assembly, then install the transfer case drive shaft assembly. See **Figure 106**. Mesh the gears.

17. Install the flange on the rear end of the transfer case drive shaft. Tighten a new flange nut finger-tight.

18. Tap the drive shaft assembly into position in the transfer case. See **Figure 107**.

19. Install the high-low fork rod, then secure it with a retaining pin. See **Figure 108**.

20. Apply gasket sealer to the edges of the front-rear shift fork plug, then tap it into the case. See **Figure 109**.

21. Install the check ball and spring. Apply gasket sealer to the check ball plug threads, than install the plug. See **Figure 110**. Tighten to 19-25 N•m (14-18 ft.-lb.).

22. Install a snap ring on the coupling sleeve hub (**Figure 111**). Select a snap ring will that will reduce hub end play to zero-0.20 mm (zero-0.008 in.). See **Figure 112**.

23. Install the shift lever shaft and differential lever.

24. Install the cross shift shaft. See **Figure 113**.

25. Apply multipurpose grease to the front case thrust washer and shims, then install them. See **Figure 114**.

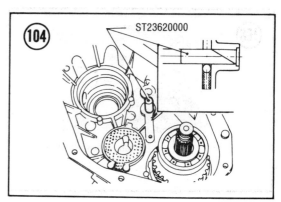

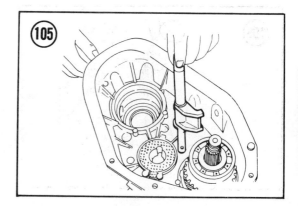

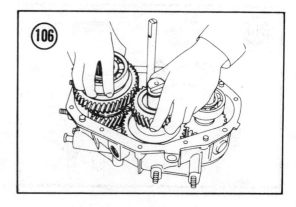

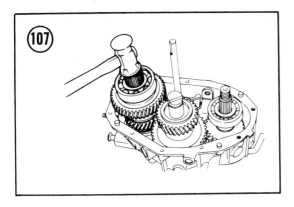

(107)

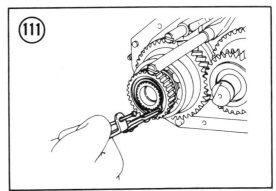

(111)

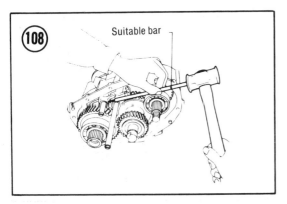

(108)

Suitable bar

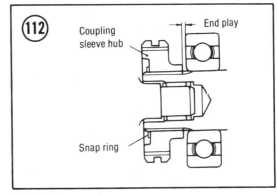

(112)

Coupling
sleeve hub

End play

Snap ring

8

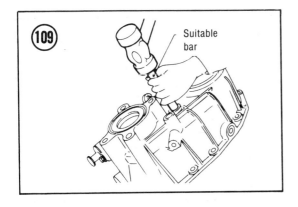

(109)

Suitable
bar

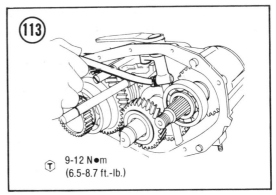

(113)

9-12 N●m
(6.5-8.7 ft.-lb.)

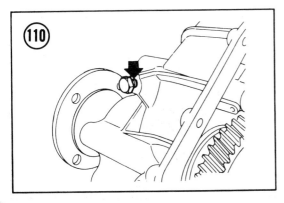

(110)

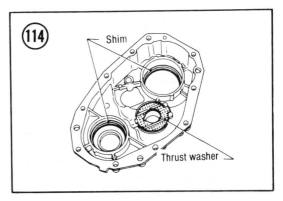

(114)

Shim

Thrust washer

26. Apply a continuous bead of gasket sealer to the front case mating surface. See **Figure 115**.

27. Tap the front case on with a soft-faced mallet (**Figure 116**). Install the front case bolts and tighten to specifications (**Table 1**).

28. Install the spacer, front-rear shift fork and coupling sleeve, spacer and snap ring. See **Figure 117**.

29. Coat the pilot bearing with gear oil, then install it. See **Figure 118**.

30. Install the front-rear drive shaft on the transfer case drive shaft.

31. Apply a continuous bead of gasket sealer to the transfer case gasket surface (**Figure 119**).

32. Install the transfer case front cover (**Figure 120**).

33. Install the flanges. Secure the flanges with new locknuts. Tighten to specifications (**Table 1**).

34. Install the switch. Tighten to specifications.

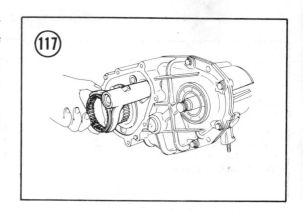

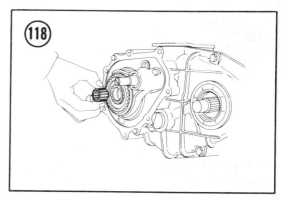

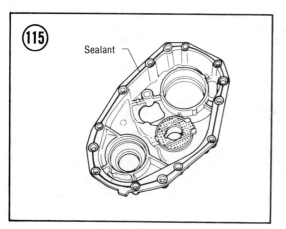

Sealant

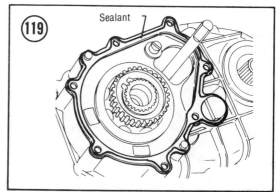

Sealant

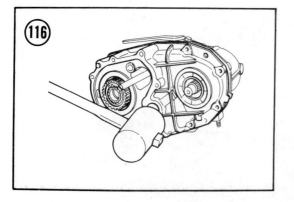

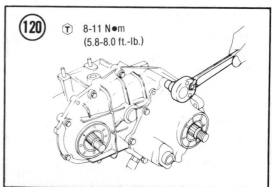

(T) 8-11 N•m
(5.8-8.0 ft.-lb.)

Table 1   TIGHTENING TORQUES

Fastener	N•m	Ft.-lb.
Clutch		
Pressure plate to flywheel	16-21	12-16
Slave cylinder bolts	30-40	22-30
Slave cylinder bleed valve	7-9	5-6.5
Master cylinder nuts	8-12	6-9
Master cylinder stopper bolt	1.5-2.9	1.1-2.2
Transmission Removal/Installation		
Transmission to engine	43-58	32-43
Engine rear plate to transmission	9-12	6.5-9
Crossmember to body	31-42	23-31
Insulator to crossmember		
1980	16-22	12-16
1981	31-35	23-26
Insulator to transmission		
1980	31-36	23-27
1981	42-49	31-36
Transmission overhaul		
Bearing retainer to adapter plate	16-23	12-17
Mainshaft locknut	137-167	101-123
Counter gear locknut (5-speed only)	98-127	72-94
Rear extension to transmission case	16-21	12-15
Front cover to transmission case	16-21	12-15
Ball pin	20-34	14-25
Striking lever locknut	9-12	6.5-9
Check ball plugs	19-25	14-18
Back-up lamp switch	20-29	14-22
Return spring plug	8-10	6-7
Drain and filler plugs	25-34	18-25
Transfer Case Removal/Installation		
Insulator to transfer case	27-35	20-26
Insulator to body	27-35	20-26
Transfer case protector	27-35	20-26
Transfer Case Overhaul		
Check ball plugs	19-25	14-18
Taper pin	9-12	6.5-9
Front case	8-11	6-8
Front cover	8-11	6-8
4wd switch	20-29	14-22
Flange	118-137	87-101
Speedometer sleeve	3-4	2-3
Drain and filler plugs	20-39	14-29

8

Table 2   GEAR END PLAY

First gear	0.27-0.34 mm (0.010-0.013 in.)
Second gear	0.12-0.19 mm (0.005-0.007 in.)
Third gear	0.13-0.37 mm (0.005-0.015 in.)
Fifth gear	0.10-0.17 mm (0.004-0.007 in.)
Reverse idler gear	
(5-speed only)	0.05-0.50 mm (0.002-0.020 in.)

Table 3   TRANSMISSION SHIMS

Distance "A"	Shim thickness
3.42-3.51 mm (0.1346-0.1382 in.)	0.1 mm (0.004 in.)
3.32-3.41 mm (0.1307-0.1343 in.)	0.2 mm (0.008 in.)
3.22-3.31 mm (0.1268-0.1303 in.)	0.3 mm (0.012 in.)
3.12-3.21 mm (0.1228-0.1264 in.)	0.4 mm (0.016 in.)
3.02-3.11 mm (0.1189-0.1224 in.)	0.5 mm (0.020 in.)
2.92-3.01 mm (0.1150-0.185 in.)	0.6 mm (0.024 in.)

Table 4   TRANSFER GEAR END PLAY

High gear	0.10-0.20 mm (0.004-0.008 in.)
Low gear	0.10-0.20 mm (0.004-0.008 in.)
Coupling sleeve hub	zero-0.20 mm (zero-0.008 in.)

Table 5   TRANSFER MAIN GEAR SHIMS

Distance L1	Shim thickness
0.06-0.15 mm (0.0024-0.0059 in.)	None
0.16-0.25 mm (0.0063-0.0098 in.)	0.1 mm (0.004 in.)
0.26-0.35 mm (0.0102-0.0138 in.)	0.2 mm (0.008 in.)
0.36-0.45 mm (0.0142-0.0177 in.)	0.3 mm (0.012 in.)
0.46-0.55 mm (0.0181-0.0217 in.)	0.4 mm (0.016 in.)

Table 6   TRANSFER DRIVE SHAFT SHIMS

Distance L2	Shim thickness
zero-0.13 mm (zero-0.0051 in.)	None
0.14-0.23 mm (.0055-0.0091 in.)	0.1 mm (0.004 in.)
0.24-0.33 mm (0.0094-0.0130 in.)	0.2 mm (0.008 in.)
0.34-0.43 mm (0.0134-0.0169 in.)	0.3 mm (0.012 in.)
0.44-0.53 mm (0.0173-0.0209 in.)	0.4 mm (0.016 in.)
0.54-0.63 mm (0.0213-0.:248 in.)	0.5 mm (0.020 in.)

CHAPTER NINE

FRONT SUSPENSION, AXLES, DIFFERENTIAL AND STEERING

This chapter provides service procedures for the front suspension, front axle, front differential and steering. **Table 1** and **Table 2** are at the end of the chapter.

Datsun 4-wheel drive pickups use upper and lower suspension links (A-arms), tube shock absorbers and torsion bar springs. The wheel hubs are supported by knuckle spindles, which pivot on ball-joints.

The steering is recirculating ball type.

Power is transmitted from the transfer case to the front differential, then through double-jointed axle shafts to the wheels.

WHEEL ALIGNMENT

Several suspension angles affect the running and steering of the front wheels. These angles must be properly aligned to prevent excessive wear, as well as to maintain directional stability and ease of steering. The angles are as follows:

    a. Caster
    b. Camber
    c. Toe-in
    d. Steering axis inclination
    e. Steering lock angles

Caster, camber, steering lock angles and toe-in can be adjusted. However, all but toe-in require a front end rack. Take the job to a dealer or alignment shop.

Pre-alignment Check

Adjustment of the steering and various suspension angles is affected by several factors. Perform the following steps before any adjustments are attempted.

1. Check tire pressure and wear. See *Tire Wear Analysis*, Chapter Two.
2. Check play in front wheel bearings. Adjust if necessary.
3. Check play in ball-joints.
4. Check for broken springs.
5. Remove any excessive load.
6. Check shock absorbers.
7. Check steering gear for wear or damage.
8. Check play in steering linkage.
9. Check wheel balance.
10. Check rear suspension for looseness.

Front tire wear patterns can indicate several alignment problems. These are covered under *Tire Wear Analysis*, Chapter Two.

Caster and Camber

Caster is the inclination from vertical of the line through the ball-joints. Positive caster shifts the wheel forward; negative caster shifts the wheel rearward. Caster causes the wheels to return to a straight-ahead position after a turn. It also prevents the wheels from wandering due to wind, potholes or uneven road surfaces.

9

Camber is the inclination of the wheel from vertical. With positive camber, the top of the tire leans outward. With negative camber, the top of the tire leans inward.

Toe-in

Since the front wheels tend to point outward when the car is moving forward, the distance between the front edges of the tire (A, **Figure 1**) is slightly less than the distance between the rear edges (B) when the car is at rest.

> *NOTE*
> *This is less true of radial tires than of bias ply or bias belted tires. The toe-in setting for radial tires is quite small; in some cases, zero.*

Although toe-in adjustment requires only a simple homemade tool, it usually isn't worth the trouble for home mechanics. Alignment shops include toe-in as part of the alignment procedure, so you probably won't save any money by doing it yourself. The procedure described here can be used for an initial toe-in setting after steering linkage overhaul.

1. With the steering wheel centered, roll forward about 15 ft. onto a smooth, level surface.

2. Mark the center of the tread at the front and rear of each tire.

3. Measure the distance between forward chalk marks (A, **Figure 1**). Use 2 pieces of telescoping aluminum tubing. Telescope the tubing so each end contacts a chalk mark. Using a sharp scribe, mark the small diameter tubing where it enters the large diameter tubing.

4. Measure between the rear chalk marks with the telescoping tubes. Make another mark on the small tube where it enters the large one. The distance between the 2 scribe marks is toe-in.

If toe-in is incorrect, loosen the tie rod clamps (**Figure 2**). Rotate the adjusting tubes as shown to change toe-in. Then tighten the clamps.

Steering Axis Inclination

Steering axis inclination is the inward or outward lean of the line through the

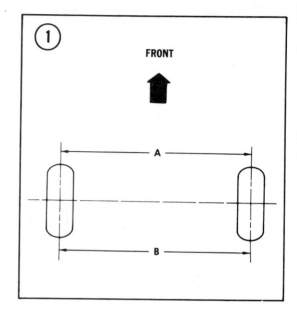

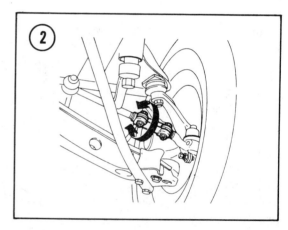

ball-joints. It is measured to check for bent suspension parts.

Steering Lock Angles

When a vehicle turns, the inside wheel makes a smaller circle than the outside wheel. Because of this, the inside wheel turns at a greater angle than the outside wheel. These angles are adjustable, but the job should be left to a dealer or alignment shop.

FRONT SUSPENSION

Figure 3 is an assembled view of the front suspension. **Figure 4** is an exploded view. Refer to them as needed for the following procedures.

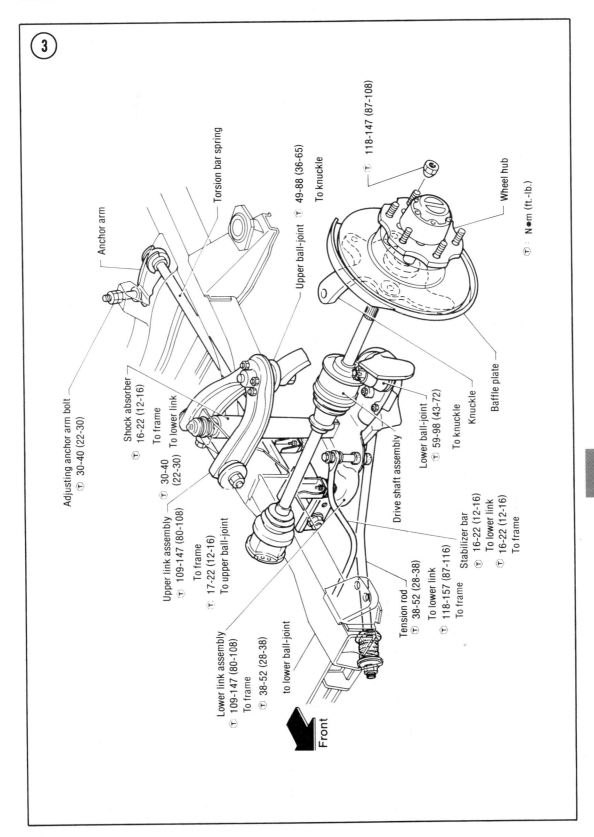

③

Torsion bar spring

Anchor arm

Adjusting anchor arm bolt
ⓣ 30-40 (22-30)

ⓣ Shock absorber
30-40 16-22 (12-16)
(22-30) To frame
To lower link

Upper link assembly
ⓣ 109-147 (80-108)
To frame
ⓣ 17-22 (12-16)
To upper ball-joint

Lower link assembly
ⓣ 109-147 (80-108)
To frame
ⓣ 38-52 (28-38)
to lower ball-joint

Upper ball-joint ⓣ 49-88 (36-65)
To knuckle

118-147 (87-108) ⓣ

Wheel hub

Baffle plate

Knuckle

Lower ball-joint
ⓣ 59-98 (43-72)
To knuckle

Drive shaft assembly

Stabilizer bar
ⓣ 16-22 (12-16)
To lower link
ⓣ 16-22 (12-16)
To frame

Tension rod
ⓣ 38-52 (28-38)
To lower link
ⓣ 118-157 (87-116)
To frame

ⓣ : N●m (ft.-lb.)

Front

9

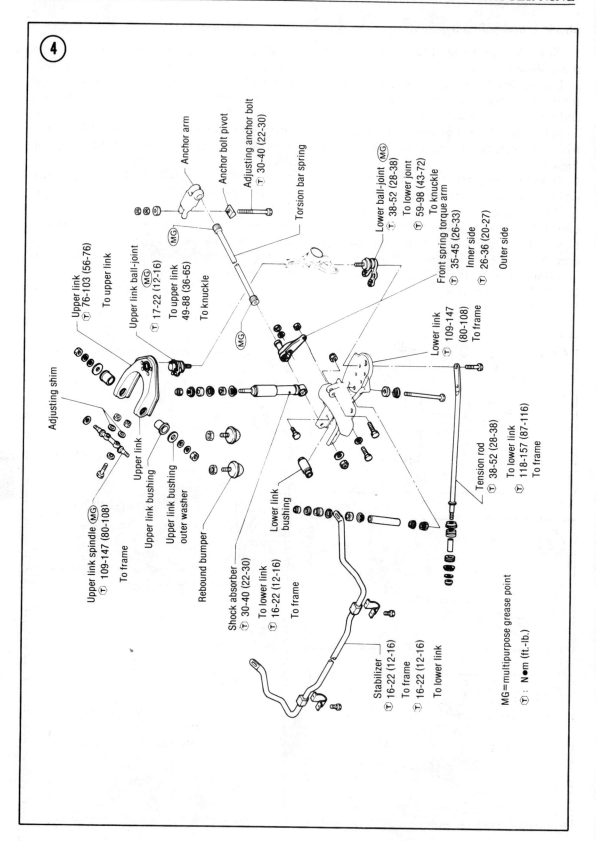

④

Anchor arm

Anchor bolt pivot

Adjusting anchor bolt
ⓣ 30-40 (22-30)

Torsion bar spring

Lower ball-joint Ⓜ🄶
ⓣ 38-52 (28-38)
To lower joint
ⓣ 59-98 (43-72)
To knuckle

Front spring torque arm
ⓣ 35-45 (26-33)
Inner side
ⓣ 26-36 (20-27)
Outer side

Upper link
ⓣ 76-103 (56-76)
To upper link

Upper link ball-joint
Ⓜ🄶
ⓣ 17-22 (12-16)
To upper link
49-88 (36-65)
To knuckle

Ⓜ🄶

Ⓜ🄶

Lower link
ⓣ 109-147
(80-108)
To frame

Adjusting shim

Upper link

Upper link bushing

Upper link bushing
outer washer

Rebound bumper

Shock absorber
ⓣ 30-40 (22-30)
To lower link
ⓣ 16-22 (12-16)
To frame

Lower link
bushing

Tension rod
ⓣ 38-52 (28-38)
To lower link
ⓣ 118-157 (87-116)
To frame

Upper link spindle Ⓜ🄶
ⓣ 109-147 (80-108)
To frame

Stabilizer
ⓣ 16-22 (12-16)
To frame
ⓣ 16-22 (12-16)
To lower link

MG=multipurpose grease point

ⓣ : N•m (ft.-lb.)

Shock Absorber Replacement

1. Set the parking brake. Place the transmission in FIRST.

2. Loosen the front wheel nuts. Jack up the front end of the truck, place it on jackstands and remove the front wheels.

3. Spray the shock absorber nuts and bolts with penetrating oil such as WD-40. See **Figure 5**.

4. Hold the shock absorber stem from turning and remove upper nuts, washers and bushings.

5. Remove the nut and bolt from the lower end of the shock absorber. Take it out.

6. Check all parts for wear and damage, especially rubber bushings. See **Figure 6**.

7. Installation is the reverse of removal. Install the lower bolt with its head toward the front of the truck.

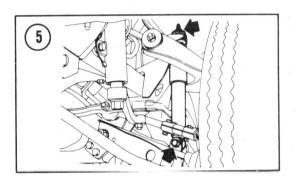

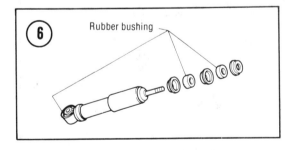

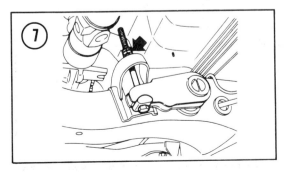

Torsion Bar Removal

At their front ends, the torsion bars are attached to torque arms, which are in turn attached to the lower suspension links. At the rear, the torsion bars are attached through anchor arms to the crossmember. As the suspension links move up and down, they twist the torsion bars. This provides a spring effect.

1. Set the parking brake. Place the transmission in FIRST.

2. Loosen the front wheel nuts. Jack up the front end of the truck, place it on jackstands and remove the front wheels.

3. Remove the adjusting anchor arm bolt from the anchor arm. See **Figure 7**.

4. Slide the anchor arm (**Figure 8**) off the rear end of the torsion bar.

5. Slide the torsion bar rearward out of the torque arm.

6. Remove the torque arm from the lower suspension link. See **Figure 9**.

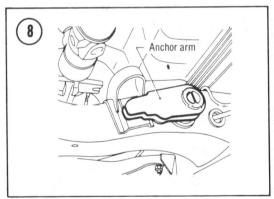

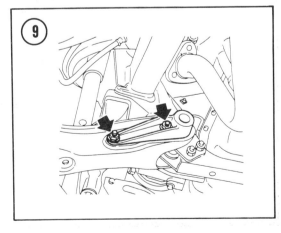

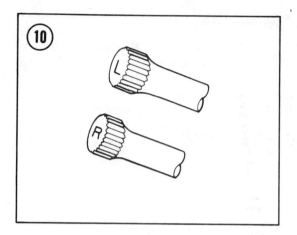

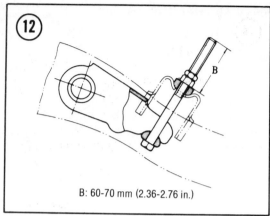

B: 60-70 mm (2.36-2.76 in.)

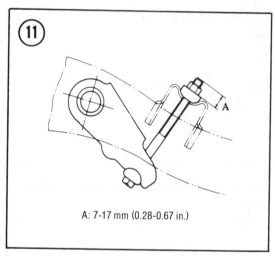

A: 7-17 mm (0.28-0.67 in.)

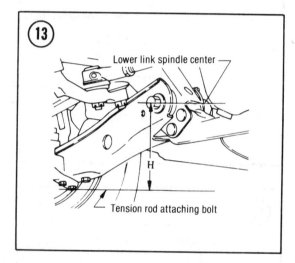

Lower link spindle center

H

Tension rod attaching bolt

Torsion Bar Inspection

1. Check torsion bars for wear, twisting, bending or damaged splines. Replace torsion bars that show these conditions.
2. Check the anchor arm, torque arm and adjusting bolt for wear or damage. Replace worn or damaged parts.

Torsion Bar Installation and Adjustment

1. Attach the torque arm to the lower suspension link. Tighten the nuts to specifications (end of chapter).
2. Grease the splines at the end of the torsion bar. Install the torsion bar in the torque arm.

NOTE
Left and right torsion bars are not interchangeable. They can be identified by the "L" and "R" marks stamped on the ends. See Figure 10.

3. Install the bolt in the anchor arm.
4. Install the anchor arm on the torsion bar. The anchor arm bolt should protrude 7-17 mm (0.28-0.67 in.). See **Figure 11**. If not, take the anchor arm off the torsion bar and reinstall it in a different position.
5. Place a jack beneath the anchor arm. Raise the jack until the anchor arm bolt protrudes 60-70 mm (2.36-2.76 in.). See **Figure 12**. Turn the anchor arm adjusting nut to hold the anchor arm in this position.
6. Install the wheels and lower the truck.

NOTE
The truck must be unloaded for the next step.

7. Turn the anchor bolt adjusting nut so dimension "H" (**Figure 13**) is 134-139 mm (5.28-5.47 in.).

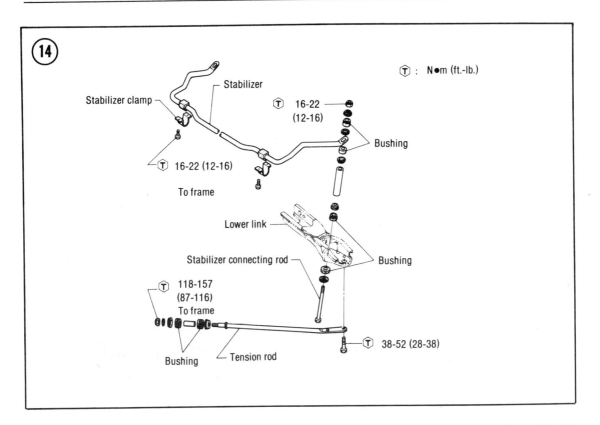

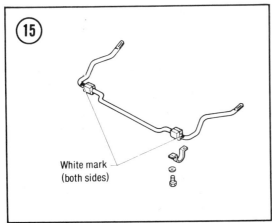

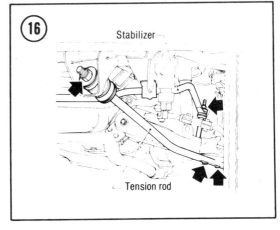

Stabilizer Bar Removal

1. Set the parking brake. Place the transmission in FIRST.
2. Jack up the front end of the truck and place it on jackstands.
3. Detach the stabilizer bar brackets from the truck frame. See **Figure 14**.
4. Check all parts for wear or damage, especially rubber bushings. Replace as needed.
5. Installation is the reverse of removal. Be sure the white paint marks (**Figure 15**) are evenly spaced on the outer sides of the bushings. Tighten all nuts and bolts to specifications (end of chapter).

Tension Rod Removal/Installation

1. Remove the tension rod nuts and bolts (**Figure 16**). Take the tension rod out.
2. Check all parts for wear or damage, especially rubber bushings.

3. Installation is the reverse of removal. Arrange the bushings as shown in **Figure 17**. Tighten nuts and bolts to specifications (end of chapter).

Upper Suspension Link and Ball-joint Removal

1. Set the parking brake. Place the transmission in FIRST.
2. Loosen the front wheel nuts. Jack up the front end of the truck, place it on jackstands and remove the front wheels.
3. Place a jack beneath the lower suspension link to relieve torsion bar tension.
4. Remove the upper ball-joint stud nut.
5. Separate the ball-joint stud from the knuckle spindle with a tool like the one shown in **Figure 18**. These are available from rental dealers.
6. Pull the ball-joint stud loose from the knuckle spindle. See **Figure 19**.
7. Remove the upper link spindle from the body. See **Figure 20**.

NOTE
There are camber shims between the upper arm spindle and body. Write down their locations so they can be returned to their original positions.

Upper Suspension Link and Ball-joint Disassembly

1. Unbolt the ball-joint from the suspension link. See **Figure 21**.

2. Remove the nut and washers from each end of the suspension link spindle.
3. Press the spindle in one direction and remove the bushings from one end (**Figure 22**). Then press it in the other direction and remove the bushings from the other end. The spindle can then be removed from the link.

NOTE
Step 3 can be done by a machine shop if you don't have a press.

Upper Suspension Link and Ball-joint Inspection

1. Check the link for bending or cracks. Replace it if these conditions are found. If the link is slightly rusty, clean and paint it. If rust is serious, replace the link.
2. Check the spindle for wear or damage. Replace it if these can be seen.

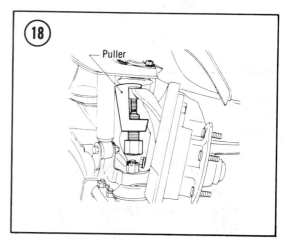

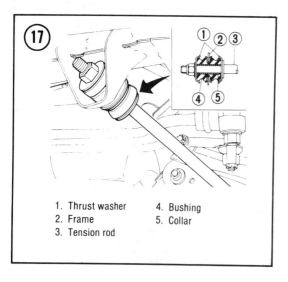

1. Thrust washer
2. Frame
3. Tension rod
4. Bushing
5. Collar

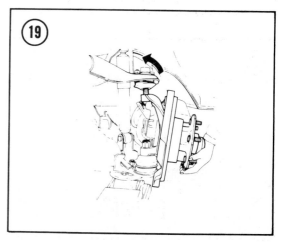

3. Check the rubber bushings for wear, damage or deterioration. Replace the bushings if there is any doubt about their condition.

4. Check the ball-joint dust cover for wear or damage. Replace the ball-joint if these can be seen.

5. Pull on the ball-joint stud and note end play (**Figure 23**). It should be 0.1-1.0 mm (0.004-0.039 in.). If beyond specifications, replace the ball-joint.

6. If the old ball-joint is to be reused, remove the grease plug and install a grease fitting in its place. Slowly pump in new grease until all the old grease is forced out. Remove the grease fitting and install the grease plug.

Upper Suspension Link and Ball-joint Assembly

1. Press new bushings into the link until the bushing flanges contact the link. See **Figure 24**.

2. Install the link spindle and inner washers (**Figure 25**).

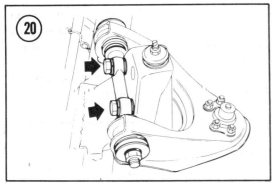

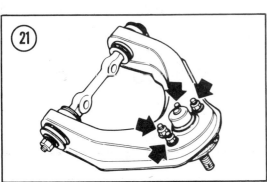

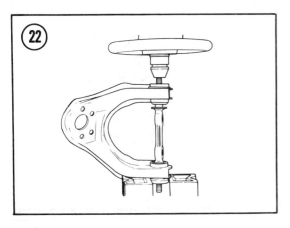

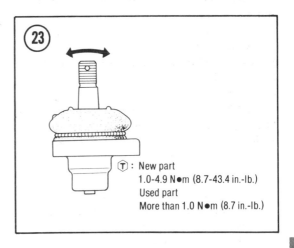

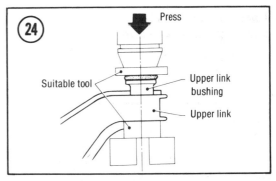

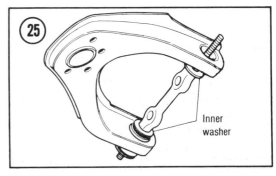

NOTE
The rounded sides of the inner washers face inward.

3. Press the remaining bushing into the link until its flange contacts the link.
4. Install the spindle nuts and tighten them slightly. See **Figure 26**.
5. Install the ball-joint (**Figure 27**).

Upper Suspension Link and Ball-joint Installation

1. Attach the link and spindle to the frame. See **Figure 28**.

NOTE
Return the camber shims to their original positions.

2. Make sure the link is centered as shown in **Figure 29**.

CAUTION
Before performing the next step, make sure there is no grease on the ball-joint stud or threads.

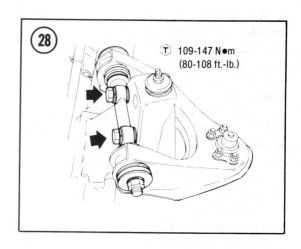

T 109-147 N•m
(80-108 ft.-lb.)

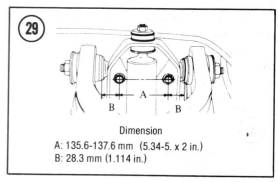

Dimension
A: 135.6-137.6 mm (5.34-5. x 2 in.)
B: 28.3 mm (1.114 in.)

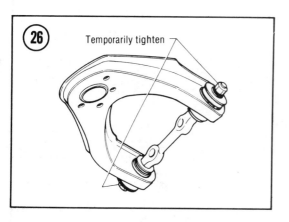

Temporarily tighten

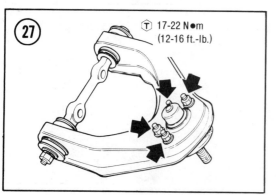

T 17-22 N•m
(12-16 ft.-lb.)

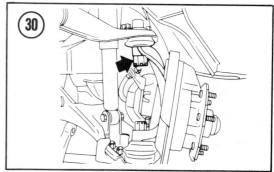

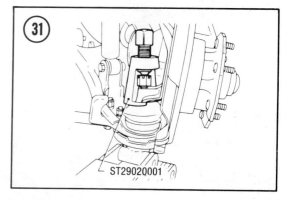

ST29020001

3. Attach the upper ball-joint to the knuckle spindle. See **Figure 30**. Tighten the nut to specifications (end of chapter), then secure it with a new cotter pin.

4. Install the wheels and lower the truck. Bounce the truck several times and roll it back and forth to settle the suspension. Then tighten the spindle nuts (**Figure 26**) to specifications with the truck's weight on the wheels.

5. After installation, have wheel alignment checked and adjusted if necessary by a dealer or alignment shop.

Lower Suspension Link and Ball-joint Removal

1. Set the parking brake. Place the transmission in FIRST.

2. Loosen the front wheel nuts. Jack up the front end of the truck, place it on jackstands and remove the front wheels.

3. Remove the torsion bar as described in this chapter.

4. Detach the lower end of the shock absorber from the lower link.

5. Loosen the lower link ball-joint nut. Separate the ball-joint from the link with a tool like the one shown in **Figure 31** (Datsun part No. ST29020001; Kent-Moore part No. J25725). These are available from tool rental dealers.

6. Disconnect the stabilizer bar and tension rod from the link. See **Figure 32**.

7. Remove the lower link pivot bolt (**Figure 33**). Take the link out.

8. Detach the ball-joint from the link. See **Figure 34**.

9. Tap the lower link bushing out of the frame with a suitable tool, such as a socket. See **Figure 35**.

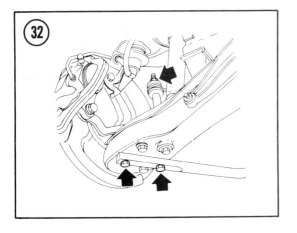

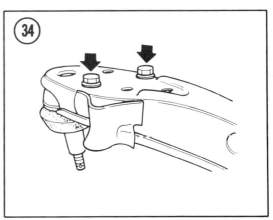

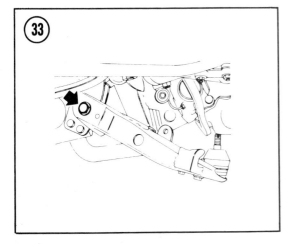

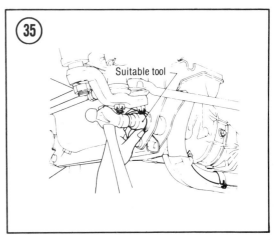

Lower Suspension Link and Ball-joint Inspection

1. Check the lower link for bending or cracks. Replace it if these are found. If the link is lightly rusted, clean and paint it. If rust is heavy, replace the link.

2. Pull on the ball-joint stud and check for movement. See **Figure 36**. If beyond specifications, replace the ball-joint. The ball-joint must also be replaced if the dust cover is cracked.

3. If the ball-joint is to be reused, remove the grease plug. Install a grease fitting and pump in multipurpose lithium grease until all the old grease is forced out. Then remove the grease fitting and install the plug.

4. Check the lower link bushing for wear or deterioration. Replace the bushing if there is any doubt about its condition.

5. Inspect the torsion bar and related parts as described in this chapter. Replace as needed.

Lower Suspension Link and Ball-joint Installation

1. Install the ball-joint (**Figure 37**).

2. Tap the spindle bushing into the frame.

3. Attach the torque arm to the torsion bar, then position them as shown in **Figure 38**.

4. Install the lower link (**Figure 39**).

5. Attach the torque arm to the lower link. Tighten bolts to specifications (end of chapter).

CAUTION
Before the next step, make sure there is no grease on the ball-joint stud or threads.

6. Jack up the lower link and connect the ball-joint to the knuckle spindle. Tighten the nut to specifications (end of chapter), then secure it with a new cotter pin.

7. Attach the torque arm to the lower link. Install the anchor arm on the torsion bar. See *Torsion Bars* in this chapter.

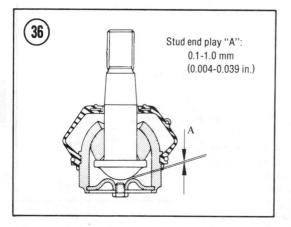

(36) Stud end play "A":
0.1-1.0 mm
(0.004-0.039 in.)

A

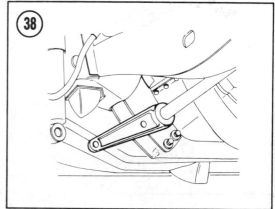

(38)

(37)

Ⓣ 38-52 N•m
(28-38 ft.-lb.)

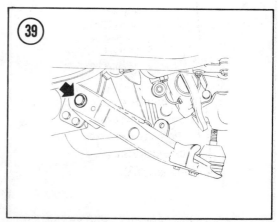

(39)

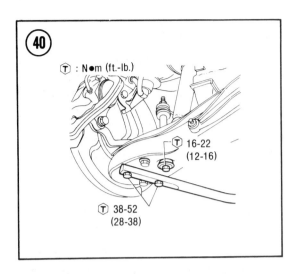

8. Attach the shock absorber lower end to the lower link. Tighten the nut and bolt to 30-40 N•m (22-30 ft.-lb.).

9. Attach the tension rod and stabilizer bar to the lower link. See **Figure 40**.

10. Install the wheels and lower the truck. Adjust the torsion bars as described in this chapter.

11. After installation, have wheel alignment checked by a dealer or alignment shop.

FRONT AXLES

The front axles consist of double-jointed axle shafts, hubs with tapered roller bearings, and free-running hubs. See **Figure 41**.

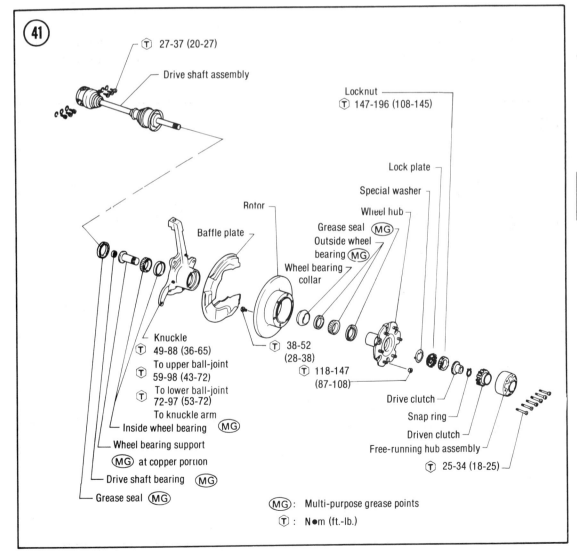

Free-running Hub
Removal/Installation

1. To remove, undo the mounting screws (**Figure 42**) and take the hub off.
2. Installation is the reverse of removal. Use a torque wrench and Phillips screwdriver bit to tighten the screws to specifications (end of chapter).

Free-running Hub
Disassembly/Inspection/Assembly

1. Set the hub in the LOCK position.
2. Attach a magnet to the driven clutch (**Figure 43**). Turn the magnet clockwise. This will pull on the lockpin and allow the driven clutch to be removed.
3. Remove the lockpin.
4. Check all parts for wear or damage. Replace as needed.
5. To assemble, place the knob in the FREE position and install the lockpin. Screw the driven clutch in counterclockwise as far as it will go, then turn it clockwise to align the screw holes. See **Figure 44**.

Axle Shaft Removal

1. Remove the free-running hub as described in this chapter.
2. Remove the snap ring and drive clutch (**Figure 45**).
3. Remove the rubber rebound bumpers.
4. Detach the stabilizer bar from the suspension link. See *Stabilizer Bar* in this chapter.
5. Detach the axle shaft from the differential. See **Figure 46**.

> *NOTE*
> *For the next step, turn the steering to the left to remove the left axle shaft or to the right to remove the right axle shaft.*

6. Pull the outer end of the axle shaft inward, out of the hub.
7. Take the axle shaft out.

Axle Shaft Inspection

1. Check the axle shaft for cracked or worn boots. Replace the axle shaft if these are found.

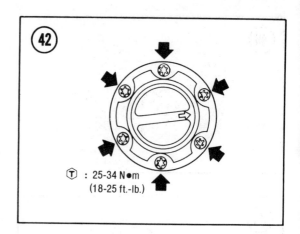

(42)

$\top$: 25-34 N●m
(18-25 ft.-lb.)

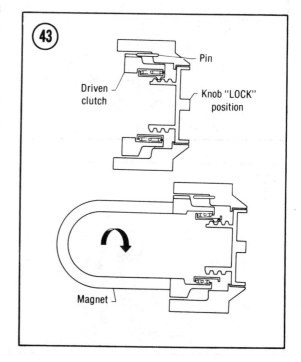

(43)

Pin

Driven clutch

Knob "LOCK" position

Magnet

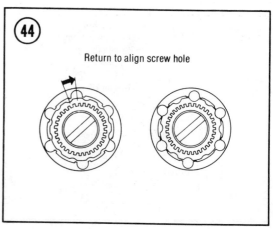

(44)

Return to align screw hole

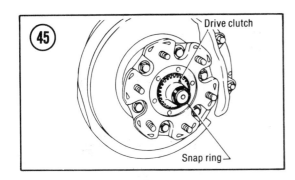

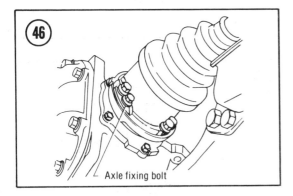

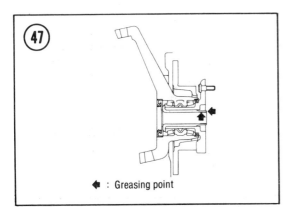

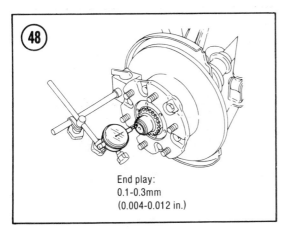

End play:
0.1-0.3mm
(0.004-0.012 in.)

2. Twist the axle shaft and check for loose joints. Replace the axle shafts if joints are loose.

NOTE
End play in joints is normal.

Axle Shaft Installation

Installation is the reverse of removal, plus the following.

1. Apply multipurpose lithium grease to the copper part of the wheel bearing support. See **Figure 47**.

2. Tighten all fasteners to specifications (end of chapter).

3. Measure axle shaft end play with a dial indicator (**Figure 48**). If not within specifications, correct with a different thickness of snap ring.

Wheel Hub and Knuckle Removal

1. Set the parking brake. Place the transmission in FIRST.

2. Loosen the front wheel nuts. Jack up the front end of the truck, place it on jackstands and remove the front wheels.

3. Remove the brake caliper. See *Front Brakes*, Chapter Eleven.

4. Remove the axle shaft as described in this chapter.

5. Remove the knuckle arm bolt (**Figure 49**).

WARNING
During Steps 6 and 7, do not remove the ball-joint nuts. The suspension is under spring tension and sudden release of the suspension links could cause serious injury.

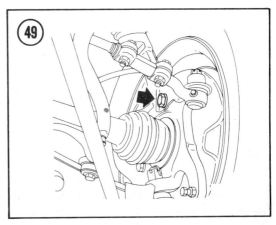

6. Loosen, but do not remove, the upper and lower ball-joint nuts. See **Figure 50**.

7. Detach the ball-joint studs from the knuckle spindle with a tool such as the one shown in **Figure 51** (Datsun part No. ST29020001; Kent-Moore part No. J25725). These are available from rental dealers.

8. Place a jack beneath the lower link to relieve spring tension. See **Figure 52**. Remove the ball-joint nuts.

9. Separate the knuckle from the upper and lower suspension links.

Wheel Hub and Knuckle Disassembly

1. Release the lockwasher with a screwdriver (**Figure 53**). Remove the lockwasher and throw it away.

2. Remove the locknut with a hub socket (Datsun part No. KV40102500). **Figure 54** shows the tool in use; **Figure 55** shows it alone. This tool is available from local dealers and from Adventure Four Wheel Drive Center, 2565 Winchester Blvd., Campbell, Calif. 95008.

3. Remove the lockwasher and special washer. See **Figure 56**.

4. Push the wheel bearing support out of the hub. See **Figure 57**.

5. Separate the knuckle from the hub with a puller. See **Figure 58**.

6. Remove the wheel bearing collar.

7. Tap out the inner wheel bearing and grease seal with a hammer and brass bar. See **Figure 59**.

8. Tap the hub assembly on a block of wood to loosen the outer bearing. See **Figure 60**.

9. Have the outer bearing pressed off by a machine shop. See **Figure 61**. Remove and discard the grease seal.

Wheel Hub and Knuckle Inspection

1. Thoroughly clean all parts with solvent and blow dry.

WARNING
Do not spin dry bearings with compressed air. They may fly apart.

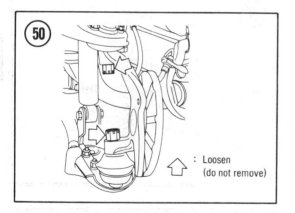

50

: Loosen
(do not remove)

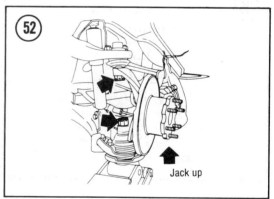

52

Jack up

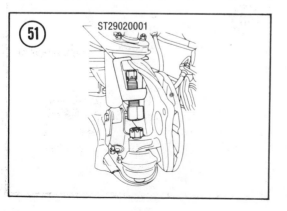

51

ST29020001

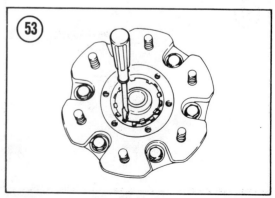

53

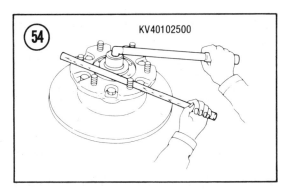

KV40102500

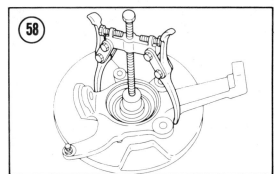

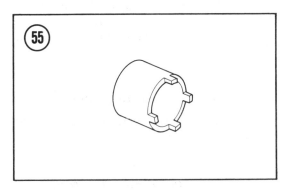

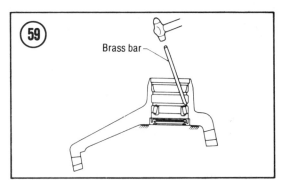

Brass bar

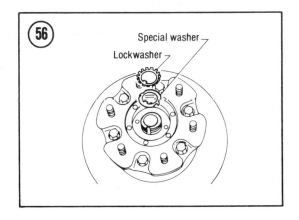

Special washer

Lockwasher

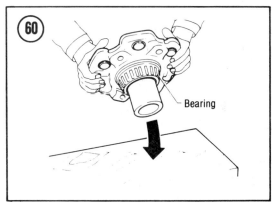

Bearing

9

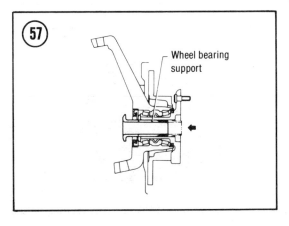

Wheel bearing support

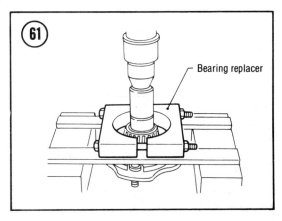

Bearing replacer

2. Check the wheel bearings for the following:
   a. Chips
   b. Cracks
   c. Pits
   d. Rust
   e. Burns (blue-tinted areas)
   f. Wear
   g. Scoring

Replace bearings that show these conditions.

3. Check the wheel hub and knuckle for cracks. If no cracks are visible and the truck has been subjected to hard use, have the hub and knuckle checked for invisible cracks by a machine shop.

4. If brake discs need to be replaced, unbolt them from the hubs.

5. Replace grease seals whenever the hub is disassembled, even if they appear to be in good condition.

Wheel Hub and Knuckle Assembly

Assembly is the reverse of disassembly, plus the following.

1. Pack wheel bearings with multipurpose lithium grease. Work as much grease between the rollers as possible.

2. Tap the bearing outer races into the knuckle with a suitable drift (**Figure 62**).

3. Pack the lip of the outer grease seal with multipurpose grease. Have the outer grease seal and wheel bearing pressed onto the hub by a machine shop. Be sure the seal lip faces in the direction shown in **Figure 63**.

> *CAUTION*
> *Press only against the bearing inner race.*
> *Do not press against the rollers or cage.*

4. Install the old bearing collar or one stamped with the same number. See **Figure 64**.

5. Have the inner bearing pressed onto the hub by a machine shop. See **Figure 65**.

> *CAUTION*
> *Press only against the inner race. Do not press against the cage or rollers.*

6. Install the special washer and lockwasher (**Figure 66**).

7. Tighten the locknut to specifications with the hub socket (**Figure 67**).

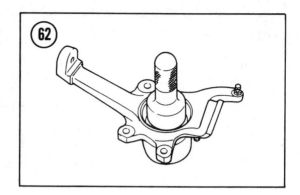

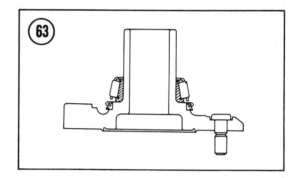

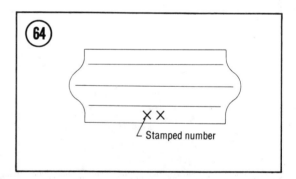

Stamped number

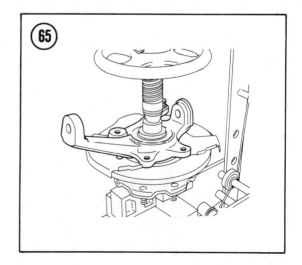

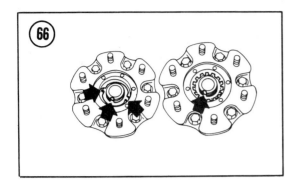

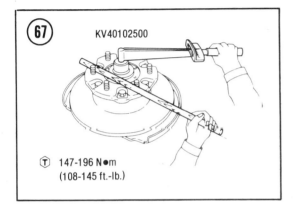

KV40102500

147-196 N•m
(108-145 ft.-lb.)

8. Turn the hub several turns in both directions to seat the bearings. See **Figure 68**.

9. Check wheel bearing preload with a spring scale (**Figure 69**).

10. If preload is more than specified, replace the bearing collar with a thicker one. If preload is less than specifications, replace the bearing collar with a thinner one.

> *CAUTION*
> *Do not try to adjust preload by tightening the locknut to more or less than specifications. This will cause bearing damage or a loose locknut.*

11. Once preload is set correctly, bend the lockwasher lip into a locknut groove. See **Figure 70**.

12. Install the grease seal on the knuckle with a suitable drift. Be sure the seal lip faces in the proper direction. See **Figure 71**.

Wheel Hub and Knuckle Installation

Installation is the reverse of removal, plus the following.

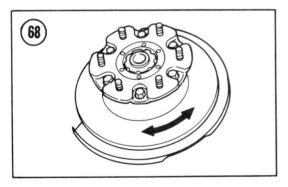

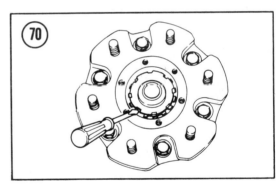

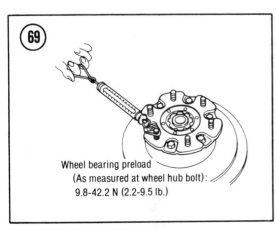

Wheel bearing preload
(As measured at wheel hub bolt):
9.8-42.2 N (2.2-9.5 lb.)

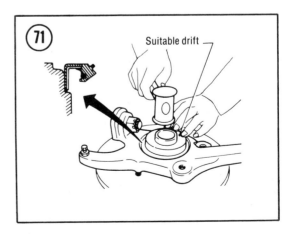

Suitable drift

1. Make sure there is no grease on ball-joint studs or threads. Support the lower suspension link with a jack while installing the ball-joint nuts. See **Figure 72**.

2. Tighten all fasteners to specifications (end of chapter).

3. Adjust axle shaft end play. See *Axle Shafts* in this chapter.

FRONT DIFFERENTIAL

Removal/Installation

This section includes removal, installation and inspection procedures. Differential repair requires special skills and many expensive special tools. The inspection procedures will tell you if repairs are needed.

Refer to **Figure 73** for this procedure.

1. Set the parking brake. Place the transmission in FIRST.

2. Jack up the front end of the truck and place it on jackstands.

3. Place a pan beneath the differential and drain the oil. See **Figure 74**.

4. Make match marks on drive shaft and differential flanges (**Figure 75**). Unbolt the drive shaft from the differential.

5. Detach the axle shafts 'from the differential. See **Figure 76**.

6. Remove the differential mounting bolts (**Figure 77**). Take the differential out.

7. Installation is the reverse of removal, plus the following.

    a. Align the match marks on differential and drive shaft.

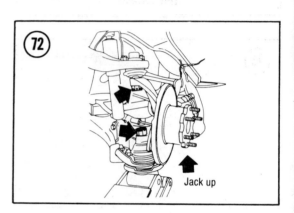

Jack up

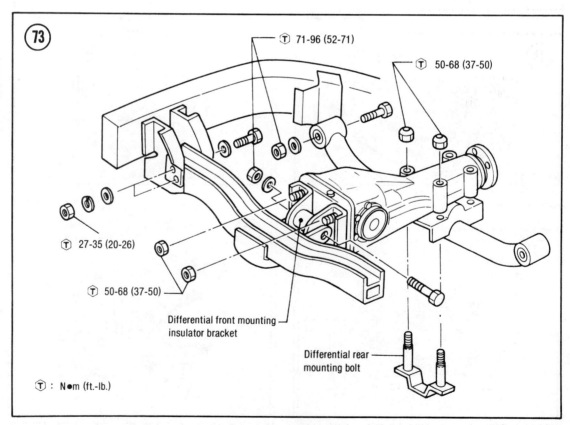

$\widehat{T}$ 71-96 (52-71)

$\widehat{T}$ 50-68 (37-50)

$\widehat{T}$ 27-35 (20-26)

$\widehat{T}$ 50-68 (37-50)

Differential front mounting insulator bracket

Differential rear mounting bolt

$\widehat{T}$: N•m (ft.-lb.)

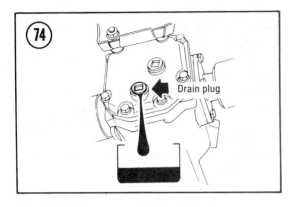

Drain plug

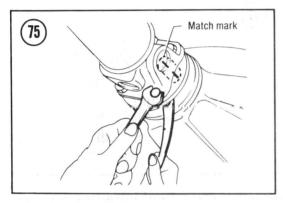

Match mark

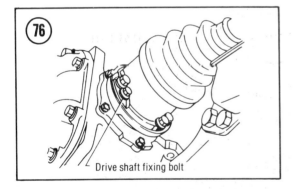

Drive shaft fixing bolt

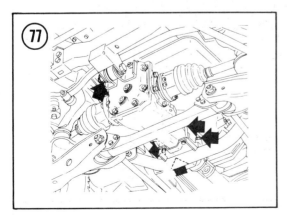

b. Tighten all nuts and bolts to specifications (end of chapter).

c. Fill the differential with an oil recommended in Chapter Three.

Inspection

1. Remove the rear cover from the differential. See **Figure 78**.

2. Turn the ring gear and look for broken, chipped or worn teeth. Check the differential for rough movement. Have the differential repaired if these conditions are found.

3. Connect a dial indicator as shown in **Figure 79**. Hold the pinion from turning with one hand and turn the ring gear against the dial indicator with the other. The reading (backlash) should be 0.13-0.18 mm (0.005-0.007 in.). If not, have the differential disassembled and adjusted.

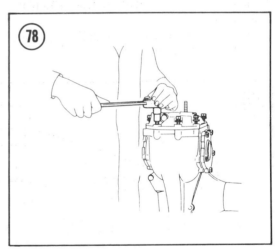

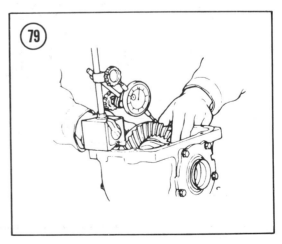

4. Connect the dial indicator as shown in **Figure 80**. Turn the ring gear and measure runout. It should not exceed 0.08 mm (0.003 in.). If it does, have the differential repaired.

5. Thoroughly clean the ring gear teeth.

6. Coat the drive side of the teeth with gear marking compound. See **Figure 81**.

7. Turn the ring gear in both directions. Compare the contact pattern pressed into the marking compound with those in **Figure 82**. If the pattern is not correct, have the differential disassembled and adjusted.

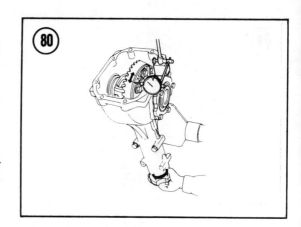

DRIVE SHAFT

The front drive shaft is covered under *Drive Shafts*, Chapter Ten.

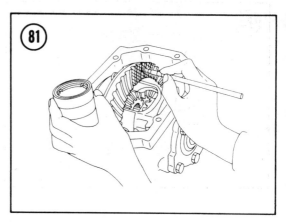

STEERING

Steering Wheel Removal/Installation

1. Disconnect the negative cable from the battery.

2. Remove the horn pad (**Figure 83**).

3. Turn the wheels so the steering column punch mark is straight up. See **Figure 84**. Make match marks on steering wheel and column.

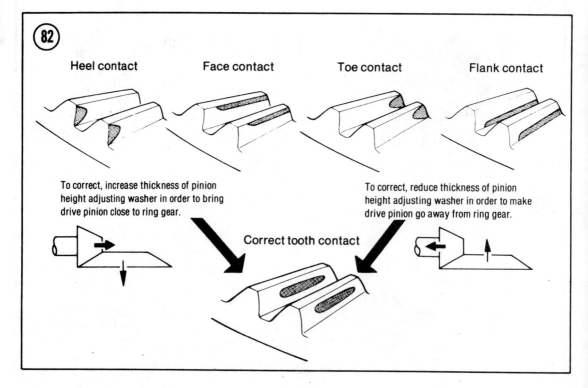

Heel contact   Face contact   Toe contact   Flank contact

To correct, increase thickness of pinion height adjusting washer in order to bring drive pinion close to ring gear.

To correct, reduce thickness of pinion height adjusting washer in order to make drive pinion go away from ring gear.

Correct tooth contact

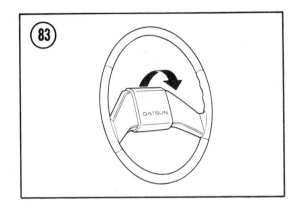

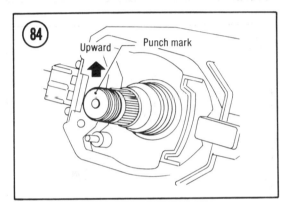

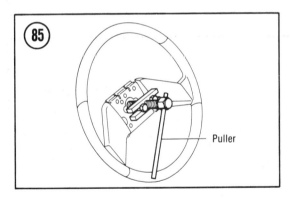

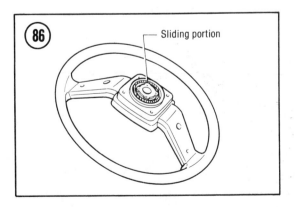

4. Remove the steering wheel with a puller (**Figure 85**). These are available from rental dealers and auto parts stores.

CAUTION
Do not pound on the steering wheel. Do not use an impact puller. These will damage the steering column.

5. Installation is the reverse of removal. Apply multipurpose grease to the friction surface (**Figure 86**). Line up the match marks on steering wheel and column.

Steering Lock Removal/Installation

1. Disconnect the negative cable from the battery.
2. Remove the steering column shell (**Figure 87**).
3. Drill out the self-shearing screws (**Figure 88**).
4. Remove the plain screws, then take off the steering lock.

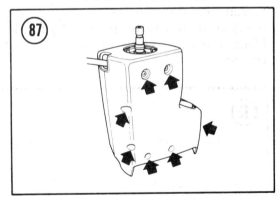

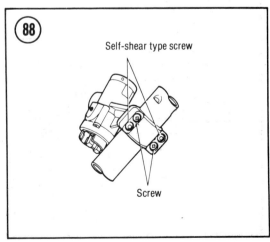

5. Installation is the reverse of removal. Align the lock with the hole in the steering column tube. Tighten the self-shearing screws until their heads snap off. See **Figure 89**.

Steering Column Removal/Installation

Refer to **Figure 90** for this procedure.

1. Disconnect the negative cable from the battery.

2. Remove the steering gear-to-column clamp bolt (**Figure 91**).

NOTE
The bolt passes through a notch in the steering gear shaft so it must be removed, not just loosened.

3. Remove the steering wheel as described in this chapter.

4. Remove the steering column shell.

5. Take the combination switch off the steering column. See **Figure 92**.

6. Remove the heater duct (**Figure 93**).

7. Detach the jacket tube bracket from the floor panel (**Figure 94**).

8. Remove the column bracket bolts (**Figure 95**). Pull the steering column into the passenger compartment.

9. Installation is the reverse of removal. Tighten all fasteners to specifications (end of chapter).

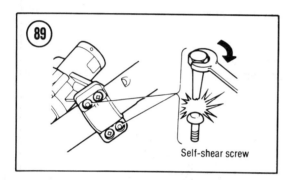
Self-shear screw

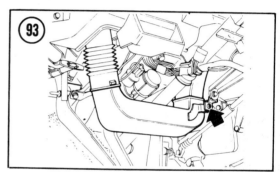

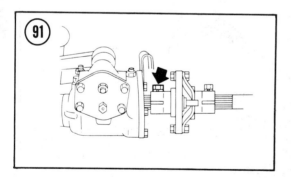

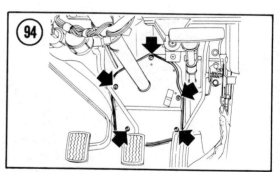

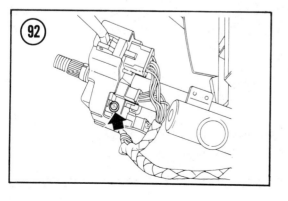

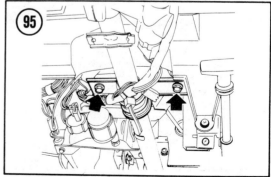

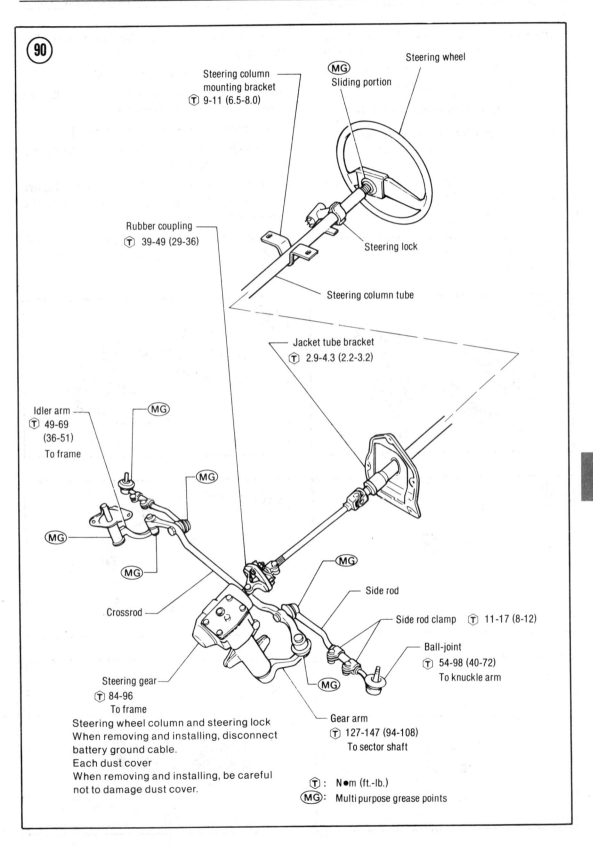

90

Steering column mounting bracket
(T) 9-11 (6.5-8.0)

(MG) Sliding portion

Steering wheel

Steering lock

Steering column tube

Rubber coupling
(T) 39-49 (29-36)

Jacket tube bracket
(T) 2.9-4.3 (2.2-3.2)

Idler arm
(T) 49-69
(36-51)
To frame

(MG)

(MG)

(MG)

(MG)

(MG)

Crossrod

(MG)

Side rod

Side rod clamp   (T) 11-17 (8-12)

Ball-joint
(T) 54-98 (40-72)
To knuckle arm

Steering gear
(T) 84-96
To frame

(MG)

Gear arm
(T) 127-147 (94-108)
To sector shaft

Steering wheel column and steering lock
When removing and installing, disconnect
battery ground cable.
Each dust cover
When removing and installing, be careful
not to damage dust cover.

(T) : N●m (ft.-lb.)
(MG) : Multi purpose grease points

9

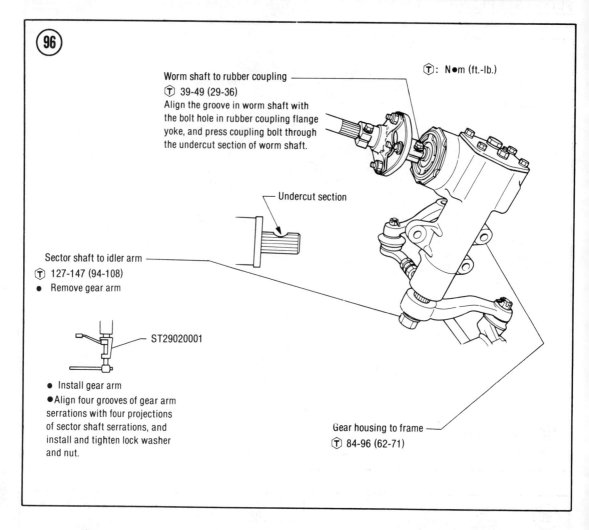

(96)

Worm shaft to rubber coupling
(T) 39-49 (29-36)
Align the groove in worm shaft with
the bolt hole in rubber coupling flange
yoke, and press coupling bolt through
the undercut section of worm shaft.

(T): N●m (ft.-lb.)

— Undercut section

Sector shaft to idler arm
(T) 127-147 (94-108)
● Remove gear arm

ST29020001

● Install gear arm
●Align four grooves of gear arm
serrations with four projections
of sector shaft serrations, and
install and tighten lock washer
and nut.

Gear housing to frame
(T) 84-96 (62-71)

Steering Gear Removal/Installation

Refer to **Figure 96** for this procedure.

1. Set the parking brake. Place the transmission in FIRST.

2. Jack up the front end of the truck and place it on jackstands.

3. Remove the steering gear-to-column clamp bolt (**Figure 91**).

> *NOTE*
> *The bolt passes through a notch in the steering gear shaft so it must be removed, not just loosened.*

4. Pull the pitman arm off the steering gear with a pitman arm puller such as Datsun tool part No. ST29020001 (Kent-Moore part No. J25725). See **Figure 97**. These are available from rental dealers.

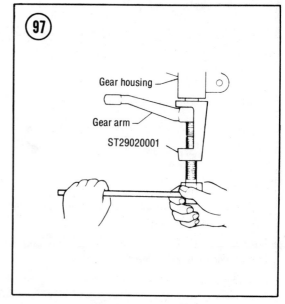

(97)

Gear housing

Gear arm

ST29020001

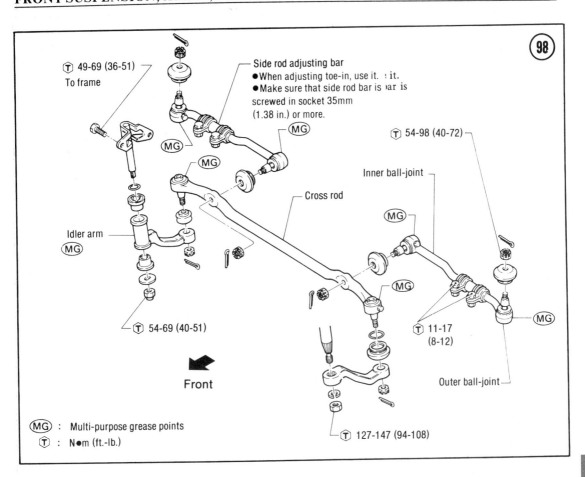

(98)

49-69 (36-51)
To frame

Side rod adjusting bar
● When adjusting toe-in, use it. ? it.
● Make sure that side rod bar is ?ar is screwed in socket 35mm (1.38 in.) or more.

54-98 (40-72)

Inner ball-joint

Cross rod

Idler arm
MG

54-69 (40-51)

Front

11-17 (8-12)

Outer ball-joint

MG : Multi-purpose grease points
T : N●m (ft.-lb.)

127-147 (94-108)

(99)

HT72520000

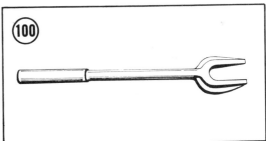

(100)

9

5. Detach the steering gear from the frame and take it out.

6. Installation is the reverse of removal. Align the 4 grooves in the pitman arm splined section with the 4 projections in the steering gear shaft splined section. Align the steering gear shaft notch with the bolt hole in the steering column. Tighten all fasteners to specifications (end of chapter).

Steering Linkage Overhaul

Refer to **Figure 98** for this procedure.

1. Set the parking brake. Place the transmission in FIRST.

2. Loosen the front wheel nuts. Jack up the front of the truck, place it on jackstands and remove the front wheels.

3. Remove the cotter pins and locknuts from the outer tie rod ends.

4. Detach the tie rod ends from the knuckle arms. Use a spreader such as Datsun tool part No. HT72520000 (**Figure 99**) or a fork-type separator (**Figure 100**). These are available from tool rental dealers.

CAUTION
Do not damage the tie rod end grease boots.

5. Detach the pitman arm from the steering gear. See **Figure 97**.

6. Unbolt the idler arm assembly from the frame (**Figure 101**).

7. Remove the steering linkage as an assembly.

8. Separate the remaining tie rod ends as described in Step 4. Disassemble the tie rods, referring to **Figure 102**.

9. Disassemble the idler arm assembly, referring to **Figure 103**.

10. Check all parts for wear and damage. Check tie rod ends for loose studs. Check idler arm bushings for wear. Replace as needed.

11. Assemble the idler arm assembly as shown in **Figure 104**. Apply multipurpose grease to the bushings.

12. Assemble tie rods as shown in **Figure 105**. Dimension A should be 275 mm (10.83 in.).

13. Install by reversing Steps 1-7. Tighten all fasteners to specifications (end of chapter). Have wheel alignment checked by a dealer or alignment shop.

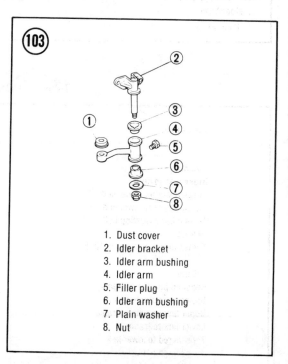

1. Dust cover
2. Idler bracket
3. Idler arm bushing
4. Idler arm
5. Filler plug
6. Idler arm bushing
7. Plain washer
8. Nut

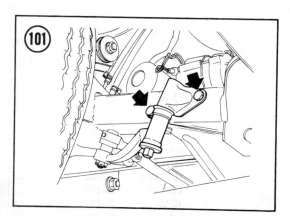

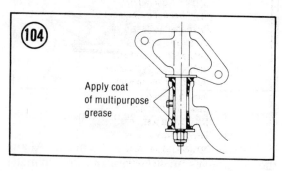

Apply coat of multipurpose grease

1. Outer side rod assembly
2. Side rod clamp
3. Side rod adjusting tube
4. Inner side rod assembly

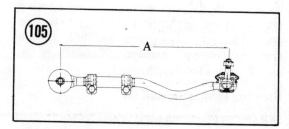

A

Table 1   SPECIFICATIONS

Camber	0 +/- 1
Caster	
1980	1-2°
1981	1° 10'-2° 10'
Steering axis inclination	
1980	10° 20' to 11° 20'
1981	10° 30' to 11° 30'
Toe-in	5-7 mm (0.20-0.28 in.)
Steering lock angles	
Inside wheel	29-33°
Outside wheel	27-29°

Table 2   TIGHTENING TORQUES

Fastener	N•m	Mkg
Hub nut	118-147	87-108
Brake disc to hub	38-52	28-38
Shock absorber upper end	16-22	12-16
Shock absorber lower end	30-40	22-30
Torsion bar adjusting bolt locknut	30-40	22-30
Torque arm to suspension link		
Inner	35-45	26-33
Outer	26-36	20-27
Rebound bumper to frame	8-11	6-8
Upper link spindle to link	76-103	56-76
Upper link spindle to frame	109-147	80-108
Lower link to frame	109-147	80-108
Tension rod to lower link	38-52	28-38
Tension rod to frame	118-157	87-116
Stabilizer bar to frame	16-22	12-16
Stabilizer bar to lower links	16-22	12-16
Drive shaft to differential	34-44	25-33
Differential cover	39-49	29-36
Differential front mount	50-68	37-50
Differential crossmember	71-96	52-71
Differential rear mount	50-68	37-50
Axle shaft bolts	27-37	20-27
Steering wheel nut	39-49	29-36
Column bracket	9-11	6.5-8
Floor hole cover	3-4	2-3
Coupling clamp bolt	39-49	29-36
Steering gear to body		
1980	45-52	33-38
1981	84-96	62-71
Pitman arm nut	127-147	94-108
Idler arm to body		
1980	31-36	23-27
1981	49-69	36-51
Idler arm nut	54-69	40-51
Tie rod end nuts	54-98	40-72

9

CHAPTER TEN

REAR SUSPENSION, DRIVE SHAFT, AXLE AND DIFFERENTIAL

This chapter provides service procedures for the rear suspension, drive shafts and rear axle. Tightening torques are listed in **Table 1** at the end of the chapter.

REAR SUSPENSION

Rear Shock Absorber Replacement

1. Securely block both front wheels so the truck will not roll in either direction. Jack up the rear end and place it on jackstands.
2. Place a jack beneath the axle to raise and lower it.
3. Detach the shock absorber from the spring plate and body (**Figure 1**), then take it out.
4. Check all parts for wear or damage, especially rubber bushings. See **Figure 2**. Replace as needed.
5. Installation is the reverse of removal. Tighten shock absorber nuts with the truck's weight on the wheels. Specifications are at the end of the chapter.

Spring Removal/Installation

1. Securely block both front wheels so the truck will not roll in either direction.

2. Loosen the rear wheel nuts. Jack up the rear end of the truck, place it on jackstands and remove the rear wheels.
3. Place a jack under the axle to support it.
4. Detach the shock absorber lower end and remove the U-bolts. See **Figure 3**.
5. Detach the parking brake cable clamp(s) from the spring. See **Figure 4**.

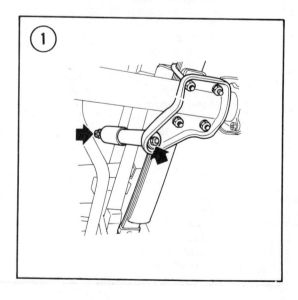

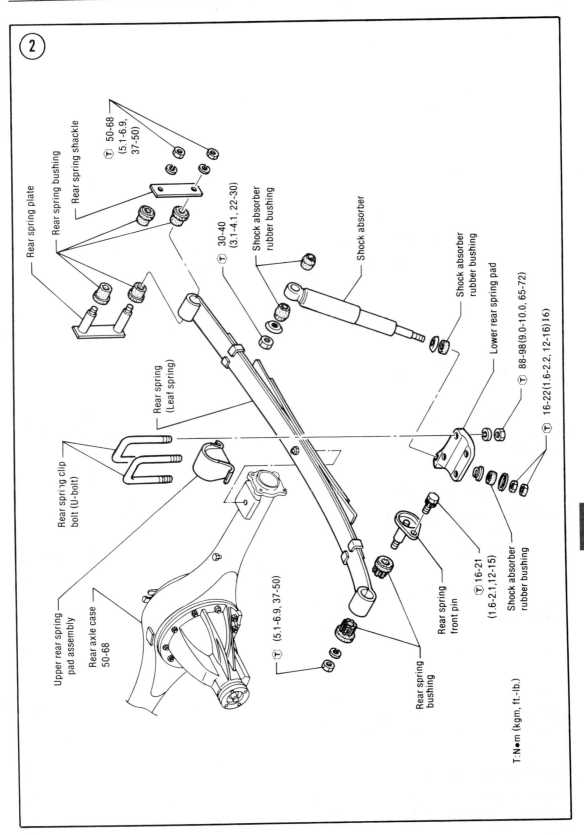

② 50-68
(5.1-6.9,
37-50)

Rear spring shackle

Rear spring bushing

Rear spring plate

T 30-40
(3.1-4.1, 22-30)

Shock absorber
rubber bushing

Shock absorber

Shock absorber
rubber bushing

Lower rear spring pad

T 88-98(9.0-10.0, 65-72)

Rear spring
(Leaf spring)

T 16-22(1.6-2.2, 12-16)16

Rear spring clip
bolt (U-bolt)

T 16-21
(1.6-2.1,12-15)

Rear spring
front pin

Shock absorber
rubber bushing

Upper rear spring
pad assembly

Rear axle case
50-68

T (5.1-6.9, 37-50)

Rear spring
bushing

T:N•m (kgm, ft.-lb.)

10

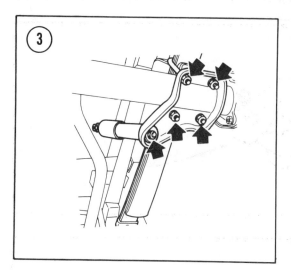

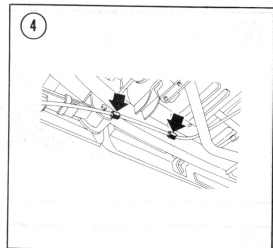

6. Lower the jack beneath the axle.
7. Detach the spring rear shackle (**Figure 5**).
8. Detach the spring front pin (**Figure 6**). Take the spring out.
9. Installation is the reverse of removal. Tighten nuts and bolts slightly, then lower the truck. Tighten nuts and bolts to specifications (**Figure 2** and **Table 1** at the end of the chapter) with the truck's weight on the wheels.

Spring Inspection

1. Check the spring for cracks. Replace cracked springs.
2. Check the spring for rust. If rust is light, sand it off and paint the spring. If rust is heavy, replace the spring.
3. Check all other parts for wear or damage, especially rubber bushings. Replace worn or damaged parts.

DRIVE SHAFTS

The Datsun 4-wheel drive pickup uses 3 drive shafts. The primary drive shaft (**Figure 7**) transmits power from the transmission to the transfer case. The front and rear drive shafts (**Figure 8**) connect the transfer case to the front and rear differentials.

Removal/Installation

1. Make match marks on the drive shaft flanges. See **Figure 9**.

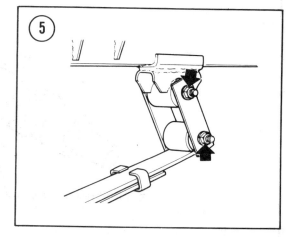

2. To remove the primary drive shaft, remove the transfer case. See *Transfer Case*, Chapter Eight.
3. Unbolt the drive shaft flanges from each other, then take the drive shaft out.
4. Installation is the reverse of removal. Align the flange match marks. Tighten all fasteners to specifications (end of chapter).

Inspection

1. Check the drive shaft for bending or other damage. Replace damaged drive shafts.
2. Check front and rear drive shafts for worn splines. Replace drive shafts if splines are worn.
3. Check universal joints for wear. If side play (**Figure 10**) is more than 0.02 mm (0.0008 in.), repair the U-joints.

6

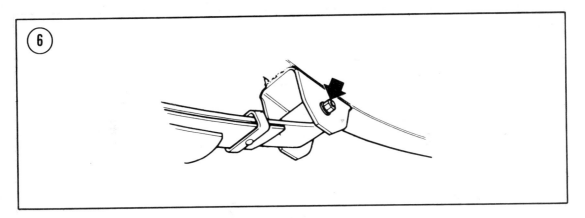

7

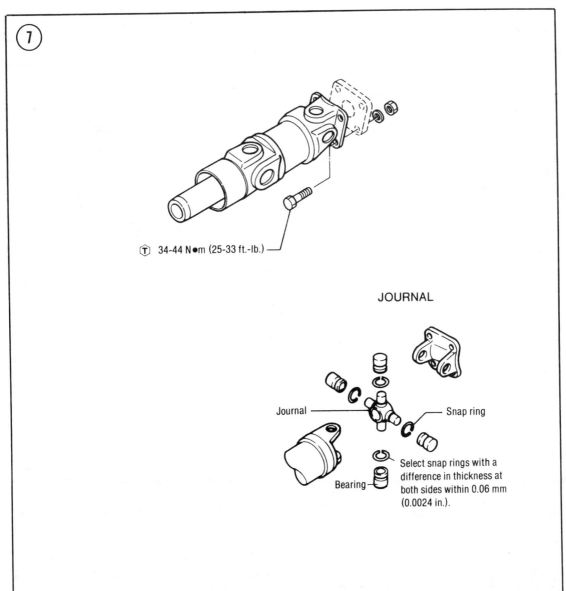

(T) 34-44 N●m (25-33 ft.-lb.)

JOURNAL

Journal

Snap ring

Bearing

Select snap rings with a difference in thickness at both sides within 0.06 mm (0.0024 in.).

10

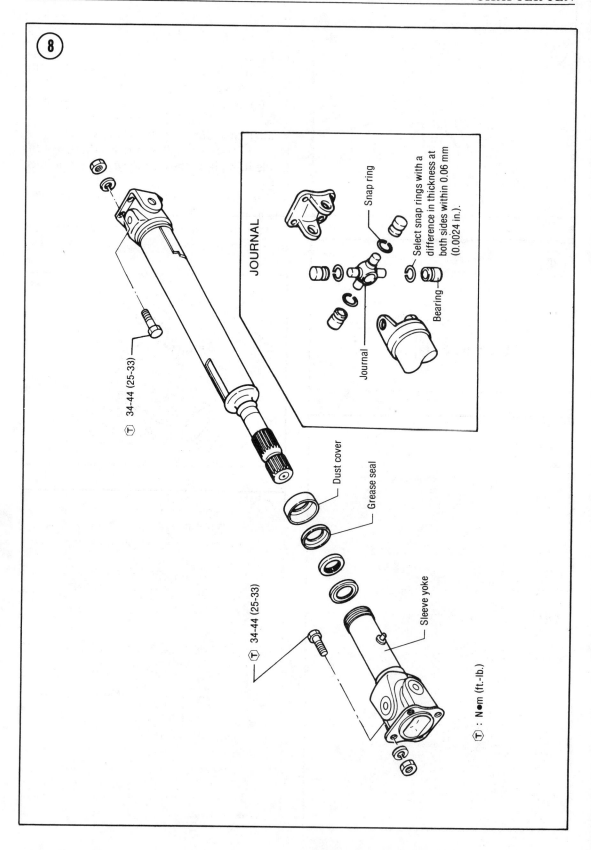

⑧

34-44 (25-33) Ⓣ

JOURNAL

Snap ring

Select snap rings with a
difference in thickness at
both sides within 0.06 mm
(0.0024 in.).

Bearing

Journal

Dust cover

Grease seal

34-44 (25-33) Ⓣ

Sleeve yoke

Ⓣ : N●m (ft.-lb.)

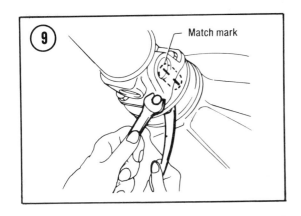

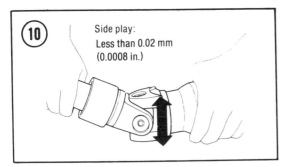

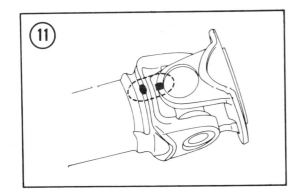

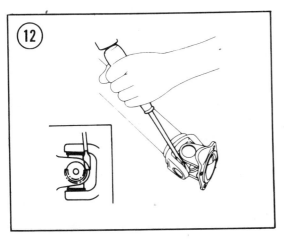

Universal Joint Repair

1. Make match marks on the drive shaft yokes. See **Figure 11**.

2. Tap out the snap rings (**Figure 12**).

3. Mount the drive shaft in a vise with 2 sockets. See **Figure 13**. One socket must be smaller than the U-joint bearings; the other must be large enough so the bearings will fit inside it. Tighten the vise to push the bearings out.

4. Tap the yoke with a hammer to remove one bearing. See **Figure 14**.

5. Turn the yoke over and tap the other side to remove the opposite bearing. See **Figure 15**.

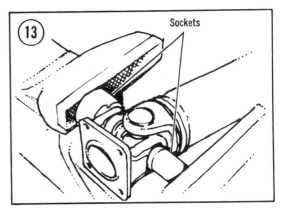

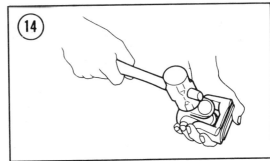

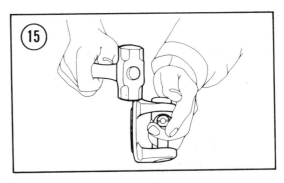

10

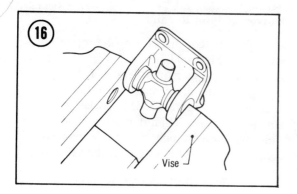

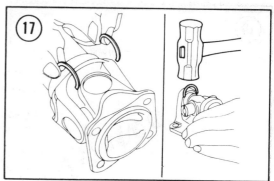

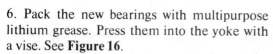

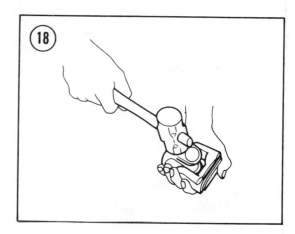

6. Pack the new bearings with multipurpose lithium grease. Press them into the yoke with a vise. See **Figure 16**.

7. Tap in new snap rings (**Figure 17**).

8. Tap the yoke to center the bearings (**Figure 18**).

REAR AXLE

Refer to **Figure 19** for these procedures.

Axle Shaft Removal

1. Securely block both front wheels so the truck will not roll in either direction.

2. Loosen the rear wheel nuts. Jack up the rear end of the truck, place it on jackstands and remove the rear wheels.

3. Remove the brake drum. See *Rear Brakes*, Chapter Eleven.

4. Disconnect the parking brake cable and brake line at the backing plate. See **Figure 20**.

5. Remove 4 nuts securing the brake backing plate (**Figure 21**).

6. Remove the axle shaft, together with the backing plate. Use a slide hammer and adapter such as Datsun tools part Nos. ST36230000 and KV40101000 (Kent-Moore part Nos. J25840-A and J25604-01). See **Figure 22**. These are available from rental dealers.

Axle Shaft Inspection

1. Carefully examine the machined surfaces of the axle shaft and housing for wear. Check the shaft for bending, twisting or damaged splines.

2. Inspect the rear wheel bearing. Rotate it and check for noise, roughness or excessive play. If in doubt about the bearing, replace it as described in this chapter.

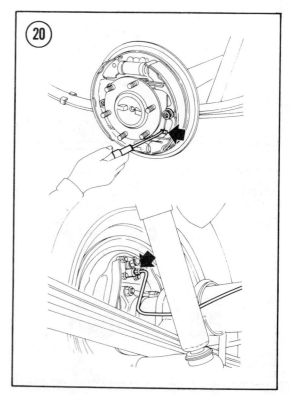

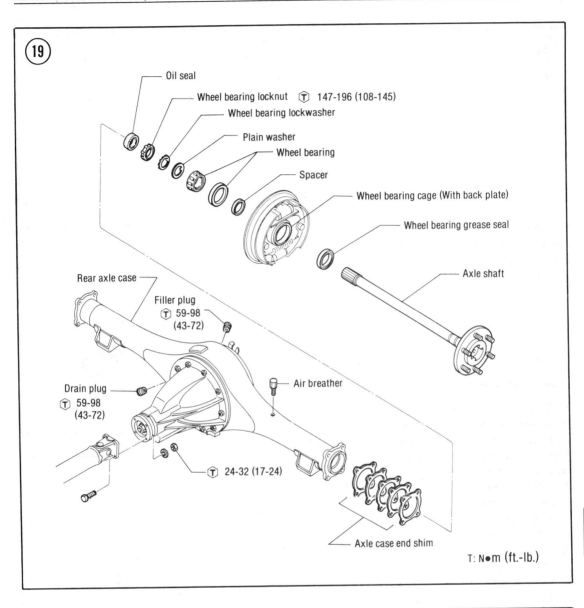

⑲

Oil seal

Wheel bearing locknut ⓣ 147-196 (108-145)

Wheel bearing lockwasher

Plain washer

Wheel bearing

Spacer

Wheel bearing cage (With back plate)

Wheel bearing grease seal

Axle shaft

Rear axle case

Filler plug
ⓣ 59-98
(43-72)

Drain plug
ⓣ 59-98
(43-72)

Air breather

ⓣ 24-32 (17-24)

Axle case end shim

T: N●m (ft.-lb.)

10

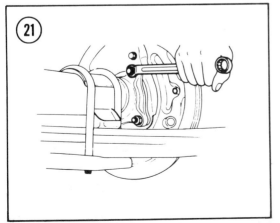

㉑

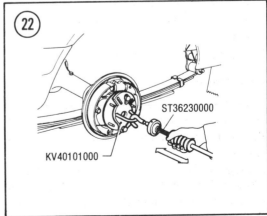

㉒

ST36230000

KV40101000

Axle Oil Seal Replacement

1. Remove the axle shaft as described in this chapter.
2. Pry out the oil seal with a screwdriver (**Figure 23**).
3. Drive in the new seal with a suitable drift.
4. Pack the space between the seal lips with multipurpose grease.

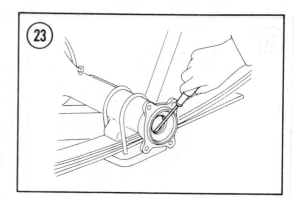

Rear Wheel Bearing Replacement

This procedure requires special equipment and should be left to a dealer or machine shop. It is included here in case you are not near a dealer and your local machine shop is not familiar with the Datsun pickup. Much of the cost of bearing replacement can be saved by removing the axle shaft yourself and having a dealer or machine shop replace the bearing.

1. Remove the axle shaft as described in this chapter.
2. Bend back the tabs on the wheel bearing lockwasher (**Figure 24**).
3. Remove the wheel bearing locknut (**Figure 25**).

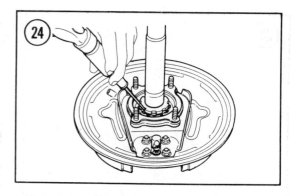

> *NOTE*
> *The locknut is tightened to 147-196 N•m (108-145 ft.-lb). A wrench like the one shown in* **Figure 25** *(Datsun part No. ST38020000; Kent-Moore part No. J25864-01) must be used to remove it.*

4. Remove the wheel bearing, bearing cage, and backing plate. Use a press and support tools like the ones shown in **Figure 26**.
5. Inspect the oil seal in the bearing cage. If worn or damaged, tap it out as shown in **Figure 27**, then tap in a new one. Pack the new seal's lip with multipurpose grease as shown in **Figure 28**.
6. If the wheel bearing outer race is worn or damaged, tap it out with a brass drift. See **Figure 29**. Install a new one as shown in **Figure 30**.

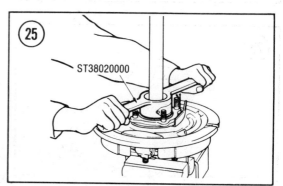

ST38020000

7. Install the spacer, then tap in the wheel bearing. See **Figure 31**.

> *NOTE*
> *The flat side of the spacer faces the wheel bearing (inboard). The chamfered side of the spacer faces outboard.*

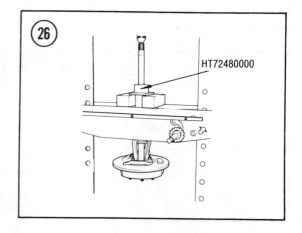

HT72480000

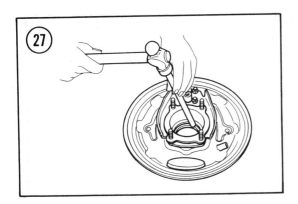

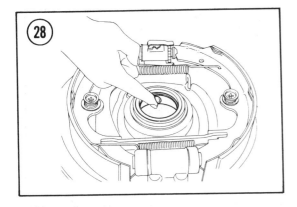

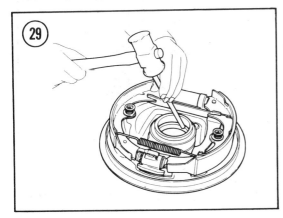

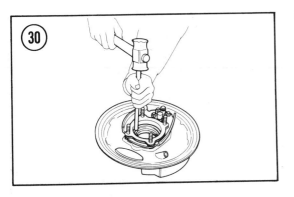

8. Install the plain washer and a new lockwasher. Install the bearing locknut with its chamfered side toward the lockwasher. Tighten the locknut to 147-196 N•m (108-145 ft.-lb.), using the tool shown in **Figure 25**. Bend up the lockwasher to secure the nut.

9. Pack the bearing with grease. Apply grease to the bearing recess in the axle housing.

Axle Shaft Installation

1. Make sure the wheel bearing is packed with grease.

2. Install the axle shaft and shims in the housing (**Figure 32**). Be careful not to damage the seal.

3. Measure axle shaft end play with a dial indicator (**Figure 33**). It should be 0.02-0.15 mm (0.0008-0.0059 in.). If not, add or remove shims to adjust.

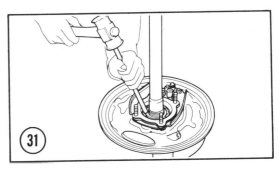

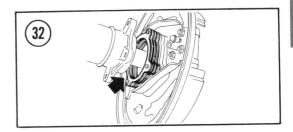

10

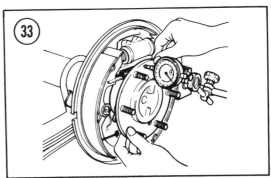

Axle Housing Removal/Installation

1. Securely block both front wheels so the truck will not roll in either direction.

2. Loosen the rear wheel nuts. Jack up the rear end of the truck, place it on jackstands and remove the rear wheels.

3. Place a jack beneath the axle to support it.

4. Remove the rear drive shaft as described in this chapter.

5. Remove the brake drums. See *Rear Brakes*, Chapter Eleven.

6. Disconnect the parking brake cable from each rear brake assembly. See **Figure 34**.

7. Disconnect the brake line from each rear brake assembly. See **Figure 35**.

NOTE

The factory recommends a flare nut wrench such as Datsun tool part No. GG94310000 for brake line nuts. See **Figure 36**. *Do not use an adjustable wrench, since it may round off the nut.*

8. Disconnect the shock absorber lower ends and remove the U-bolts. See **Figure 37**.

9. Raise the axle housing off the springs and remove it to one side. See **Figure 38**.

10. Installation is the reverse of removal. Tighten all fasteners to specifications (end of chapter). Bleed the brakes as described under *Brake Bleeding*, Chapter Eleven.

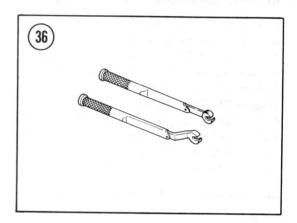

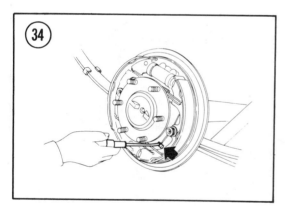

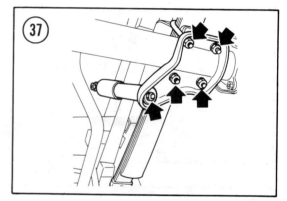

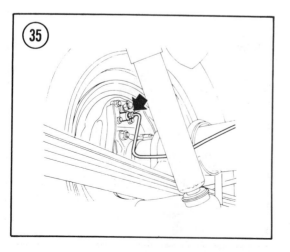

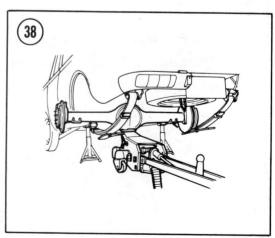

DIFFERENTIAL

This section includes removal, installation and inspection procedures. Differential repair requires special skills and many expensive special tools. The inspection procedures will tell you if repairs are needed.

Removal/Installation

1. Place a pan beneath the differential and drain the oil. See **Figure 39**.
2. Disconnect the drive shaft and remove the rear axle shafts as described in this chapter.
3. Remove the differential mounting nuts (**Figure 40**). Take the differential out.
4. Installation is the reverse of removal. Tighten all nuts and bolts to specifications (end of chapter). Fill the differential with an oil recommended in Chapter Three.

Inspection

1. Turn the ring gear and look for broken, chipped or worn teeth. Check the differential for rough movement. Have the differential repaired if these conditions are found.

2. Connect a dial indicator as shown in **Figure 41**. Hold the pinion from turning with one hand and turn the ring gear against the dial indicator with the other. The reading (backlash) should be 0.15-0.20 mm (0.006-0.008 in.). If not, have the differential disassembled and adjusted.

3. Connect the dial indicator as shown in **Figure 42**. Turn the ring gear and measure runout. It should not exceed 0.08 mm (0.003 in.). If it does, have the differential repaired.

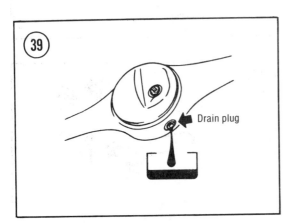

(39) Drain plug

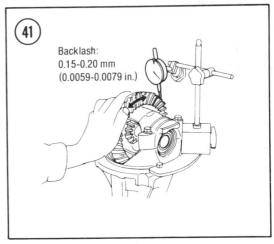

(41) Backlash:
0.15-0.20 mm
(0.0059-0.0079 in.)

10

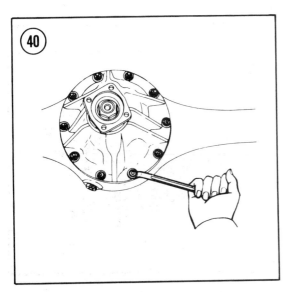

(40)

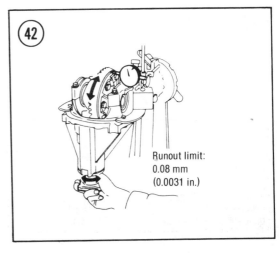

(42) Runout limit:
0.08 mm
(0.0031 in.)

4. Thoroughly clean the ring gear teeth.

5. Coat the drive side of the teeth with gear marking compound. See **Figure 43**.

6. Turn the ring gear in both directions. Compare the contact pattern pressed into the marking compound with those in **Figure 44**. If the pattern is not correct, have the differential disassembled and adjusted.

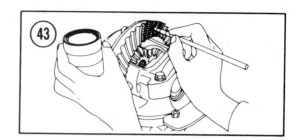

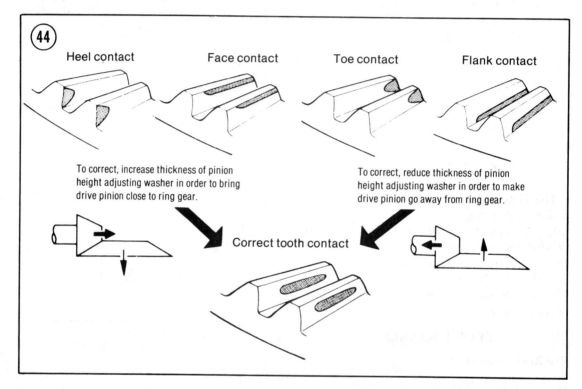

Heel contact   Face contact   Toe contact   Flank contact

To correct, increase thickness of pinion height adjusting washer in order to bring drive pinion close to ring gear.

To correct, reduce thickness of pinion height adjusting washer in order to make drive pinion go away from ring gear.

Correct tooth contact

Table 1   TIGHTENING TORQUES

Fastener	N•m	Ft.-lb.
Shock absorber upper nut	30-40	22-30
Shock absorber lower nut	16-22	12-16
Spring U-bolt nuts	88-98	65-72
Spring front pin nut	50-68	37-50
Spring shackle	50-68	37-50
Backing plate bolts	53-63	39-46
Wheel bearing locknut	147-196	108-145
Differential mounting nuts	17-25	12-18
Differential drain and filler plugs	59-98	43-72
Rebound bumpers	16-22	12-16
Drive shaft to differential	24-32	17-24

CHAPTER ELEVEN

BRAKES

The Datsun 4-wheel drive pickup uses disc brakes at the front and drum brakes at the rear. A Master-Vac brake booster (power brakes) reduces pedal effort. A load sensing valve proportions hydraulic pressure according to the amount of load in the bed. The handbrake is a mechanical type that operates the rear brakes.

FRONT BRAKES

Pad Replacement

1. Set the handbrake. Place the transmission in FIRST.
2. Loosen the front wheel nuts. Jack up the front end of the truck, place it on jackstands and remove the front wheels.
3. Remove the clip securing the pad retaining pins. Hold down the anti-squeal springs, then pull the pins out. See **Figure 1**.
4. Release the anti-squeal springs, then pull out the pads (**Figure 2**).

> *CAUTION*
> *Do not press the brake pedal with the pads removed or the pistons will fall out.*

5. Inspect the pads. Light surface grease or oil stains may be sanded off. If oil or grease has penetrated the surface, replace the pads. Since brake fluid will ruin the friction material,

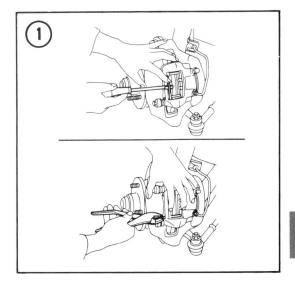

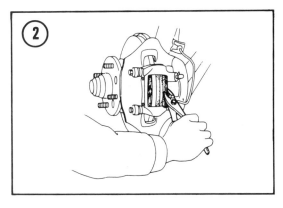

brake pads must be replaced if any brake fluid has touched them. Pads must also be replaced if the friction material is worn to less than 2 mm (0.008 in.) thick.

> *NOTE*
> *Always replace pads in complete kits. These include all pads, retaining pins, retaining pin clips and anti-squeal springs necessary to service both front brake assemblies.*

6. Check the cylinder body for brake fluid leaks. If fluid has leaked from the cylinder, overhaul the caliper as described later.
7. Carefully clean the space which holds the brake pads. Use alcohol or spray brake cleaner. Do not use gasoline, kerosene or solvent. These leave residues which can cause rubber parts to soften and swell.
8. Open the bleed valve.

> *CAUTION*
> *During the next 2 steps, do not push the pistons in past the normal position (**Figure 3**). This will cause the pistons to hang up on the seals. The caliper will then have to be disassembled and the seals replaced with new ones.*

9. Push piston B into the cylinder with a pry bar (**Figure 4**). Install the inner pad.
10. Push piston A in by prying the caliper yoke outward (**Figure 5**). Install the outer pad.
11. Apply high-temperature disc brake grease to the friction points shown in **Figure 6**.

> *CAUTION*
> *Apply very small amounts of grease. Do not let grease touch the disc or pad friction surfaces. Do not use ordinary multipurpose grease, since it may melt and contaminate the pads or disc.*

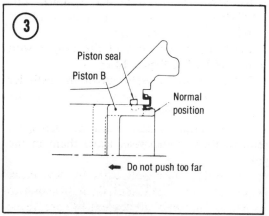

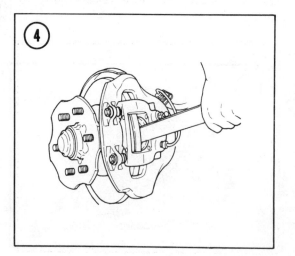

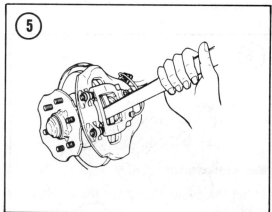

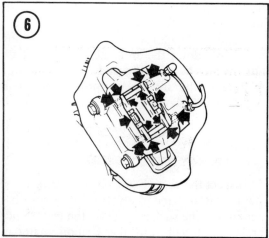

12. Close the bleed valve. Install the wheels, lower the truck and tighten the wheel nuts.

13. Press the brake pedal several times to seat the pads. If the pedal doesn't feel firm, bleed the brakes. See *Brake Bleeding* in this chapter.

Caliper Removal/Installation

1. Remove the brake pads as described in this chapter.

2. Place a pan under the caliper to catch dripping brake fluid.

3. Disconnect the brake line from the caliper (**Figure 7**).

NOTE
*The factory recommends a flare nut wrench such as Datsun tool part No. GG94310000 (**Figure 8**) to connect and disconnect brake lines. Do not use an adjustable wrench, since it may round off the nut.*

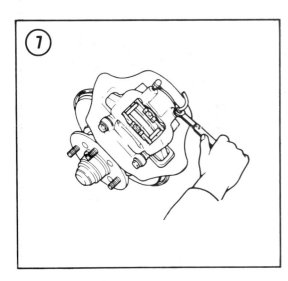

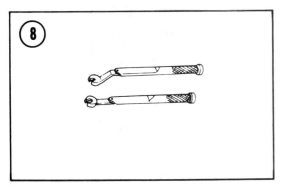

4. Remove the caliper mounting bolts (**Figure 9**). Take the caliper off.

5. Installation is the reverse of removal. Tighten the caliper mounting bolts to 72-97 N•m (53-72 ft.-lb.). Tighten the brake line nut to 15-18 N•m (11-13 ft.-lb.).

6. Bleed the brakes as described under *Brake Bleeding* in this chapter. Tighten the bleed valve to 6.9-8.8 N•m (5-6.5 ft.-lb.).

Caliper Overhaul

Refer to **Figure 10** for this procedure.

1. Pour the brake fluid out of the caliper. Clean the outside of the caliper with new clean brake fluid or spray brake cleaner. Do not clean with gasoline, kerosene or solvent. These leave residues which can cause rubber parts to soften and swell.

2. Remove the fixing bolts (**Figure 11**).

3. Remove the yoke (**Figure 12**).

4. Remove the yoke holder (**Figure 13**). Remove the retaining ring and dust seal from each end of the caliper.

5. Push the pistons out of the caliper with your thumbs. See **Figure 14**.

6. Take the piston seals out of the cylinder bore. See **Figure 15**. Use fingers only so the bore won't be scratched.

7. If the grippers are worn or damaged, remove them. Otherwise, leave them in the yoke.

8. Thoroughly clean all parts in new clean brake fluid or brake cleaner. Do not clean with gasoline, kerosene or solvent. These leave residues which can cause rubber parts to soften and swell.

11

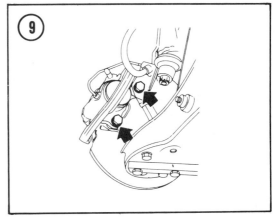

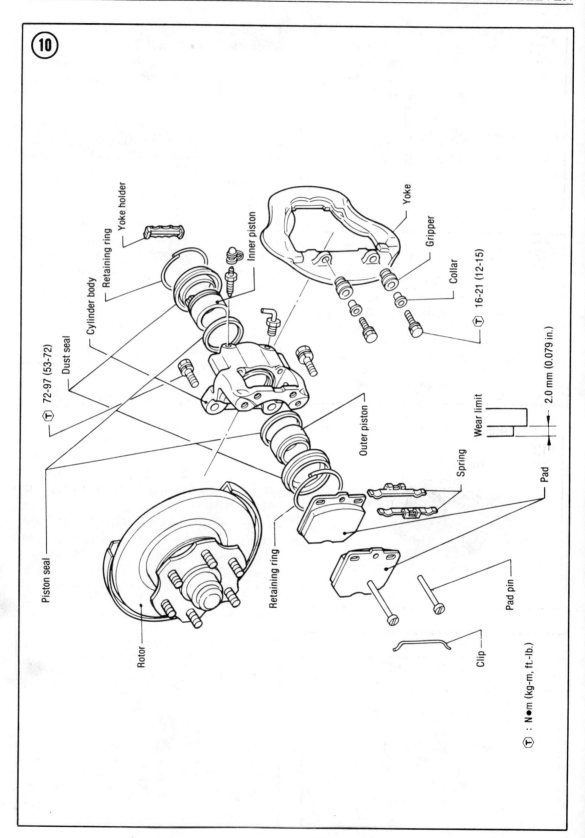

10

Yoke holder

Retaining ring

Inner piston

Yoke

Gripper

Collar

(T) 16-21 (12-15)

Cylinder body

Dust seal

(T) 72-97 (53-72)

Piston seal

Outer piston

Wear limit

2.0 mm (0.079 in.)

Spring

Pad

Retaining ring

Rotor

Pad pin

Clip

(T) : N•m (kg-m, ft.-lb.)

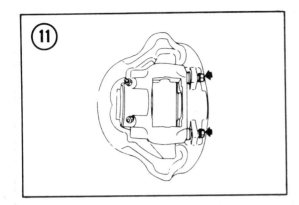

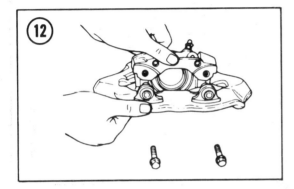

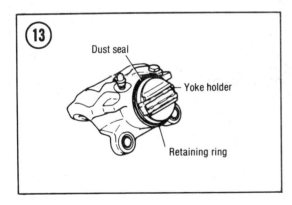

Dust seal

Yoke holder

Retaining ring

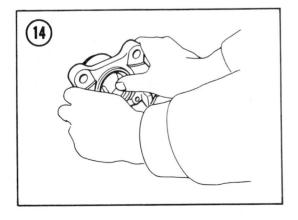

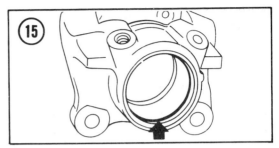

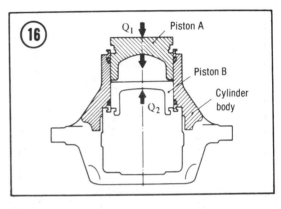

Q_1 Piston A

Piston B

Cylinder body

Q_2

9. Check the yoke for wear, cracks or other visible defects. Replace if any of these can be seen.

10. Inspect the cylinder bore. Replace the cylinder body if wear or damage can be seen. Light rust or dirt may be removed with fine emery paper. Replace the cylinder body if dirt or rust is heavy.

11. Inspect the pistons. Since they are plated, the pistons can't be sanded. If the pistons can't be cleaned with a rag, replace them.

12. Coat the piston seals and their grooves with rubber grease or brake fluid. Install new piston seals, using fingers only so the cylinder bore won't be scratched.

NOTE
Never reuse piston seals. In addition to stopping leaks, the seals retract the pistons when the brakes are let up. Very minor damage or deterioration can ruin the seals.

13. Coat the cylinder bore with new clean brake fluid. Apply rubber grease or brake fluid to the pistons, then install them in the cylinder. Insert piston A from direction Q1 and piston B from direction Q2. See **Figure 16**. Align the yoke groove in piston A with the yoke groove in the cylinder body.

11

CAUTION
*Do not push the pistons in past the point shown in **Figure 16** or they will hang up on the piston seals. If this happens, the seals will have to be thrown away and replaced with new ones.*

14. Apply high-temperature disc brake grease to the sealing surfaces of the dust seals. Install the dust seals and retaining rings (**Figure 17**). Wipe off any excess grease with alcohol.

15. Install the yoke holder in piston A.

16. If the grippers were removed, install them (**Figure 18**). Use a one per cent soap solution (one teaspoon of soap in 2 cups of water) to lubricate the grippers. Do not use a stronger soap solution.

17. Install the yoke in the yoke holder. Align the yoke holder with the yoke, then press them together (**Figure 19**). This requires a force of 20-30 kg (44-66 lb.).

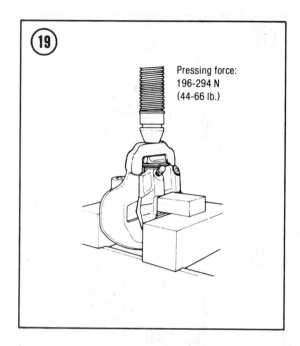

Pressing force:
196-294 N
(44-66 lb.)

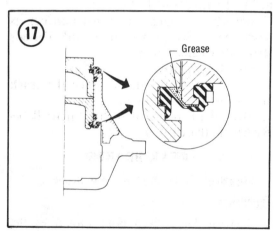

Grease

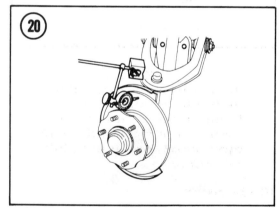

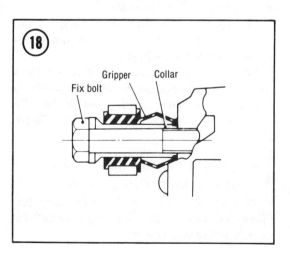

Fix bolt Gripper Collar

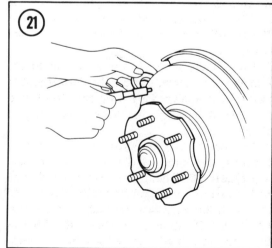

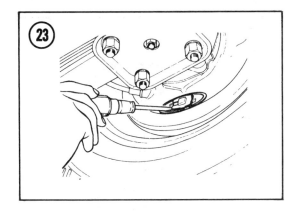

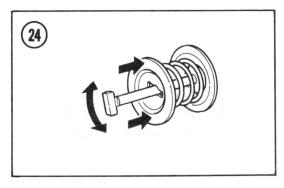

NOTE
Don't improvise a press. If you don't have one, have the job done by a machine shop. Be sure there is no clearance between piston and yoke after pressing. Be sure the grippers are not caught between cylinder body and collars.

Disc Inspection

1. Remove the caliper. See *Caliper Removal/Installation* in this chapter.
2. Check wheel bearing adjustment. See *Wheel Hub and Knuckle Installation*, Chapter Nine.
3. Check the disc for rust, scratches or cracks. If cracks are visible, replace the disc. If rust is visible or if scratches are deep enough to snag a fingernail, have the disc turned by a machine shop.
4. Set up a dial indicator so its pointer contacts the center of the disc's swept area. See **Figure 20**. Rotate the disc one full turn and measure runout. Maximum permissible runout (total indicator reading) is 0.15 mm (0.006 in.). If runout is excessive, the disc can be reconditioned by a machine shop.

Minimum disc thickness is 10.5 mm (0.413 in.). If it would have to be cut thinner than this to correct it, the disc must be replaced.
5. Check thickness at several points around the disc with a micrometer (**Figure 21**). Variation in thickness must be 0.07 mm (0.0028 in.) or less. If it is more than this, have the disc turned by a machine shop.

Disc Removal/Installation

1. Remove the caliper as described under *Caliper Removal/Installation* in this chapter.
2. Remove the brake disc together with the hub. See *Wheel Hub and Knuckle Removal*, Chapter Nine.
3. Unbolt the brake disc from the hub.
4. Make sure the hub and disc mating surfaces are completely clean. Very small amounts of dirt can cause excessive disc runout.
5. Bolt the disc to the hub. Tighten the bolts to 38-52 N•m (28-38 ft.-lb.).
6. Repack and adjust the wheel bearings as described under *Wheel Hub and Knuckle Assembly*, Chapter Nine.
7. Install the caliper.
8. Install the front wheels, lower the truck and tighten the wheel nuts.
9. Bleed the brakes as described under *Brake Bleeding* in this chapter.

REAR BRAKES

Figure 22 shows the rear drum brakes.

Removal

1. Securely block both front wheels so the truck will not roll in either direction.
2. Loosen the rear wheel nuts. Jack up the rear end of the truck, place it on jackstands and remove the rear wheels.
3. Make sure the parking brake is off, then remove the brake drum. If the drum is difficult to remove, pry upward on the adjuster wheel to retract the shoes. See **Figure 23**.

WARNING
Do not inhale brake dust. It contains asbestos, which may cause lung injury.

4. Turn the anti-rattle pin 90° with pliers. See **Figure 24**. Remove the pins, retaining collars, springs and spring washers.

11

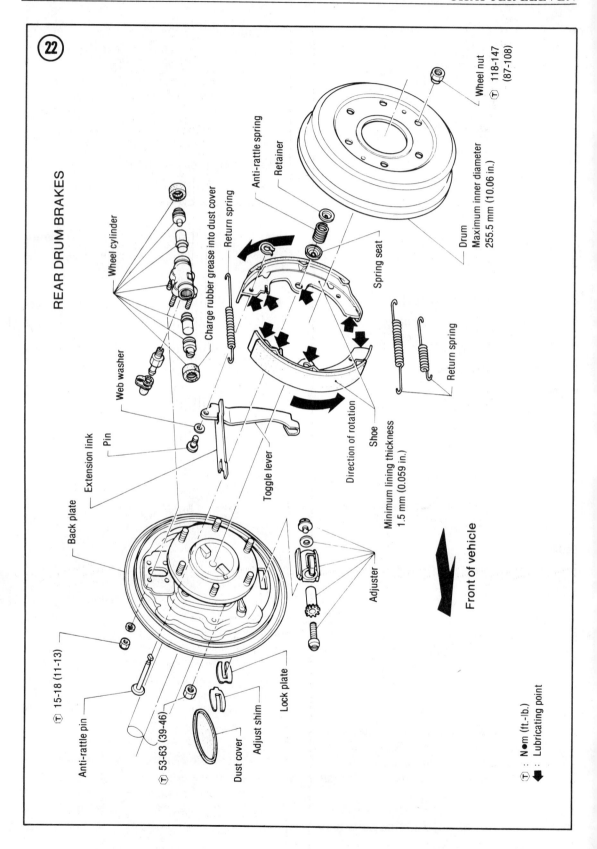

REAR DRUM BRAKES

22

Wheel nut
118-147
(87-108)

Anti-rattle spring

Retainer

Drum
Maximum inner diameter
255.5 mm (10.06 in.)

Spring seat

Return spring

Return spring

Charge rubber grease into dust cover

Wheel cylinder

Web washer

Pin

Extension link

Direction of rotation

Shoe

Minimum lining thickness
1.5 mm (0.059 in.)

Toggle lever

Back plate

Front of vehicle

Adjuster

15-18 (11-13)

Anti-rattle pin

53-63 (39-46)

Dust cover

Adjust shim

Lock plate

N•m (ft.-lb.)
: Lubricating point

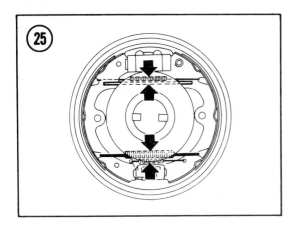

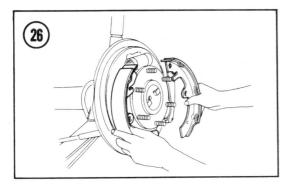

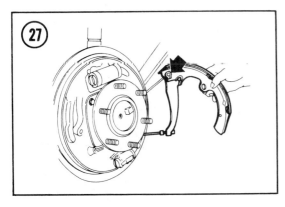

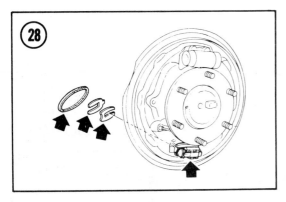

5. Remove the 2 lower return springs (**Figure 25**). Spread the brake shoes, then remove the upper return spring and extension link.

6. Lift off the brake shoes (**Figure 26**).

7. Disconnect the rear brake shoe from the toggle lever (**Figure 27**), then take it off.

8. Pull back the rubber wheel cylinder boots. Slight moisture inside is normal. If brake fluid runs out of the boots, disconnect the brake line and remove the wheel cylinder.

9. Remove the adjuster cover and securing shims (**Figure 28**), then take the adjuster out.

10. Backing plate removal—not necessary for normal brake service—requires removal of the rear axle shaft. See *Axle Shaft Removal*, Chapter Ten.

Inspection

1. Clean all parts with spray brake cleaner or alcohol. Do not use gasoline, kerosene or solvent. These leave residues which may cause rubber parts to soften and swell.

2. Check drums for visible scoring, excessive or uneven wear and corrosion. If you have precision measuring equipment, measure the drum for wear and out-of-roundness. If you do not have the equipment, this measurement can be done by a machine shop. Maximum permissible out-of-roundness is 0.02 mm (0.0008 in.). If the drum is out-of-round or otherwise defective, it can be turned to correct it. However, the inside diameter must not exceed 255.5 mm (10.06 in.). If it would have to be cut larger than this to correct it, the drum must be replaced.

3. Inspect the lining material on the brake shoes. Make sure it is not cracked, unevenly worn or separated from the shoes. If it is, replace the shoes.

4. Check for oil, grease or brake fluid on the linings. Light surface oil or grease stains may be sanded off. If oil or grease has penetrated the surface or if any brake fluid has touched the linings, replace the shoes.

5. Check linings for wear. Replace the shoes if linings are worn thinner than 1.5 mm (1/16 in.).

6. Check the anti-rattle pins, adjuster mechanism and handbrake operating arm for worn or damaged parts. Replace as needed.

11

7. Check return springs for weakness or deformation. Replace if these conditions are detected.

8. Check adjuster parts for wear or damage. Replace as needed.

Wheel Cylinder Overhaul

Figure 29 shows the wheel cylinder parts.

NOTE
Nabco and Tokico brand wheel cylinders are used in production. Rebuild kits for these cylinders are not interchangeable. Be sure to get the right brand.

1. Remove the dust covers from the cylinder.
2. Push the piston heads, pistons and piston cups out of the cylinder.
3. Remove the bleed valve and its cap.
4. Discard all rubber parts.
5. Clean metal parts in spray brake cleaner or clean brake fluid. Do not clean with gasoline, kerosene or solvent. These leave residues which can cause rubber parts to soften and swell.
6. Check the cylinder bore and piston for scoring, cracks, corrosion, dirt or excessive wear. Check the piston heads for worn brake shoe slots. Replace cylinder and piston if any of these conditions is found.
7. As a final check on a suspect cylinder and piston, measure diameter of the piston and cylinder bore. If the difference between these measurements is more than 0.15 mm (0.006 in.), replace the cylinder.
8. Apply rubber grease to new piston cups. Install them on the pistons. The wide sides of the cups face into the cylinders.
9. Coat the cylinder bore and pistons with rubber grease or brake fluid. Install the pistons in the cylinder.
10. Install the piston heads and dust boots.
11. Install the bleed valve and dust cap.

Installation

Installation is the reverse of removal, plus the following.

1. Apply high-temperature brake grease to the adjuster friction points (**Figure 30**).

CAUTION
Do not use ordinary multipurpose grease. This may melt and contaminate the linings.

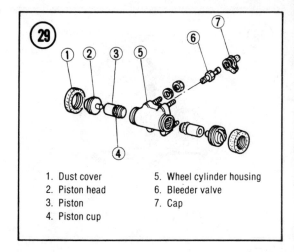

1. Dust cover	5. Wheel cylinder housing
2. Piston head	6. Bleeder valve
3. Piston	7. Cap
4. Piston cup	

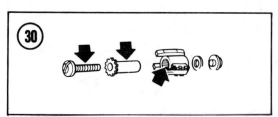

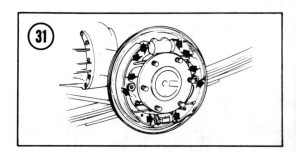

2. If the wheel cylinder was removed, tighten its mounting nuts to 15-18 N•m (11-13 ft.-lb.).

3. Apply high-temperature brake grease to the metal-to-metal friction points shown in **Figure 31**.

CAUTION
Use small amounts of grease. Do not let grease touch the brake linings.

4. Adjust and bleed the brakes as described in this chapter.

MASTER CYLINDER

All models use a dual-piston master cylinder. See **Figure 32** (1980) or **Figure 33** (1981).

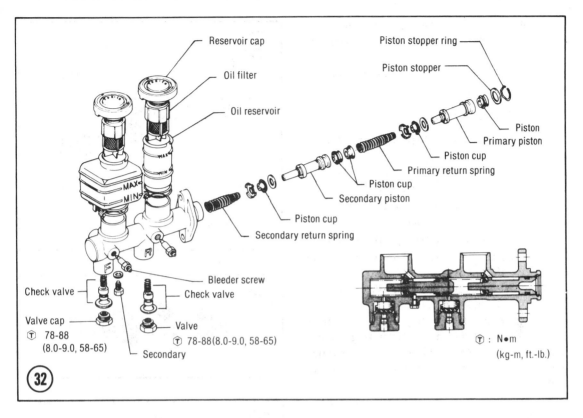

Reservoir cap

Oil filter

Oil reservoir

Piston stopper ring

Piston stopper

Piston

Primary piston

Piston cup

Primary return spring

Piston cup

Secondary piston

Piston cup

Secondary return spring

Bleeder screw

Check valve

Check valve

Valve cap

ⓣ 78-88
(8.0-9.0, 58-65)

Secondary

Valve

ⓣ 78-88(8.0-9.0, 58-65)

ⓣ : N●m
(kg-m, ft.-lb.)

32

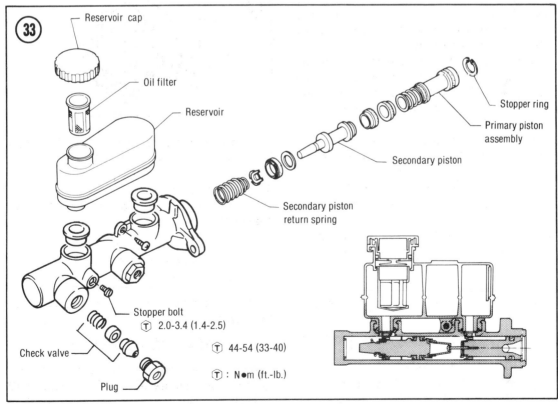

33

Reservoir cap

Oil filter

Reservoir

Stopper ring

Primary piston
assembly

Secondary piston

Secondary piston
return spring

Stopper bolt
ⓣ 2.0-3.4 (1.4-2.5)

ⓣ 44-54 (33-40)

ⓣ : N●m (ft.-lb.)

Check valve

Plug

11

Removal/Installation

1. Place rags beneath the master cylinder to catch dripping brake fluid.

CAUTION
Brake fluid will damage paint. Wipe up any spilled fluid immediately, then wash the area with soap and water.

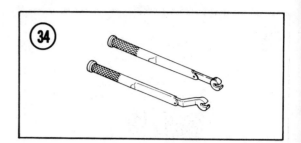

2. Disconnect the brake lines from the master cylinder. A flare nut wrench such as Datsun tool part No. GG94310000 (**Figure 34**) is recommended. Do not use an adjustable wrench, since it may round off the nuts.
3. Detach the master cylinder from the brake booster. Lift the master cylinder out.
4. Installation is the reverse of removal. Tighten the mounting nuts to 7.8-10.8 N•m (6-8 ft.-lb.). Tighten the brake lines to 15-18 N•m (11-13 ft.-lb.). Bleed the brakes as described under *Brake Bleeding* in this chapter.

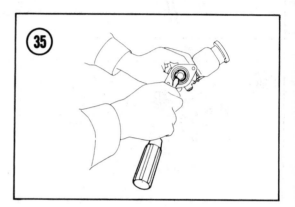

Disassembly

Refer to **Figure 32** (1980) or **Figure 33** (1981).

NOTE
Nabco and Tokico brand master cylinders are used in production. Rebuild kits for the 2 brands are not interchangeable. Be sure to get the right brand.

1. Remove the reservoir cap(s) and filter(s). Pour out the brake fluid.

NOTE
Do not remove the reservoir tanks unless you plan to install new ones.

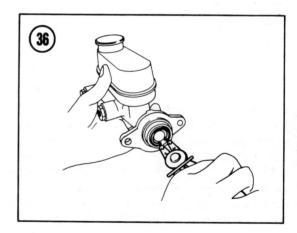

2. On 1980 models, remove the stopper ring with a screwdriver. See **Figure 35**.
3. On 1981 models, remove the snap ring with snap ring pliers. See **Figure 36**.
4. Remove the stopper screw. See **Figure 37** (1980) or **Figure 38** (1981). Take out the pistons and springs.
5. Unscrew the plugs and take out the check valves.
6. On 1980 models, unscrew the bleed valves.

Inspection

1. Discard the piston cups.

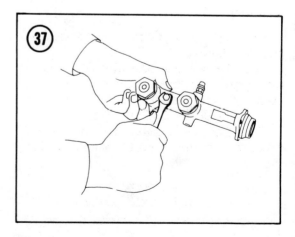

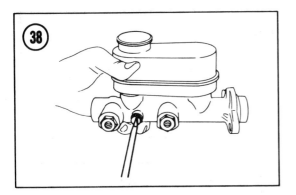

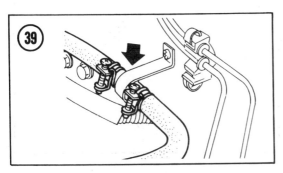

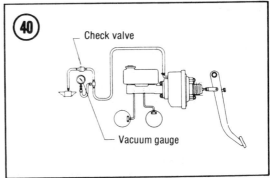

2. Thoroughly clean all remaining parts in brake fluid. Do not clean with gasoline, kerosene or solvent. These leave residues which can cause rubber parts to soften and swell.

3. Check the cylinder bore and pistons for excessive or uneven wear, scoring or corrosion. Wear is excessive if clearance between pistons and cylinder walls exceeds 0.15 mm (0.006 in.). Replace the master cylinder if these conditions can be seen.

4. Check springs for wear, damage or weakness. Replace as needed.

Assembly

Assembly is the reverse of disassembly, plus the following:

1. Coat the piston cups with brake fluid or rubber grease before installing them on the pistons. Be sure the cups face in the directions shown in **Figure 32** and **Figure 33**.

2. Coat the cylinder bore and pistons with brake fluid or rubber grease before installing the pistons.

CAUTION
Do not scratch the cylinder bore or pistons while installing.

3. After installation, bleed the brakes as described under *Brake Bleeding* in this chapter. Carefully check the master cylinder for fluid leaks.

BRAKE BOOSTER

The Master-Vac brake booster uses intake manifold vacuum to reduce braking effort. The booster and its check valve should be tested at intervals specified in Chapter Three.

Check Valve Test

1. Remove the check valve (**Figure 39**).

2. Disconnect the hose from the brake booster side of the valve. Connect a vacuum gauge in its place.

3. Run the engine at a fast idle. Turn the engine off when the vacuum reaches approximately 500mmHg (20 in.Hg).

4. With the engine off, watch the vacuum gauge for 15 seconds. Any vacuum drop, even a slight one, indicates a defective check valve or vacuum line. If no defect can be seen in the vacuum line, replace the check valve.

Airtightness Test (No Load)

1. Using a T-fitting, connect a vacuum gauge into the line between the check valve and brake booster. See **Figure 40**.

2. Run the engine at a fast idle. Turn it off when the vacuum reaches approximately 500mmHg (20 in.Hg).

3. With the engine off, watch the vacuum gauge for 15 seconds. Any vacuum drop indicates a defective vacuum line or brake booster. If no defects can be found in the vacuum line, replace the brake booster as described in this chapter.

11

Airtightness Test (Under Load)

1. Connect a vacuum gauge as described in Step 1 of the preceding section. Place the gauge where it can be seen from the driver's seat or have an assistant watch it for you.

2. With the engine running, press the brake pedal as far as it will go.

3. When vacuum reaches approximately 500 mmHg (20 in.Hg) shut the engine off. Keep the brake pedal down.

4. Watch the vacuum gauge for 15 seconds after the engine is shut off. Any vacuum drop indicates a defective brake booster. Replace as described in the following section.

Booster Removal

Refer to **Figure 41** for this procedure.

1. Remove the master cylinder as described under *Master Cylinder Removal/Installation* in this chapter.

2. Disconnect the booster pushrod from the brake pedal.

3. Working under the dash, remove the booster mounting nuts.

4. Lift the booster off the firewall.

Booster Installation

Installation is the reverse of removal, plus the following:

1. Before installing a new booster, check its pushrod length (dimension A, **Figure 42**). This should be 9.75-10.0 mm (0.384-0.394 in.). If necessary, loosen the pushrod locknut and turn the pushrod to change its length. See **Figure 43**. Then tighten the locknut.

> *NOTE*
> *If the pushrod is more than 0.5 mm (0.020 in.) from the correct length, replace the brake booster.*

2. Check operating rod length (dimension B, **Figure 44**). On 1980 models, this should be 180 mm (7.09 in.). On 1981 models, it should be 275 mm (10.83 in.). If incorrect, loosen the locknut and turn the clevis to change length.

3. Tighten the booster mounting nuts to 7.8-10.8 N•m (6-8 ft.-lb.).

4. Bleed the brakes as described under *Brake Bleeding* in this chapter.

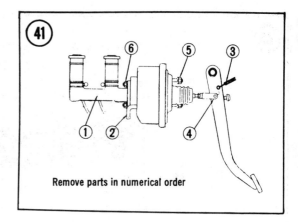

(41)

Remove parts in numerical order

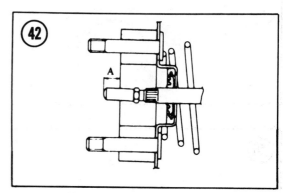

(42)

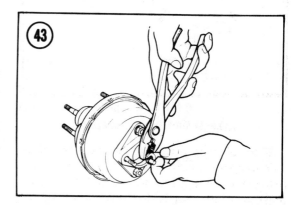

(43)

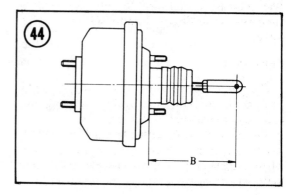

(44)

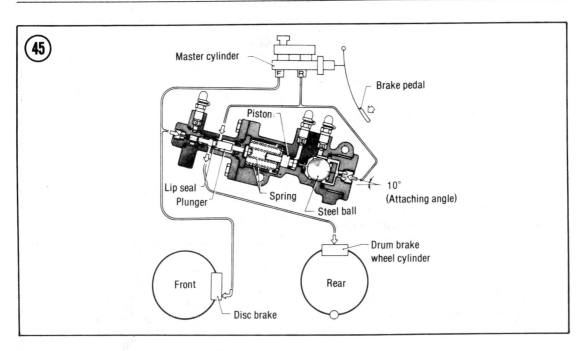

Master cylinder

Brake pedal

Piston

10°
(Attaching angle)

Lip seal
Plunger

Spring

Steel ball

Drum brake
wheel cylinder

Front

Rear

Disc brake

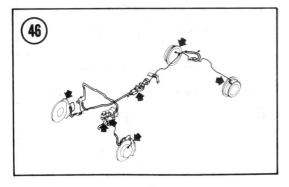

LOAD SENSING VALVE

This valve prevents premature rear wheel lockup by regulating pressure to the front and rear brakes. When the truck is lightly loaded, pressure to the rear brakes is reduced. As the load increases, pressure to the rear brakes increases accordingly. **Figure 45** shows the valve.

Valve Test

The braking system must be in good condition to test the valve. Make any necessary repairs before testing.

1. Drive at 25 mph with the truck unloaded. Apply the brakes hard enough to lock the wheels *slightly*. The front wheels must lock before or at the same time as the rear wheels.

2. Repeat Step 1 with a load in the truck's bed. Again, the rear wheels must not lock before the front wheels.

3. If the valve fails either part of this test, replace it.

BRAKE BLEEDING

The hydraulic system should be bled whenever air enters it. This is because air in the brake lines will compress, rather than transmitting pedal pressure to the brake operating parts. If the pedal feels spongy or if pedal travel increases considerably, brake bleeding is usually called for. Bleeding is also necessary whenever a brake line is disconnected.

This procedure requires handling brake fluid. Be careful not to get any fluid on brake discs, pads, shoes or drums. Clean all dirt from bleed valves before beginning. Two people are needed, one to operate the brake pedal and the other to open and close the bleed valves.

Bleeding should be done in the following order: master cylinder (1980 only), load sensing valve, right rear, left rear, right front, left front. See **Figure 46**.

1. Clean away any dirt around the master cylinder reservoirs. Top up the master cylinder with brake fluid marked DOT 3.

11

NOTE

DOT 3 means the brake fluid meets current Department of Transportation quality standards. If the fluid doesn't say DOT 3 somewhere on the label, buy a brand that does.

2. Attach a plastic tube to the bleed valve (**Figure 47**). Immerse the other end of the tube in a jar containing several inches of clean brake fluid.

NOTE

Do not allow the end of the tube to come out of the brake fluid during bleeding. This could allow air into the system, requiring that the bleeding procedure be done over.

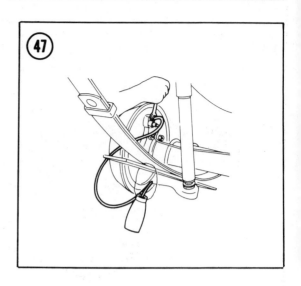

BRAKE LINES

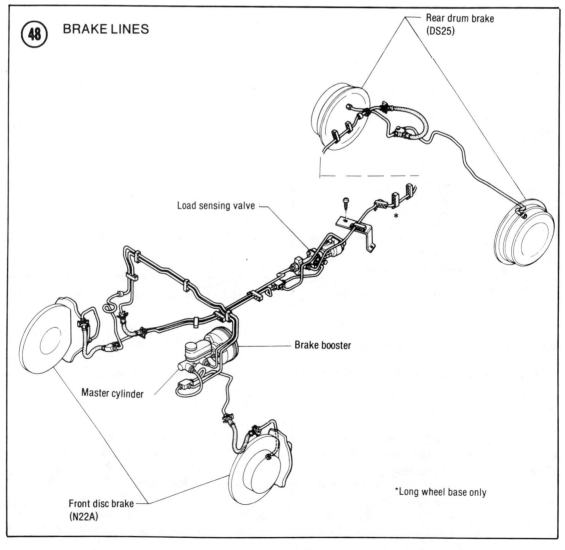

Rear drum brake
(DS25)

Load sensing valve

*

Brake booster

Master cylinder

Front disc brake
(N22A)

*Long wheel base only

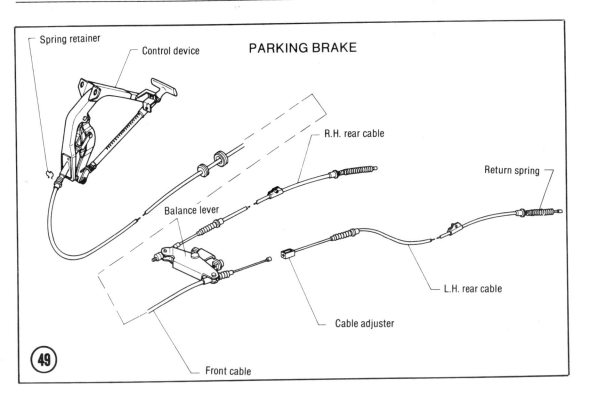

PARKING BRAKE

Spring retainer
Control device
R.H. rear cable
Return spring
Balance lever
L.H. rear cable
Cable adjuster
Front cable

49

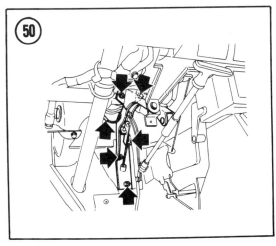

50

NOTE
Keep an eye on the brake fluid level in the master cylinder during bleeding. If the fluid level is allowed to drop too low, air will enter the brake lines and the entire bleeding procedure will have to be repeated.

BRAKE LINES

Brake lines should be checked for wear, damage or leaks at intervals specified in Chapter Three. **Figure 48** shows the lines.

PARKING BRAKE

Figure 49 shows the parking brake mechanism.

Handle Removal/Installation

1. Disconnect the brake warning switch wiring. See **Figure 50**.
2. Disconnect the parking brake cable from the control lever.
3. Remove the control bracket fasteners.
4. Working in the engine compartment, remove the spring retainer.
5. Take the handle out.
6. Installation is the reverse of removal.

3. Slowly press the brake pedal 2 or 3 times, then hold it down.
4. With the brake pedal down, open the bleed valve 1/3-1/2 turn. Let the brake pedal sink to the floor, then close the bleed valve. Do not let the pedal up until the bleed valve is closed.
5. Let the pedal back up slowly.
6. Repeat Steps 3-5 until the fluid entering the jar is free of air bubbles.
7. Repeat the process for the other bleed valves.

11

Front Cable Removal/Installation

1. Securely block the wheels so the truck will not roll in either direction. Place the transmission in FIRST.

2. Make sure the parking brake is all the way off.

3. Loosen the adjuster nut at the balance lever. See **Figure 51**.

4. Disconnect the front cable from the handle. See **Figure 52**.

5. Disconnect the right rear cable from the balance lever. Disconnect the left rear cable from the front cable. See **Figure 53**.

6. Detach the balance lever (**Figure 54**). Take out the balance lever and front cable.

7. Installation is the reverse of removal. Lubricate all friction points with multipurpose lithium grease. Adjust the parking brake as described under *Adjustments* in this chapter.

Rear Cable Removal/Installation

1. Securely block both front wheels so the truck will not roll in either direction.

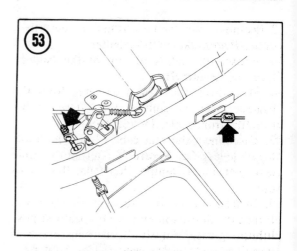

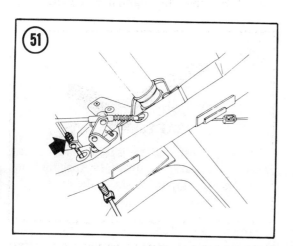

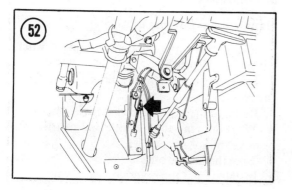

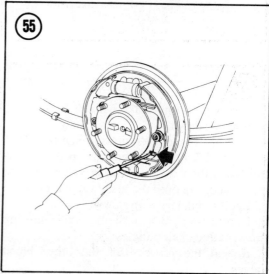

2. Remove the brake drums as described under *Rear Brakes* in this chapter.

3. Loosen the adjusting nut at the balance lever. See **Figure 51**.

4. Disconnect the right rear cable from the balance lever. Disconnect the left rear cable from the front cable. See **Figure 53**.

5. Disconnect the rear cables from the brake toggle levers. See **Figure 55**. Detach the cable lock plates and clamps, then take the cables out.

6. Installation is the reverse of removal. Lubricate all friction points with multipurpose lithium grease. Adjust the parking brake as described under *Adjustments* in this chapter.

STOP LAMP SWITCH REPLACEMENT

The stop lamp switch is mounted on the brake pedal bracket (**Figure 56**).

1. To remove, disconnect the switch wires. Loosen the locknut and unscrew the switch.

2. Installation is the reverse of removal. Adjust the switch as described under *Adjustments, Brake Pedal* in this chapter.

ADJUSTMENTS

Brake Pedal

1. Check pedal height from the floor (**Figure 57**). It should be 168-174 mm (6.61-6.85 in.). To adjust, loosen the stop lamp switch locknut. Rotate the stop lamp switch to change pedal height, then tighten the locknut.

2. Push the pedal by hand until resistance is felt. The distance traveled is pedal free play. It should be 1-5 mm (0.04-0.20 in.). To adjust, loosen the locknut on the brake booster input rod. Rotate the rod to change its effective length, then tighten the locknut.

Parking Brake

The handbrake lever should rise 6 to 10 notches when pulled with a force of 20 kg (44 lb.). See **Figure 58**. To adjust, loosen the locknut on the cable adjuster under the car. See **Figure 59**. Turn the aduster to tighten or loosen the cable, then tighten the locknut.

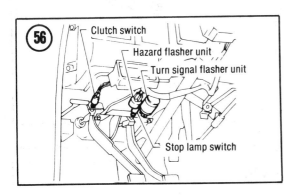

(56) Clutch switch
Hazard flasher unit
Turn signal flasher unit
Stop lamp switch

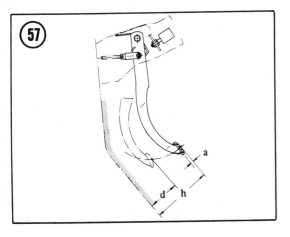

(57)

a
d   h

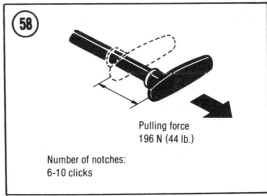

(58)
Pulling force
196 N (44 lb.)
Number of notches:
6-10 clicks

(59)
Locknut

11

Rear Drum Brakes

1. Securely block both front wheels so the truck will not roll in either direction.
2. Jack up the rear end of the truck and place it on jackstands.
3. Remove the adjusting hole plug (**Figure 60**).
4. Lightly tap the adjuster toward the front of the truck.
5. Turn the adjuster wheel downward to spread the brake shoes. Keep turning until the shoes lock the drum.
6. Turn the adjuster upward 12 notches. Make sure the brake drum turns without dragging.
7. Install the wheels. Lower the truck and tighten the wheel nuts.

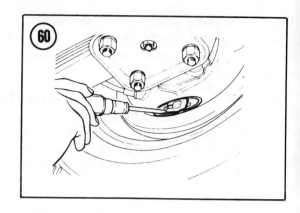

Front Disc Brakes

Front disc brakes are adjusted automatically by the piston seals. No means of manual adjustment is necessary or provided.

CHAPTER TWELVE

BODY

This chapter provides service procedures for the seats, instrument panel, console, bumpers, grille, hood, doors, tailgate, bed and cab. Other body repairs require special skills and should be left to a dealer or body shop.

SEATS

Front Seat Removal/Installation

1. Slide the seat back and remove its front mounting bolts. See **Figure 1**.
2. Slide the seat forward and remove its rear mounting bolts. Lift the seat out.
3. Installation is the reverse of removal.

Jump Seat Removal/Installation (King Cab)

1. Lift up the seat cushion, remove its mounting screws and take the cushion out.
2. Remove the screws securing the lower edge of the seat back. Lift the seat back up and out.
3. Installation is the reverse of removal.

INSTRUMENT PANEL REMOVAL/INSTALLATION

This section covers removal of the entire instrument panel assembly. To remove just the gauge cluster, see *Instruments*, Chapter Seven.

Refer to **Figure 2** for this procedure.
1. Disconnect the negative cable from the battery.
2. Remove the steering column shell. See *Steering Column Removal/Installation* in this chapter.

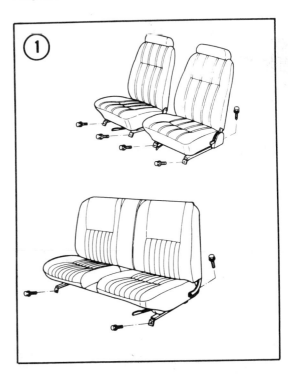

3. Remove the package tray (**Figure 3**).

4. Reach behind the speedometer and disconnect the speedometer cable.

5. Working behind the instrument panel, disconnect all wiring connectors.

6. Remove the instrument panel upper mounting bolts (**Figure 4**).

7. Remove the instrument panel lower mounting bolt (**Figure 5**).

8. Remove the instrument panel center mounting bolt (**Figure 6**).

9. Remove the mounting bolts from each end of the instrument panel, then lift the panel out.

CAUTION
The panel should come out easily. If not,

check to make sure all fasteners have been removed.

10. Installation is the reverse of removal.

CONSOLE REMOVAL/INSTALLATION

Refer to **Figure 7** for this procedure.

1. Remove the center armrest plug and mounting screws, then take out the center armrest.

2. Remove the console mounting screws, then take the console out.

3. Installation is the reverse of removal.

GRILLE REMOVAL/INSTALLATION

Figure 8 shows the grille and related parts.

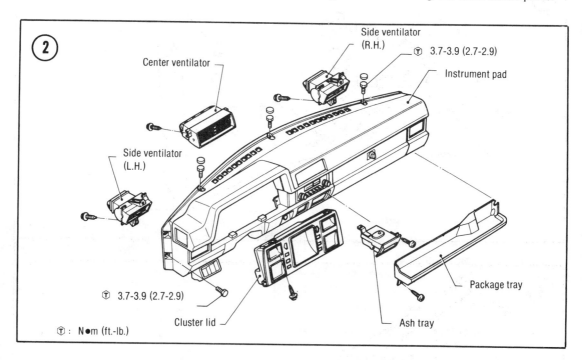

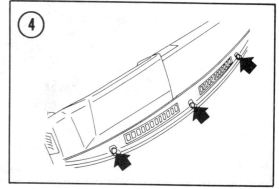

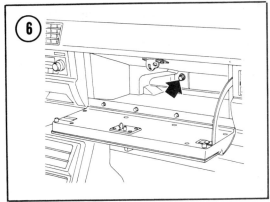

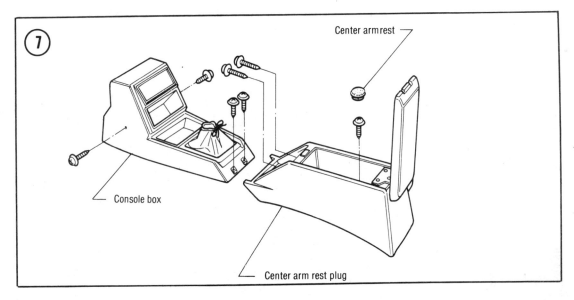

Center armrest

Console box

Center arm rest plug

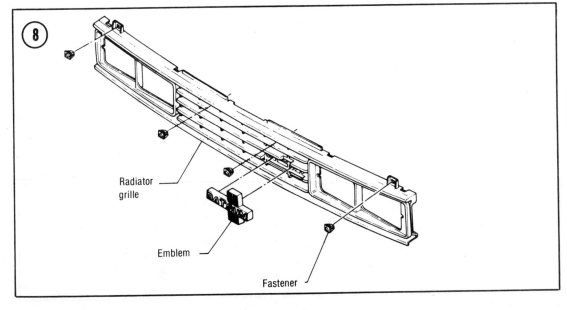

Radiator grille

Emblem

Fastener

12

1. Referring to **Figure 9**, turn the grille fasteners 1/4 turn with a standard screwdriver. Detach the fasteners and lift the grille out.
2. Installation is the reverse of removal. Insert the fasteners into the grille from the rear, then turn them 1/4 turn to lock. See **Figure 10**.

BUMPERS

Front Bumper Removal/Installation

1. Disconnect the negative cable from the battery.
2. Remove the bumper mounting bolts (**Figure 11**). Take the bumper partway out, disconnect the wiring for the front combination lamps, then remove the bumper.

3. Installation is the reverse of removal.

Rear Bumper Removal/Installation

To remove the rear bumper, remove its mounting bolts and take it out. See **Figure 12**. Installation is the reverse of removal.

HOOD

Adjustment

Refer to **Figure 13** for the following procedures.
1. To move the hood forward, back or to one side, loosen the hinge-to-hood bolts. Reposition the hood as needed, then tighten the bolts.

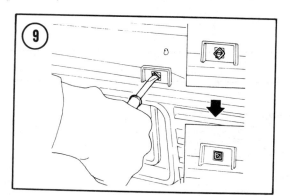

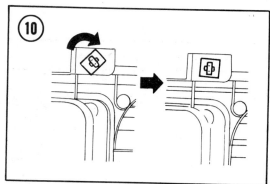

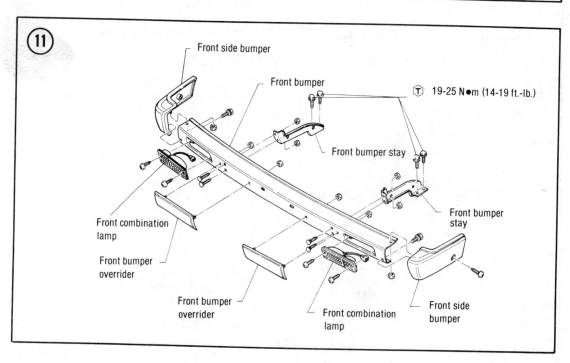

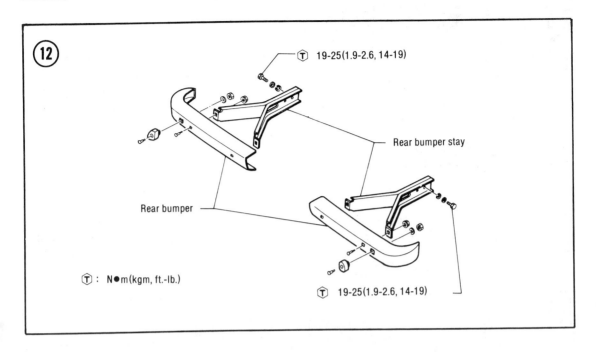

(12)

Ⓣ 19-25(1.9-2.6, 14-19)

Rear bumper stay

Rear bumper

Ⓣ : N●m(kgm, ft.-lb.)

Ⓣ 19-25(1.9-2.6, 14-19)

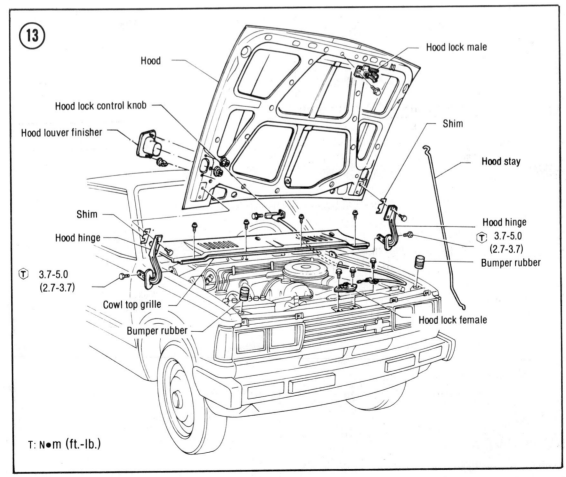

(13)

Hood lock male

Hood

Hood lock control knob

Hood louver finisher

Shim

Hood stay

Shim

Hood hinge
Ⓣ 3.7-5.0
(2.7-3.7)

Hood hinge

Bumper rubber

Ⓣ 3.7-5.0
(2.7-3.7)

Cowl top grille

Hood lock female

Bumper rubber

T: N●m (ft.-lb.)

12

2. If the hood moves forward, back or to one side when closed, loosen the upper side of the hood latch. Reposition the latch as needed, then tighten the latch.

3. To adjust hood height, turn the rubber bumpers to raise or lower them.

4. If the hood is too tight or too loose when closed, loosen the locknut on the dovetail bolt (**Figure 14**). Turn the dovetail bolt as needed to adjust, then tighten the locknut.

Removal/Installation

This procedure requires 2 people.

1. Open the hood. Place a thick layer of rags beneath the trailing edge of the hood to protect the paint.

2. With a soft lead pencil, make alignment marks around the hood hinges directly onto the hood. The marks will ease installation.

3. Have your assistant support one side of the hood. Detach the hinge from the hood on your side, then support the hood while the assistant unbolts the other side.

4. Lift the hood off.

5. Installation is the reverse of removal. Adjust the hood as described in the preceding section.

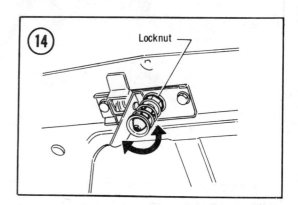

2. With a soft lead pencil, make alignment marks around the hood hinges directly onto the hood. The marks will ease installation.

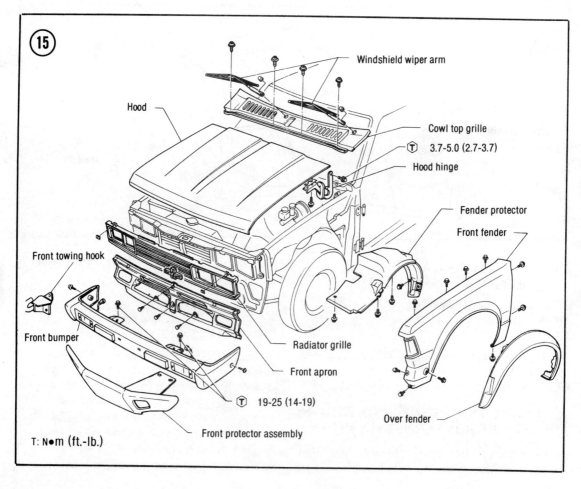

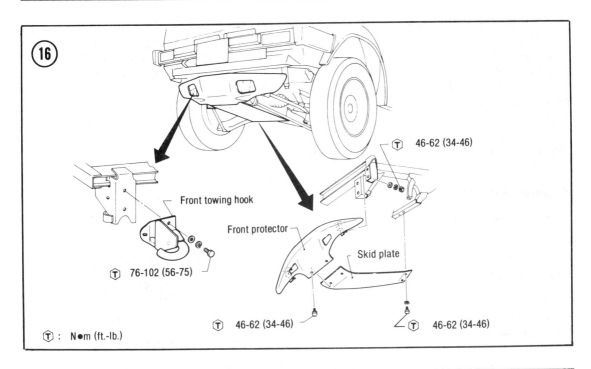

(16)

46-62 (34-46)

Front towing hook

Front protector

Skid plate

76-102 (56-75)

46-62 (34-46)

46-62 (34-46)

(T) : N•m (ft.-lb.)

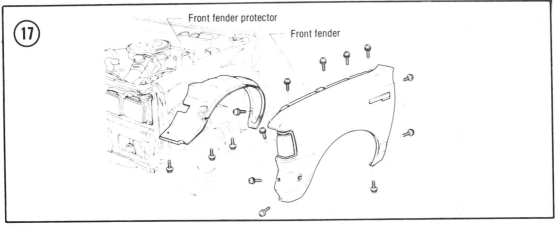

(17)

Front fender protector

Front fender

FRONT APRON REMOVAL/INSTALLATION

Refer to **Figure 15** for this procedure.

1. Remove the front bumpers. See *Bumpers* in this chapter.
2. Detach the front apron from the truck and take it off.
3. Installation is the reverse of removal.

FRONT PROTECTOR AND SKID PLATE REMOVAL/INSTALLATION

To remove the front protector and skid plate, undo the mounting nuts and bolts, then take them off. See **Figure 16**. Installation is the reverse of removal.

FENDER REMOVAL/INSTALLATION

Refer to **Figure 17** for this procedure.

1. Disconnect the negative cable from the battery.
2. Remove the front bumper. See *Bumpers* in this chapter.
3. Remove the front fender protector.
4. Disconnect the side marker light wiring.
5. Detach the fender and take it off.
6. Installation is the reverse of removal.

12

FENDER FLARE
REMOVAL/INSTALLATION

To detach the flare, undo its fasteners and take it off. See **Figure 18**. Installation is the reverse of removal.

DOORS

Refer to **Figure 19** for the following procedures.

Removal

1. Open the door and place a jack beneath it. Use a rag between door and jack to protect the paint.

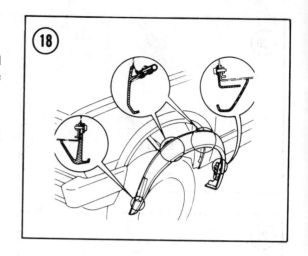

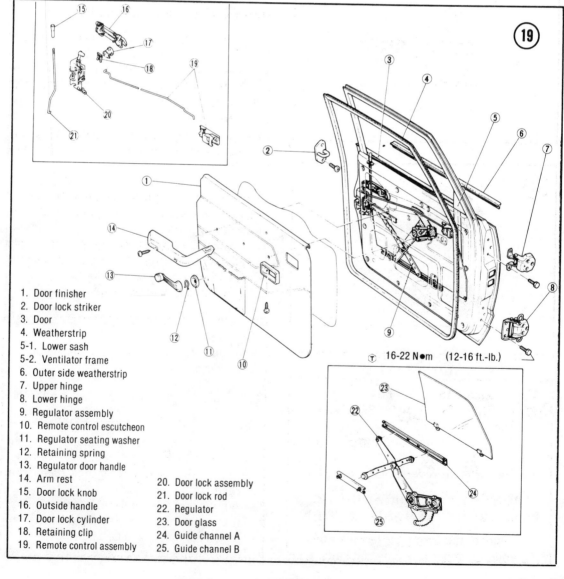

1. Door finisher
2. Door lock striker
3. Door
4. Weatherstrip
5-1. Lower sash
5-2. Ventilator frame
6. Outer side weatherstrip
7. Upper hinge
8. Lower hinge
9. Regulator assembly
10. Remote control escutcheon
11. Regulator seating washer
12. Retaining spring
13. Regulator door handle
14. Arm rest
15. Door lock knob
16. Outside handle
17. Door lock cylinder
18. Retaining clip
19. Remote control assembly
20. Door lock assembly
21. Door lock rod
22. Regulator
23. Door glass
24. Guide channel A
25. Guide channel B

16-22 N•m   (12-16 ft.-lb.)

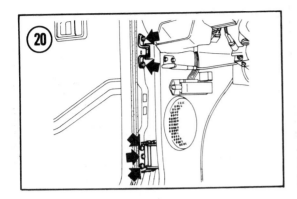

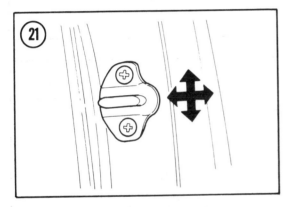

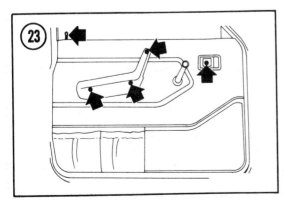

2. While an assistant supports the door, unbolt the hinges (**Figure 20**). Lift the door off.

Installation and Adjustment

1. Inspect the door weatherstripping. Replace if deteriorated or damaged.
2. Remove the door striker plate (**Figure 21**).
3. Remove the fender protector (**Figure 17**).
4. Loosen the hinge-to-pillar bolts (**Figure 22**). Align the door with the body, then tighten the bolts.
5. Install the striker plate. Position the striker plate so the door closes evenly, then tighten its mounting screws.

Door Panel Removal/Installation

1. Remove the armrest, lock knob and door handle trim. See **Figure 23**.
2. Make a wire hook. Press in on the door panel around the window crank and pull the crank clip out. See **Figure 24**.
3. Insert a wide-bladed screwdriver or similar tool between door panel and door. Carefully pry the panel clips out of the door, then take the panel off.
4. If necessary, carefully peel the plastic sealing screen away from the door. Be careful not to let the sealing screen adhesive stick to surrounding parts.
5. If necessary, carefully pry out the door outside weatherstripping. Use a screwdriver wrapped with a rag to protect the paint.
6. Installation is the reverse of removal.

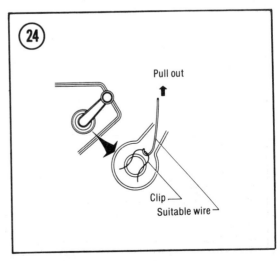

12

Door Glass Removal/Installation

1. Remove the door trim panel as described in the preceding section.

2. If equipped with vent windows, remove the vent window frame. If not equipped with vent windows, remove the lower sash (**Figure 25**).

3. Detach the door glass from the regulator (**Figure 26**).

4. Lift the glass up and out of the door.

5. If necessary, detach the regulator from the door and remove it through the access hole.

6. Installation is the reverse of removal. Adjust the glass as described in the following section.

Door Glass Adjustment

Refer to **Figure 27** for this procedure.

1. To adjust glass tilt, loosen the nuts securing guide channel B. Tilt the guide channel to straighten the glass, then tighten the nuts.

2. To slide the glass to front or rear, loosen guide channel A. Push the glass up and back into its run, then tighten guide channel A.

3. If the glass doesn't slide easily, loosen the vent window frame or lower sash. Reposition the vent window frame or lower sash as needed, then tighten it.

Lock Mechanism Removal/Installation

1. Remove the door panel as described under *Door Panel Removal/Installation* in this chapter.

2. Detach the clip from the inside handle rod (**Figure 28**).

3. Remove the inside door handle (**Figure 29**).

4. Pull out the lock cylinder retaining clip (**Figure 30**), then take out the lock cylinder.

5. Detach the rod holder from the door lock rod. See **Figure 31**.

6. Remove the lock assembly mounting screws, then take the lock assembly out.

7. Remove the outside handle.

8. Installation is the reverse of removal. Apply multipurpose grease to all friction points.

SIDE WINDOW REMOVAL/ INSTALLATION (KING CAB)

1. Undo the mounting screws (**Figure 32**).

2. Take out the window and weatherstripping (**Figure 33**).

3. Installation is the reverse of removal. Replace the weatherstripping if deteriorated or damaged.

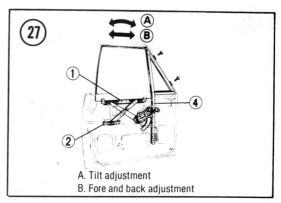

A. Tilt adjustment
B. Fore and back adjustment

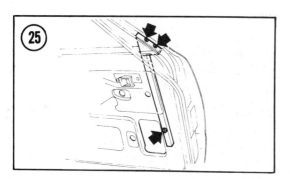

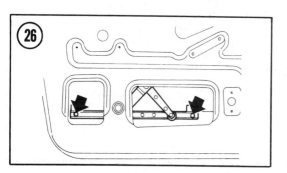

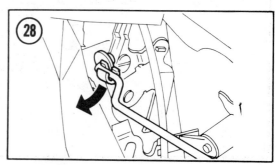

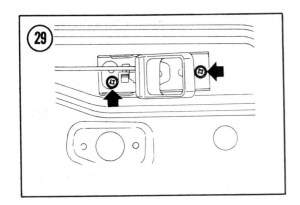

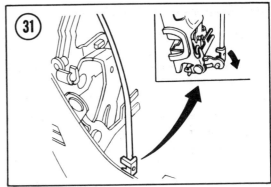

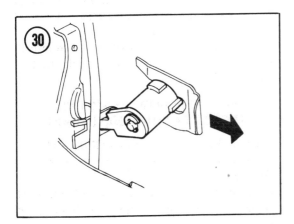

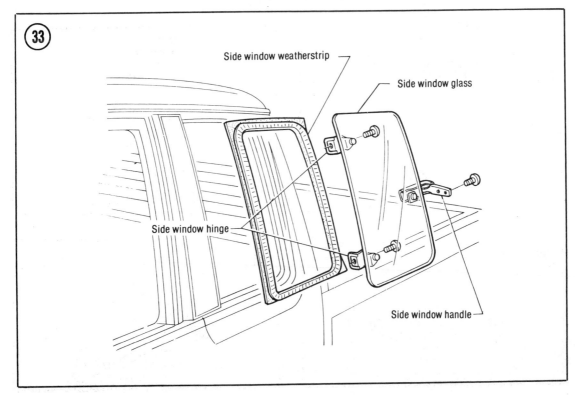

Side window weatherstrip

Side window glass

Side window hinge

Side window handle

12

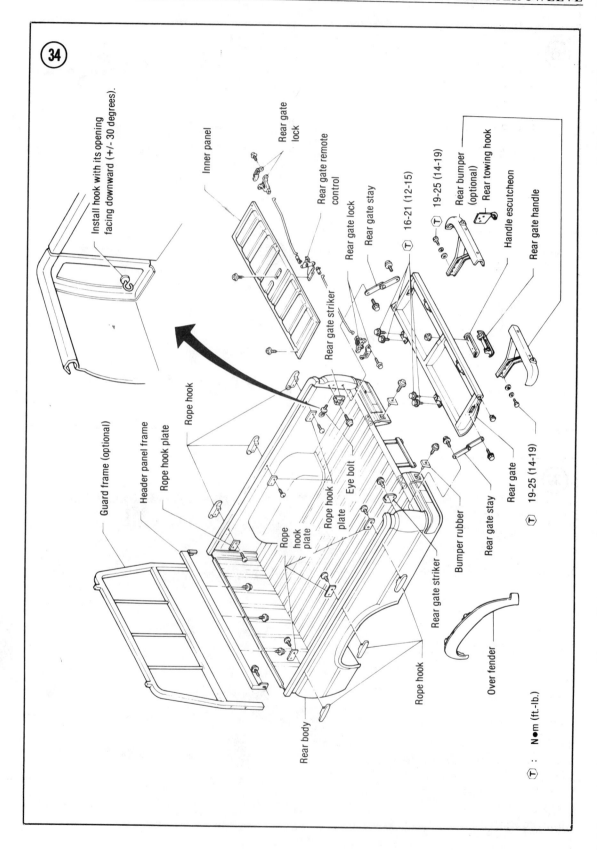

(34)

Install hook with its opening facing downward (+/- 30 degrees).

Inner panel

Rear gate lock

Rear gate remote control

Rear gate lock

Rear gate stay

Rear gate striker

16-21 (12-15)

19-25 (14-19)

Rear bumper (optional)

Rear towing hook

Handle escutcheon

Rear gate handle

Guard frame (optional)

Header panel frame

Rope hook plate

Rope hook

Rope hook plate

Rope hook plate

Eye bolt

Bumper rubber

Rear gate stay

Rear gate

19-25 (14-19)

Rear body

Rope hook

Rope hook

Rear gate striker

Over fender

(T) : N•m (ft.-lb.)

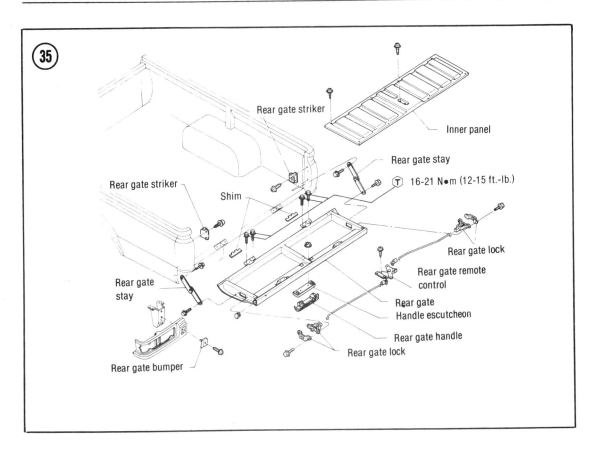

(35)

Rear gate striker

Inner panel

Rear gate stay

(T) 16-21 N•m (12-15 ft.-lb.)

Rear gate striker

Shim

Rear gate lock

Rear gate remote control

Rear gate stay

Rear gate Handle escutcheon

Rear gate handle

Rear gate lock

Rear gate bumper

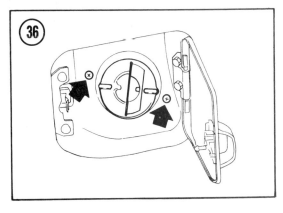

(36)

REAR BODY

Refer to **Figure 34** for these procedures.

Tailgate Removal/Installation

1. With a soft lead pencil or felt pen, make alignment marks around the tailgate hinges onto the bed. The marks will ease installation.
2. Have an assistant support one side of the tailgate. Unbolt your side, then support it while the assistant unbolts the other side.

3. Lift the tailgate off.
4. Installation is the reverse of removal.

Lock Assembly Removal/Installation

1. Remove the inner tailgate panel.
2. Detach the lock assembly (**Figure 35**), then take it out.
3. If necessary, remove the outside handle screws, then remove the outside handle.
4. Installation is the reverse of removal.

Bed Removal/Installation

1. Disconnect the negative cable from the battery.
2. Disconnect the wiring for rear combination lamps and license plate lights.
3. Remove the fuel filler neck screws (**Figure 36**).
4. Detach the rear body from the frame. See **Figure 37**.

NOTE
Mark the locations of all shims for reinstallation.

12

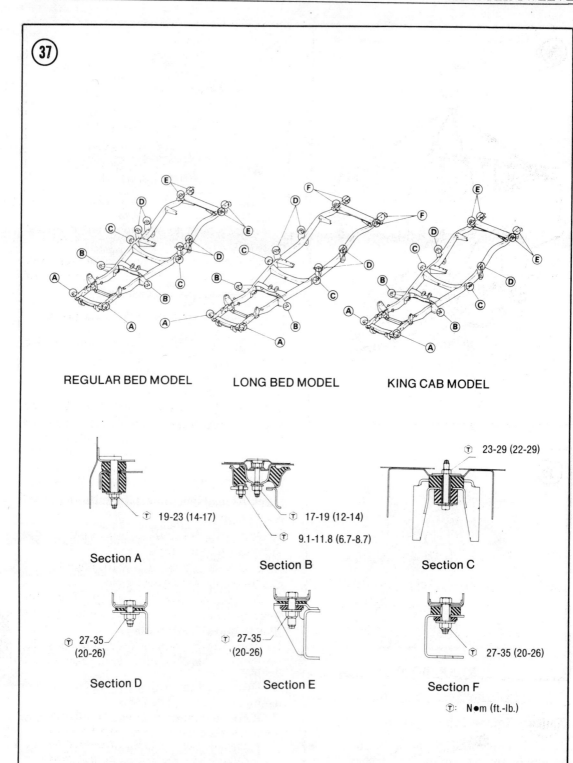

(37)

REGULAR BED MODEL   LONG BED MODEL   KING CAB MODEL

Ⓣ 19-23 (14-17)

Section A

Ⓣ 17-19 (12-14)

Ⓣ 9.1-11.8 (6.7-8.7)

Section B

Ⓣ 23-29 (22-29)

Section C

Ⓣ 27-35
(20-26)

Section D

Ⓣ 27-35
(20-26)

Section E

Ⓣ 27-35 (20-26)

Section F

Ⓣ: N•m (ft.-lb.)

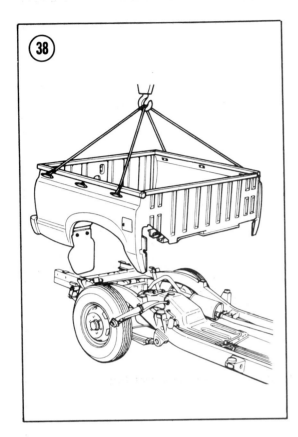

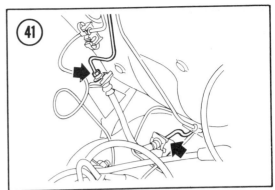

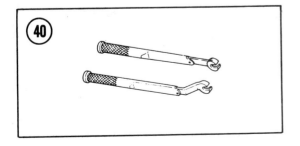

5. Attach a hoist to the body and lift it off (**Figure 38**).

6. Installation is the reverse of removal. **Figure 37** shows the arrangements of mounting fasteners and bushings.

CAB REMOVAL/INSTALLATION

1. Remove the hood and front bumpers. See *Hood* and *Front Bumpers* in this chapter.

2. Remove the battery.

3. Remove the air cleaner.

4. Detach the emission control lines from the engine compartment sidewalls. See *Emission Controls* in Chapter Five of this supplement.

5. If equipped with air conditioning, have the system discharged by a dealer or air conditioning shop. Detach the engine-mounted components from the cab-mounted components.

6. Disconnect the brake booster vacuum hose fom the intake manifold.

7. Disconnect all wiring from the engine.

8. Disconnect the throttle cable.

9. Detach the steering column from the steering gear at the rubber coupling. See **Figure 39**.

10. Remove the radiator mounting bolts. Tie the radiator and shroud back against the engine.

NOTE
*For the next 2 steps, the factory recommends a flare nut wrench such as Datsun tool part No. GG94310000 (**Figure 40**). Do not use an adjustable wrench, since it may round off the nuts.*

11. Disconnect the brake and clutch lines in the engine compartment (**Figure 41**).

12

12. Disconnect the brake lines under the truck (**Figure 42**).

13. Disconnect the speedometer cable from the transmission.

14. Remove the shift lever.

15. Disconnect the handbrake lever and cable.

16. Disconnect all wiring harnesses securing the cab to the frame.

17. Attach a hoist to the cab as shown in **Figure 43**.

18. Detach the cab from the frame. See **Figure 37**.

19. Hoist the cab off.

20. Installation is the reverse of removal. **Figure 37** shows the arrangement of mounting fasteners and bushings.

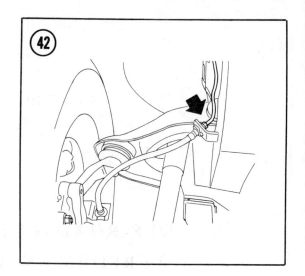

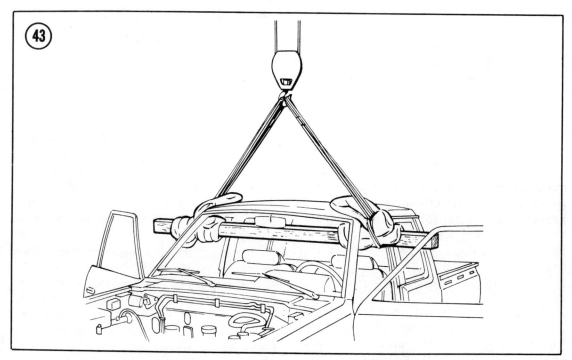

CHAPTER THIRTEEN

OFF-ROAD PREPARATION AND PERFORMANCE IMPROVEMENT

This chapter talks about the many modifications and accessories available for your truck. It covers off-road equipment and preparation, engine and drive train modifications and load-hauling and custom accessories. **Tables 1-3** are at the end of the chapter.

TIRES AND WHEELS

This should be the first area you look at. Tires affect traction, braking, handling (on and off road), rolling resistance, ride quality and noise level. Wheels affect the performance of the tires. The right wheel and tire selection can offer solid improvement in all these areas, at relatively low cost and with little time and trouble.

Tires

An enormous variety of tires is available for every type of surface. However, selection need not be a difficult task if you analyze your needs carefully. First, determine the weight category of your truck: light weight, up to

3,200 pounds; medium weight, 3,200 to 5,000 pounds; or heavy weight, over 5,000 pounds. Don't guess at the weight and don't assume that the weight on the rating plate is correct. Instead, have the truck weighed at a public scale. The cost is usually no more than a couple of dollars. If you think the truck may be in the heavy category, weigh the front and rear individually to determine actual axle rates.

As much as practical, the truck should be weighed with the same load and equipment it carries in actual use. Also, the fuel tank or tanks should be full, as well as auxiliary gas and water cans.

When the true weight is known, use **Table 1** to determine size and rating requirements.

The next step is to determine what the truck will be used for. For the average owner, the truck is probably used as a first or second car with some off-road driving. Off-road mileage in such a case would be from 5-10 per cent, rarely more. An ideal tire for this situation should have excellent highway performance, long tread life and reasonable traction off road.

Since gains in highway performance mean losses in off-road performance (and vice versa), a compromise is required. A well-designed mud and snow tire, like that shown in **Figure 1**, provides reasonable pavement performance. The randomly spaced side and interior tread blocks eliminate the harmonics that cause tire noise. A highly aggressive tread like that shown in **Figure 2** is necessary for very rough terrain. However, its tread design and stiff sidewall construction would give it a harsh, noisy ride and short tread life on pavement.

Tire cost should be seriously considered along with tire performance. Cost is not simply the price of the tire, but the cost per mile as well. Tire mileage depends heavily on vehicle loading and correct pressure, so it is a good idea to talk to owners of similar trucks, similarly equipped, that use the tires you are interested in.

Tire height is also an important consideration because it will affect gear ratios. First, measure the circumference of your present tires. Then measure the circumference of the new tire, mounted on an appropriate wheel and inflated. A significant difference will raise the gear ratios and cause an unacceptable power loss with the stock engine. Although tall tires are the best way to increase clearance (since they raise the axles as well as the body), sizes larger than L78-15 are not practical on a stock Datsun 4-wheel drive pickup.

NOTE
If possible, buy the wheels and tires from the same source. Otherwise, if problems occur, the tire dealer may blame the wheel supplier or vice versa.

Wheels

Wheels should be selected as carefully as tires. There are numerous excellent wheel manufacturers in this country—and there are probably as many more who have little or no knowledge of what is required to produce a safe, quality wheel. As with tires, wheel selection can be simplified if you deal with a supplier familiar with off-road vehicles.

There are several guidelines you can use to decide whether the wheels you are considering are right for your needs and safely constructed.

First, make sure rim width is correct for the tires you have selected. See **Table 2**.

If the wheel is too narrow for the tire, it will pull the tire beads too close together and cause the tire to crown. Off road, crowning will reduce flotation. On pavement, crowning will cause the tire to wear rapidly in the center of the tread. If the wheel is too wide for the tire, the wheel will be vulnerable to rock damage.

Make sure wheel offset is correct for your truck. Wheel offset (**Figure 3**) is the relationship of the wheel center to the wheel rim. Positive offset moves the wheel rim outward (the truck's track is wider). Negative offset moves the wheel rim inward (the

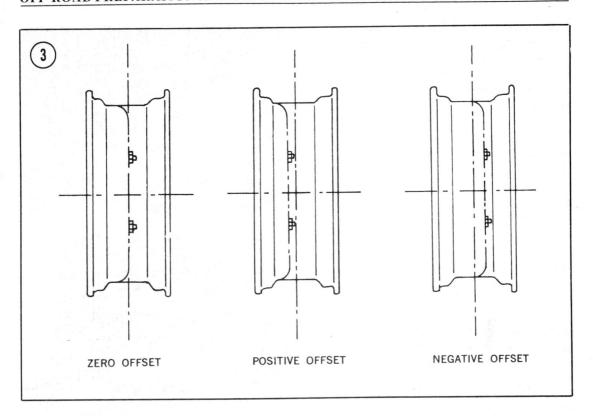

ZERO OFFSET   POSITIVE OFFSET   NEGATIVE OFFSET

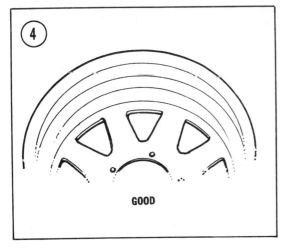

GOOD

truck's track is narrower). Too much negative offset can cause clearance problems between tires and wheel wells. Too much positive offset increases the strain on wheel bearings and hubs. Some positive offset is necessary because the inside of the wheel and tire must not interfere with tie rods or suspension.

The best way to check offset is to install a wheel and tire on the front and rear of the truck. If the supplier won't do this (and you don't feel like finding another supplier), offer to pay the mounting charge if the tires and wheels don't fit. When you're spending hundreds of dollars to last thousands of miles, it's worth $10 or so to avoid a bad purchase.

The most important thing to look for in wheels is their construction. Aluminum wheels are still very popular despite the inroads the steel spoke types have made into the market. Cast wheels remain the most popular of the aluminum types, although in spite of the vast amount of technical information that has grown out of their long history, inferior cast wheels are still being manufactured. Brands like Cragar, E-T and Turbo-Vector are safe bets in that they are correctly engineered, heat treated and machined for balance and roundness. There are good cast wheels other than those mentioned—but beware of bargain wheels.

The most popular ORV wheel is the steel spoke type. While these may appear to be all the same, quality varies significantly. A few simple checks will identify good wheels.

Note whether the wheel has a full circumference mating surface (**Figure 4**),

13

rather than stub spokes (**Figure 5**). The full circumference center is stronger, distributes the load better and allows some necessary flexing.

Check the weld quality. A good weld will be uniform and free of large pits. The weld should be continuous around the circumference, but if not, it should be applied between the spokes rather than in line with them. See **Figure 6**.

Inspect the wheel centers around the inside of the bolt pattern. The center should be machined or stamped so the wheel will "crush" when the lug nuts are tightened. See **Figure 7**. This places tension on the lug nuts so they won't loosen.

Disc wheels are still common and generally less expensive than aluminum or steel spoke wheels. However, caution should be used when selecting disc wheels, despite their safe-looking stock appearance. A common cost saver used by shady manufacturers is a 2- or 3-piece steel rim (**Figure 8**). The wheel on the left was made up of 2 rim halves welded together to obtain a wider rim. The one on the right is made up of 2 outer sections connected by a straight center section. Both types are invariably made from old wheels. They are seldom round, usually have excessive runout and their strength is questionable. It's possible

to build a good wheel in this manner, but it requires costly machining, an expensive jig and expert welding—hardly what you would expect from a manufacturer who is maximizing his profit by using salvage wheels. Not long ago, before wide one-piece rims were available to wheel manufacturers, this type of construction was common. But today, with wide rims available, there is no reason to build wheels in this manner—certainly not so far as the consumer is concerned.

Riveted centers in disc wheels are a good indicator that the manufacturer knows what he is doing. Because of the equipment required, riveting is much more expensive than welding, although there are many good welded wheels on the market.

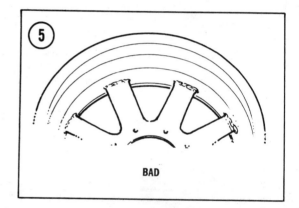

BAD

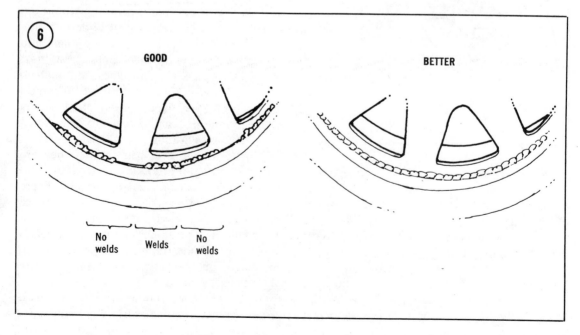

GOOD

BETTER

No welds   Welds   No welds

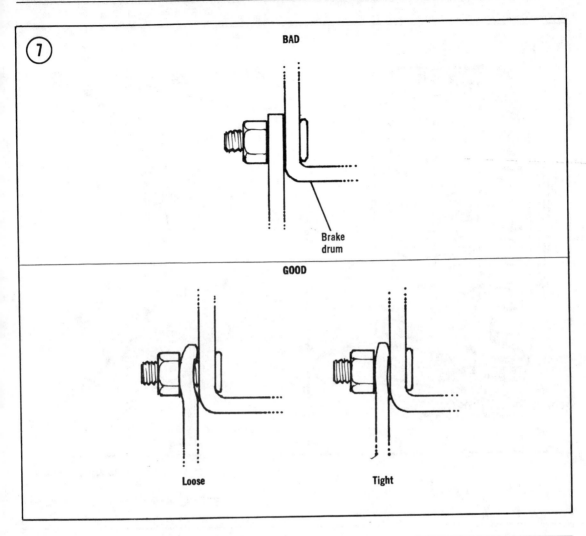

(7)   **BAD**

Brake
drum

GOOD

Loose   Tight

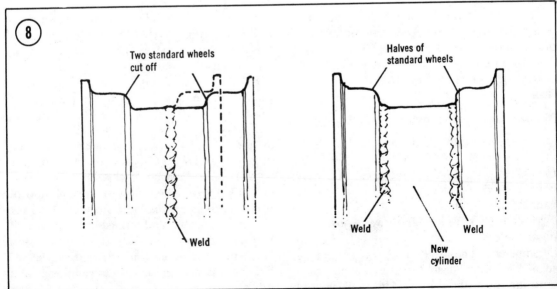

(8)

Two standard wheels
cut off

Halves of
standard wheels

Weld

Weld   Weld

New
cylinder

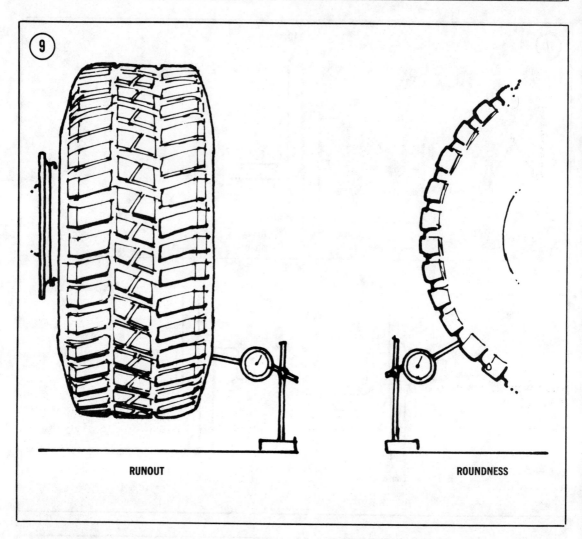

RUNOUT

ROUNDNESS

As a final check on a wheel, have each wheel in the set checked for runout and out-of-roundness (**Figure 9**). Runout and out-of-roundness should not exceed 1.5 mm (0.059 in.). Good wheels will pass this test easily.

Mounting and Balancing

Correct mounting and balancing of ORV tires is essential. It's wise to have this done by the seller. Use caution, however—he may have a good product but not know how to handle the job correctly.

Mounting is a straightforward job, but nevertheless it can be botched by an incompetent. The beads and rim should be soaped beforehand so the tire can be eased onto the rim without force. The beads should be evenly and completely seated before the tire is inflated to operating pressure. Misalignment of the tire on the rim will cause it to be out-of-round.

Balancing is a bit more difficult than mounting. Because of the size and weight of most ORV tires, bubble balancing is ineffective and may indicate that weight should be added where it is not needed. The only accurate way of balancing ORV tires is with a spin balancer, with the tire-wheel combination off the truck. If this method of balancing is not available from the seller, ask him for a discount and then shop around until you find someone who can do precision spin balancing. It may cost a little extra to begin, but it will pay off in increased tire mileage and ride comfort.

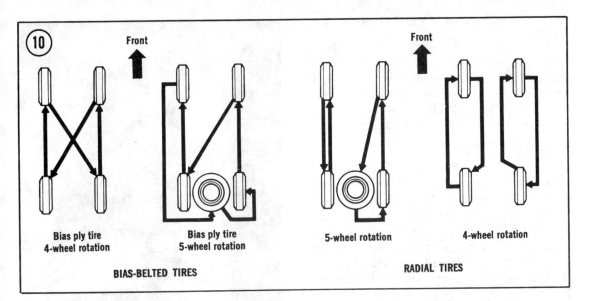

Bias ply tire
4-wheel rotation

Bias ply tire
5-wheel rotation

BIAS-BELTED TIRES

5-wheel rotation

4-wheel rotation

RADIAL TIRES

Balance weights on the outsides of the wheels may be unavoidable, especially if a great deal of weight is required. Good dynamic balance can be difficult to obtain when weights are used only on the insides of the wheels.

Tire Pressure

A good quality, accurate tire gauge should be carried in the truck at all times and used regularly. Check tire pressures once a week, when tires are cold. The recommended pressures listed in **Table 1** will serve as a guideline.

Most drivers will increase pressure when increasing the vehicle load, but may forget to reduce pressure after the load is removed. This causes a harsh ride and increased wear in the center of the tread.

In special situations, such as operating in deep sand or mud when maximum flotation is required, tire pressure can be reduced to as low as 10 psi to provide a wider contact patch with the ground. However, tires should be run at low pressure for no longer than necessary and then only at very low speeds to prevent overheating caused by increased rolling resistance.

Inspection and Care

Tire and wheel inspection should begin with the weekly pressure check. Incorrect inflation pressures will show up rapidly as incorrect wear patterns and once this has begun, there's no correcting it—wear will accelerate.

Inspect the tread and the sidewalls for cuts and slices. If the surface is cut deep enough to expose cord, have the tire inspected by a tire shop to determine whether it is still usable.

Check for bubbles, especially on the sidewalls. Bubbles indicate that the plies have separated. If you find a bubble, deflate the tire to a low pressure and press in on the bubble to check for resistance. Compare the bubbled area to an unaffected area of the sidewall. If the bubbled area feels mushy, there is likely to be a star break inside the tire. There is nothing to do for it but replace the tire as soon as possible. If the truck must be driven with a tire damaged in this manner, it's a good idea to dismount the tire and install a heavy rubber patch over the damaged area.

Inspect rims for dents and fractures. Have them repaired or replace them as soon as possible. Periodically, check the wheel and tire for runout and out-of-roundness as shown in **Figure 9**.

Tire balance should be checked periodically and corrected if necessary. Changes in balance occur as the tire wears.

Tires should be rotated if they wear unevenly. See **Figure 10**.

13

SUSPENSION AND CHASSIS

For most applications, stock suspension—with the exception of original equipment shock absorbers—is adequate. In fact, for any use other than racing or extensive travel over very rough terrain, heavy duty suspension kits are an unnecessary expense.

Shock Absorbers

For light and moderate duty, stock shock absorbers should be replaced with any one of a number of good aftermarket units that are available from the suppliers recommended at the end of this chapter or from auto supply stores. Most shock absorber manufacturers offer shock absorbers tailored to off-road use. These include the more common brands such as Gabriel, Monroe and Koni, as well as specialist companies such as Rough Country. No matter what your brand choice, the added cost of adjustable units is worth consideration. Their softest settings provide a comfortable ride for highway use and their firmer settings provide increased damping for off-road applications.

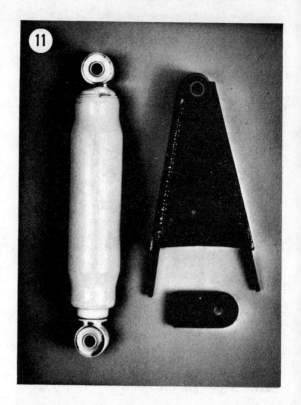

If you occasionally carry heavy loads (such as a camper), air shocks should be considered. These provide a smooth highway ride and can be pumped up to compensate for increased weight in the bed.

Dual-shock setups (**Figure 11**) are useful for high-speed travel over rough terrain such as dirt roads or slower speeds on extremely rough surfaces. For slower speeds or smoother surfaces, the extra damping is unnecessary. On pavement, they cause a harsh ride.

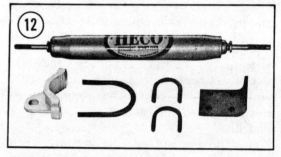

Dual shocks won't cure a suspension that frequently bottoms. Although they will help for a while, the lack of spring stiffness will overwork the shocks and cause them to wear out rapidly. If bottoming is a problem, install stiffer springs and torsion bars.

Springs and Torsion Bars

The stock parts are adequate for most uses. If the truck bottoms frequently, replace the stock springs and torsion bars with heavy duty units. These are carried by the Datsun Competition Department and can be ordered through local dealers.

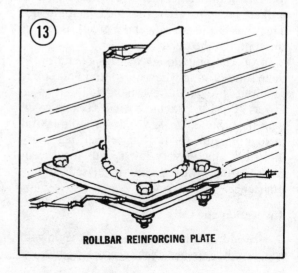

ROLLBAR REINFORCING PLATE

Lift Kits

Lift kits raise the truck higher off the suspension. This increases body-to-ground clearance, but does not increase axle-to-ground clearance. For this reason, lift kits should only be used to provide clearance for tall tires. Avoid super-high lift kits (over 4 inches). These raise the truck's center of gravity excessively, causing serious handling problems and increasing rollover potential.

Axle Trusses

For very hard use or in cases where the truck is likely to become airborne, axle trusses are invaluable because they strengthen the axle housing and greatly reduce the possibilities of bending or breaking the outer tube. On Datsuns, this applies to the rear axle only.

Skid Plates

Skid plates for the differentials, fuel tank and transfer case are essential for operation in rough, rocky terrain. They provide damage protection to expensive drive components and allow the truck to slide over large obstacles.

Steering Stabilizer

The steering stabilizer (**Figure 12**) is a hydraulic damper which controls movement of the steering lnikage. It prevents sudden wheel movements (caused by rocks, potholes, etc.) from twisting the wheel out of the driver's hands. It also reduces shimmy caused by wide tires.

ROLLOVER PROTECTION

Rollover protection is essential for rough terrain, especially on sidehills or on soft surfaces where the bank or trail can break away.

It is important to note that the subject here is rollover protection—not flipover protection. Even the best commercially available roll bar or cage won't guarantee the occupants' safety in a high-speed, end-over-end flipover.

Ideally, a roll bar or cage should attach directly to the frame, but this is not always possible. It *should not* be attached only to unreinforced sheet metal. A well-designed bar should have large mounting plates to distribute the load over a wide area (**Figure 13**) and they should be located as closely as possible to the door jambs or corners of the cargo bed (**Figure 14**).

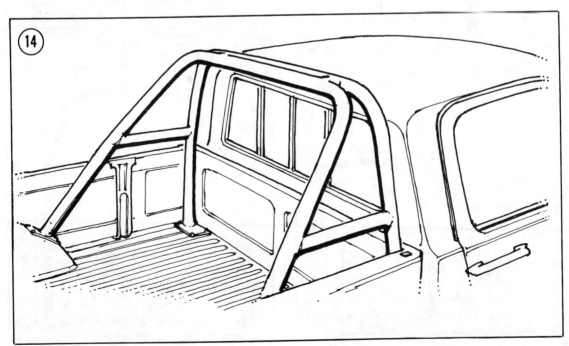

13

There are several important points to look for when buying a roll bar or cage. First, the tubing should have mandrel bends that are smooth along the inner diameter (**Figure 15**). Wrinkling along the inner diameter (**Figure 16**) is characteristic of a bend that was made without a mandrel. The wrinkles will allow the bend to collapse during a rollover.

Second, check tubing thickness. If the bar is 1-3/4 to 2 inches in diameter, wall thickness should be 0.125 in. and 3-inch bars should have a wall thickness of 0.095 in.

Third, inspect the welds (**Figure 17**). They should be uniform and clean. If they are rough, pitted and vary in width, don't buy the roll bar or cage.

Primary use of the truck should be considered when selecting a rollover structure. Good single- and double-tube bars work well for most situations where operating speeds are low and the surface is reasonably

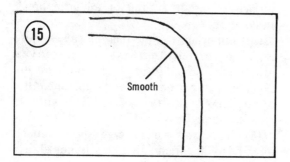

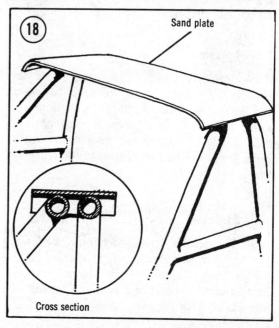

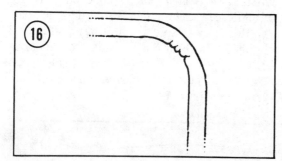

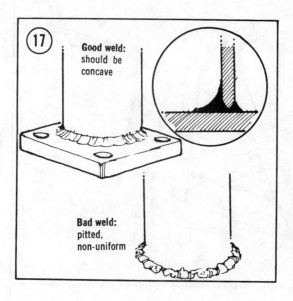

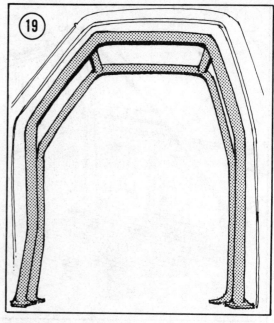

firm. If the truck is used extensively in deep sand, a sand plate (**Figure 18**) is an essential to keep the bar from sinking. For rough, high-speed running, a full cage is a must. See **Figure 19**.

WINCHES

For most off-roaders, a winch is an expensive frill. But for the really adventurous back-country traveler a winch is an essential piece of equipment that could mean the difference between riding and walking.

There are a number of good winches available from several manufacturers, offering choices in installation type and location, pulling capacity and price. **Figures 20-23** show typical winch types and installations. When installing a winch system, locate the switch relay as close to the battery as possible to minimize current loss.

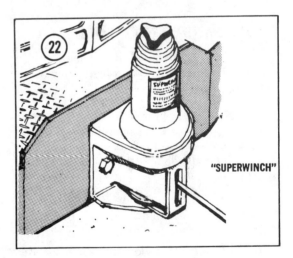

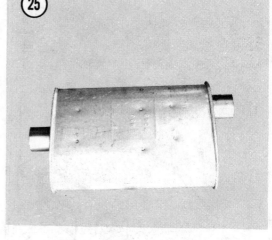

The cost of an installation kit should be taken into consideration when choosing a winch. A kit can add as much as $150 to the price.

TOOLS AND SAFETY EQUIPMENT

The following equipment will enable you to handle the more common problems that occur in off-roading.

1. *Tire gauge:* This should be used frequently—not just during outings. Correct tire pressure is important during daily driving to ensure good ride and handling, as well as long tire life.

2. *First aid kit:* Even minor cuts and scrapes can become serious injuries if the wound isn't cleaned, disinfected and covered immediately.

3. *Survival kit:* A good kit, such as the SURVIVIT from Dick Cepek, Inc., could mean the difference between life and death. This one contains signal devices, compass, sawknife, weather protection and more.

4. *Water:* For man and machine. At least two 5-gallon containers are needed in dry regions.

5. *Gas and oil:* Always top off your tanks and make sure you have a full 5-gallon can extra. A couple of quarts of motor oil take up little space and there's no substitute for your engine's lifeblood.

6. *Hand tools:* Pliers, screwdrivers (both standard and Phillips), a couple of adjustable

wrenches, some combination wrenches (from 10 mm to 19 mm), a spark plug wrench and a pocket knife.

7. *Tire equipment:* High-lift jack, bead breakers, spare inner tube, tire boot, tire repair kit, valve core remover and tire pump.

8. *Vehicle spares:* Fan belt, radiator hoses, fuses and fusible links, radiator stop-leak, electrical tape, muffler tape, assorted metric screws, nuts and bolts, lug nuts and mechanic's wire.

9. *Fire extinguisher:* Should be rated for gasoline and electrical fires.

10. *Digging out kit:* Shovel, axe, sand mats and towstrap.

11. *Fuel tank and line stop-leak:* There are commercially available stop-leak compounds. In an emergency, a bar of soap can be rubbed over a small fuel leak to stop it.

DRIVE TRAIN

Differentials

The front differential is the R180 unit used in the Z-car. The rear differential is the same design used on the 2-wheel drive pickup. The Z-car limited slip differential can be used in the 4-wheel drive pickup. A Detroit Locker limited slip unit is available for the rear differential. Both are carried by the Datsun Competition Department and can be ordered through local dealers.

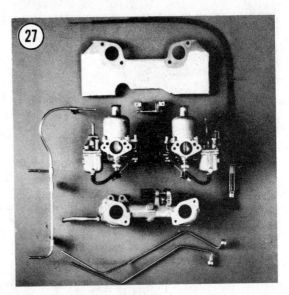

NOTE
Installation of the limited slip unit in the rear differential requires special tools and should be done by a dealer or other competent shop.

Transmission

The Datsun Competition Department carries a 5-speed rally transmission with direct drive fifth gear, rather than overdrive. Gear ratios are closer than with the stock 5-speed. Ratios are listed in **Table 3**.

ENGINE MODIFICATIONS

Available modifications for Datsun 4-wheel drive pickups include exhaust systems, carburetors, turbocharger kits and engine conversions.

NOTE
Engine modifications may violate emission laws and regulations. Consult with local authorities before modifications are made.

Headers and Exhaust Systems

Headers (**Figure 24**) reduce exhaust system back pressure, so less horsepower is used to push exhaust gases out of the engine. This improves performance and mileage.

Low-restriction exhaust systems also reduce back pressure. The system carried by

the Datsun Competition Department includes a "turbo" muffler (**Figure 25**). Although it looks stock, the muffler's 2-inch diameter and free-flow interior reduce exhaust restriction, while keeping noise at acceptable levels.

Carburetors

The Holley model 5200 carburetor (**Figure 26**) is available in a kit from Low Manufacturing. The kit includes the carburetor, adapter, chrome air cleaner and linkage. According to the company, the carburetor produces a 10-15 per cent improvment in performance and mileage.

SU-type carburetors (**Figure 27**) are available from the Datsun Competition Department for use with the L20B engine (1980 only). These provide good low end and mid-range power.

Turbocharging

Turbocharging is a relatively easy way to gain a large power increase. The turbocharger (**Figure 28**) is a pump driven by exhaust gases leaving the engine. It pulls or pushes air through the carburetor, which increases the density of the incoming air/fuel charge. **Figure 29** shows a turbocharger system.

Truck turbocharger kits generally operate at low boost levels. This provides a smaller total power increase than high-boost applications,

13

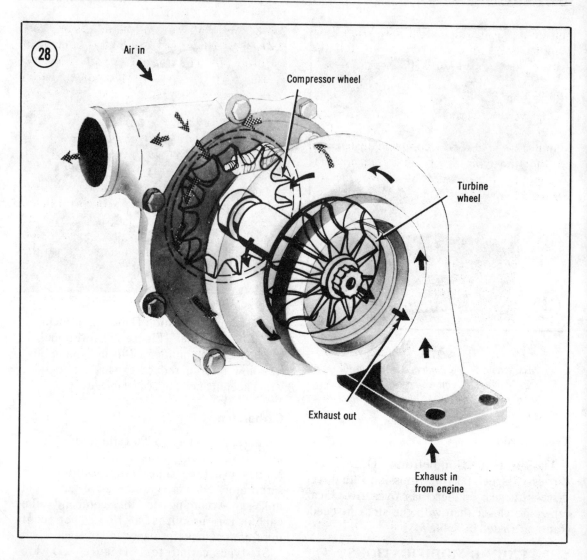

(28) Air in

Compressor wheel

Turbine wheel

Exhaust out

Exhaust in from engine

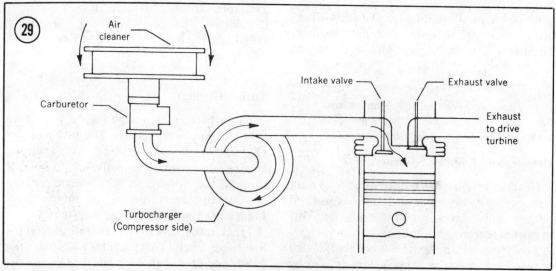

(29) Air cleaner

Carburetor

Intake valve

Exhaust valve

Exhaust to drive turbine

Turbocharger (Compressor side)

but the power is available at lower rpm. Low Manufacturing offers a turbo kit for the Datsun pickup. See **Figure 30**.

Engine Conversion

One very effective means of increasing power is to install a V6 engine. Low Manufacturing offers a complete installation kit (not including engine and transmission) for about $400. **Figure 31** shows the kit. **Figure 32** shows an installed engine. The kit can be used with the General Motors or AMC 255 cubic inch V6 or the GM 231 cubic inch even-fire V6. The transmission must also be replaced with a 2-speed Powerglide, Turbo 350, Muncie 4-speed, Buick 5-speed or equivalent.

ACCESSORIES

Lights

There are 2 basic types of off-road light—spot beam and flood. Spot beam lights provide maximum range, but do not provide good beam dispersion to the sides. Flood beams offer wide dispersion and light up the sides of the road or trail, at the cost of reduced range.

The ideal combination is 2 spot beams on the roll bar (**Figure 33**) and 2 floods in front of the grille.

Driving lights should not be connected to the truck's fuse panel, since all fuses are already protecting other circuits. The simplest hookup is directly to the battery (**Figure 34**).

> *NOTE*
> *Laws and regulations covering driving lights vary from area to area. Check with local authorities before buying lights.*

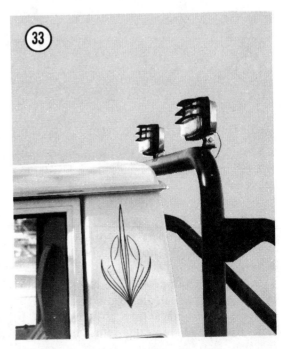

13

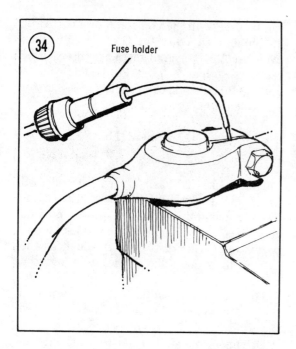

Fuse holder

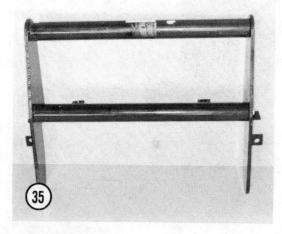

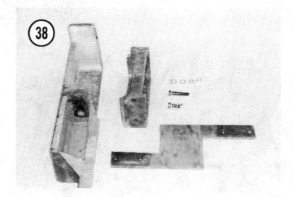

Grille Guards

Grille guards (**Figure 35**) mount in front of the grille to prevent damage from brush, tall grass, etc.

Bumpers

Heavy duty bumpers are a must for trailer towing. **Figure 36** shows a tube bumper, a type popular among off-roaders.

Step-type bumpers are also popular. Although they usually have good front-to-rear stiffness, their brackets may allow them to flex from side to side. This may cause handling problems when towing a heavy trailer. To solve the problem, install mounting and reinforcing brackets of heavy steel plate. These can be made by a welding shop. **Figure 37** shows the brackets installed; **Figure 38** shows the separate pieces.

Bed Liners

Some manufacturers offer fiberglass bed liners to protect the bed from damage. Another method is to make a bed liner of 3/4-inch plywood (**Figure 39**). Securing the plywood with screen door hooks as shown allows easy removal.

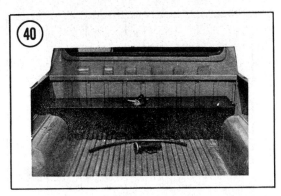

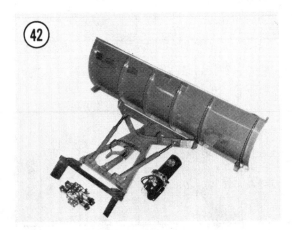

Gas Tank

Low Manufacturing offers a 20-gallon cross-bed gas tank (**Figure 40**). The tank comes with all mounting hardware and electric crossover valves and uses the stock fuel gauge.

Snow Plow

The Low Manufacturing snow plow (**Figure 41** and **Figure 42**) has a 6 foot blade which can be raised, lowered and angled from inside the truck. The 275-lb. unit is connected to the truck frame with 3 pins and 3 quick-disconnect hoses. A light bar is optional.

13

Table 1 TIRE PRESSURES AND CAPACITIES

Tire Size	Load Range	Maximum Load Capacities Per Tire (lb.) At Cold Tire Inflation Rates (psi)								
		20	25	30	35	40	45	50	55	60
L78-15	B	1520	1715	1900						
7.9-14	C	790	900	1000	1090	1180	1260			
9-15	C	1230	1400	1560	1710	1850	1980			
10-15	B	1390	1580	1760						
10-15	C	1390	1580	1760	1930	2080	2230			
11-15	B	1500	1710	1900						
11-15	C	1500	1710	1900	2080	2250	2410			
12-15	B	1780	2020	2250						
12-15	C	1780	2020	2250	2460	2660	2850			
14-15	C	1780	2020	2250	2460	2660	2850			
16-15	C	1780	2020	2250	2460	2660	2850			
8.00-16.5	D			1360	1490	1610	1730	1840	1945	2045
8.75-16.5	D			1570	1720	1850	1990	2110	2240	2350
9.50-16.5	D			1860	2030	2190	2350	2500	2650	2780
10-16.5	C			1840	2010	2170	2330			
10-16.5	D			1840	2010	2170	2330	2480	2620	2750
12-16.5	B			2370						
12-16.5	D			2370	2590	2800	3000			
12-16.5	E			2370	2590	2800	3000	3190	3370	3550
14-16.5	C	1780	2020	2250	2460	2660	2850			
16-16.5	C	1780	2020	2250	2460	2660	2850			
14-17.5	D			2820	3080	3210	3500	3790	4060	

Table 2   TIRE AND WHEEL SIZES

Tire Size	Wheel Size (Width Bead to Bead)	Tire Size	Wheel Size (Width Bead to Bead)
E or ER 78-14	5–7 in.	7.9-14LT	6–7 in.
F or FR 78-14	5÷7 in.	9-15LT	7–8 in.
G or GR 78-14	5½–7 in.	10-15LT	7–8 in.
H or HR 78-14	5½–8 in.	11-15LT	8 in.
J or JR 78-14	6–8 in.	12-15LT	10 in.
F or FR 78-15	5–7 in.	12R-15LT	8–10 in.
G or GR 78-15	5½–7 in.	14-15LT	10 in.
H or HR 78-15	5½–7 in.	16-15LT	10–12 in.
J or JR 78-15	5½–8 in.	8.00-16.5	6 in.
L or LR 78-15	6–8 in.	8.75-16.5	6¾ in.
M or MR 78-15	6–8 in.	9.50-16.5	6¾ in.
N or NR 78-15	6½–9 in.	10-16.5	8¼ in.
F or FR 60-14	6–8 in.	12-16.5	9¾ in.
G or GR 60-14	6½–9 in.	14-16.5	9¾ in.
G or GR 60-15	6–8 in.	16-16.5	9¾ in.
L or LR 60-15	7–10 in.	14-17.5	10½ in.

Table 3   GEAR RATIOS

Gear	Stock 5-speed	Rally 5-speed
First	3.592	3.321
Second	2.246	2.270
Third	1.415	1.601
Fourth	1.000	1.240
Fifth	0.813	1.000

13

SUPPLEMENT
1982 SERVICE INFORMATION

This supplement provides information for 1982 models. All procedures not covered in this Supplement are the same as for 1981 models.

The chapter headings for this supplement correspond to those in the main body of the book. If a procedure is not included in the supplement, there are no changes in the 1982 models.

CHAPTER THREE

LUBRICATION, MAINTENANCE, AND TUNE-UP

SCHEDULED MAINTENANCE

The maintenance schedule is basically the same as for 1981. The interval for drive belt adjustment is every 30,000 miles or 24 months on all models. On trucks equipped with power steering, fluid level should be checked and the lines checked for leaks every 15,000 miles or 12 months.

Drive Belts

Adjustment procedures are the same as for 1981 models, except for the addition of the power steering pump belt on 1982 models so equipped. Belt deflection specifications are listed in **Table 1**.

To adjust the power steering belt, loosen the idler pulley locknut (**Figure 1**). Turn the adjusting bolt as needed to change belt tension, then tighten the locknut.

Power Steering

Check fluid level and look for leaks as described in the Chapter Nine section of this supplement.

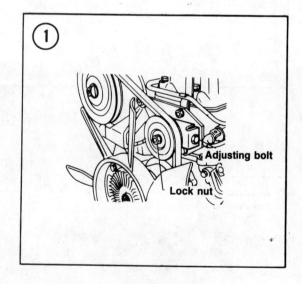

TUNE-UP

Tune-up procedures are the same as for 1981 models. Periodic idle speed adjustment is not required on U.S. trucks. On Canadian models, idle speed should be adjusted every 15,000 miles or 12 months.

Some tune-up specifications differ from 1981. These are listed in **Table 2**.

Table 1 BELT DEFLECTION SPECIFICATIONS

Fan belt	
New	8-11 mm (5/16-7/16 in.)
Used	12-15 mm (1/2-5/8 in.)
Air conditioning compressor belt	
New	5-8 mm (3/16-5/16 in.)
Used	7-10 mm (1/4-1/3 in.)
Power steering pump belt	
New	12-15 mm (1/2-5/8 in.)
Used	15-18 mm (5/8-3/4 in.)

Table 2 TUNE-UP SPECIFICATIONS

Spark plug type (NGK brand)	
Intake side	
Standard	BPR6ES
Hot type	BPR5ES
Cold type	BPR7ES
Exhaust side	
Standard and hot type	BPR5ES
Cold type	BPR6ES, BPR7ES
Ignition timing and idle speed	3 ±2° BTDC @ 650 ±100 rpm

CHAPTER FOUR

NAPS-Z ENGINE

ENGINE REMOVAL

This is the same as for 1981 models. On trucks equipped with power steering, unbolt the power steering pump from the engine and tie it back out of the way. It is not necessary to disconnect the pump hoses.

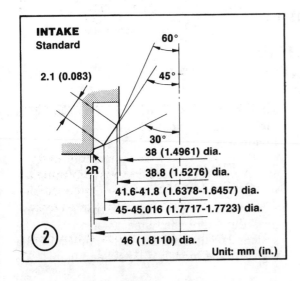

INTAKE
Standard
60°
2.1 (0.083)
45°
30°
38 (1.4961) dia.
2R
38.8 (1.5276) dia.
41.6-41.8 (1.6378-1.6457) dia.
45-45.016 (1.7717-1.7723) dia.
② 46 (1.8110) dia.
Unit: mm (in.)

VALVES AND VALVE SEATS

Valve seat dimensions differ from 1981 models. See **Figures 2-5**.

14

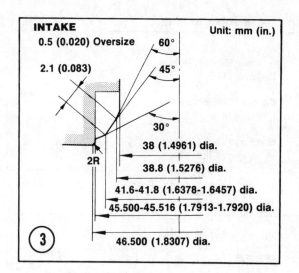

INTAKE   Unit: mm (in.)
0.5 (0.020) Oversize   60°
2.1 (0.083)   45°
                            30°
                      38 (1.4961) dia.
2R   38.8 (1.5276) dia.
                41.6-41.8 (1.6378-1.6457) dia.
                45.500-45.516 (1.7913-1.7920) dia.
3   46.500 (1.8307) dia.

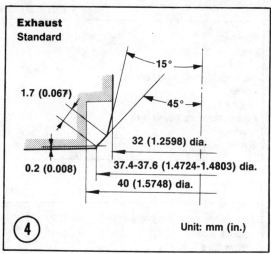

Exhaust
Standard   15°
1.7 (0.067)   45°
                            32 (1.2598) dia.
0.2 (0.008)   37.4-37.6 (1.4724-1.4803) dia.
                   40 (1.5748) dia.
4   Unit: mm (in.)

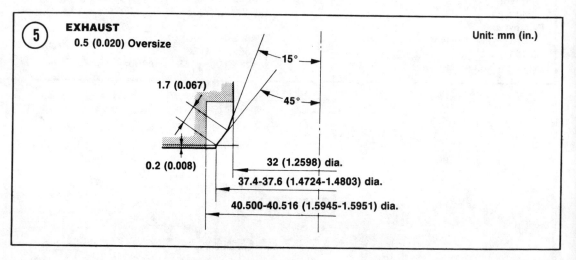

5   EXHAUST   Unit: mm (in.)
     0.5 (0.020) Oversize
                                15°
     1.7 (0.067)   45°

     0.2 (0.008)   32 (1.2598) dia.
                 37.4-37.6 (1.4724-1.4803) dia.
                 40.500-40.516 (1.5945-1.5951) dia.

CHAPTER FIVE

FUEL, EXHAUST AND EMISSION CONTROL SYSTEMS

CARBURETOR

Service procedures are the same as for 1981 trucks. Some specifications differ (see **Table 3**).

VACUUM LINES

Vacuum lines for all models except non-California high altitude trucks are the same as for 1981. The 1982 non-California high altitude vacuum lines are shown in **Figure 6**.

EVAPORATIVE EMISSION CONTROL SYSTEM

Evaporative emission control inspection procedures are the same as for 1981. The system layout used on 1982 non-California high altitude models differs. See **Figure 7**.

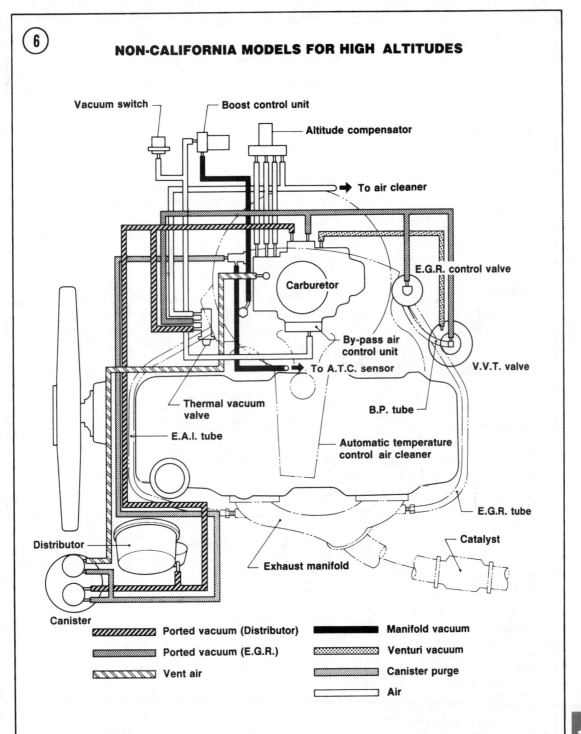

6

NON-CALIFORNIA MODELS FOR HIGH ALTITUDES

Vacuum switch

Boost control unit

Altitude compensator

→ To air cleaner

E.G.R. control valve

Carburetor

By-pass air control unit

V.V.T. valve

→ To A.T.C. sensor

Thermal vacuum valve

B.P. tube

E.A.I. tube

Automatic temperature control air cleaner

E.G.R. tube

Distributor

Catalyst

Exhaust manifold

Canister

//////// Ported vacuum (Distributor)	▬▬▬ Manifold vacuum
Ported vacuum (E.G.R.)	Venturi vacuum
Vent air	Canister purge
	Air

14

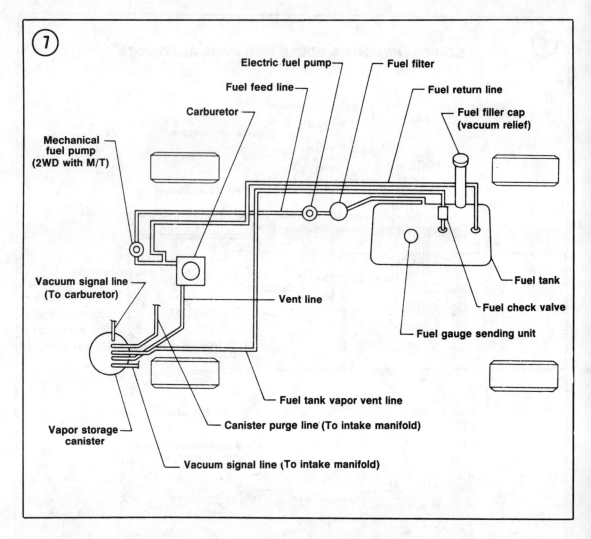

⑦

Electric fuel pump —   — Fuel filter

Fuel feed line —

Carburetor —

Fuel return line —

Fuel filler cap
(vacuum relief) —

Mechanical
fuel pump
(2WD with M/T) —

Vacuum signal line —
(To carburetor)

Vent line

Fuel tank —

Fuel check valve —

Fuel gauge sending unit —

Fuel tank vapor vent line

Vapor storage —
canister

Canister purge line (To intake manifold)

Vacuum signal line (To intake manifold)

Table 3 CARBURETOR SPECIFICATIONS

Jets and air bleeds	
Primary main jet	
California	112
49-state and Canada	105
Secondary main jet	155
Primary main air bleed	80
Secondary main air bleed	60
Primary slow jet	47
Secondary slow jet	100
Power valve	
California	35
49-state and Canada	40
Float adjustment	
Dimension "h" (needle valve stroke)	1.3-1.7 mm
	(0.051-0.067 in.)
Dimension "H" (float level)	23 mm (0.91 in.)
Fast idle cam adjustment (second step)	0.81-0.95 mm
	(0.032-0.037 in.)

CHAPTER SEVEN

ELECTRICAL SYSTEM

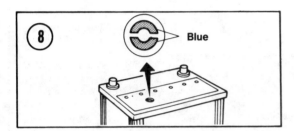

BATTERY

The 1982 models use a sealed, maintenance-free battery with a built-in condition indicator. A blue indicator (**Figure 8**) indicates that the battery is in good condition. If the indicator is transparent, the battery needs to be recharged.

CHAPTER EIGHT

CLUTCH AND TRANSMISSION

Service procedures for the 4-speed transmission are the same as for the 1981 models. The 5-speed is almost identical, but the center of the 3 lockballs on the main shaft has been replaced by a roller. See **Figure 9**. Fifth gear end play for 1982 trucks is 0.10-0.17 mm (0.004-0.007 in.).

14

5-SPEED TRANSMISSION
(MODEL FS5W71B)

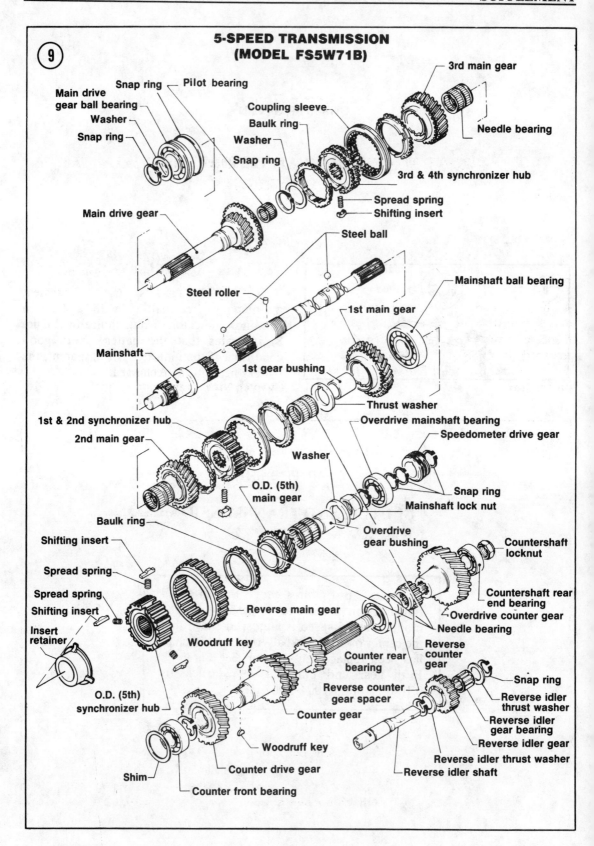

⑨

Snap ring — Pilot bearing

Main drive gear ball bearing

Washer

Snap ring

Coupling sleeve

Baulk ring

Washer

Snap ring

3rd main gear

Needle bearing

3rd & 4th synchronizer hub

Main drive gear

Spread spring

Shifting insert

Steel ball

Steel roller

Mainshaft ball bearing

1st main gear

Mainshaft

1st gear bushing

Thrust washer

Overdrive mainshaft bearing

Speedometer drive gear

1st & 2nd synchronizer hub

2nd main gear

Washer

Snap ring

Mainshaft lock nut

O.D. (5th) main gear

Overdrive gear bushing

Countershaft locknut

Baulk ring

Shifting insert

Spread spring

Spread spring

Shifting insert

Insert retainer

Reverse main gear

Countershaft rear end bearing

Overdrive counter gear

Needle bearing

Reverse counter gear

Woodruff key

Counter rear bearing

Reverse counter gear spacer

Counter gear

O.D. (5th) synchronizer hub

Snap ring

Reverse idler thrust washer

Reverse idler gear bearing

Reverse idler gear

Reverse idler thrust washer

Reverse idler shaft

Woodruff key

Counter drive gear

Shim

Counter front bearing

CHAPTER NINE

FRONT SUSPENSION, AXLES, DIFFERENTIAL AND STEERING

AXLE SHAFTS

Disassembly

The inner ends of 1982 axle shafts can be disassembled. The outer ends can be inspected, but the axle shafts must be replaced if the outer ends are worn or damaged. Refer to **Figure 10** for this procedure.

NOTE
During reassembly, the axle shaft must be packed with a special axle shaft grease available from Datsun dealers. Obtain the necessary grease before starting.

1. Remove the axle shaft as described in Chapter Nine, main body of book.

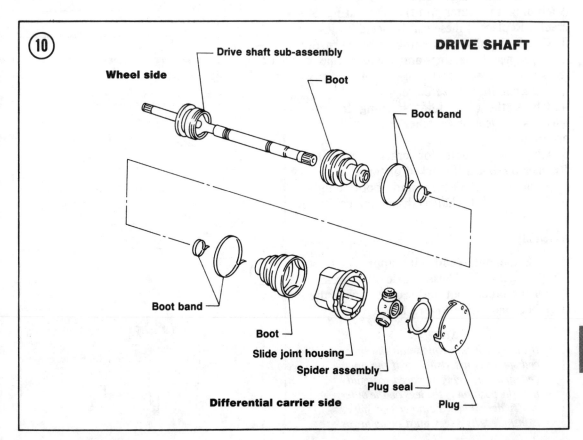

DRIVE SHAFT

⑩

Wheel side

Drive shaft sub-assembly

Boot

Boot band

Boot band

Boot

Slide joint housing

Spider assembly

Plug seal

Plug

Differential carrier side

14

2. Place the axle shaft in a soft-jawed vise. Remove the end plug (**Figure 11**), then take out the plug seal.

3. Remove and discard the boot bands. See **Figure 12**.

4. Make match marks on the shaft and spider assembly. See **Figure 13**.

> *CAUTION*
> *During the next step, hold the axle shaft by hand to keep it from falling.*

5. Press the spider assembly off. See **Figure 14**. A machine shop can do this if you don't have a press.

6. Remove the boot.

7. Place the axle shaft in a soft-jawed vise as shown in **Figure 15**. Remove the boot bands, then take off the boot.

Inspection

1. Thoroughly clean all parts with solvent and blow dry.

2. Check the axle shaft sub-assembly (including the outer joint) for twisting or cracks. Replace if these can be seen.

3. Check the spider assemblies for worn or damaged needle bearings and washers. Check the splines for wear or damage. Replace if any of these conditions can be seen.

4. Check the slide joint housing friction surfaces for wear or scratches. Replace if these are found.

5. Check the boots for cracks or tears. Replace the boots if cracked or torn.

6. Replace the O-ring and boot bands whenever the axle shaft is disassembled.

Assembly

1. Pack the outer end with approximately 240 g (8 1/2 oz.) of Nissan axle shaft grease. Install the outer boot and secure it with the large boot band. See **Figure 16**.

> *NOTE*
> *If the match mark made on the inner end spider is not visible or if the inner end spider is being replaced, carefully note the position of the legs on the outer end spider. When the inner end spider is installed, its 3 legs must be as far as*

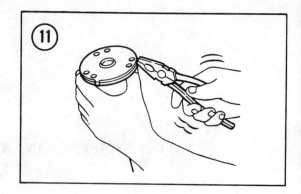

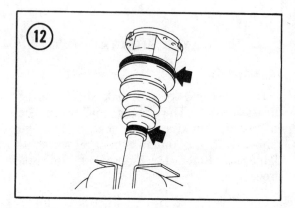

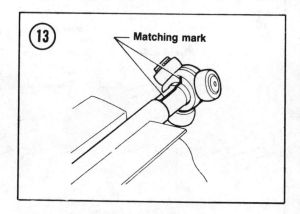

Matching mark

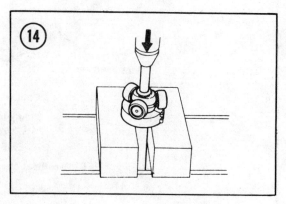

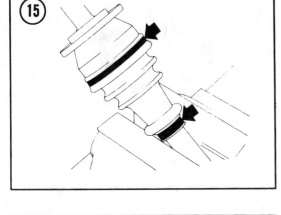

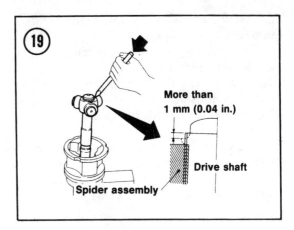

More than
1 mm (0.04 in.)

Drive shaft

Spider assembly

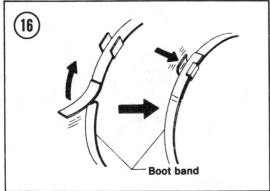

Boot band

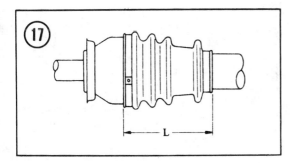

L

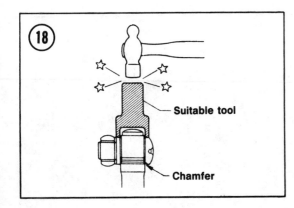

Suitable tool

Chamfer

*possible out of alignment with the outer
end spider's 3 legs.*

2. Position the boot so dimension L, **Figure
17**, is 118 mm (4.65 in.). Make sure the boot
is not distorted, then secure it with the small
boot band.

CAUTION
*During the next step, do not damage
the boot on the end of the axle shaft.*

3. Slide new boot bands and the inner boot
onto the axle shaft.
4. Place the slide joint housing on the axle
shaft, then place the axle shaft in a soft-jawed
vise.

NOTE
*During the next step, align the match
marks made during disassembly. If
there are no match marks, install the
spider assembly so its 3 legs are as far
as possible out of alignment with the 3
legs of the outer joint's spider assembly.*

5. Tap the spider assembly onto the axle
shaft with a suitable drift as shown in **Figure
18**.
6. Stake the axle shaft at 3 evenly spaced
points. See **Figure 19**. Do not stake it at
points where it has been staked before. Make
sure each staking covers 2 splines and is at
least 1 mm (0.04 in.) wide.
7. Place the slide joint housing on the spider
assembly and pack with approximately 160 g
(5 5/8 oz.) of Nissan axle shaft grease.

14

8. Install the boot and secure it with the large boot band. See **Figure 20**.

9. Coat the plug seal with Nissan axle shaft grease, then install it.

10. Install the plug. Temporarily secure the plug with nuts and bolts as shown in **Figure 21**, then secure it with the locktabs. Remove the nuts and bolts.

11. Position the inner boot so its length (dimension L, **Figure 22**) is 103 mm (4.06 in.). Make sure the boot is not distorted, then secure it with the small boot band.

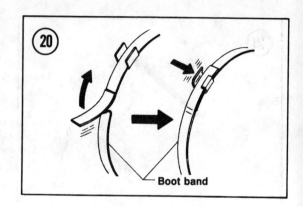

Boot band

STEERING

Service procedures for non-power steering are the same as for 1981 models. Power steering is optional on 1982 trucks.

**Fluid Level and
Leak Inspection (Power Steering)**

1. With the engine cold, unscrew the reservoir cap and check fluid level on the dipstick. See **Figure 23**. Top up if necessary with DEXRON type automatic transmission fluid. Do not use any other type of fluid.

2. Warm the engine to normal operating temperature. Make sure the power steering fluid is at operating temperature (40-60° C; 104-176° F) with a thermometer.

3. Run the engine at idle. Do not run it over 1,000 rpm.

4. Have an assistant turn the steering wheel from full left lock to full right lock several times.

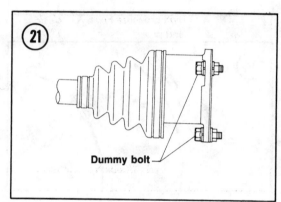

Dummy bolt

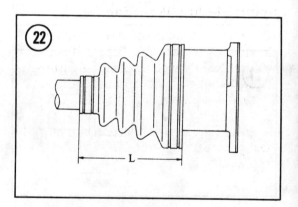

L

CAUTION
Turn the wheel slowly to prevent scrubbing damage to the tires.

5. Hold the steering wheel at each lock position for 5 seconds. Carefully check the power steering pump gaskets, seals and hose connections for fluid leaks. See **Figure 24**.

CAUTION
Do not hold the steering wheel at full lock for more than 15 seconds at a time.

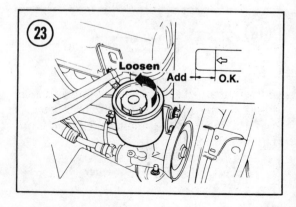

Loosen   Add ⟶| O.K.

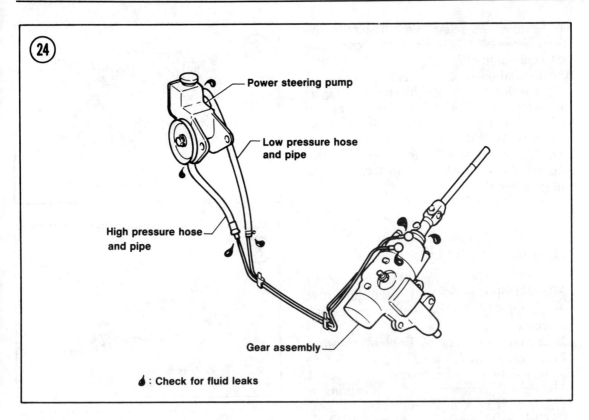

(24)

Power steering pump

Low pressure hose and pipe

High pressure hose and pipe

Gear assembly

💧 : Check for fluid leaks

System Bleeding (Power Steering)

1. With the engine cold, check fluid level on the dipstick (**Figure 23**). Top up if necessary with DEXRON type automatic transmission fluid. Do not use any other type of fluid.
2. Jack up the front end of the car and place it on jackstands.
3. With the engine off, quickly turn the steering wheel from full left to full right lock 10 times.

CAUTION
Make sure the linkage contacts the stops lightly. Do not turn the steering hard against the stops.

4. Recheck fluid level and top up if necessary.
5. Warm the engine to normal operating temperature. Make sure fluid temperature is 40-60° C (104-176° F) with a thermometer.
6. Turn off the engine and recheck fluid level. Top up if necessary.
7. Run the engine for 3-5 seconds.
8. Turn off the engine and recheck fluid level. Top up if necessary.

9. With the engine off, quickly turn the steering all the way to right and left 10 times.

CAUTION
Make sure the linkage contacts the stops lightly. Do not turn the steering hard against the stops.

10. Check the power steering fluid. It should be free of bubbles. If not, repeat Steps 6-9.
11. If there are still bubbles in the fluid after repeating Steps 6-9, check the system for leaks.

Pump Removal/Installation (Power Steering)

1. Before removal, steam clean the pump and surrounding area, then let dry completely. Blow dry with an air compressor if available.
2. Loosen the idler pulley locknut (**Figure 25**). Turn the adjusting bolt counterclockwise to loosen the drive belt. Take the belt off.
3. Loosen the hoses at their connections to the pump (**Figure 26**). Do not remove the hoses.

14

4. Remove the pump mounting nuts and bolts (**Figure 27**). Disconnect the hoses, then take the pump off.

5. Installation is the reverse of removal. Tighten fasteners to specifications in **Figure 26** and **Figure 27**. Add fluid if the pump was drained or a new pump is being installed. Capacity is 900-1,000 ml (30-33 fl. oz.). Check fluid level, check for leaks and bleed the system as described in this section of the supplement.

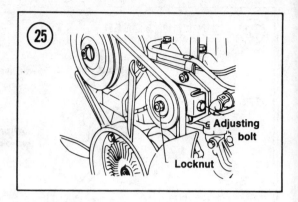

Steering Gear Removal/ Installation (Power Steering)

1. Before removal, steam clean the steering gear and surrounding area, then allow it to dry thoroughly. Blow dry with a compressor if available.

2. Disconnect the gear at the points shown in **Figure 28**, then lift it out.

3. Installation is the reverse of removal. Tighten all fasteners to specifications in **Figure 28**. Check fluid level, look for leaks and bleed the system as described in this section of the supplement.

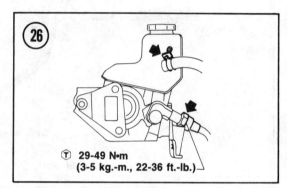

Steering Linkage Overhaul (Power Steering)

Refer to **Figure 29** for this procedure.

1. Set the handbrake. Place the transmission in FIRST (manual) or PARK (automatic).

2. Loosen the front wheel nuts. Jack up the front end of the truck, place it on jackstands and remove the front wheels.

3. Remove the cotter pins and lock nuts from the outer tie rod ball-joints.

4. Detach the tie rod ball-joints from the knuckle arms. Use a puller of the type shown in **Figure 30** or a fork-type separator (**Figure 31**). These are available from rental dealers.

5. Detach the pitman arm from the shaft with a pitman arm puller such as Datsun tool part No. ST29020001 (Kent-Moore part No. J 25725). See **Figure 32**. These are available from rental dealers.

6. Detach the idler arm assembly from the frame.

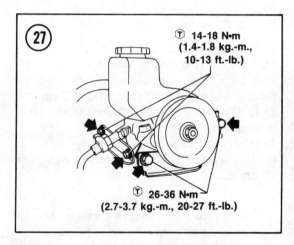

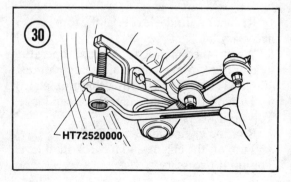

(28) **STEERING GEAR**

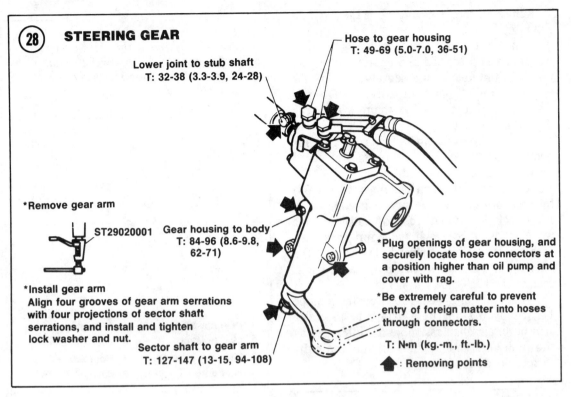

Hose to gear housing
T: 49-69 (5.0-7.0, 36-51)

Lower joint to stub shaft
T: 32-38 (3.3-3.9, 24-28)

*Remove gear arm

ST29020001

Gear housing to body
T: 84-96 (8.6-9.8, 62-71)

*Install gear arm
Align four grooves of gear arm serrations with four projections of sector shaft serrations, and install and tighten lock washer and nut.

Sector shaft to gear arm
T: 127-147 (13-15, 94-108)

*Plug openings of gear housing, and securely locate hose connectors at a position higher than oil pump and cover with rag.

*Be extremely careful to prevent entry of foreign matter into hoses through connectors.

T: N•m (kg.-m., ft.-lb.)

◆ : Removing points

(29) **STEERING LINKAGE**

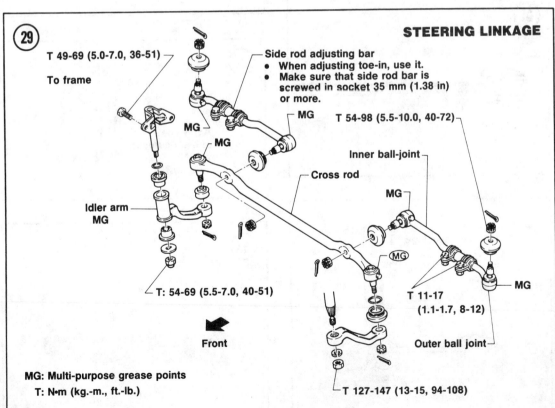

T 49-69 (5.0-7.0, 36-51)

To frame

Side rod adjusting bar
• When adjusting toe-in, use it.
• Make sure that side rod bar is screwed in socket 35 mm (1.38 in) or more.

MG

T 54-98 (5.5-10.0, 40-72)

MG

Inner ball-joint

Cross rod

MG

Idler arm
MG

T: 54-69 (5.5-7.0, 40-51)

Front

MG

T 11-17
(1.1-1.7, 8-12)

Outer ball joint

MG: Multi-purpose grease points
T: N•m (kg.-m., ft.-lb.)

T 127-147 (13-15, 94-108)

14

7. Remove the steering linkage as an assembly.

8. Separate the remaining steering linkage ball-joints as described in Step 4. Remove the nut from the idler arm assembly.

9. Clean metal parts in solvent. Do not immerse ball-joints. Wipe them with a rag dipped in solvent.

10. Check tie rods and the cross rod for bends, cracks or damaged threads. Replace if these conditions are found.

11. Check the idler arm bushings (**Figure 33**) for wear or damage. Replace as needed.

12. Check tie rod and cross rod ball-joints for worn studs. Place each ball-joint in a vise with the stud facing upward. Try to pull the stud up and down. If any play can be felt, replace the ball-joint.

13. Assemble and install by reversing steps 1-8. Apply multipurpose grease to the idler arm bushings, then assemble the idler arm as shown in **Figure 34**. Tighten all nuts and bolts to specifications (**Figure 29**).

NOTE
*If tie rod ball-joints are removed, make sure the tie rod is the correct length when installing the new ball-joints. Dimension A, **Figure 35**, should be 275 mm (10.83 in.).*

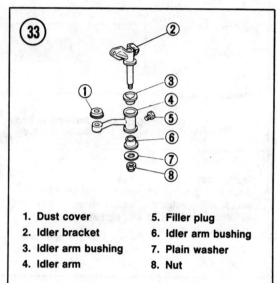

1. Dust cover
2. Idler bracket
3. Idler arm bushing
4. Idler arm
5. Filler plug
6. Idler arm bushing
7. Plain washer
8. Nut

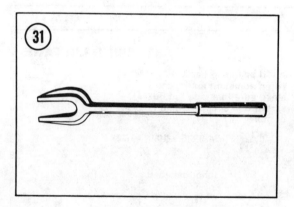

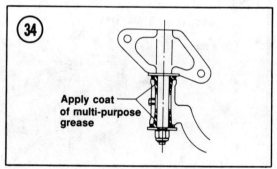

Apply coat of multi-purpose grease

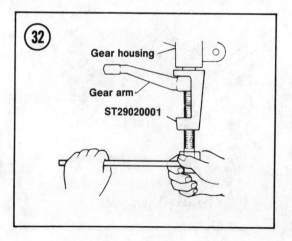

Gear housing

Gear arm

ST29020001

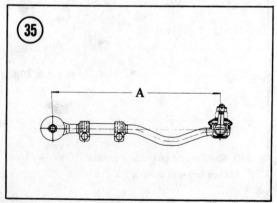

A

CHAPTER ELEVEN

BRAKES

Service procedures are the same as for 1981 models, except that the front brakes use pad shims. See **Figure 36**.

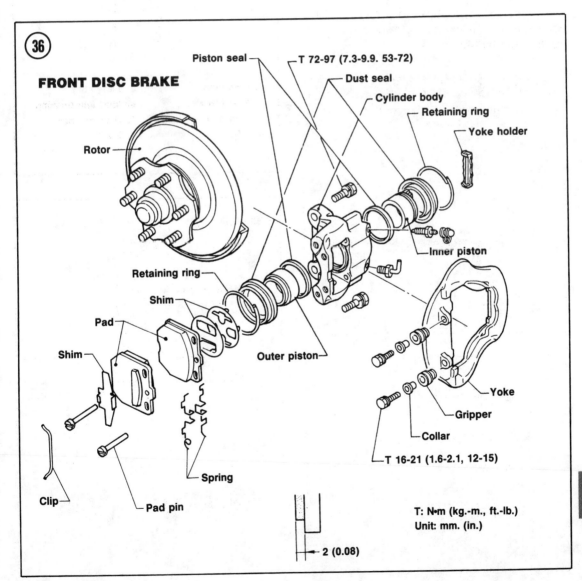

36

FRONT DISC BRAKE

Piston seal

T 72-97 (7.3-9.9. 53-72)

Dust seal

Cylinder body

Retaining ring

Yoke holder

Rotor

Inner piston

Retaining ring

Shim

Pad

Shim

Outer piston

Yoke

Gripper

Collar

T 16-21 (1.6-2.1, 12-15)

Spring

Clip

Pad pin

2 (0.08)

T: N•m (kg.-m., ft.-lb.)
Unit: mm. (in.)

14

INDEX

15

15

NOTES

NOTES

NOTES

NOTES

NOTES

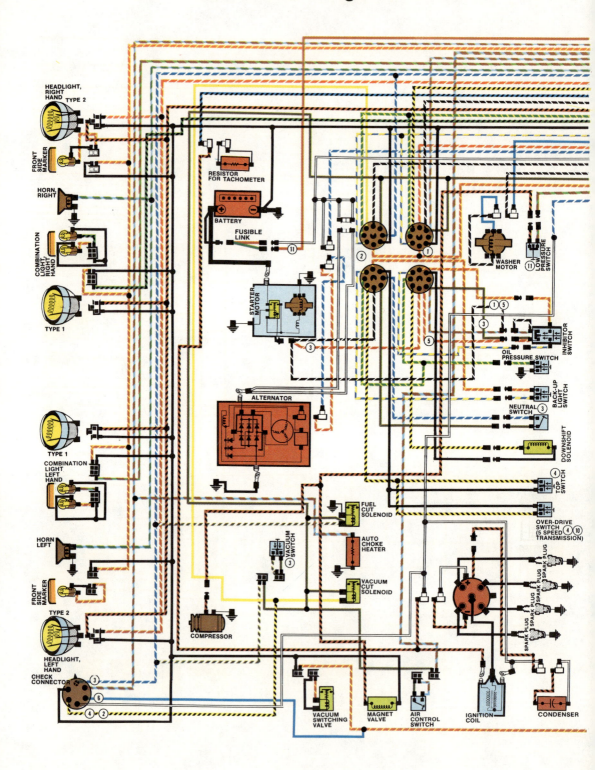

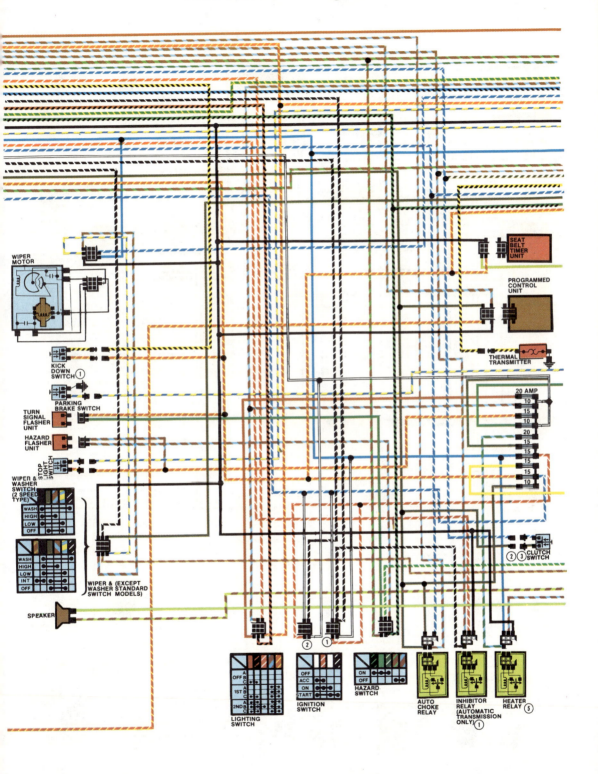

1 Automatic transmission	5 Canada	9 Base models
2 Manual transmission	6 Heavy-duty/California	10 5-speed manual transmission
3 All U.S. models	7 Deluxe/King cab	11 Air conditioned
4 California	8 King cab	

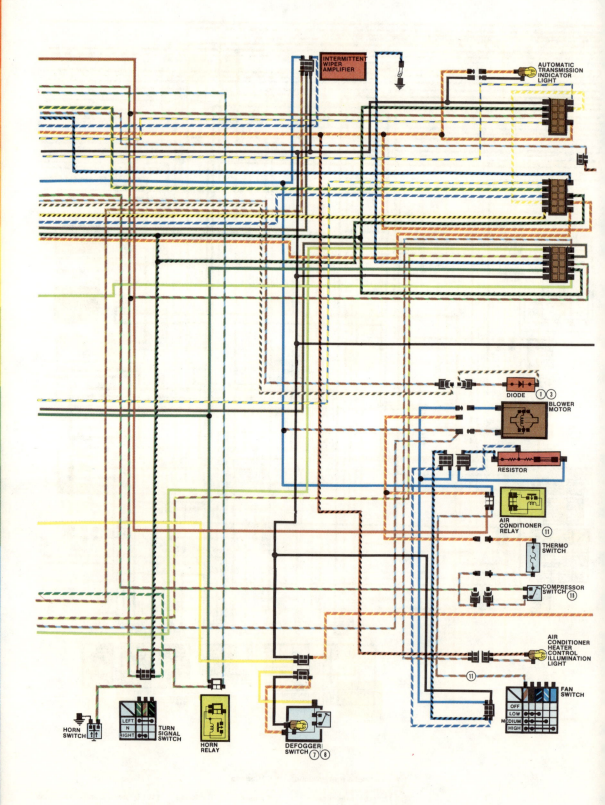

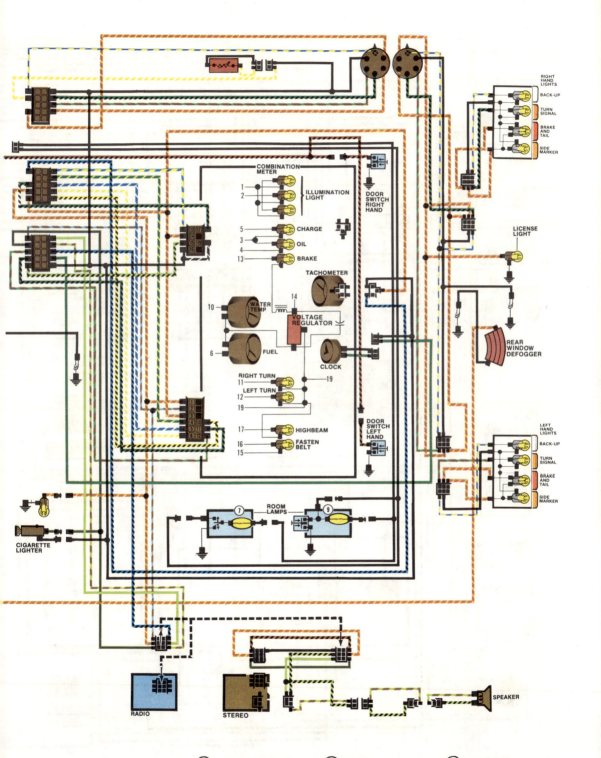

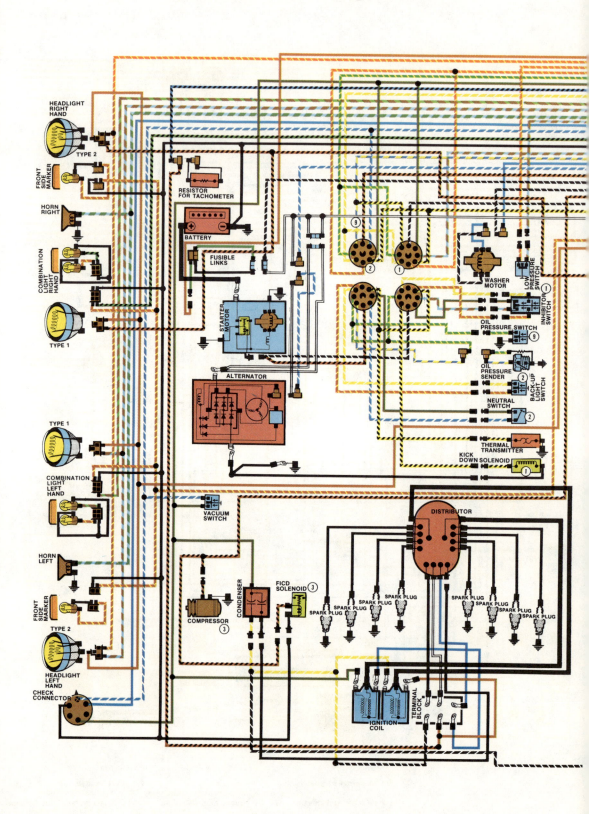

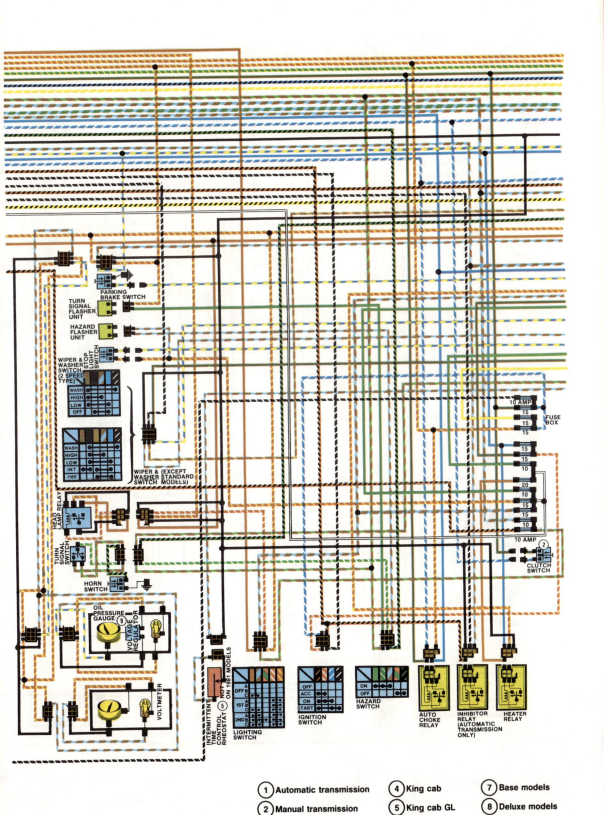

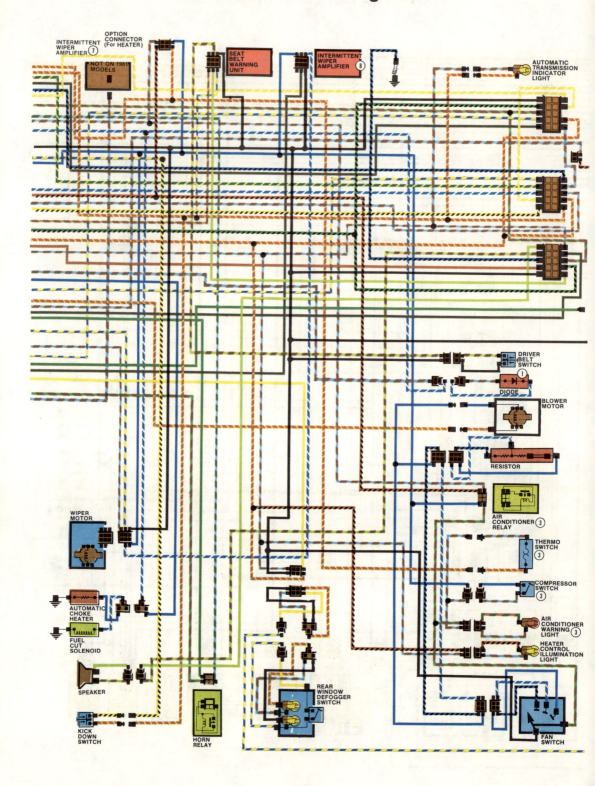

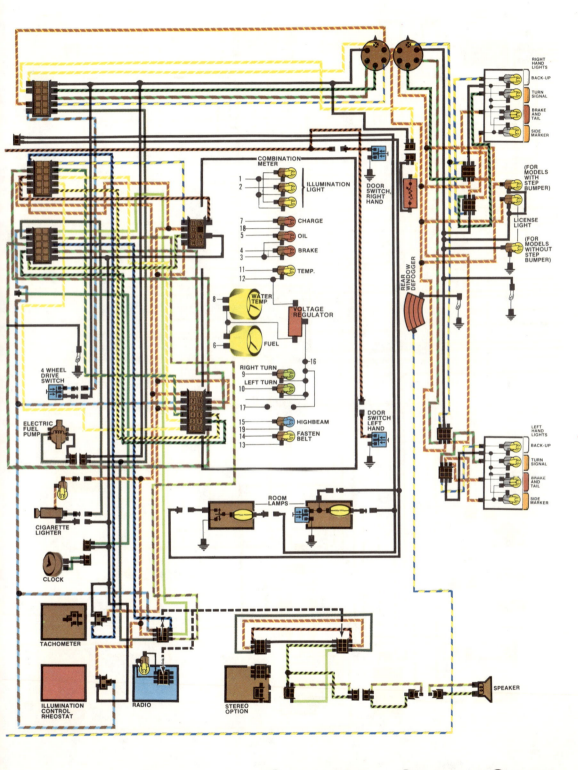

1. Automatic transmission
2. Manual transmission
3. Air conditioned
4. King cab
5. King cab GL
6. Cab & chassis
7. Base models
8. Deluxe models
9. 4-wheel drive

NOTES

NOTES

NOTES